SOCIAL CAPITAL
AND SOCIAL
COHESION IN
POST-SOVIET
RUSSIA

SOCIAL CAPITAL
AND SOCIAL
COHESION IN
POST-SOVIET
RUSSIA

Judyth L. Twigg
and
Kate Schecter, Editors

M.E.Sharpe
Armonk, New York
London, England

Library of Congress Cataloging-in-Publication Data

Social capital and social cohesion in post-Soviet Russia / edited by Judyth L. Twigg
and Kate Schecter.
    p. cm.
Includes bibliographical references and index.
ISBN 0-7656-1223-2 (cloth: alk. paper) — ISBN 0-7656-1224-0 (pbk.: alk. paper)
    1. Russia (Federation)—Social conditions—1991- 2. Social capital (Sociology)—Russia
(Federation) 3. Post-communism—Russia (Federation) I. Twigg, Judyth L.
II. Schecter, Kate.

HN530.2.A8S647 2003
306'.0947—dc21   2003041562

Printed in the United States of America

The paper used in this publication meets the minimum requirements of
American National Standard for Information Sciences
Permanence of Paper for Printed Library Materials,
ANSI Z 39.48-1984.

MV (c)   10   9   8   7   6   5   4   3   2   1
MV (p)   10   9   8   7   6   5   4   3   2   1

Table of Contents

List of Tables and Figures

Tables

Figures

About the Editors and Contributors

Judyth L. Twigg is an associate professor of political science at Virginia Commonwealth University. She holds a B.S. in physics from Carnegie Mellon University, an M.A. in political science and Russian studies from the University of Pittsburgh, and a Ph.D. in political science and security studies from MIT. Her current work focuses on the health and demographic crisis in Russia, with a particular emphasis on health system reform and health-care financing. She is the co-editor of *Russia's Torn Safety Nets: Health and Social Welfare during the Transition* (2000) and the author of many published articles on Russian health system reform.

Kate Schecter is a program officer for the American International Health Alliance (AIHA), where she is responsible for health reform activities in Georgia, Armenia, and Azerbaijan. She is also the manager of a project in Odessa, Ukraine, to prevent the transmission of HIV/AIDS from mothers to their babies. Before joining AIHA she worked as a consultant for the World Bank for three years, specializing in health-care reform and child welfare issues in the former Soviet Union and Eastern and Central Europe, and taught at the University of Michigan from 1993 to 1997. Schecter received her M.A. in Soviet studies from Harvard University, and Ph.D. in political science from Columbia University. She has made three documentary films for PBS about the former Soviet Union and is the co-author of *Back in the USSR* (1988) and *An American Family in Moscow* (1975), two journalistic accounts of living in the former USSR.

Tatyana V. Barchunova, Ph.D., is a teacher of philosophy and a researcher of discriminative practices and stereotypes. She is affiliated with Novosibirsk State University. Barchunova has participated in a number of research and social projects in Russia and internationally and has published widely on the methodology of science and cultural stereotypes. In addition, she has edited a collection of essays entitled *The Gender Ceiling* (in Russian, Novosibirsk, 1998) and co-edited *Western Feminism: A Reader* (St. Petersburg, 2000).

Linda J. Cook, Ph.D., Columbia University, is a professor of political science at Brown University, where she is director of Brown's International Relations Program. She is also an associate of the Davis Center for Russian Studies at Harvard University. She previously authored *The Soviet Social Contract and Why It Failed* (1993) and co-edited (with Mitchell Orenstein and Marilyn Rueschemeyer) *Left Parties and Social Policy in Post-Communist Europe* (1999). Her current project concerns the politics of social policy reform in the Russian Federation.

Stephen Handelman is author of *Comrade Criminal: Russia's New Mafiya* (1995), considered the definitive account of the rise of organized crime in post-Soviet Russia. Handelman is an associate fellow at Columbia University's Harriman Institute on Post-Soviet Studies and has served as a consultant to law enforcement agencies in the United States and Canada. A prizewinning foreign correspondent and investigative journalist, Handelman has reported from Europe, Africa, Asia, the Middle East, and Latin America, as well as the former Soviet Union. Between 1987 and 1992 he was Moscow Bureau Chief of the *Toronto Star*, and he now writes a regular column on international affairs for that newspaper.

Boris Kagarlitsky is an internationally published author and journalist who originally trained as a theater critic. His opposition activities and work as editor of the samizdat journal *Left Turn* led to his imprisonment in the early 1980s. On his release, Kagarlitsky entered formal politics, and he has maintained an active role in current Russian affairs and the labor movement. His book *The Thinking Reed* was awarded the Deutscher Memorial Prize in 1988.

Andrew Konitzer-Smirnov received his Ph.D. from the University of Pittsburgh's Department of Political Science. He has worked extensively with the Samara and Ulyanovsk oblasts both as the field director of a USIA-sponsored university partnership program and conducting research on regional development and the political economy of regional executive elections.

Sapar M. Kulianov graduated from Moscow State University and began a career as a physicist but increasingly devoted time to working with children and on child welfare issues. Since September 1995 he has been director of a Moscow children's shelter.

Maria Lagus was assistant technical attaché at the Swedish Embassy in Moscow from 1979 until 1990. In 1992 she became manager for the Swedish Save the Children's office for the East European region, and more recently she has been a senior manager for the Swedish International Development Agency (SIDA). Lagus holds an M.S. in economics from the University of Uppsala.

Augusto Lopez-Claros served as the International Monetary Fund's resident representative in the Russian Federation from 1992 to 1995. Trained at Cambridge and at Duke University, Lopez-Claros was a professor of economics at the University of Chile in Santiago. He is now Senior International Economist and Executive Director with Lehman Brothers International (London).

Tatyana Matsuk is an independent analyst of social systems and a senior research consultant with Ekonomika Publishing House. She holds a Ph.D. in computer science and has worked in the Russian Academy of Sciences Institute for Control Studies and the Institute for Employment Studies. From 1992 to 1995 she was a program director and deputy chairman of the Russian Cultural Foundation's Classical Heritage Association. She is widely published in both English-language and Russian-language journals.

Boris Nemtsov is the leader of the Union of Right Forces faction in the State Duma of the Russian Federation, as well as the chairman of the Federal Political Council of the Union of Right Forces political party. Prior to holding these positions, he was the elected governor of Nizhny Novgorod, having earlier been the Yeltsin administration's presidential representative there. Nemtsov also served as first deputy prime minister of Russia and minister of fuel and energy and was a member of the Russian Security Council. He is the author of *A Provincial*. Nemtsov holds a Ph.D. in physics and mathematics from Gorky State University.

Natalia Rimashevskaya is director of the Russian Academy of Sciences Institute for Socioeconomic Studies of the Population, a professor at the High School of Economics, and editor in chief of the quarterly journal *Narodonaselenie* and the yearbook *Russia's Sociodemographic Situation*. Rimashevskaya is a member of the State Commission on the All-Russian Population Census, vice-president of the International Social Science Council, and president of the Crisis Center for Women. She is the author of hundreds of publications covering a wide range of social policy issues.

Richard Rose is the founder-director of the Centre for the Study of Public Policy, University of Strathclyde, Glasgow. In his research, he draws on a wide range of social science concepts, including epidemiology and demography, to analyze problems of government comparatively across the developed world. Since 1991, he has conducted more than 100 representative sample surveys across seventeen post-Communist countries of Central and Eastern Europe and the former Soviet Union (see www.cspp.strath.ac.uk). Rose has published hundreds of articles and dozens of books, including his latest book (with Neil Munro), *Elections Without Order: Russia's Challenge to Vladimir Putin.*

Elena Vinogradova, Ph.D., is a senior research fellow in the Russian Academy of Sciences Institute of Economics. She has participated in research projects supported by the European Union's TACIS program, the World Bank, and the government of the Russian Federation. Her work on social policy in Russia and regional sociological surveys has been published in Russia and the United States.

Acknowledgments

The editors would like to thank the Carnegie Corporation of New York, and particularly its president, Vartan Gregorian, and program officers Deana Arsenian and David Speedie, for their remarkable support. This project is the result of a grant that emerged from the Carnegie Corporation's Russia Initiative, a multiyear, interdisciplinary assessment of Russia's current political, economic, and social challenges.

The Russia Initiative provided a forum for informative and sometimes heated debate. We would like to thank our colleagues in the Russia Initiative's two working groups on social cohesion for their insights and for the opportunity to discuss these issues openly with such a varied group of experts. In addition to the authors of this volume, those groups also included Jonas Bernstein, Elizabeth Brainerd, Robert Kushen, Vladimir Shkolnikov, and Elena Varavikova. In Moscow and Washington, essential commentary on earlier generations of this work was provided by Valery Chervyakov, Andrei Demine, Svetlana Misikhina, Eugene Rumer, Igor Sheiman, Leonid Sholpo, and Natalia Zinovieva.

The American International Health Alliance, headed by Jim Smith, and the National Bureau of Asian Research, led by Rich Ellings, provided institutional bases for the Carnegie Corporation's generous grant funding. We appreciate their infrastructural and logistical support.

Our three research assistants, Catalina Villamizar, Piers Merrick, and especially Roslyn Stein, have been invaluable and indefatigable. They have done a remarkable job with conference planning and communications among an array of scholars and institutions spanning several continents. Roz's ongoing work copyediting the manuscript and maintaining an electronic information dissemination network for the project participants has been exemplary.

Finally, we would like to acknowledge the steady and constant support of our husbands. Ari and Bill have been there over the past four years while Judy had a baby, and while we celebrated numerous birthdays, dance recitals, and graduation ceremonies. The mothers are grateful to their terrific kids and to the fathers for making possible a rewarding balance of work and family.

Social Capital and Social Cohesion in Post-Soviet Russia

1

Introduction

Judyth L. Twigg and Kate Schecter

Despite numerous predictions to the contrary, Russia emerged intact from the chaotic turbulence of the post-Soviet 1990s. Characterizations of Russia's political and economic condition, however, range all over the map: Russia as a successfully established market economy versus Russia as an impoverished basket case; Russia as a fledgling but stable democracy versus Russia as a country falling into the throes of soft authoritarianism; Russia as a beneficiary of smart U.S. and international policy versus Russia "lost." Most analyses, however, agree that despite a veneer of political stability, a considerable portion of Russian society remains in turmoil. Many Russians' economic and social circumstances are still shattered by the loss of the Soviet-era social safety net.

This book is the result of a collaborative effort to understand the social dynamics of the post-Soviet transition. Its central theme is the role played by social capital in Russia during the course of the last decade. It examines the fate of residual sources and stockpiles of social capital left over from the Soviet period. It also explores potential wellsprings of new social capital created by Russia's more recent challenges and opportunities. Fundamentally, it asks whether the decidedly Western concept of social capital is applicable to the Russian case. Social capital and its counterpart, civil society, are normally conceptualized as standing apart from, even in opposition to, the state. They are distinctly nongovernmental or antigovernmental qualities. Must the role of the state vis-à-vis social capital be reconceptualized when thinking about a traditionally authoritarian society like Russia? Can—or must—the state play a role as a provider or guarantor of Russian social cohesion? In any case, what are the implications of these social dynamics for Russia's broader socioeconomic and political development? What are the implications for Russian and Western policy?

Social capital is a notoriously elusive and diffuse concept. This work will accept a broad definition of the term, encompassing the norms, relationships or networks, and resulting formal or informal institutions that determine the nature and quality of a society's public and private interactions.[1] Social cohesion is the result of effective and abundant social capital. A cohesive society enjoys a sense of common purpose, shared values, a stable identity, and a widely agreed-upon vision of the future and the framework within which to pursue that vision.

Sociologists and other scholars have convincingly demonstrated that social cohesion is critical for societies to achieve and maintain political stability and economic prosperity.[2] Effective social networks, by facilitating coordination and cooperation, increase economic productivity by reducing both direct and indirect business costs. Vertical social ties that bridge socioeconomic, ethnic, or religious categories—ties based on some coherent sense of national identity—facilitate progress toward genuine democratic institution-building and pluralism. The absence of broadly distributed social capital can lead disaggregated groups to pursue narrow parochial interests counter to national goals. Indeed, in its most encompassing sense, social cohesion creates the contextual environment within which state, private, and community interests can converge.[3]

Within Russia, these necessary convergences have been the exception rather than the rule in recent years. Throughout the 1990s, rich were pitted against poor, the healthy against the sick, Russians against non-Russians, urban against rural, Russian Orthodox against other religions, generation against generation—the list could continue indefinitely. The Russian state under Yeltsin demonstrated limited willingness or capacity to exercise leadership and to address effectively either the symptoms or the underlying causes of this "disease." The first post-Soviet decade gave the Russian people increasing reason to lose faith in their public institutions, given the repeated examples of government complacency in the face of shocking social crises (for example, Russia's burgeoning AIDS epidemic, or its alarmingly high rates of alcoholism also manifest in the large population of abandoned and neglected children) and seemingly substantiated allegations of widespread corruption, including massive fraud in the March 2000 first round of presidential elections. In public opinion polls, over three-quarters of Russians still consistently view their public authorities as absolutely corrupt at all levels.

On the surface, Soviet society appeared far more cohesive than the disenfranchised and disillusioned population of today's Russia. Despite the repression and material hardships of the Soviet era, many Russians profess nostalgia for the old days. Now life has been reduced to a scramble and rules of the game have become unclear. Trust in a close-knit circle of family and friends once helped people to endure the hardships of Soviet life. In some cases, these ties still bind small groups of people together, but far too many of those bonds have been broken.

The most evident social chasm in today's Russia is the large and growing gap between the haves and the have-nots—a dramatic change from Soviet times, when income disparities were far less pronounced and hidden from public view. Official Russian estimates claim that between 20 and 30 percent of the Russian people live in poverty, existing below a subsistence level of less than one dollar per day. Single women with children have been hardest hit, resulting in a marked feminization of poverty. There has been an explosion of young Russian women duped by false promises of an escape from their dismal circumstances. Meanwhile, the rich are getting richer, with a 42-fold difference between the highest and lowest income deciles.

Income disparities have also revealed and exacerbated generational cleavages. The story is a familiar one—pensioners vote, and children do not—but the implications in the Russian environment are particularly dire. While it is true that elderly beggars hover outside subway stations, pensioners have fared relatively well as the primary group targeted by government social policy. Pensions can reach as high as three or four times the level of single-parent aid, and they consistently dwarf child benefits. When the costs of raising children are taken into account, the needs of single-parent families are two to three times higher than those of pensioners, but their income is on average twice as low. The neglect of children extends to decay of the country's public educational infrastructure, with recent tests revealing that standards have fallen precipitously. The growing number of street children, with estimates of their number ranging from one to four million, is testament to many Russian families' inability to cope with the financial and psychological challenge of raising their offspring.

Little wonder, then, that many Russian women are simply opting not to have children at all. As a result of declining birthrates and rising death rates, Russia now faces a demographic crisis unprecedented for a peacetime industrial society. Recent official government estimates (actuarial forecasts from its Pension Fund) predict that Russia's population shrinkage, currently at around 750,000 people per year, will accelerate to 1,000,000 per year through the year 2016. In essence, Russia is being depopulated. President Vladimir Putin placed this issue at the top of the country's agenda during his year 2000 annual presidential address to the Federal Assembly. Yet the policies, and the resources to back them, have not emerged to cope with a situation in which only 30 percent of Russian newborns are considered healthy and more than two-thirds of pregnancies are marred by serious complications.

Many Russians have experienced the post-Soviet years as a decade of fear—not only of each other, with violent crime so prevalent that "routine" bombings and shootings scarcely even make it into the local news, but also of the direction of their society itself. In a September 2000 survey conducted by the All-Russian Center for the Study of Public Opinion, sixty percent of Russians said they foresaw and feared anarchy, chaos, and the collapse of the country. No wonder survey data consistently indicated that a majority of them longed for a "strong hand" that might restore "order."

If the Russian state has failed as a generator or even as an effective caretaker of social capital and social cohesion, are there other potential untapped sources that might be harnessed? Nations throughout history have managed to weather difficult times, indeed have even pulled together to overcome tremendous strife, thanks to a sense of common purpose and national identity. In the post-Soviet environment, however, Russia continues to lack a cohesive sense of "self" to replace the Communist ideology that was imposed from above. Recent efforts to recreate at least the trappings of a coherent identity—the restoration of the Soviet anthem and flag, for example—have served only to further divide a society still uncertain about the meaning of its past. It is not merely that a significant portion of the population is unwilling to jettison much of its Soviet identity. More importantly, there has yet to emerge a satisfying national idea to put in its place, to satisfy the need of post-Soviet generations for a set of unifying themes around which Russia can congeal.

Some politicians have attempted to harness Russian nationalism for this purpose. But the results of these efforts—increasingly visible anti-Semitism, two brutal wars against Chechnya, growing hostility toward the very immigrants who might help mitigate the effects of the country's demographic crisis—bode poorly for the building of productive social capital. Unifying the majority against an array of minority groups is a false cohesion, unsustainable in the long run and unable to produce the necessary economic and political benefits. A similar dynamic is discernible where spirituality and religion are concerned. Legislation passed in recent years has deliberately favored the Russian Orthodox Church over virtually all other faiths, creating outright legal harassment against Jews, Mormons, Jehovah's Witnesses, and others. This official discrimination against religious minorities not only furthers a climate of divisiveness and intolerance, it also threatens to deprive many people of a primary source of strength during the difficult post-Soviet transition.

Some pockets of improvement, however, brighten this gloomy picture. Survey research across the country indicates that, since the year 2000, the mood of the Russian people has steadily improved. From 1998 to the present, the number of people who feel that life is fundamentally unfair has decreased by 30 percent, and the percentage of those who feel as though they have control over their own lives has doubled. For the first time since the Soviet collapse, a majority of Russians think that their country's current path will yield positive results for themselves and their society, with the percentage characterizing Russia's situation as "catastrophic" dropping from 51 percent in 1999 to 14 percent today.

Quite probably, policies pursued by the Putin administration—in addition to a general perception that the country is finally in the hands of energetic, competent leadership—are responsible for this tentative upswing. Around one-quarter of Russians still live in abject poverty, but many more are for the first time in years enjoying pensions and government wages being paid out regularly and promptly. Real wages, including those of government workers, are rising steeply, covering, and in some instances exceeding, the rate of inflation. Almost half of Russians think that Putin has made meaningful efforts to stamp out corruption.

Two-thirds of people say that they are satisfied with their current social status, and more than 40 percent define themselves as "middle class." This emergent middle class, however defined, now peppers the socioeconomic landscape not just in Moscow and St. Petersburg, but in numerous large and medium-sized cities across the country. Literally thousands of nongovernmental organizations have begun to take responsibility for issue areas and social services abandoned or neglected by the Russian government.[4] While foreign assistance has offered a critical helping hand for many of these efforts, by and large these successes spring wholly from the ingenuity, sweat, and community-mindedness of the Russian people themselves. In sum, the Russian people see progress, or at least what they interpret as genuine attempts at progress, along an array of issue areas central to their well-being— a distinct change from the Yeltsin years.

To be sure, some of these opinions may be based more on perception than reality, and some may prove to be illusory once Russia's economic boost from relatively high world oil prices comes to an end. As Putin asks people to make further sacrifices for the sake of economic reform—for example, paying nearer-to-market prices for their currently heavily subsidized housing and utilities—the confidence he inspires may rapidly wane. Yet for the time being, Russia's traditional fatalism, combined over the last decade with pervasive resentment over the country's decline and loss of superpower status, is making way, however tentatively, for a glimmer of societal confidence and cautious optimism.

* * *

The contributors to the present volume provide fresh and diverse perspectives on these themes. Linda Cook's chapter tackles one of the central questions of social capital and cohesion in the Russian context: the role of the state as a contributor to, or a detractor from, social capital. She introduces an important dynamic element to her analysis. During the Yeltsin period, she argues, the state did little to overcome the Soviet-era lack of social capital; indeed, much of what the public sector represented to the Russian people during the 1990s—poor management, corruption, and a seemingly endless string of promises made and promises broken—generated "large-scale societal distrust and defection from state-mediated social security programs." Although it is still early in the Putin administration, Cook demonstrates that many of Putin's policies hold significant potential for top-down restoration of public trust and social cohesion. By constructing streamlined, more responsive, and transparent government bureaucracies and services, the Russian government in recent years has engendered "an increase of trust and a greater willingness to cooperate in the provision of public goods." Wage and pension arrears have diminished or disappeared in conjunction with a decline in tax evasion, barter, and "other forms of defection from the formal sector." Although Putin's progress in this area remains tentative, and a number of important questions remain concerning the sustainability and inclusiveness of his social policy agenda, the record thus far under the Putin regime may finally have broken a decade-long "vicious cycle" of inefficiency and mistrust.

A cautionary note on Putin's ultimate success in reforming the public sector comes from Elena Vinogradova's chapter. Through extensive surveys of employees in federal and municipal institutions, Vinogradova and her colleagues find that standards and practices inherited from the Soviet era continue to plague the provision of state social services. Modern incentives for responsive customer service are still lacking, as are effective strategic planning and managerial techniques. While state employees' attitudes embody much of the empathy and community-mindedness that lie at the core of social cohesion—they derive genuine satisfaction from helping members of the public, particularly the needy—they lack the skills and motivation to do so with cost-efficiency. The implementation of their duties, however well intended, still centers around management of allotted funds (the core of the Soviet-era command-economy bureaucratic system) rather than results-oriented service to society. Vinogradova ends, however, on an optimistic note: The development of individual initiative and administrative efficiency may emerge from the embryonic social capital within the public employee community.

The next chapters turn to the potential for social cohesion to develop and thrive from within various nodes of Russian society. Boris Kagarlitsky begins this discussion with an analysis of ethnicity and nationality in contemporary Russia. Unfortunately, the landscape he constructs is not a hopeful one. Ethnicity, he argues, has emerged as a fall-back source of identity within a Russia whose umbrella social and economic structures have disintegrated. Within this context, a blame game has developed, where members of ethnic minority groups have become scapegoats for all of society's ills: crime, corruption, and unemployment. Within-group ties have become stronger: "Having found themselves in alien, unusual, and sometimes hostile environments, the ethnic minorities in large cities show considerably more solidarity and readiness to help one another than does the prevailing population." But in a classic illustration of the "dark side" of social capital, an "us-them" dynamic now prevails between ethnic Russians and many non-Russian diasporas. Kagarlitsky argues that the state's prosecution of the war in Chechnya has grossly exacerbated this phenomenon, resulting in "permissible," or officially sanctioned, racism against people from the Caucasus or Muslims in general. The Putin administration has literally institutionalized these attitudes as state policy through its tightening of citizenship laws, its project for national integration (asserting the primacy of the Russian nation), its continued political partnership with the Orthodox Church, and its stepped-up campaign against Chechens as Muslim terrorists. According to Kagarlitsky's analysis, Russian society stands at a crossroads. Will it choose to integrate non-Russian nationality groups into a "continuously self-renewing and inclusive Russian nation"? Or will it pursue "a strategy of state development based on the narrow definition of the nation as a union of Eastern Orthodox Christian Slavs, transforming all other residents of the country into second-rate citizens who are subjects of the Empire"? As Kagarlitsky so eloquently concludes, the choice may spell either "the preservation and development of society, or the ruin thereof."

Tatyana Matsuk's assessment of Russian religion and spirituality parallels Kagarlitsky's findings. Religious extremism, like ethnonational extremism, is derived from the country's socioeconomic and political problems. And even though freedom of worship might be expected to function as a source of solace and cohesion for a fractured society, in Russia the dynamic has been just the opposite, at least in part due to intolerant state policies. The war in Chechnya (against Muslim "terrorists") and the elevation of Russian Orthodoxy almost to "official" status, along with the flurry of regional and federal laws restricting the activities of "nontraditional" religions, have led to increased atomization and intolerance. Matsuk finds the continued politicization and authoritarian imposition of the Orthodox Church to be particularly troublesome; she worries that the interests of colluding secular and religious elites will trump "the rights of each citizen—including the right to have his or her own beliefs and world outlook." If this continues, she argues, the innate "mysterious Russian soul" of a "highly spiritual people ready to help a neighbor at any time and work with others for a common benefit" will be trampled.

Crime and corruption certainly represent one of the major detractors from social cohesion; many scholars use crime rates as one of their primary indicators of the presence or absence of social capital. Stephen Handelman eloquently details the presence of crime as "the most vivid failure of the post-Communist experiment," asking why a crime-fighting culture has failed to emerge in Russia. He reports that, in perhaps an ultimate irony, the withdrawal of the state from its social obligations has invited "Mafiya" groups to emerge as in some cases the primary source of cohesion, mutual trust, predictability, and social security in many small towns and far-flung regions across the country. Under Putin, Handelman argues, the state has taken steps not so much to eliminate the Mafiya in this guise, as to make it no longer necessary. As economic and social responsibilities once again fall under effective state purview, "the Mafiya will be pushed back into the margins again." Continued widespread high-level corruption, however, and popular perceptions that anticorruption measures remain selectively targeted and enforced, do not bode well for enhanced levels of trust throughout society. And all indicators point toward a Putin government that wants to defeat crime and corruption problems without sacrificing any of its prerogatives—that is, offering as little transparency and citizen participation as it can get away with. Handelman concludes with a lament that a crime-fighting culture, and the enhanced levels of social cohesion that would go hand in hand with that culture, cannot emerge without the very citizen involvement that Putin seems deliberately to be quelling.

Natalia Rimashevskaya turns from macro- to micro-level analysis, examining the role and potential of the Russian family to preserve and nurture social cohesion. Here, too, the picture is rather pessimistic. Rimashevskaya cites a litany of statistics pointing to the demise of the family across Russia: declining birthrates, lower marriage and higher divorce rates, increasing numbers of out-of-wedlock births, a degradation of maternal and child health, and an increase in social orphanhood. An array of economic and social factors—unemployment, declining social status for many families, widespread poverty, social polarization, the deterioration of social protection mechanisms, and ironically, newly found freedom to move and travel—has contributed to conflict within families and family destabilization. Here a "vicious cycle" is particularly cruel. Just as the state has abdicated much of its previous role as social protector, the family—which should emerge as Russians' primary physical and psychological survival tool during difficult times—has lost much of its economic and emotional wherewithal. As a result, "instead of a social explosion, we have seen social degradation, which is more dangerous for Russia's development in the long run than a social explosion. . . . The social price of reforms . . . has turned out to be so high that it calls into question whether the Russian gene pool will be preserved."

Not all Russians, however, have reacted to the turmoil of the last decade in the same manner. Richard Rose has already demonstrated that social capital and health are strongly correlated with one another.[5] In his chapter, he further explores this topic by asking why some people have remained relatively healthy—have, indeed, thrived—in the face of transformation while others have suffered severe health consequences. By linking the societal with the individual level of analysis, he demonstrates that social confidence, defined as a person's belief that he has control over his own life, is a crucial mitigating factor explaining differential responses to Russia's socioeconomic transition. Based on data from an early 2000 survey of 1,600 Russians, Rose finds that high self-reported social confidence can "more than [offset] the impact on physical health of the shocks of societal transformation." Both social integration and social confidence have significant impacts on emotional and physical health.

It is well known that, for reasons as yet unfathomed by scholarly analysis, women's health has not suffered to the same degree as men's during the post-Soviet transition. Tatyana Barchunova explores the gender dimension of social capital in Russia. In contrast to the national-level statistical and survey methodologies employed by other authors in this volume, Barchunova offers observations of small groups of social agents tackling their particular problems in just one geographic region, Novosibirsk. She finds the state to be marginal in this analysis; instead, the important activity takes place among communities of people taking charge of the learning, doing, and construction of meaning in their own lives to pursue their own interests and solve their own (and their communities') social problems. These "communities of practice" are highly concentrated, although the issue areas they cover are quite broad. And while on the surface, not surprisingly, the organizations representing these communities seem to be predominantly female—women addressing "women's" issues—in reality, according to Barchunova, the underlying principles and ideas behind them are not gendered. Rather than a study of women's oppression and suffering, therefore, Barchunova has offered glimpses of hope that women and men working together in a nongovernmental context can effectively solve ordinary Russians' problems regardless of the policies and machinations of the state.

In the study of social capital, it is important to acknowledge that Russia is a large and diverse society. Two of this volume's chapters explicitly address that heterogeneity. Judyth Twigg provides a dynamic, quantitative analysis of social capital variations across the country. Using a host of indicators to construct an "index" of social capital along with regional rankings, she finds wide variation but surprising consistency across time (throughout the 1990s) in the stocks of social capital enjoyed by Russia's regions. She demonstrates that geography matters, with regions in European Russia closer to Moscow (on average) exhibiting higher levels of social cohesion, and those in Siberia and the Far East generally ranking lower on social capital indicators. Perhaps most importantly, she reports no consistent statistically significant relationship between a region's wealth, its urbanness, its ethnic homogeneity, or the quality of its political leadership and its ranking on the composite Social Capital Index. Twigg argues that these findings beg for further study of the operationalization of social capital as a concept, and of the implications of this difficult-to-measure commodity for Russian and Western policy toward particular regions.

Andrew Konitzer-Smirnov tackles the regional level of analysis with an explicit, in-depth comparison of two particular regions: Ulyanovsk and Samara. Based on extensive field research in both areas, Konitzer-Smirnov demonstrates convincingly that variations in social policy and social capital "are often as strong between [Russian] federal subunits as between sovereign states." While Ulyanovsk and Samara are neighboring regions that share many common economic and demographic features, they vary in one important respect (which makes them ideal for comparison in this context): the former has tried to preserve the Soviet social contract at all costs, while the latter has restructured its economic and social service sectors to take full advantage of the opportunities and efficiencies of market-oriented reform. As a result, despite rhetoric about protection of its people from the "ravages of the market," Ulyanovsk has suffered from a still "bloated and poorly managed" health and social sector. Its people lack adequate support but have not been given the opportunity to substitute goods and services from the private sector. The supposedly most productive sectors of that region's society—the educated, young, and working-age populations—have been alienated. In contrast, Samara has enjoyed "better quality, more broadly distributed public goods and employment opportunities" that have "created wide-based political support for an outwardly liberal regime."

The role played by international assistance to Russia during its transition decade has been hotly debated in recent years, and the social impacts of International Monetary Fund and World Bank policies have frequently assumed center stage in these discussions. Former World Bank chief economist and senior vice president Joseph Stiglitz, for example, has recently written that "by ignoring the impacts of its policies on the poor and on social capital, the IMF actually impeded macroeconomic success."[6] Kate Schecter and Augusto Lopez-Claros here provide complementary assessments of the international community's role in fostering social cohesion during Russia's transition decade. Schecter focuses on the shortcomings of World Bank assistance to Russia, particularly its health sector, observing that the Bank "is caught in a web of its own requirements and therefore fails to address the most demanding issues." She highlights, by contrast, the past and potential future successes of aid models that involve genuine partnership from a grassroots perspective.

Lopez-Claros's powerful examination of International Monetary Fund activity similarly finds fault with a major international financial institution. He claims that, while paying lip service to social protection in Russia, the IMF in reality ignored the sharp decline in living standards for a significant portion of the population. The ultimate result was an "undermining [of] the effectiveness of its overall approach." Again, the "vicious cycle" rears its ugly head: "lack of adequate progress on structural reforms delayed the economic recovery, prolonged the plight of vulnerable groups and ended up undermining public support for the reforms." Overall, Lopez-Claros judges IMF efforts in Russia during 1995–98 to have been largely detrimental. The loans enabled the Russian government to neglect the development of its own state capacity (IMF money substituted for tax collection), failed to solicit significant actual economic reform, and were alarmingly ineffectively used.

Maria Lagus, a former official with the Swedish International Development Agency, provides a more positive view of her country's experience with aid to Russia's social sector. She outlines four broad target areas in which Sweden inaugurated cooperation programs with Russia in the 1990s: the promotion of common security, deepening the culture of democracy, supporting the development of a functioning market economy, and supporting environmentally sustainable development. Lagus indicates that Sweden's success stems from two key philosophical tenets that underlay its aid efforts: the efficient distribution of scarce public resources to those most in need (that is, a shift from universal to targeted benefit programs), and the inculcation of Russian citizens no longer dependent on state largesse but instead active agents responsible for their own individual and societal well-being. Perhaps Lagus's most important observation, and one with important lessons for international assistance programs, is this: "Russia is neither poor nor unable to run its own business." The problem has not been *under*development, but *mis*development inherited from the Soviet period. The challenge is therefore to respect Russia enough to trust its own enormous capacity and potential—and to convince the Russian people to do the same.

Sapar Kulianov's description of the Moscow children's shelter he directs is a stunning example of what can be achieved. His detailed case study provides a social and operational history of this successful nongovernmental organization (NGO), which exists on a combination of state and private funding. Kulianov's conclusions, however, sound an alarm concerning the relationship between state and NGO activity. It is state policy (at least in part),

Kulianov claims, that is causing the problem of child homelessness and abandonment. Until the state undertakes systematic crisis-prevention work with high-risk families across the country, NGO efforts will at best amount to a "fire department" principle, in which firefighters arrive at the peak of the blaze, or worse, after everything has already burnt.

Boris Nemtsov's concluding chapter echoes Kulianov's sentiment in this regard, arguing that the lack of effective implementation mechanisms (particularly financial) have reduced public social assistance largely to just another unfulfilled promise. Detailing the litany of social ills that have plagued the Russian landscape during the transition period—poverty, illicit drug use, crime, depopulation, family decay—Nemtsov writes that the costs of transition have been highest for the already poor, and that transition-era policies have caused even more families to descend into poverty. But Nemtsov also holds the Russian people themselves at least partly responsible for their plight. In his assessment, most people have yet to overcome Soviet-era norms and habits of dependence and passivity; they have not yet internalized and exercised responsibility for themselves and each other on an individual, family, and community basis.

Several common themes emerge from these individual chapters. Primary among them is a general agreement that, in addition to networks of individuals and nongovernmental organizations—the traditional, Western-conceived repositories of social capital—the state and state policy can also act as a provider or detractor of social cohesion. Among all of this volume's authors, only Barchunova explicitly finds the Russian state to be irrelevant to social capital. Cook, of course, faults Yeltsin-era policy for the continued demise of social cohesion because of its erosion of important social benefits. While she and Handelman find some cause for hope that the Putin administration has reversed that trend, Rimashevskaya and Nemtsov maintain a more pessimistic appraisal. Kagarlitsky and Matsuk even more sharply criticize the Putin government for policies seemingly designed to alienate large communities of Russian citizens from one another along ethnic or religious lines. Their underlying message is clear: Efforts to manipulate social relations for short-term political gain will, in the long run, doom the Russian Federation to a fractured and uncertain future.

Surprisingly, another thread running through many of these analyses is the continued legacy of the Soviet past, even after more than a decade of transition. Vinogradova's analysis indicates that Russian public-sector workers continue to struggle to overcome command-economy work habits, inhibiting what seems to be their genuine desire to provide a useful set of products to their customers. Lagus and Nemtsov lament a parallel phenomenon among a general public still too lacking in individual initiative and adaptability. At the regional government level, Konitzer-Smirnov eloquently illustrates the dire social consequences of efforts to preserve rather than discard the vestiges of the Soviet system. Again, a single lesson emerges, this time focusing on the importance of policy that empowers individual Russians to shed their Soviet-era passivity. The Russian people must instead become agents of change for their own lives and for the lives of others in their communities.

Nemtsov ends on a note that explicitly echoes Kagarlitsky's conclusions, following an ultimate theme that is implicit in each of the works presented here: Social capital and cohesion, and Russia's social conditions in general, matter. Frequently the social sector has been overlooked as developments in democratization, marketization, free media, and the institutionalization of the rule of law have taken center stage. Yet the well-being of Russian citizens and communities clearly underlies each of these macro-level reform processes. Virtually every chapter in this volume, for example, touches on the intimate connection between social capital and economic development; progress along both lines runs in classic "vicious" or "virtuous" cycles. Nemtsov's concluding words are an appropriate wrap-up to this introduction as well: "The prospects for tackling these problems are connected to the stability of a democratic system in Russia, accompanied by an ability to adopt and accept the value of an open society. The accumulation of social problems cannot stimulate the acceleration of the transition but rather threaten to break it and to send the country into a situation even worse than in the 1990s."

Notes

1. Richard Rose, "How Much Does Social Capital Add to Individual Health? A Survey Study of Russians," *Social Science and Medicine* 51 (2000): 1421–1435; Robert D. Putnam, *Making Democracy Work: Civic Traditions in Modern Italy* (Princeton, NJ: Princeton University Press, 1993); Bruce Kennedy, Ichiro Kawachi, and Elizabeth Brainerd, "The Role of Social Capital in the Russian Mortality Crisis," *World Development* 26 (1998): 2029–2043.

2. Putnam, *Making Democracy Work*; Thomas R. Cusack, "Social Capital, Institutional Structures, and Democratic Performance: A Comparative Study of German Local Governments," *European Journal of Political Research* 35 (1999): 1–34; Gerry Veenstra and Jonathan Lomas, "Home Is Where the Governing Is: Social Capital and Regional Health Governance," *Health and Place* 5 (1999): 1–12; Alejandro Portes and Patricia Landolt, "Social Capital: Promise and Pitfalls of Its Role in Development," *Journal of Latin American Studies* 32 (2000): 529–547; Paul F. Whiteley, "Economic Growth and Social Capital," *Political Studies* 48 (2000): 443–466.

3. Christopher Marsh, "Social Capital and Democracy in Russia," *Communist and Post-Communist Studies* 33 (2000): 183–199; James S. Coleman, *Foundations of Social Theory* (Cambridge, MA: Harvard University Press, 1990), 315.

4. See Sarah E. Mendelson and John K. Glenn, eds., *The Power and Limits of NGOs: A Critical Look at Building Democracy in Eastern Europe and Eurasia* (New York: Columbia University Press), 2002; and two recent special issues on the subject of civil society in Russia from the journal *Demokratizatsiya*, Vol. 10, Nos. 2–3, Spring and Summer 2002.

5. Richard Rose, "How Much Does Social Capital Add to Individual Health? A Survey Study of Russian," *Social Science and Medicine* 51 (2000): 1421–1435; see also Bruce Kennedy, Ichiro Kawachi, and Elizabeth Brainerd, "The Role of Social Capital in the Russian Mortality Crisis," *World Development* 26 (1998): 2029–2043.

6. Joseph Stiglitz, *Globalization and Its Discontents* (New York: W. W. Norton & Company, 2002), 161.

2

Social Cohesion in Russia

The State and the Public Sector

Linda J. Cook

This chapter focuses on the public sector in Russia over the decade of transition (1992–2002), addressing three questions: How has the public sector functioned as a source of or a detractor from cohesion and social cohesion in Russian society? How has this dynamic changed over the course of the transition? What policies could be applied to the sector in order to encourage a rebuilding of social cohesion and capital? The chapter argues that throughout the Yeltsin period the public sector functioned mainly as a detractor from social cohesion, generating large-scale societal distrust and defection from state-mediated social security programs. The Putin administration has begun efforts to restore trust by constructing a more effective and transparent public sector. It is at the same time streamlining that sector, shrinking the state's role and responsibilities, and bringing taxing and redistributive practices more into sync with the inegalitarian realities of present Russian society.

Social capital is often defined as a purely societal resource, inhering in a "structure of relationships" in society, separate from the state and, indeed, determining the quality of governance.[1] However, the literature also presents a "statist" view which holds that the state can promote or destroy social capital, that "social capital needs formal institutions to flourish."[2] According to this view, "the state can actively nurture a stable, progressive, and predictable environment in which it is possible for a vibrant civil society to emerge and flourish."[3] Here social capital facilitates coordinated action in society, and it may be measured by looking at "norms of reciprocity sustained by socialization and sanction—trust in public institutions."[4] The present study subscribes to this "statist" view, arguing that the poor quality of governance in Russia's public sector over much of the past decade has eroded social cohesion, as measured by levels of trust in public institutions. Recent improvements in the stability and predictability of governmental performance correlate with marked improvements in trust.

Trust, cooperation, and reciprocity are central to the functioning of the public sector. The post-authoritarian state can provide social goods—education, social security, poverty relief—only if the society minimally trusts it to manage redistribution of resources fairly and reliably across age and income groups and individual life cycles, and so pays taxes and social security contributions. Obviously trust is not the only factor here; the state's capacity to enforce payment compliance also matters greatly. But the argument that in the Russian system, with its large potential for escape into the informal sector, the state must establish credibility as a condition for generalized compliance.

Here, then, cohesion is defined, as a society's capacity to cooperate in the provision of public goods, effectively, to accept state-mediated coordination in funding and administering such goods. Large-scale defection from an established system of public provision indicates a decline in cohesion; return to participation indicates an increase. In theory, of course, society could respond by forming or finding cohesive communities that compensate for the state's failures, and many Russians do rely on such networks.[5] But the inadequacy of this option is clearly evidenced by the substantial rates of poverty, family breakdown, and premature mortality in Russia, and the stark rise in income disparities as the state's taxing and redistributive capacities withered.[6] In a large, complex, urbanized society such as Russia's, cohesion implies trust in some coordinating mechanisms in the public sphere.

It is an oversimplification to say, as analysts sometimes do, that the Russian state under Yeltsin "withdrew" from the public sector. Rather, the state inherited a set of obligations in the social sphere that it could neither reform nor sustain in the face of economic decline. Problems created by a declining revenue base were compounded by blatant misuse of public sector funds, payment offsets, and tax exemptions. The results were deficits in social sector accounts, falling payment levels, and delays in public sector wages and pensions, leading in turn to large-scale defection from the system. The Yeltsin administration's few reform initiatives were poorly designed and largely ineffective.[7] By the mid-1990s a "vicious cycle" of tax evasion and public sector payment arrears had developed, undermining social services, social insurance, and pension security, as well as trust in the government's capacity to provide public goods and services.

The Putin administration began a multifaceted effort to break this cycle, an effort that includes changes in the state's performance, the restructuring of social policy and benefits, tax reform, shifts in institutional responsibilities, and the creation of some new, limited consultative mechanisms. These

Table 2.1

Poverty in the Russian Federation

	1990	1992	1995	1997	1998	1999	2000	2001
% population below sub-sistence level	11	33.5	24.7	20.7	23.3	28.4	29.1	27.6

Sources: Jeni Klugman, *Poverty in Russia: Public Policy and Private Responses* (Washington: World Bank, 1997), p. 29; Goskomstat, *Rossiia v Tsifrakh, 2002* (Moscow: Goskomstat, 2002), p. 100.

measures seem designed to create a "virtuous cycle," in which a more effective state funds a leaner but more reliable public sector. We will next look more closely at the state and the public sector in both the Yeltsin and Putin periods, focusing especially on pension security and poverty policy.

The Yeltsin Period: Less Cohesion, More Defection

During the 1990s, Russia's social sector suffered a crisis. According to the OECD, total public social expenditures declined from almost 18 percent of GDP in 1994, to 16 percent on average in the mid-1990s and an estimated 13 percent in 1999, while the GDP itself declined through these years.[8] The sector's resources could not keep pace with mandated benefits. From 1994, social assistance payments were increasingly in arrears because of both insufficient funds and the collapse of delivery mechanisms. Salaries of public sector workers such as teachers and doctors fell to poverty levels and frequently went unpaid, and their conditions of work deteriorated. A substantial part of the population lived in poverty (see Table 2.1), unemployment grew to over 13 percent in 1998, and inequality increased.[9] While negative trends pervaded the public sector, the following discussion will focus on two key policy areas, pensions and poverty, because they affected large and vulnerable population groups that were especially dependent on the state.

Decline in Pension Security

Russia inherited from the Soviet state a solidaristic pension system based on the Pay-As-You-Go (PAYG) principle, with current pensions paid from current wages—effectively, a government-mediated intergenerational transfer of funds. Pensions, based on years of employment, wages, and other factors, were low but reliable, eligibility was broad, and the system had a modest redistributive effect that benefited the poorer within the retiree age cohort. As participation in the state pension scheme was mandatory for most and no alternative old-age insurance existed, the system represented a kind of "enforced cohesion" that nonetheless sustained pensioners in the low-wage, low-disparity Soviet economy. By the mid-1990s more than one-fourth of Russia's population was eligible for pension payments, with revenues coming from a comparatively high payroll tax of 28 percent financed by employers and 1 percent from employee incomes.[10] The system confronted two serious structural problems: the demographic dilemma, common to aging industrial societies, of worsening worker-retiree ratios; and a radical decline in the national wage bill that formed its tax base. Overlaying these factors were several others relating to governmental performance, trust, and social cohesion that both exacerbated the system's problems and undermined efforts to resolve them.

The first and most obvious problem was the government's failure to pay pensions regularly or in legally mandated amounts. From 1994, arrears in pension payments, varying in length of delay and across regions, became endemic and a major political issue. In 1997, arrears amounted to more than 10 percent of the annual expenditures of the Pension Fund. In the run-up to the 1996 presidential election, Yeltsin, vying with a Communist challenger who relied heavily on the pensioner vote, promised to eliminate arrears. Over the next year he did so, relying on the executive's excessive disposition over federal budgetary allocations to transfer a large pool of funds into the pension system. During the following year, arrears again mounted, to 17 percent of annual expenditures by the end of 1998, until they were paid off with the aid of another budget transfer in 1999.[11] The central cause of arrears was inadequate contributions to regional pension funds, but the government's erratic payment schedules and opaque budgetary processes, when combined with its apparent ability to pay pensions when politically motivated, bred cynicism and distrust about its claims.

Pensions also underwent a severe decline in real value, frequent changes in benefit formulas, and compression, or leveling, during the 1990s. The government complied poorly with provisions for indexation that would have protected the value of pensions, so that by 1999 the real value of average pensions stood at about 60 percent of their 1991 level. Frequent changes in legislation and manipulation of benefit formulas rendered the system, in the words of a recent OECD study, "not sufficiently transparent to enable people to fully comprehend what they can expect from it."[12] Compression resulted in part from one of the Yeltsin administration's more socially responsible policies, a commitment to keep average pensions above the subsistence level and supplement minimum pensions. This was accomplished through presidentially decreed compensation payments as well as restrictions on the upper limit of pension payments.[13] Compression pushed all pensions toward a common level: By 1999 most retirees received nearly the same pension, irrespective of their wage levels or payments into the fund. By severing the connection between earnings and pensions, compression drove away from the system the middle- and upper-income groups in an increasingly stratified society.

The main institutional pillar of Russia's pension system is the Pension Fund, a federal off-budget fund created in 1991 to collect, administer, and pay pensions throughout the federation. Pensions are by far the largest social security program in Russia, with payments accounting for 5–6 percent of GDP in the mid-1990s. The Pension Fund, which manages billions of rubles, has from its beginning been mired in administrative and legal problems. Local offices have inadequate administrative capacity to keep up with the frequent recalculation of pensions, contributing to delays and arrears.[14] More importantly, legal regulation of the Fund has been very weak, and informed observers view it as badly managed or corrupt. Government ministers, academic experts and pensioners' organizations regularly claim that the Fund's management has diverted money from pension payments, borrowed from commercial banks at high interest rates, refused audits, and generally operated with a serious lack of transparency or accountability.[15] This combination of factors—high social security taxes, low and erratic payment of pensions, arrears, manipulation of benefit formulas, compression, and distrust—contributed to large-scale defection from the pension system. Social security taxes were paid almost entirely by enterprises, and enterprise debts to the Pension Fund rose throughout the decade, with three-fourths of corporate entities failing to pay punctually by 1997 (see Table 2.2). In that year, enterprises owed over R87 trillion, nearly 50 percent of the total inflow. Enterprises also evaded the taxes by reporting only a fraction of their true wage bill while paying the remaining wages in kind or in illegal cash transactions, and by accumulating wage arrears. At the same time, an indeterminate but substantial part of the labor force also began to work in the informal economy for part or all of their wages, and these could not be taxed. The government itself ran arrears to the Pension Fund, equaling R14.1 trillion in 1996, for the payment of "social pensions."[16] Debts and tax evasion undermined the Pension Fund's revenue base and its capacity to provide social security for Russia's elderly. From 1995, average pensions hovered above the pensioners' subsistence minimum (psm), and, in the aftermath of the 1998 financial crisis, dipped well below it, leaving large numbers of pensioners in poverty.[17]

The Russian government did make attempts to address the problems of the pension system during the 1990s, proposing a variety of reforms that would have restructured eligibility rules to reduce the severe financial pressures on the Fund. Most of these reforms necessarily involved limiting rights

Table 2.2

Debts of Payers to the Pension Fund (trillions of rubles at end of year for 1993–97; billions of new rubles from 1998–2000)

1993	1994	1995	1996	1997	1998	1999	2000
1.1	7.0	22.7	59.5	87.8	129.3	142.7	145.9

Sources: For 1993–1997, *Statisticheskii biulleten'* No. 3 (42), Goskomstat, June 1998, 147; for 1998–2000, *Pension Fund of the Russian Federation: The main data on the financial-economic activities for 1990–2000* (Moscow: Contemporary Economy and Law, 2000).

(for example, raising the age for pension eligibility, or eliminating benefits for those who continued to work), or taking away established prerogatives and privileges. They were met with hostility by the left in the Duma and by pensioners who distrusted the government's claims and who were determined to resist further losses. The government lacked the credibility to conduct a public dialogue about the need for pension reform, and despite the encouragement of Western advisers it seldom tried. Policymaking was strongly elite-dominated, with prominent participation by international financial institutions such as the World Bank, and little involvement by Russian society.[18]

One especially significant reform effort was the introduction of private or Non-State Pension Funds (NSPFs). Authorized by a 1992 presidential decree, NSPFs were designed to provide a market alternative for additional pension savings and eventually to allow for off-loading from the state system of some special (occupational) pensions. A number of NSPFs were established, mostly connected to large corporations.[19] They proved easily subject to corruption, however, and many were hurt and some destroyed in the 1998 financial crisis. While the larger funds survived, the experience contributed to distrust of private funds and market mechanisms as a means of providing social security.[20]

Social Benefits and Poverty Policy

In the areas of social benefits and subsidies and also poverty policy, the Yeltsin years brought a decline in government-mediated redistribution in Russian society. Moreover, those funds that were spent often failed to reach the poor or were inadequate to alleviate poverty. The groups most at risk for poverty were children and the unemployed and their households. The benefit programs in place did little to help them. Unemployment benefits amounted to less than 20 percent of the subsistence level; the minority of eligible workers who received benefits remained poor.[21] Payment of child benefits experienced months-long delays in some regions and de facto suspension in others. The failures of Russia's public sector are most starkly reflected in statistics on poverty among these groups: According to Goskomstat, in 1997 (before the financial crisis) 38 percent of families with children under age 16 were poor; in 1998 these numbers rose to 45 percent. A substantial majority of households with three or more children were poor in the late 1990s.[22] Despite the problems with the pension system, pensioners experienced considerably lower rates of poverty than children and multi-child households.

Several factors contributed to the ineffectiveness of social spending. First, the inherited system of subsidies and entitlements provided many benefits to non-poor households. According to experts' analyses, only one-third of social spending shown in official accounting went to those below subsistence, a low level by international standards.[23] The government talked a great deal about creating a new system of targeted benefits for the poor, but the political and administrative obstacles to such reform proved high, and little was accomplished. Second, responsibility for payment of many social benefits had been transferred to the regional level in 1992, cumulating disadvantages in the poorest regions. Third, funding and administration of the social sphere were rife with confusion and obfuscation. Unfunded federal mandates were regularly (and illegally) passed down to regional and local governments that lacked the resources to pay for them. The system was characterized by complex assignments of responsibilities among different levels of government, often leading to mutual recriminations between federal, regional, and local administrations over nonpayments and arrears, a pattern that was also common in public sector wage disputes. Those attempting to hold authorities accountable, including teachers and doctors striking over wage arrears, commonly faced frustration and blame-avoidance.[24]

Conclusion: The Yeltsin Period

The performance of Russia's social sector during the Yeltsin period contributed to the erosion of trust in the state. The government's de facto reliance on pension and social sector wage arrears to fund its deficits—its failure to fulfill these fundamental obligations—was an especially deep betrayal that sapped public confidence. Beyond this, the public sector was poorly organized and administered, opaque, and ineffective at meeting the needs of the young, the elderly, and the poor. And if the state itself could not provide social security, blatant corruption, financial malfeasance, and the 1998 collapse left serious doubts that it could administer or regulate private alterna-

Table 2.3

Russian Population's Trust in Government Authorities

	1999		2000	
	March	November	March	November
Toward President of Russian Federation				
Fully	3	2	48	45
Partially	21	16	29	33
Not at all	71	75	9	9
Toward Parliament				
Fully	4	4	13	10
Partially	40	35	42	43
Not at all	37	37	18	30
Toward the Government				
Fully	12	8	20	20
Partially	45	38	43	43
Not at all	28	35	18	20

Source: Obshchestvennoe mnenie—2000, Vserossiiskii tsentr izucheniia obshchest-vennogo mneniia (VTsIOM), December 2000, 57.

tives. Levels of trust in the various institutions of government at the end of the Yeltsin period reached abysmally low levels. According to a survey by VTsIOM (All-Russian Center for the Study of Public Opinion), the percentages of Russians who "fully" trusted the president, government, or parliament in 1999 could be counted in the single digits (see Table 2.3).

The Putin Administration and the Social Sector

Under Putin, the Russian state initiated a serious effort to restore trust by crafting policies to rescue the ailing social sector and to overcome the legacy of administrative incompetence and failed reform initiatives. This effort has been facilitated by economic and political conditions. The Russian economy has grown steadily since 1999, providing the state with critical financial resources, and the Duma elected in December of that year has been far more cooperative with the executive than its predecessors. The Putin strategy includes measures designed to increase confidence in the state, to make responsibility for financing and delivery of social benefits more transparent, to create compensation mechanisms for those who lose benefits in rationalizing measures, to restructure tax obligations, and to consult more broadly in the planning of major reforms. It is also intended to streamline the social sector, reduce the state's role, and privatize some aspects of social security provision. We will consider each of these elements in more detail below.

Improving the State's Effectiveness in the Social Sector

The Putin administration has used the state's increased revenues to rebuild confidence in the public sector first and foremost, by consistently meeting the state's obligations for public sector wage, pension, and other social payments. Nonpayments and most arrears were eliminated in 1999. The focus moved to bringing payments back to their pre-1998 levels, then to increasing benefit levels. By mid-2000, for example, the Pension Fund had been stabilized, R26 billion in arrears paid, and average pensions returned to 105 percent of the psM. Pensions continued to rise in 2000 and 2001.[25] The government has also set an agenda to raise the minimum wage gradually toward the subsistence level (it currently stands below 20 percent of that level).[26] Public sector wages have been increased. Along with these concrete measures, the Putin administration has committed itself to rebuilding a public sector that will provide mandated benefits and effective poverty relief. Though payments remain very low in real terms (and some subsidies, for example on housing and utilities, have been simultaneously removed), the Russian state has consistently met, and gradually increased, most social payments over a three-year period.

The Putin administration has also made progress in reorganizing, streamlining, and rationalizing the system of social benefits and payments. It is implementing measures to centralize responsibility for all federally mandated benefits, to cut some and limit eligibility for others, and to equalize payments across regions. Federal laws on social protection of the disabled, veterans, and children, for example, will now be funded fully from the federal budget rather than from local budgets, so that benefits no longer depend on the varying prosperity of regions. These changes should make social payments more reliable and fairly distributed, but at the same time more limited. The administration's ultimate goal is a rather minimalist welfare state that relies on means tests to target aid exclusively to the poor. As stated by Deputy Prime Minister Valentina Matvienko, "Only families whose income does not exceed the subsistence minimum per person—mainly large families, pensioners, and the disabled—can count on state assistance."[27]

Rationalizing the social sector inevitably means taking away benefits from some. The inherited benefit system included myriad entitlements for almost all population categories, from high-ranking civil servants to elderly World War II veterans. Efforts by the Yeltsin administration to cut and rationalize met political opposition from the left, resistance from a population that was suffering a nearly universal decline in living standards, and general skepticism that the state would use the savings constructively.[28] The Putin administration is trying to ease acceptance of benefit cuts by partially compensating groups that will lose eligibility, for example, by simultaneously increasing their wages or by "monetizing" benefits.[29] It also has the advantage of carrying out cuts while wages and incomes are gradually rising for many. The current strategy relies on partial compensation mechanisms to gain acceptance of retrenchment from current beneficiary groups.

The key to all of these measures—reliable pension and public sector wage payments, increased federal financing of benefits, and compensation mechanisms—is increased revenue sources, and these can be secured in the longer term only by expanding the amount of effectively taxed income. The Putin leadership understands that the current economic recovery is based on an import-substitution response to the 1998 currency devaluation as well as favorable world market prices for its energy exports, conditions likely to be temporary. The key to consolidating Putin's efforts is to overcome tax evasion, especially to get middle- and upper-income Russians to declare and pay on their full incomes. Here the situation improved little in the early Putin years. In the spring of 2001 the government estimated that only about one-third of the real income of citizens was reported as official earnings,[30] while Pension Fund head Mikhail Zurabov calculated that 60 percent of employers were paying minimal Pension Fund contributions that would make their employees eligible for "subsistence-level pensions at best."[31]

The administration has relied on two main sets of measures in its efforts to overcome tax evasion: reform and reorganization of the tax system, and pension reform. The tax reform includes three main elements. The first applies to general income rather than social security taxes. In 2001 a flat, 13 percent tax was instituted across all income levels, replacing a complex, graduated tax structure and substantially lowering the rate for those in higher income brackets. The rationale was that a simple, reduced tax—one that is quite low by international standards, and that actually raised the rate slightly for poorer strata—would encourage middle- and upper-income Russians to make honest income declarations.

The second reform affects social taxes specifically, and involves a regression of the tax rate against wages. According to this system, the (now unified) social tax, is to be paid as follows:

> 35.6 percent on incomes up to R100,000
> 20   percent on incomes of R100–300,000
> 10   percent on incomes of R300–600,000
> 5   percent on incomes above R600,000

The tax is, again, paid by employers, and is paid not on individuals' incomes but on the general wage bill. As the average wage paid by the enterprise increases, the social tax drops dramatically, to near exemption on the highest incomes. It was designed to give employers a strong financial incentive to pay a legal, high wage, which would, in turn, increase income tax receipts. Social security tax collections have reportedly increased under the new system.

The third reform was intended, *inter alia*, to remove control over pension revenues from the Pension Fund to the Federal Tax Service, a reassignment of institutional responsibilities that could be expected to increase public confidence. The reform involved consolidating payroll taxes for the four off-budget social funds—employment, social insurance, medical insurance, and pension (by far the largest)—into a lower, "unified social tax" to be collected by the Tax Service and held in Treasury accounts. In the words of Deputy Prime Minister Valentina Matvienko, who has responsibility for the social sector, the government thinks the "transfer of functions to collect these taxes to the Tax Service will increase efficiency, tighten control, and improve collection."[32] The Pension Fund, however, effectively resisted the reform, and incorporation of pension contributions into the unified tax was delayed until 2003. [33]

The Putin administration also addressed the problem of pension-leveling, which is seen as a major disincentive to participation in the system. Measures were quickly adopted to lift restrictions on the upper limit of wages on which pensions could be computed. The coefficient that tied payouts to the current average wage was to be raised in stages, then eliminated, so that higher-income Russians would receive pensions that bore a closer relationship to their wages.[34]

Pension Reform

A more radical, long-term reform that would partially privatize pension provision was also initiated in 2000. It was designed to replace the present, state-guaranteed, PAYG system with a three-tiered system: the first tier, a basic, guaranteed, minimum pension; the second tier, based on a personal account and differentiated according to earnings; and the third, funded tier, an investment or accumulative account to which an increasing percentage of individuals' pension savings would be contributed. The Putin administration promised that this reform would place the pension system on a firm financial footing in the long term, that it would avoid the inevitable bankruptcy of the current system when the large postwar generation retires, and that the second and third tiers would provide for a differentiation of pension earnings that would reduce incentives for evasion of social taxes and keep higher incomes in the legal sphere. The pension reform has completed its passage through the legislature. It provides a good case for judging to what extent the Putin administration is rebuilding trust and cooperation in its relations with Russian society through its reform of the social sector.

The introduction of a funded or accumulative tier follows broad international trends in pension reform, but it has been subject to a great deal of contention in the Russian context. The most prominent division has emerged within the government, between Mikhail Dmitriev in the Ministry of Economic Development and Trade and Mikhail Zurabov, head of the Pension Fund.[35] Dmitriev, since 1997 a strong proponent of transition to an accumulative system, sees investment accounts as both a long-term benefit to individual pensioners and a potential pool of investment funds for the financially starved Russian economy. Investment of pension funds is expected to put into government and corporate securities $1 billion in the first year and $2 billion within two years. According to one report citing the views of financial analysts, this reform would be a "boon for the Russian financial market and industry, desperate for long-term money."[36] Zurabov has resisted the move toward an accumulative system, partly on the grounds of financial risk to pensioners, but also, many believe, because the Pension Fund would lose control over the money in investment accounts. The "Pension War" between the Ministry of Economic Development and the Pension Fund over different conceptions of the future system, overlaid and partly driven by different institutional interests in the outcome, has punctuated the reform process.[37] Concerns have also been raised that the reform will lead to reductions in payments to current pensioners, will disadvantage women and lower-paid workers, and will eliminate the modest redistributive effects of the current system.

With pension reform, as with social sector reform generally, the Putin administration has relied more than its predecessor on consultative mechanisms that bring a somewhat broader strata of actors into the policy deliberation process. At the outset of his presidency, Putin created a highly influential committee under the leadership of German [Herman] Gref to map out the administration's social sector and economic reform programs. The Gref committee included in its consultations social policy experts and professionals whose widely differing views had been excluded or marginalized earlier, though the final program was drafted by a very narrow group. Similarly, in February 2001, Putin created the National Council on Pension Reform (NCPR), which brought together representatives of government, the Duma, veterans' and employers' organizations, Russia's main (and weak) trade union federation, and others, to thrash out a final set of policy proposals.[38]

These consultative mechanisms represent a small step forward in building a consensus on social sector reform among the elite. They have contributed to improvements in the coherence and effectiveness of adopted policies. But they are not designed to activate public participation or to create a genuine social dialogue about policy. Both the Gref Committee and the NCPR were heavily weighted toward government representatives and other establishment organizations. They did create a more authentic domestic policy process, restricting the role, for example, of representatives of the World Bank, which had been heavily involved in pension policy during the Yeltsin period. Still, the Council was created rather late in the policy-making process, holding its first meeting only in mid-March, when most aspects of the reform had already been decided, and it was viewed partly as a mechanism to resolve the disputes between Dmitriev and Zurabov. The Council did produce a legislative package, though debates continued.[39]

Concerns about the investment mechanism and management of the proposed accumulative accounts, in fact, extend far beyond the Pension Fund, to experts and professionals as well as much of the public. Meetings of the NCPR included "many criticisms and doubts about guarantees of the safety of the pension savings and about the mechanism for multiplying them."[40] The skeptics question who would hold the accumulative accounts, how and by whom decisions would be made about their investment, etc. The underlying issue here is broad distrust, both in the market and in the government's capacity to regulate it. There is a sense that Russia's financial, economic, and legal systems remain too unstable to provide long-term social security, and that there is an absence of investment projects into which the money of the future old can be reliably placed.[41]

The government has made a variety of proposals to assuage these fears. Yevgeny Gontmakher, head of the Social Development Department of the Russian Federation Government Staff, has proposed that investments be handled by an investment commission with representatives of the ministries of Economic Development and Trade and Finance and the Federal Securities Commission—the state agencies that make economic policy— as well as representatives of employers and labor unions, with a Council of Experts to recommend investment strategies to the commission.[42] Putin has proposed that the state would ensure a guaranteed accumulation for these investments, while Deputy Prime Minister Matvienko promised that the state would guarantee pension money, indexed to inflation "until our securities market really gets operating."[43] There have also been proposals to invest part of the funds abroad, where markets are presumably more stable. Nevertheless, continued conflict over the investment mechanism held up the pension reform package for months.

Is the pension reform process, then, helping to rebuild trust and cooperation in relations between the Russian state and society? Is the Putin administration seeking to define a public interest in its redesign of the social sector? This is surely part of the story. The problems of the pension system's demographics are real enough; reform would arguably give middle- and upper-income Russians more incentives to participate in the system, and new consultative mechanisms have been used. On the other hand, the range of participants in policy deliberations has remained narrow, and the major divisions look mainly like a conflict between government ministries with their own agendas, agendas in which the financial security of future pensioners stands as a secondary consideration at best. The Putin administration appears determined to push through pension reform, as evidenced by the range of proposals it has made to gain acceptance. Much of the public, however, has remained skeptical as the reform proceeded through the legislature; a public opinion poll conducted in April-June 2001 by the Romir service showed that, while one-third of those surveyed believed the purpose of pension reform was to improve the situation for pensioners, one-third viewed reform as "an affair of the authorities." The majority have little confidence in the financial institutions in which pension funds could be accumulated (18 percent trust Sberbank; 2 percent trust commercial banks; 41 percent would trust a pension fund that accumulates the "state" part of pensions; 45 percent would not trust it). A large percentage had doubts about the honesty of the government's intentions.[44] One pension expert was more starkly critical in viewing the reform: "Only financial circles are interested in the accumulative system. . . . Banks will have cheap money to invest in the economy . . . the government needs money to invest in the domestic economy . . . but [it is] very risky . . . the economy is to be supported at the expense of future pensioners . . . it is a crime to take [this] money from workers who often earn less than the subsistence minimum.[45]

Conclusion

In the public sector under Putin, pensions and wages are paid, administrative efficiency and (to a lesser extent) transparency have improved, and rationalizing reforms have begun to take effect. The contrast with the Yeltsin period is striking. Governmental performance has correlated with, and I argue contributed to, an increase of trust and a greater willingness to cooperate in the provision of public goods. Levels of public trust rose through 2000, appreciably in the government and dramatically in the president (see Table 2.3 on page 24). According to polls of the Public Opinion Research Foundation and the Russian Public Opinion Research Institute, 40 percent of respondents named the reduction of wage and pension arrears among Putin's accomplishments.[46] The federal government's taxing capacity has also improved as evasion, barter, and other forms of defection from the formal sector declined. According to Finance Minister Kudrin, federal budget revenues increased from 13.7 percent of GDP in the first quarter of 1999 to 17.6 percent in the first quarter of 2000. The drop in defection rates indicates an increased willingness on the part of Russian society to accept state-mediated coordination in funding and administering public goods, and, according to our conception, greater social cohesion.

If the Putin-era reforms are increasing trust and cohesion in Russian society, they are doing so partly by institutionalizing a social security system that is far less solidaristic and redistributive, and more individualistic and differentiated, than its predecessor. Russia now has in place a low, flat income tax, a regressive social security tax that virtually legalizes tax avoidance at the highest income levels, a pension system that is shedding its intergenerational transfer mechanism and seeking to reproduce the wage system's income differentiation, and a declared goal of creating a minimalist social benefits system. Putin has sought to draw the better-off into the system mainly through concessions. The social benefits system is being re-created around new and different norms, institutionalizing within the social sector the inequality that characterizes the broader socio-economy. The state under Putin has made a greater accommodation with society, but especially with its better-off strata.

There remain a number of questions about whether the Putin strategy can successfully build and sustain the effectiveness of the public sector and the trust of Russian society. First are the financial uncertainties, over whether economic recovery will continue and whether the current tax structure, particularly extension of the regressive social tax, will lead to diminished receipts for funding of the sector. Second are the problems of effective implementation; administration of new pension systems and targeted poverty relief may prove more difficult and expensive than anticipated. Third, the intention to shrink the state's role to provision of relief only for those below subsistence has longer-term implications for the social sector. Such an approach may have two types of negative effects on social cohesion: to limit and delegitimate any state-mediated redistribution between upper-income Russians and the lower-income who manage to stay above subsistence, and to create a residual, politically vulnerable public sector in which the majority of Russians have no stake. Finally, the Putin administration's major public-sector reform—the move toward an accumulative pension system—raises important questions about the state's responsiveness and responsibility toward society. The administration appears determined to privatize despite much public concern over the reliability of the investment mechanism, giving little priority to the building of public trust.

Notes

1. See, for example, Robert Putnam, *Making Democracy Work: Civic Traditions in Modern Italy* (Princeton: Princeton University Press, 1993); Christopher Marsh, "Social Capital and Democracy in Russia," *Communist and Post-Communist Studies* 33 (2000): 183–199; Alejandro Portes, "Social Capital: Its Origins and Applications in Modern Sociology," *Annual Review of Sociology* 24 (1998): 1–24.

2. Nicolai Petro, "Creating Social Capital in Russia: The Novgorod Model," *World Development* 2 (2001): 229.

3. Michael Woolcock, "Social Capital and Economic Development: Toward a Theoretical Synthesis and Policy Framework," *Theory and Society* 27 (1998): 157.

4. Petro, "Creating Social Capital," 230.

5. See Richard Rose, "How Much Does Social Capital Add to Individual Health? A Survey Study of Russians," *Social Science and Medicine* 51 (2000): 1421–1435; on informal social protection mechanisms see also OECD, *The Social Crisis in the Russian Federation* (Paris: OECD, 2001): 23–27.

6. See UNICEF, *A Decade of Transition* (Florence: UNICEF, 2001).

7. See Linda J. Cook, "The Russian Welfare State: Obstacles to Restructuring," *Post-Soviet Affairs* 4 (2000): 355–378.

8. OECD, *The Social Crisis*, 11, 27, 37.

9. The Gini Coefficient for the Russian Federation increased from 24 in 1987–88 to 31 in 1993 and 48 in 1996; see World Bank, *World Development Indicators* (Washington, D.C.: 1994; 1996).

10. World Bank, *Russian Federation: Toward Medium-Term Viability* (Washington, D.C.: World Bank, 1996), 67; *Statisticheskii Biulleten'*, No. 3 (42), Goskomstat, June 1998, 146.

11. OECD, *The Social Crisis*, 22–23.

12. OECD, *The Social Crisis*, 119.

13. "The State Is Always in Debt to the People," *Rossiiskaya Gazeta*, 29 July 2000.

14. Vladimir Mikhailev, "Social Security in Russia Under Economic Transformation," *Europe-Asia Studies* 1 (1996): 5–25.

15. Marina Baskakova, Senior Researcher, Moscow Center for Gender Studies, Russian Academy of Sciences, interview by author, Moscow, 4 February 1999; Valentina Bochkareva, Senior Researcher, Institute for Social and Economic Problems of the Population, Russian Academy of Sciences, interview by Elena Vinogradova, Moscow, 25 June 1998; Oksana Dmitrieva, "Fate of Pension Reform Discussed," in *FBIS*, 22 February 2001, citing *Obshchaya Gazeta*, 22 February 2001, 5.

16. Tatyana Maleva, ed., *Sovremennye Problemy Pensionnoi Sfery: Kommentarii Ekonomistov i Demografov* (Moscow: Carnegie Center for International Peace, 1997).

17. "Social Funds: Adding to Them According to and Above the Plan," *Rossiiskaya Gazeta*, 19 May 2000.

18. For an account of international involvement in Russian pension policy during this period see: Andrea Chandler, "Globalization, Social Welfare Reform and Democratic Identity in Russia and Other Post-Communist Countries," *Global Social Policy* 3 (2001): 324–326.

19. Tamara Pushkina and Maria Turovskaya, "Negosudarstvennym pensionnym fondam trebuetsya gosudarstvennaya podderzhka," *Chelovek i Trud* 4 (1999): 36–37.

20. Irina Denisova, Maria Gorban, and Ksenia Yudaeva, "Social Policy in Russia: Pension Fund and Social Security," *Russian Economic Trends* 1 (1999): 12–24.

21. Marc Foley, "Static and Dynamic Analyses of Poverty in Russia," in *Poverty in*

Russia: Public Policy and Private Response, ed., Jeni Klugman (Washington, D.C.: World Bank, 1997).

22. Goskomstat, *Rossiiskii Statisticheskii Ezhegodnik* (Moscow: Goskomstat, 1999), 166.

23. Lilia Ovcharova and Daria Popova, "What Kind of Poverty Alleviation Does Russia Need?" *Russian Economic Trends* 1 (2000): 7–14.

24. See Debra Javeline, *Protest and the Politics of Blame: The Russian Response to Unpaid Wages*. (Ann Arbor: University of Michigan Press 2003).

25. "Social Funds: Adding to Them According to and Above the Plan," *Rossiiskaya Gazeta*, 19 May 2000.

26. "What is the Government Thinking There? Deputy Premier Valentina Matvienko Pays a Visit to *Trud*," *Trud*, 25 September 2001. The minimum wage was held very low in part because it was used as an index for determining other social benefits; this connection has been severed by new legislation.

27. "The State is Always in Debt to the People," *Rossiiskaya Gazeta*, 29 July 2000.

28. Linda J. Cook, Mitchell Orenstein, and Marilyn Rueschemeyer, *Left Parties and Social Policy in Post-Communist Europe* (Boulder: Westview, 1999), 65–68.

29. "Minister Kalashnikov on Aid to Poor," *Rossiiskaya Gazeta*, 21 January 2000.

30. "Can Savage Capitalism be Tamed?" *Rossiiskaya Gazeta*, 5 April 2001.

31. "Labor Code in the Morning, Pension Reform in the Evening. Government Envisions Approval of New Labor Code and Pension Legislation by End of Year," *Rossiiskaya Gazeta*, 20 March 2001.

32. "Matvienko Says Tension over Social Tax Artificial," *FBIS*, 7 June 2000, citing ITAR-TASS.

33. "Unified Social Tax," *Rossiiskaya Gazeta*, 10 June 2000.

34. "The State is Always in Debt to the People," *Rossiiskaya Gazeta*, 29 July 2000.

35. "Labor Code in the Morning, Pension Reform in the Evening," *Rossiiskaya Gazeta*, 20 March 2001.

36. Svetlana Kovalyova, "Russia's New Pension System Launch Said at Risk," *Johnson's Russia List*, #5422, 13 September 2001, citing Reuters, 13 September 2001.

37. "Pension War between Pension Fund and Ministry of Economic Development," *Segodnya*, 6 March 2001, cited in *Current Digest of the Post-Soviet Press*, 4 April 2001, 11.

38. "Sostav natsional'nogo soveta pri Prezidente Rossiiskoi Federatsii pri pensionnoi reforme" (Copy of memo was given to author).

39. "National Council Approves Concept of Pension Reform," *FBIS*, 19 March 2001, citing ITAR-TASS.

40. "Putin's National Council Approves Four Main Pension Reform Bills," *FBIS*, 30 May 2001, citing *Rossiiskaya Gazeta*, 30 May 2001.

41. See, for example, "Government Reaches Pension Impasse Instead of Promised Reform," *Obshchaya Gazeta*, 22 February 2001.

42. "Pension Reform: Everyone Will Participate. The State Will Be Responsible," *Rossiiskaya Gazeta*, 24 April 2001.

43. "What is the Government Thinking There?" *Trud*, 25 September 2001.

44. "Russian Surveys on Pension Reform Support Examined," *FBIS*, 18 July 2001, citing *Vremya MN*, 18 July 2001.

45. Author's interview with pension expert, Moscow, 2 May 2001.

46. "Can Savage Capitalism be Tamed," *Rossiiskaya Gazeta*, 5 April 2001.

47. "Revenue Rising," *Rossiiskaya Gazeta,* 12 May 2000.

3

Public Administration in Social Services

The Need and Capacities for Reform

Elena Vinogradova

The difficult path of social reform in Russia does not end with the adoption of legislative acts. Implementation of new legislative provisions depends largely on the institutions responsible for social protection, poverty and unemployment reduction programs, and realization of youth and family policies. A new social policy, which is more targeted, will set higher requirements for the effectiveness and efficiency of these organizations. Without a new type of public administration to replace the traditional nomenklatura and bureaucracy, state institutions will be incapable of fostering social capital and citizens' trust in the state, and thus of building greater social cohesion.

A decade of post-Soviet development has resulted in the emergence of a number of new state institutions in charge of social policy. Those state bodies inherited from the Soviet social sector have gone through multiple reorganizations affecting many aspects of their operations. All these changes have certainly increased the responsiveness of these institutions, but to a large extent they have preserved many characteristics of the previous bureaucratic system.

What is the relative weight of the old and the new managerial culture in Russian social policy institutions? What are the state institutions' capacities for reform, capacities created by social transformation, brought by new generations of managers and rank-and-file employees, and encouraged by developments in the consciousness of citizens and civil servants?

A series of sociological surveys carried out in 1999 and 2000 sought answers to these and other questions.[1] The surveys were conducted in institutions involved with various areas of social policy, including social protection departments of local and regional administrations, divisions of the Federal Employment Service, committees and departments for youth and family policies, and financial departments of local and regional administrations. They comprised about 150 focused interviews with managers as well as polling of with the staffs of the above-mentioned institutions.

The study involved two parts. Phase I was a pilot study; it included focused interviews conducted in Moscow, St. Petersburg, Tula, and the Altai Republic from fall 1999 through spring 2000, along with a survey conducted in Tula and the Altai Republic in spring 2000 (with 96 respondents). The second part took place in summer 2000 and involved large-scale polling in six regions of the Russian Federation: the Chelyabinsk, Khabarovsk, Samara, Belgorod, Vologda regions, and the Chuvash Republic, including the cities of Chelyabinsk, Magnitogorsk, Khabarovsk, Komsomolsk-na-Amur, Samara, Novokuibyshevsk, Belgorod, Stary Oskol, Vologda, Cherepovets, Cheboksary, and Yadrin, as well as six rural municipalities in the above-mentioned regions.

The results presented in this chapter are drawn mainly from the latter survey, which involved 1,150 respondents. Each region was represented more or less equally. In rural settlements and small towns, almost the entire staffs of the organizations took part in the polling. In large cities, where the number of staffers was much higher, between 30 percent to 60 percent of employees completed the survey. The majority of respondents were middle-aged: 30 percent of the individuals polled were 30 to 39 years old, and 37 percent were 40 to 49 years old. The shares of respondents under 30 and over 49 years old were approximately equal.

Old and New Public Management

Serving society, modern public institutions are important contributors to creating and maintaining social capital. On the other hand, the goal of traditional bureaucratic entities is mainly to serve the state. This fundamental difference has important implications for how these bodies operate; these implications can be seen in how an entity recruits, evaluates, promotes, compensates, manages, and communicates with its employees, as well as in the ways it makes and implements decisions, evaluates its own performance, and communicates with other organizations and with society at large.

When an entity is serving the state, for example, the formal execution of instructions sent down from a higher authority takes precedence over any actual accomplishments in serving society. Organizations of the old bureaucratic type react primarily to orders and guidelines from above, whereas professional bodies of the new type tend to be self-motivated and welcome innovations and initiative.

Confidentiality and lack of transparency are intrinsic in the internal lives of traditional bureaucratic organizations, in contrast to institutions in which transparency and accountability is the norm. The former display a high degree of centralization of decision-making, while the latter delegate responsibilities to all levels of employees. Traditional bureaucracies have virtually unlimited access to resources, as opposed to organizations under the new model, which pursue a policy of responsibility for economic efficiency in using budgetary funds.

One of the key objectives of the survey was to assess where a participating organization fell on the spectrum of organizational types (we will call the two poles "traditional" and "new," respectively) by looking at which of the models best described their standards and the nature of their work. We hypothesized that Russian state bodies continue to be dominated by a managerial culture and bureaucratic practices typical of the Soviet period. Although we confirmed this hypothesis in many respects, we found considerable differences in some areas. Some of the organizational practices observed can be characterized as progressing toward modernization, while other changes in practice resulted from a collapse of the old standards with no new standards to replace them.

Education and Professional Skills

A new model of public administration provides that the education and professional skills of the staff be optimized, that employees' skills match the organization's purposes, and that the number of people employed be limited. Traditional bureaucratic institutions typically have had relatively free access to many resources, including human resources. Their often excessive number of staff have been well-educated, but their composition has been far from optimal.

The data from the survey revealed some of the characteristics of the personnel at federal and municipal social service institutions today. Survey data do not confirm the commonly accepted opinion that Russian governmental organizations are staffed predominantly by old administrative personnel— those who were trained at Soviet educational institutions affiliated with the Communist Party, Komsomol, or trade unions and who matured in Soviet organizations. The overall share of graduates of Soviet managerial schools is only 13 percent of the employees surveyed. Among the employees occupying relatively high positions, that percentage is slightly higher. The dominant group among employees working in the organizations surveyed comprises people who have taken on their jobs since the start of the market reforms in Russia. Only 35 percent of the respondents have been working for federal or municipal organizations for over 10 years.

The overall level of education of the staff is high. Almost all of the respondents have higher educational degrees, which is a legal requirement for those working in public service. Exceptions are rare and occur mainly in rural areas. However, the composition of human resources in terms of skills and training is less satisfying. To a large extent the personnel as a whole continue to display qualities largely representative of public administration during the Soviet period, such as the predominance of experts with basic engineering training. The share of professional public administrators, economists, lawyers, and psychologists—those who normally form the basis of successful public service entities—is meager.

Lack of fit between their professional skills and the demands of their jobs is well understood by employees themselves. Respondents were asked to rate their need to have certain professional knowledge and skills, as well as to evaluate the adequacy of their own professional training. As it turns out, the discrepancy between what is available and what is needed was very large, especially in the areas of economics, information technologies, social legislation, labor law, and psychology—those fields that are key to public administration in social services. Not surprisingly, when asked about the reasons for low effectiveness and quality of work in their organizations, about one-third of respondents pointed to insufficient professional training of employees.

The new model of public administration has in place an effective system of personnel training, which includes professional development and retraining of existing employees and support of new ones. Respondents showed varying levels of awareness of the availability of advanced training. About 50 percent believe that advanced training is available to them and consider this an attractive feature of their jobs, and about 40 percent say that they have no access to advanced training.

The data tell us that the current situation is a long way from the "personnel paradise" of the Soviet period, where all the needs of the governmental institutions were easily satisfied, but likewise it is far from the optimal structure of human resources under a new organizational model. Opportunities to change the structure of human resources in social-sector organizations within the framework of the existing administrative model are quite limited.

Personnel Recruitment and Promotion

The traditional and new models of public administration employ different principles and procedures for enacting personnel policies. The core criteria for employee promotion under the new model are personal achievement, initiative, and the capability for self-improvement. The recruitment and promotion procedures of the contemporary merit-based administrative model envisage competition, transparency, and team decision-making. The traditional bureaucratic model takes into account such criteria as the ability to promptly and diligently carry out instructions, accuracy in fulfilling everyday responsibilities, subjective performance evaluation, and personal recommendations, all procedures that are devoid of competition, and transparency.

When considering the basis for employee promotion, only a little more than half (56 percent) named "effectiveness and quality of work carried out in accordance with official duties" as being "decisive in employee promotion," while education and "skills and experience necessary to work at a new position" were marked by an even smaller number of respondents (40 percent and 32 percent, respectively). Although these three criteria were marked more often than other response options, their significance is far from overwhelming. Initiative and ability to learn and exceed the bounds of official duties are not of primary importance. In other words, a large part of respondents do not appear to see a connection between effective performance and initiative and their career growth (see Table 3.1).

Objective and open personnel recruiting and promotion procedures have not yet become prevalent in the organizations surveyed. Over 70 percent of respondents reported that the recruiting tool most frequently used in their organization is interviewing potential candidates, with the next most popular method, informal criteria such as connections through relatives and friends, chosen by 27 percent of respondents (see Table 3.2).

In the realm of promotional practices, 72 percent selected "recommendations from supervisors" as most frequently used to determine promotions, with "official evaluation and rating of professional skills" chosen by 45 percent of respondents (see Table 3.3).

Many employees know little about the actual process of personnel recruitment and promotion in their organizations (see Table 3.4). Only 23 percent of respondents were aware to some degree of promotion opportunities in their own organization, while 86 percent were unaware of such opportunities.

Answers to questions about the overall assessment of personnel policies also confirm that in the eyes of a very significant proportion of respondents, personnel policies carried out in their organizations are not connected to the professional achievements of employees and their level of responsibility and independence. Many respondents consider personnel recruiting and promotion procedures not sufficiently transparent, clear, and objective. Others, believing that these procedures have no bearing on them and their careers, are indifferent to them.

Table 3.1

Distribution of responses to the question: "Which criteria are decisive in employee promotion?"

Response categories	Share of positive answers as a percentage of the total number of respondents			Total % choosing this response
	Rated 1st	Rated 2nd	Rated 3rd	
Total length of service	6	4	6	16
Age	1	2	2	5
Gender	0	0	2	2
Education (doctoral degree, additional training, degree in public administration, etc.)	18	13	9	40
Level of responsibility	9	12	9	30
Effectiveness and quality of work carried out in accordance with official duties	26	18	12	56
Ability to learn to carry out new responsibilities and exceed the bounds of official duties	6	12	11	29
Relations with coworkers, teamwork	3	9	14	26
Relations with management	10	7	7	24
Connections through relatives and friends and other connections	4	5	1	10
Skills and experience necessary to work at a new position	11	9	12	32
Hard to say	3	0	0	3
No answer	3	9	15	27

Table 3.2

Distribution of responses to the question: "What recruitment tools are most frequently used in your organization?"

Response categories	Share of positive answers as a percentage of the total number of respondents			
	Yes	No	Hard to say	No answer
Open competition	16	55	23	6
Interviews with various candidates selected for their skills and work experience	72	10	15	3
Candidate testing	14	52	26	8
Primarily informal criteria, such as connections through relatives and friends and other connections	27	29	38	6

Table 3.3

Distribution of responses to the question: "What procedures are employed in your organization to determine which employees to promote?"

Response categories	Share of positive answers as a percentage of the total number of respondents			
	Yes	No	Hard to say	No answer
Open competition	7	64	22	7
"Attestation" (official evaluation and rating of professional skills)	45	29	21	5
Promotion of employees who form the administrative reserve	34	22	38	6
Supervisor's recommendation	72	6	18	4
Human Resources Department's recommendation	17	38	37	8

Table 3.4

Distribution of responses to the question: "To what extent are you aware of the following career opportunities?"

Response categories	Share of positive answers as a percentage of the total number of respondents				
	Well aware	Somewhat aware	Somewhat not aware	Not aware	No answer
Vacancies that open in your organization	21	20	27	29	3
Vacancies that open in other organizations in federal and municipal social service	4	7	36	50	3
Promotion opportunities	7	16	37	36	4
Competitions to fill vacancies in your organization	10	16	26	43	5
Competitions to fill vacancies in other organizations	1	5	28	51	15

Remuneration, Benefits, and Privileges

The new type of public administration recognizes personal merit, and its remuneration systems are based on qualifications and personal contribution, rather than on age or seniority. A public employee's prestige comes from competitive labor market salaries.

Unlike Soviet state institutions, where high salaries were unquestionably an attractive factor, the Russian public sector today fails to compete with

Table 3.5

Distribution of responses to the questions: "What—other than position— most affects the level of compensation in your organization? What qualities in employees and the actual work they do influence the level of compensation?"

Response categories	Share of positive answers as a percentage of the total number of respondents			Total % choosing this response
	Rated 1st	Rated 2nd	Rated 3rd	
Total length of service	16	11	5	32
Age	0	1	0	1
Gender	0	1	2	3
Education (doctoral degree, additional training, degree in public administration, etc.)	15	13	9	37
Level of responsibility	14	12	11	37
Effectiveness and quality of work carried out in accordance with official duties	16	13	13	42
Ability to learn to carry out new responsibilities and exceed the bounds of official duties	2	7	7	16
Relations with coworkers, teamwork	1	3	7	11
Relations with management	8	7	6	21
Experience at this job	1	5	5	11
Connections through relatives and friends and other connections	3	5	4	12
Seniority	22	14	12	48
Other	0	0	0	0
No answer	2	8	19	29

other sectors for human resources. The private sector offers much higher remuneration to those experts needed for state bodies to function effectively, e.g., lawyers, economists, and specialists in finance, information technologies, and public relations, etc.[2] "Low salary" was named a disadvantage of the job by 96 percent of respondents. According to half of the individuals surveyed, it is the main reason people quit their current jobs and seek other employment.[3]

Under Soviet administration, along with monetary compensation that could compete in the labor market, civil servants had access to a great number of social benefits. In this regard, the situation has changed dramatically. The social benefits offered today as part of a civil servant's compensation package are gradually becoming less valuable; they are no longer as abundant as they used to be and their quality is lower, contrary to what is commonly thought. Rank-and-file employees working for federal and municipal social services often receive no social benefits at all or social benefits that are merely comparable to those of employees at many other Russian companies. Among the available services, 42 percent of respondents reported receiving vouchers for vacation centers free of charge or at a discount; only 18 percent receive housing assistance; and only 13 percent have access to better-quality medical services than those provided by municipal medical facilities.[4]

The survey results indicate that the majority of staffers are not sure that their performance is the leading determinant of the size of their compensation. Seniority is likely to be more important (42 and 48 percent respectively). Respondents virtually did not mark as important either the ability to learn to carry out tasks exceeding the bounds of their official duties or relations with colleagues and teamwork (see Table 3.5).

Managerial Techniques

Opportunities to carry out a mass survey of employees in order to study managerial techniques used at their organizations are relatively limited. However, the results of the survey allow us to explore some aspects of this issue. The main characteristic of modern administration and the feature that distinguishes it from the highly centralized traditional bureaucratic system is the delegation of decision-making authority throughout the system. Responsibility is distributed to various levels in the managerial structure.

The survey results show that delegation of authority to lower levels in the organization—a reserve that can improve the efficiency of administration—has not been utilized. The questionnaire contained the following question: "In the process of work you prepare proposals to the management on certain issues. Do you believe that you can make decisions on some of these issues independently?" Over half of respondents answered the question affirmatively; 18 percent said that it was possible regarding all issues; and 60 percent said that it was possible in some cases. Over 40 percent of respondents name the lack of decision-making authority as a negative feature of their work. Over half (55 percent) believe that the requirement to internally coordinate on issues with various superiors significantly impedes their work, and 38 percent mention the negative effect of external coordination.

The current practices for planning work are typical for state institutions of the Soviet period. Planning is nothing more than compiling a list of activities, their dates, and the resources needed to carry them out. Plans reflect only the activities of an organization and the departments within it; they do not include goals and target results, which could then serve as evaluation criteria. Within this approach, strategic and long-term planning are practically nonexistent. In the majority of cases, planning horizons in the institutions surveyed do not exceed one year. Staffers participate primarily in monthly and quarterly work planning. Fewer than 20 percent of respondents said that they take part in designing long-term plans that go at least one year into the future. The majority of individuals surveyed considered this state of affairs to be reasonable, and only the same 20 percent believe that strategic planning is necessary.

The results of the survey testify to the fact that federal and municipal public employees often encounter problems with access to information and legal expertise in their work. Approximately one-third of respondents reported having difficulty receiving information necessary for their work from other federal and municipal establishments and institutions. In general, 48 percent talked about a lack of information needed to do their work.

Many staffers (57 percent) said that the fact that many effective pieces of legislation are undeveloped is a serious problem. In their opinion, the regulations they rely on in their everyday work are often not functional and contain a great deal of vague and contradictory language. Time and again, their work is hindered by the absence of needed regulation (39 percent of respondents mentioned this problem). In addition, some important social and employment issues have no proper legislative regulations.

Modern information technology and computerized document-sharing have not yet become widespread. Fewer than one-fourth of staffers in the organizations polled actively use e-mail, the internet, or intranet. One-third of respondents (33 percent) said that they never or almost never use contemporary means of communication and data access. They believe that this lagging behind in the use of up-to-date document-sharing technology is related to a shortage of computers and means of communication.

The study of operational practices at federal and municipal social service institutions allows us to conclude that their personnel potential, personnel relations, and managerial techniques hardly correspond with the requirements of the new model of public administration. The positive effect of social reforms may be significantly diminished and in some cases nonexistent because of the low efficiency of the operation of institutions responsible for implementation of the innovations.

Willingness to Renew

Insofar as state institutions may affect (positively or negatively) the formation of social capital, the community of public employees in turn creates social capital within these institutions. The development of this process then exerts a powerful influence on the effectiveness, dynamics, and ability of these organizations to respond to public needs.

Table 3.6

Distribution of responses to the question: "What attracts those who leave other sectors for the federal and municipal services sector?"

Response categories	Share of positive answers as a percentage of the total number of respondents			Total % choosing this response
	Rated 1st	Rated 2nd	Rated 3rd	
Prestige	13	13	10	36
Stability	51	15	6	72
Social benefits	2	5	6	13
Opportunities to receive unofficial income	1	0	1	2
Opportunities to exert unofficial influence	0	1	1	2
Professional reputation	4	12	9	25
Moral satisfaction from work	17	19	11	47
Career growth opportunities	2	5	9	16
Educational and advanced training opportunities	2	8	10	20
Other (name)	1	1	1	3
Hard to say	3	0	1	4
No answer	4	21	35	60

Among the factors that determine the formation of social capital within the public service sector are, employees' motivation; proper understanding of their mission as public employees, particularly as employees in the social-service sector; the ability to critically and independently evaluate their organizations; and the readiness to bear responsibility. The list also includes a certain amount of trust in the state as employer, in management of their organizations, and in society as represented by its citizens and institutions. Employees should be open and ready to cooperate with colleagues, citizens, civic organizations, and the media. Our analysis of the survey results and observations made while polling allow one to draw some conclusions about this.

Motivation and Understanding of Mission

As can be seen in Table 3.6, 72 percent of federal and municipal employees consider the stability their work to be its most appealing characteristic. Stability is by far more important than a prestigious job, a professional reputation, career growth opportunities, or availability of advanced training.

The respondents perceive the concept of stability as having several aspects. Stability means invariability and routineness of professional functions, no need to "invent anything exceptional," and the guaranteed absence of mistakes resulting from the division of responsibility and multiple coordination procedures. Stability is also understood as a relatively low likelihood of losing one's job. At the same time, for a large number of respondents who have come through multiple reorganizations, changes in leadership, and waves of layoffs at their institutions, stability means the provision of labor rights and the absence of outright lawlessness. (Lawlessness, in their opinion, is omnipresent in the private sector.)

Respondents agreed that those who come to work for organizations connected with solving social problems are attracted, among other things, by the moral satisfaction that this job provides. Asked to relate their own attitude to the profession, over 80 percent of individuals polled mentioned "an opportunity to benefit society" as the most attractive aspect. Obviously, in choosing this, respondents may be making a response choice based on an established stereotype of socially approved values. However, it must be acknowledged that many observations confirm that this choice is to a large extent sincere. Some employees display a real compassion for the unemployed, low-income families, and retirees, and are "happy to help them." Quite often this attitude is generated by a specific social solidarity with these clients, solidarity of people who lost the social and financial status that previously had made them respect themselves and be respected by others.

Employees often perform selfless actions, such as working overtime with no compensation or pursuing nonstandard solutions to help their clients. For instance, employees at one of the departments of social protection polled acted on their own initiative by growing vegetables and distributing them among low-income families as a form of social assistance. In some rural areas, the delivery of food packages, one type of social assistance, is very challenging due to harsh climate conditions and the poor quality of roads, and requires an extraordinary organizational and physical effort from social service employees, often women of retirement age. Many staffers working for employment services show exceptional commitment and resourcefulness as they organize psychological support groups for the long-term unemployed. Often these are former schoolteachers and industrial sociologists who have no special training for that job, but mobilize all of their life experience and emotional resources to do this work.

Observations made while working on this and other studies in which the author participated lead to the conclusion that many social service employees who truly find moral satisfaction in their work display their dedication in specific cases where they "took care of people," rather than in consistent improvement in the overall effectiveness of the organizations in which they work. The majority of workers lack virtually any understanding of their mission as employees of public institutions sanctioned by society; they view their main task as "helping the poor from the bottoms of our hearts" rather than as providing the population with stable and professional services. The best of the employees are usually motivated primarily by humane kindheartedness, rather than by a sense of responsibility to society, their customer. Incentives such as responsibility for effective use of resources allotted by society and the reliable functioning of the social protection system are virtually nonexistent.

This is evident in particular in responses to questions related to the potential for improving labor efficiency. Practically all respondents admitted that the amount of work their departments are responsible for could be done by a smaller number of employees. Pessimists who reject this possibility are in a minority of 11 percent. About 60 percent of the individuals polled believe that "higher salaries and a simultaneous increase in workload" can solve this issue. Forty-five percent think that it can also be achieved "if organization of work in their departments is improved." At the same time, when asked, "What hinders effective operation of your department?" the respondents primarily named insufficient financing and technological capability and the fact that employees were overloaded with work.

Responses to questions about ways to find reserve working hours produce a similar picture. The respondents believe that it would benefit the business if they devoted *more* time to the following: data analysis (40 percent), evaluation of the results of their work (39 percent), activities related to information gathering (33 percent), preparation of decisions (30 percent), and long-term planning (27 percent). The respondents were practically unable to identify activities on which they needed to spend *less* time. Obviously, this attitude corresponds poorly with the idea of doing the same amount of work with a smaller number of people.

However, about one-quarter to one-third of employees surveyed are of a different opinion. They believe that effectiveness can be improved by suspending rules or rejecting excessive centralization and micromanagement and by expanding the authority of the staff to make independent professional decisions.

It is also important to stress that the mission interpretation and opinions on work-effectiveness improvement potential mentioned above are less typical of employees of the Federal Employment Service. This institution was established during the reform period when it became apparent that unemployment was a problem that Russia would have to tackle over the long term. The employment service was founded by new people, a significant number of whom, especially those entering management, received related professional training. Employees of this agency are more likely to think in market-economy terms and perceive the citizens whom they serve as clients.

Interestingly, the word "client" is intrinsic in their vocabulary when talking about their work.

The employment service also shows a higher level of responsibility regarding the resources it uses. It is possible that this is partially due to the fact that over a long period of time, including the time of the survey, the service's departments were involved in raising money for the Employment Fund (which they no longer do).[5] Targeted payments into the Employment Fund were similar—albeit very marginally so—to insurance payments, which made them different from impersonal budgetary resources.

Significantly, the overwhelming majority of employees (95 percent) at all organizations surveyed consider staff training, advanced training, and retraining an important work-effectiveness improvement tool. In keeping with this, the majority of respondents displayed a readiness to study and retrain.

Responsibility and Trust in the State as Employer

The attitude of employees toward contract work speaks of their readiness to bear more responsibility for the results of their work. Respondents were asked to comment on the possibility of working on a contract basis, where the contract is renewable, or not, after a few years (e.g., two to five years), with the arrangement providing for more independence, responsibility, and a higher wage.[6] Respondents divide into three nearly equal groups in regard to this issue: those willing to work on a contract basis, those unwilling to do so, and those unsure about their preferences. Similar results are found in the analysis of responses to the question of how the staff would react if such an innovation became reality (see Tables 3.7 and 3.8).

The idea of working on a fixed-term contract basis is more highly favored by men than by women: 45 percent of men indicated a willingness to work on a contract basis, while only 27 percent of women welcomed the idea. The attitude to this hypothetical innovation significantly depends on age as well. Respondents under 30 years of age were slightly more willing to switch to a fixed-term contract basis: 37 percent of them said they would do so, as compared to 27 percent in relatively older age groups (30–40 and 40–50 years old).

Doubts and negative attitudes toward the fixed-term contract system appear to be largely related to the overall inertia and stability considerations mentioned earlier.[7] However, another important factor is also the bias suspected in an employer's performance evaluation. During interviews, many respondents spoke with even greater anxiety about the possibility that the contract renewal process may be arbitrary. In their opinion, this process could easily become a source of unscrupulous manipulations on the part of deci-

Table 3.7

Distribution of responses to question regarding contract work

Question	Share of positive answers as a percentage of the number of respondents		
	Yes	No	Hard to say
"Would you personally be interested in working on a contract basis, meaning working more than you currently do, bearing more responsibility for the quality of work and decisions made, and being prepared for the possibility that your contract would not necessarily be renewed, but receiving a significantly higher salary?"	29	39	31

Table 3.8

Distribution of responses to question regarding fixed-term contract work

Question	Share of positive answers as a percentage of the number of respondents				
	Very interested	Somewhat interested	Somewhat uninterested	Uninter-ested	Hard to say
"Would you or *your colleagues* be interested in working on a fixed-term contract basis if this meant that your salaries would be significantly higher?"	12	25	19	18	26

sion-makers, leaving employees with little protection from the state, which no longer guarantees protection of labor rights in the private sector and will most likely stop doing so in the public sector as well. Respondents remained unconvinced, even when confronted with the obvious concept that management might want to continue labor relations with good employees.

Insufficient trust in the state as employer and fair partner reveals itself in the responses to questions about the possibility of open and objective competition in Russian public service, as can be seen from the survey results in Table 3.9.

At the same time, there is a significant number of respondents who depart from the rest in their views regarding the correlation between responsibility and trust. These respondents do not rule out the possibility of establishing partnership relations with the state. They were also willing to assume responsibility and expect responsible treatment of themselves and their work from the state as employer despite existing problems. This group of respon-

Table 3.9

**Distribution of responses to question concerning competitive
hiring practices**

	Share of positive answers as a percentage of the number of respondents				
Question	Do not believe	Somewhat not believing	Somewhat believing	Believe	Hard to say
"Do you believe that there is a real possibility that open and objective competition to fill vacancies in the Russian federal and municipal service can be organized?"	23	29	15	6	26

dents makes up from one-quarter to one-third of all individuals surveyed and is essentially the same group that held positive opinions about work-effectiveness improvement potential.

Willingness to Cooperate and Openness

The ability of a group and its members to establish and maintain a relationship of cooperation, which allows issues to be resolved more effectively, is an important element in social capital formation.

It must be stressed that a "good moral and psychological climate in personnel relations" and the possibility of establishing "extended networks with useful and interesting people" are considered attractive features of a job in the eyes of a large number of employees; 63 percent and 56 percent of respondents, respectively, mentioned these qualities. As for the most typical reasons that people quit their jobs, human relations play a relatively insignificant role. The excessive emotional commitment that working with the population requires was mentioned as a common reason to resign by only 10 percent of respondents; 7 percent named bad relations with management; and 1 percent blamed bad relationships with coworkers.

The survey also offered the individuals polled the opportunity to express their opinions on the possibility of cooperation with other public and private institutions, as well as with outside experts, in order to help solve the issue of the shortage of a quality work force, which the majority of respondents named as a serious obstacle in their work. In recent years, the Russian market of managerial, financial, legal, accounting, and information services was replenished by many organizations that have a good reputation in the business world and can be contracted by state bodies to do certain types of work. In this case, the staff of state institutions can supervise and monitor their work.

Table 3.10

Distribution of responses to the question: "If you believe that you and your coworkers lack the necessary knowledge and skills in some area, what would be a reasonable solution to this problem?"

Response categories	Share of positive answers as a percentage of the total number of respondents			Total % choosing this response
	Rated 1st	Rated 2nd	Rated 3rd	
Organize training and retraining of existing employees (advanced training classes, etc.)	89	5	1	95
Employ new experts	3	45	15	63
Outsource for outside consultants	2	17	16	35
Sign contracts to do specific types of work with specialized outside organizations, including private entities	1	11	23	35
Other solutions (name)	1	3	2	6
Hard to say	1	1	4	6
No answer	3	18	39	60

This scenario is currently being discussed by experts on public administration reform. However, the idea of outsourcing organizations to fulfill this or that professional function was only marginally popular among public employees; only 35 percent of respondents said that this idea made sense (see Table 3.10). The overwhelmingly negative opinion on this issue may be due to a lack of trust in "outsiders," who live and work in accordance with their own rules and "pursue their own interests."

In contrast with organizations employed as consultants, independent experts involved as consultants and essentially incorporated into the organization in general are viewed more positively. The idea of cooperation with independent experts is backed by sixty-three percent of employees.

Respondents had different reactions to the question about what they and their coworkers thought of a situation in which outside experts with high-quality, rare professional skills take upon themselves a large amount of responsibility, carry a heavier workload, and are paid much better wages. Thirty-nine percent of respondents said that they approved of this, while 30 percent stated their opposition.[8]

Opinions also split on the hypothetical possibility that the organizations in which employees were surveyed become more open, adopting practices of administration utilized in many developed countries (see Table 3.11). The majority of respondents believe that better openness will to a greater or lesser degree affect federal and municipal institutions. In the eyes of

Table 3.11

Distribution of responses to the question: "Many countries require that their federal and municipal organizations give the population, civic organizations, and the media free access to any information and files (excluding information legally treated as state, trade, or personal secrets). If this requirement were introduced in Russia, what in your opinion would happen?"

| | Share of positive answers as a percentage of the total number of respondents | | | |
Response categories	Yes	No	Hard to say	No answer
Disorganize organizations' work	23	36	33	8
Increase responsibility of employees	55	16	22	7
Improve understanding and trust	44	19	29	8
Limit corruption and abuse of office	32	20	39	9
Lead to incompetent interference with operation of institutions	36	20	36	8
Produce work overload	49	18	27	6
Change nothing	9	27	40	24
Other	0	2	14	84

employees, the main threats posed by greater openness are work overload (49 percent) and "incompetent interference with operation of institutions" (36 percent). A significantly smaller but nonetheless considerable proportion of respondents (23 percent) think that this would lead to disorganization in their work. At the same time, 55 percent of individuals polled are convinced that greater openness would increase employees' responsibility, 44 percent said that it would improve understanding between the government and society, and 32 percent believe that it would help reduce corruption and abuse of office.

In other words, as citizens, respondents agree that openness of public institutions is an important factor in the country's development. However, as employees, they display defensive reactions typical of corporate psychology, manifested in particular in worries regarding "incompetent interference." There is little doubt that rejection of the idea of openness results from bureaucratic traditions. But concerns expressed by respondents have other grounds as well: Staffers are afraid that cooperation between citizens and state institutions will not be properly organized and managed.

Conclusion

Despite the limited resources Russian society has available to allot to financing social services and the entities that carry them out, a functioning system rendering assistance to the needy, unemployed, retired, and disabled has been established in Russia. The internal life of these institutions and their relationships with society still display many qualities inherent in the traditional bureaucratic system. The performance evaluation criteria, principles and mechanisms of compensation and promotion, managerial techniques, and the types of internal and external relations in the entities surveyed in many ways correspond to this model.

The biggest obstacle to modernizing state social service institutions is the continuing presence of standards and practices inherited from the Soviet era. They include the mechanism of financial resources allocation and spending, decision-making techniques and coordination procedures, and the system of distribution of responsibility backed by multiple guidelines. Another impeding factor is the predominance of the old type of labor relations, which together with limited financial resources for employee compensation, leads to a shortage of qualified labor, including a shortage of those employees who can promote new technologies and implement more flexible personnel policies even within the framework of the existing system.

The fact that problems facing the modernization of the public service are rooted in the omnipresent concept of public service organization and operation, used across the board in Russia, reveals itself in particular in the striking homogeneity of our survey results. The analysis of the survey data was performed both across the entire sample and separately in each pilot region, across levels of organization (regional level, cities, and rural municipal entities), across groups of respondents (management and rank-and-file employees), and across the functional areas in which the entity operated. As it turned out, variations across regions, departments, employee positions, and even age in the data set are minimal. In the prosperous and rapidly developing city of Samara, the economically troubled Komsomolsk-na-Amur, the city of Vologda in the northern European part of Russia, and the rural area of Lazo near the Chinese border, officials work and think the same.

This observation—unusual for Russian comparative studies, which typically show enormous variation among regions—is very disappointing, though it does not rule out completely an optimistic forecast in terms of modernizing state institutions. Rejection of the traditional bureaucratic model of public administration with its inflexibility and monotony, accompanied by a transition to new methods of administration, can spur the development of initiative and solutions to tackling emerging problems.

The study showed that potential for change, albeit very limited, exists in the institutions surveyed. Reforms in public administration in the social sector at least initially can rely on the seed of social capital that has formed in the public employee community. Changes may be generated within the small but nonetheless significant portion (one-third, as it appears) of staffers who believe that fair partnership with the state is possible, are willing to make independent decisions, and realize that the flip side of independence is responsibility. Further reform development might attract to the public-administration sector those who believe that the goal of the existence of an organization and their own involvement with it is not to preserve the modest but stable prosperity of officials, but to work for society's benefit and receive merit-based compensation for this work.

Notes

1. The research project on which this chapter is based was implemented with the financial support of the Carnegie Moscow Center. The second part was carried out as part of the program "Technical Assistance for Reforming the Regional Budgetary System: A Review of Budgetary Expenditures on Social Protection," whose principal investigator was the Leontief Center in St. Petersburg. The International Bank for Reconstruction and Development (IBRD) financed the project.

Mikhail Dmitriev, who at the time this project was launched was a member of the Scientific Council of the Carnegie Moscow Center and who is now Deputy Minister of Economic Development and Trade of the Russian Federation, initiated the survey and was the leader of the research team that carried it out. Pavel Kudyukin and Olga Kirichenko developed the concept and scenario of the focused interviews and conducted the majority of the interviews, analyzed the materials, and drew conclusions based on interview results. The author of this chapter prepared the questionnaires for large-scale polling and analyzed and interpreted the data. Although the overall survey was a group effort, the author is exclusively responsible for the interpretations and conclusions in this chapter.

2. Studies of public administration often mention that state officials receive non-official or illegal profits, which make up for at minimum the discrepancy between low wages in the public sector and higher wages in similar entities in the nongovernmental sector. This is an urgent problem, not addressed here, as in those organizations the study focused on, opportunities to gain additional nonofficial profits are minimal. In addition, this issue calls for its own study with separate conceptual and methodological approaches, which is beyond the goals set for this study.

3. Even though about 70 percent of respondents believe that their professional skills and work experience may be in demand in nongovernmental financial organizations, only 24 percent of them think that they could find a job in these entities in the near future. Over 40 percent of individuals surveyed are of the opinion that, educational level and work experience being equal, wages are considerably higher in the industrial sector, but only 19 percent believe that they would be able to find a job in this sector. Respondents consider moving to another job in the public sector a more likely possibility (32 percent), but expect their wages to increase insignificantly if they do so.

4. According to survey results, the number of social services employees have access to differs depending on the institution, which may reflect an unofficial hierarchy. Only 7 percent of those employed by the Federal Employment Service said that workers in their organization receive "assistance in solving housing problems," whereas 17 per-

cent of employees with the social protection bodies and 38 percent of those working for financial establishments within the social sector can lay claim to the same.

5. The Employment Fund was abolished in 2000, and unemployment reduction programs in Russia are currently financed from the budget.

6. This practice is utilized in state institutions in many countries, and the possibility of introducing it to Russian public service is under expert consideration.

7. These concerns are further reinforced by the relatively low rating employees give to their competitiveness in the labor market mentioned above.

8. At the same time, the majority of respondents believe that compensation for those working on a temporary contract basis should not exceed average wages in the organization by more than two fold (the majority of them said that the difference in wages should be from 20 percent to 100 percent). They virtually denied the possibility of a larger discrepancy.

4

Ethnic Problems and National Issues in Contemporary Russian Society

Boris Kagarlitsky

The Historical Context of Ethnic Relations in Russia

It is impossible to discuss ethnic problems and national issues in contemporary Russia without touching upon the Soviet and pre-Soviet past. Likewise, it is impossible to understand relationships between nations without taking into account the history of those relations, and without considering the history of relations between various ethnic groups and the government authority.

Russia was formed as a multinational state, with the overwhelming majority of peoples it included being indigenous. Therefore, on the one hand, Russia has always been a "melting pot" assimilating various cultures, religions, and lifestyles; on the other hand, the majority of the ethnic groups had their own distinctive history. After 1917, they even had quasi-sovereign status.

The revolution of 1917 terminated the old system, which had incorporated formal and legal inequality between those from Greater Russia, defined as Russians belonging to the Orthodox Church, and those Russians from all other nations in the country. Representatives of other Eastern Orthodox Christian nations, such as those populating Little Russia (Ukraine), Belarus, and Georgia, enjoyed a relatively privileged position. In 1922, Lenin set forth the principles of new national policies. First of all, these policies envisaged formal equality of all nations, which included the possibility of appointment to government positions, and the right to use their indigenous languages in office and record management, as well as in education and other areas. Secondly, each more or less major ethnic group received its own state administrative unit (autonomous republics and districts) within the Soviet Union or the Russian Republic. Third, the policies envisaged positive discrimination in favor of nations that were oppressed the most during the reign of the czars. The first and second principles are still formally acknowledged in Russian legislation, including the Constitution of 1993, adopted by Boris Yeltsin. Positive discrimination was never actually included in the legal system, but rather, in practice as early as the late twenties, was turned into a system of preferential treatment for representatives of minorities appointed to bureaucratic positions in the autonomous republics and in the regions populated by multiple ethnic groups. This practice persists until the present day, but more as a bureaucratic custom that has degenerated into a method for maintaining a type of equilibrium between various ethnic clans in the government.

Within a framework of established quasi-sovereignty within the autonomous administrative units, the representatives of "title nations" had the advantage of being appointed to various positions over Russians, as well as over other nationalities who were, in turn, supposed to make up for this discrimination by having preferred status within their own autonomous administrative unit. Obviously, in practice, ethnic borders were never the same as administrative ones, simply due to migrations of the population. Therefore, Bashkirs were at a disadvantage within the Tatar Republic, Tartars were at a disadvantage in Chuvashia and the Saratov Region, and so on. This created a peculiar "layer cake" of discrimination, in which the same ethnic groups could find themselves alternately privileged, or underprivileged depending on the situation.

This "layer-cake" effect explains why dissatisfaction with this Soviet national policy was widespread not only among ethnic minorities but also among Russians who represented the "imperial nation." Some members of the nationalistically inclined bureaucracy and intelligentsia were unhappy because of the "oppressed position" of the Russian Republic (RSFSR) with regard to other republics within the Soviet Union. For example, within the Communist Party of the Soviet Union, each republic had its own Central Committee as well as a State Security Committee, the Russian Republic being the only exception.

As for language policy, throughout Soviet history we observe a number of controversial processes. On the one hand, it was during the Soviet regime that the languages of "national minorities" attained official status. They began to be taught in schools and were used in office management and in official documents. Under Soviet administration, some of the minor nations were able to develop their languages in written form and to create their own literature for the first time. In the autonomous republics, knowing the local language became an important prerequisite for being promoted at work. On the other hand, ethnic minorities were actively involved in the process of modernization and urbanization. Before the revolution in Russia, ethnic villages whose residents did not understand Russian were common, but during the

Soviet era, comprehension of Russian became universal. Ethnic minorities were actively integrated to become part of Russian culture, which became to a considerable extent synonymous with urban culture. An illustration of this tendency can be seen in the city of Cheboksary in the sixties and seventies, where Chuvash felt too embarrassed to speak their native language, even though official documents were being issued in it. Mixed marriages became more common, as did migration of the representatives of local minorities to regions outside the traditional areas of their residence.

National policy underwent numerous changes throughout the existence of the Soviet regime. The consistent internationalism of the twenties was replaced by the declarative, formal internationalism of the thirties, and then by a revival of Russian nationalism in the late forties. The slogan "Friendship of the Peoples" was supplemented by the acknowledgment that the Russian nation was the "big brother" of the other nations within the USSR.

The situation of the Jews is a special issue. The revolution of 1917 as well as the Soviet regime itself assured civil rights for the majority of Jews and provided them with access to education and high-level management positions. However, during the forties, in connection with the overall change of national policy within the USSR, Jews experienced restrictions on their promotion to management positions and, later, on their access to the most prestigious educational establishments. The situation was further exacerbated by the creation of the state of Israel. Relations between Israel and the Soviet Union were extremely hostile. Therefore, by the end of the Soviet regime, Jews living in Russia came to see themselves yet again as victims of discrimination perpetrated by the authorities, and those authorities, in turn, viewed the Jews as potentially disloyal citizens.

Ethnic problems are closely related to religious problems. The Soviet system supported gradual and consistent secularization of national relationships, but that strategy very frequently failed. For many groups, national self-identification is closely tied to religion. This is particularly true of the Muslim nations. At the same time, de-Islamization in Asia and Africa was universally evident as a prerequisite for development of secular nationalism. In the Soviet Union, a similar path of development can be observed. Therefore, having undermined the old ethnic system of self-identification, the Soviet system was promoting development of a new one. Within the framework of the new rules of the game, ethnic bureaucracy and intelligentsia clans emerged and began actively competing with their Russian counterparts in the Russians' own field. One can say that bureaucratic integration gave rise to nationalism within the structure of the state government.

Finally, the Soviet system created victimized nations. Chechens, Ingush, Kalmyk, Crimean Tartars, and other nations were subject to mass deportations on the basis of nationality during the forties. During the "thaw" of the fifties and sixties, the rights of some, (but not all) of those nations, were reinstated, and the majority of the autonomous formations within the Russian Republic were restored.

In a certain sense, disintegration of the USSR was caused not by the failure, but by the success, of Soviet national policies. National minorities within the former Russian empire did not have their own elite groups, either political or cultural in nature. This situation enabled the empire to maintain its integrity through the revolution and the civil war and transform itself into the USSR. On the contrary, those elite groups were formed during the existence of the Soviet Union and actively participated in its partition. Meanwhile, bureaucratic clans that had formed in the autonomous administrative units and stayed within the composition of Russia had staked their claims to a significant share of power and assets.

The Post-Soviet Situation: The Nineties

In 1991, the Soviet Union was liquidated by a joint decision of the governments of Russia, Ukraine, and Belarus. It was replaced by an amorphous Commonwealth of Independent States. The disintegration of the Soviet Union led to an acute identity crisis for the majority of its residents. Even those who did not support the Soviet system were still part of it, to a greater or lesser extent. Belonging to a large country was perceived as natural by the majority of its citizens; the identity crisis affected not only Russians as the "imperial nation," but members of other ethnic groups as well.

The disintegration of the Soviet system was accompanied not only by changes in political and economic structures, but also by the disruption of traditional economic connections. Under those circumstances the significance of ethnic ties increased, and they became an important factor of social cohesion. The role and authority of various national societies, cultural societies, as well as political unions based on ethnicity, became more prominent. The more stressful the situation became and the graver the problems of disintegrating social structures, the more valuable "ethnicity" became, and the more the demand for it grew. This led to an exacerbation of international controversy, which in turn enhanced the meaning of ethnic solidarity. "Under the circumstances of the disintegration of the USSR, and against the background of interethnic conflicts growing more radical, ethnicity defined as the sense of belonging to one's 'blood' group becomes a value in itself—the only one capable of providing psychological protection in complex social conditions," notes sociologist Zinaida Sikevich.[1]

In response to the disintegration of the USSR, "imperial" and "democratic" tendencies arose in popular thinking. The "democratic" tendency spoke about the backwardness of Soviet society, its lack of conformity with the norms of the "civilized world," cultivating an inferiority complex in those harboring Soviet tendencies. This was accompanied by a guilt complex, or a feeling of imperial responsibility toward those nations drawn into the state by force.

On the contrary, the "imperial" tendency expressed nostalgia for the past greatness of the country. While the "democratic" tendency was suspicious of Russian culture and denied the value of inherent political and ideological tradition, the "imperial" tendency underscored the role of the Russian nation as empire-builder. It was suspicious of national minorities, seeing in peculiarities of nationality, culture, and religion only a potential menace to the unity of the state.

One can say that it has only been since the disintegration of the Soviet Union that Russians have fully recognized their cultural and national unity. After the USSR disintegrated, a considerable share of the Russian population found itself outside the boundaries of Russia. A serious problem of "compatriots abroad" arose in the political life of Russia. The statement claiming that after 1991 the Russians became a "divided nation" cannot be considered just another form of nationalistic propaganda. The majority of the republics that seceded from the Union retained privileges for the "title nation," and the status of their national languages acquired even greater importance. Respectively, the status of the Russian language was diminished.

It is important to note that those privileges that had been introduced to ensure protection of national languages as well as the rights of ethnic minorities within an integrated state, became at the very least redundant when the Union republics themselves became independent states. Thus the positive discrimination in favor of the old "imperial minorities" turned into negative discrimination against the new "post-Soviet" minorities, first and foremost Russians and Jews.

The new minorities who found themselves outside of Russia were referred to by the press as "Russian speakers." The point is that the question did not always concern ethnic Russians. As we already mentioned, the Russian language dominated the urban culture of the USSR, and the "Russian-speaking" milieu of the large cities included migrants from other ethnic groups who relocated to the cities at the time of industrialization and became integrated into Russian culture. After the disintegration of the Soviet Union, all of these "Russian speakers" found themselves in a political environment that rejected them. In particular, the official status of the Russian language declined dramatically in Ukraine; and in Estonia and Latvia most of the Russian-speaking population was unable to attain the right to become citizens.

As a result, "non-citizens" in both of those states constituted over one-third of the total population. In some cities they were the majority. The closing of Russian schools and other forms of cultural oppression occurred in almost all the newly independent states that seceded from the USSR.

Infringement upon the rights of the Russian-speaking population in the "newly independent countries" became an important topic in Russian policy. From 1992 to 1995, the repatriation of Russians from Central Asia and Azerbaijan grew to massive proportions. As a general rule, those repatriated had an unflattering assessment of the situation in the neighboring republics, as well as extremely unpleasant memories regarding the behavior of the indigenous population. This was the environment that, in 1993 and 1995, produced a considerable number of votes in favor of the Liberal Democratic Party of Russia under the leadership of Vladimir Zhirinovsky. Zhirinovsky himself came from Kazakhstan and was able to present himself not only as an aggressive nationalist, but also as a person capable of earnest discussion of problems shunned by other politicians either for diplomatic reasons or out of political correctness. However, other political organizations interpreted Zhirinovsky's success as a sign that nationalism and xenophobia would lead to success in elections. In the period from 1996 to 2000, these themes appeared in the statements of politicians of widely varying types, the liberal party "Yabloko" being the only exception.

The Communist opposition, which resisted neo-liberal reforms in 1992 and 1993, originally perceived itself purely as the protector of the Soviet regime, and declarative internationalism was widely known to be one of the principles of that regime. However, by the spring of 1993 the situation began to change. Reinstatement of the Communist Party of the Russian Federation (CPRF) headed by Gennady Zyuganov played a significant role in this process. Unlike more radical leaders of the Communist opposition, Zyuganov supported a synthesis of the "red" and "white" principles of Russian history. In other words, the matter in question was to unite the traditions of Stalinism and Czarism on the basis of "greater power," or the cult of a national state. In the late nineties, it was the CPRF that became the main party of Russian nationalists, having shunted the LDPR with Zhirinovsky away from that position.

Of course, Zyuganov's success was based on objective premises. In general, the opposition of the nineties was gradually losing its connections with Soviet traditions and was becoming more and more open to nationalistic ideas. This can be explained as Soviet society sinking further and further into its past, its framework fraying, and new realities emerging. At the beginning of the nineties, the disintegration of both the customary lifestyle and the Soviet economy was accompanied by a generalized disintegration of social classes among the population. On the one hand, events of the time drew protests both from those who suffered directly as a result of the changes and from those who resented the erosion of the scientific, technical, and intellectual potential created during the Soviet era. On the other hand, these protests sought very little like a juxtaposition of classes in the Marxist sense of the word. People were thrown out of their social classes and disoriented. Having lost their traditional social ties, they sought to ground themselves in their ethnic identities.

The disintegration of the Soviet Union was accompanied by an influx into Russia of residents of the former "brotherly republics." From 1992 to 1996, the population of the country grew by 2.9 million people due to migration from the CIS and the Baltic States.[2] Along with ethnic Russians fleeing from discrimination, representatives of other nations that had once been part of the empire or of the Soviet Union were relocating to Russia as well. As a general rule, they migrated for economic reasons. Despite the acuteness of the crisis in Russia, other republics suffered even greater disruptions. In some republics, economic crises were exacerbated by military conflict and humanitarian disaster. In Russia, which is rich in natural resources, the average wage in the nineties was considerably higher than in all the other former republics except for the Baltic countries, and unemployment continued to remain at a relatively low level. Even during the acute industrial crisis certain sectors showed some growth, primarily those requiring only low levels of investment and unskilled labor such as construction, retail trade, the service industry, and so on. This led to a considerable number of migrants coming to Russia to seek work. Most of them planned to earn some money and return to their homeland, but the most successful ones tended to stay in the Russian cities. For example, the Azerbaijani population in Russia exceeded 2 million people, about a quarter of which remained in Moscow.[3]

From 1989 to 1993, most of the migrants were Russians repatriated from former Soviet republics. But the situation changed in the period from 1994 to 1998, due to the growing number of members of other nations arriving in Russia from CIS countries. Moscow, St. Petersburg, and port cities (such as Vladivostok, Kaliningrad, and so on) were the main centers of attraction for these immigrants. According to the Moscow Industry Newspaper, about five thousand enterprises in the capital alone used foreign labor on a regular basis (mostly in construction).[4] According to official statistics, foreign workers accounted for only 1.5 percent of the total number of people employed in Moscow; however, other sources suggest that the number of illegal workers alone in Moscow reached about half a million people. A considerable share of this number cames from the countries of Southeast Asia.[5]

Before the year 2000, Russia had relatively liberal immigration laws which allowed for naturalization of all immigrants from former Soviet Union republics. At the same time, large cities continued to utilize the old residence assignment system ("*propiska*"), which was merely renamed "registration" in 1996. Even though this system, or at least the Moscow version of it, openly violated the law, it continued to remain in place. In order to be registered in Moscow or St. Petersburg, new arrivals had to have a legal job and an official place of residence. In turn, employers preferred to hire immigrants illegally for tax-evasion purposes. Police systematically checked the streets for illegal residents and extorted bribes from them, threatening deportation. These trials befell not only foreigners, but internal migrants as well, especially those who did not look like ethnic Russians.

Local conflicts and soaring unemployment in the Northern Caucasus regions of Russia led to massive migrations of Chechens, Ingushetians, and Dagestanis into large Central Russian cities. Remembering the perpetual military conflict in Chechnya, police considered every person in the street who looked likely to be from the Caucasus a potential terrorist and also a potential source of income.

Along with immigrants from CIS countries and internal migrants, an influx of "new immigrants" from Afghanistan, China, Vietnam, and the tropical countries of Africa began arriving in the larger Russian cities. After the disintegration of the Soviet Union, border control weakened. Corruption among the authorities led to illegal (or sometimes even legal) entry into the country being simply a question of money. The majority of the "new immigrants" viewed Russia simply as a stopover in their quest for the West, but, as often seems to be the case, a growing proportion of them began settling in Russia, having found work and a place to live.

Mass immigration resulted in an ethnic division of labor. The Russian press used the German term *Gastarbeiter* ("guest worker") and coined a new one—*Gastgeschofter* ("guest businessman"). The first category included hired labor (mostly in construction, sales, and the service industry), and the second encompassed businessmen who came to Moscow, St. Petersburg, and other Russian cities in order to open small businesses. From a legal standpoint, the *Gastgeschofters* had as few rights as the *Gastarbeiters*; moreover, since the former had more funds, they were a much more attractive target for corrupt officials and police. At the same time, their level in the social hierarchy was much higher, and they frequently employed others, usually illegal immigrants. In the established system of the ethnic division of labor, illegal vendors from Ukraine and Moldova frequently worked for illegal businessmen from Azerbaijan; construction teams from Tajikistan and Moldova had a lower status and drew lower wages than those from Ukraine; small tradesmen from Azerbaijan frequently hired former Chechen militants as security staff, and so on.

Having found themselves in alien, unusual, and sometimes hostile, environments, the ethnic minorities in large cities show considerably more solidarity and readiness to help one another than does the prevailing population. Besides that, they are ready to work longer and more intense hours for less money. During the days preceding the New Year, Ukrainian and Belarussian street vendors are ready to stand for eight to ten hours when the temperature is twenty degrees below zero F (-30 °C); Moldovan construction workers are ready to sleep right where they work, breathing in glue and paint vapors. Ethnic construction teams are generally known for their high level of discipline and absence of internal conflicts (at least those obvious to an outside observer). Even when the quality of their work is not as high as that of local labor, the low cost of hiring them makes them extremely competitive in the labor market.

The nineties was a time of rapid criminalization of Russian society. This can be attributed to the general social crisis, the erosion of belief in traditional values (even the concepts of "good" and "evil" as taught in the Soviet schools were questioned), and most importantly, to the overall pirate nature of privatization in Russia. This situation led to the demand for organized criminal gangs, not only for toll collection from small vendors and participation in illegal business, but also for protection of the dubious results of privatization by force. Most of the organized crime groups originated based on the "compatriot" principle, but there was also an element of spontaneous "ethnic grouping" within organized crime. The worse the living conditions in the country of origin, and the fewer the attractive job opportunities for migrants, the more candidates were available for ethnic and "compatriot" criminal groups. "Young men who came from a patriarchal village into a huge city, having no advantages offered by education, money, or street smarts, have revived and altered to suit the new environment, the traditional institutes of clan solidarity and military behavior. This enabled them to fight out a niche for themselves in an indifferent or hostile social environment," writes sociologist Georgy Derlugian. Further, Derlugian remarks: "Unlike Azerbaijanis or Georgians, Chechens had no valuable commodities to bring to Moscow from their homeland. These few Chechen migrants had to count only on themselves and on showy expressions of violence. Contempt of Soviet law, honed during the years of forced deportations, was mixed with traditional codes of behavior. This resulted in the creation of one of the most effective criminal networks in modern Russia (it would be hard to call this precarious phenomenon an organization)."[6] It is also characteristic that the Russian criminal groups competing with the Caucasus groups tried to politicize the conflict by underscoring its "racial" nature. For example, in Irkutsk one of the racket gangs was concurrently involved in organizing the Movement for Freedom of Siberia, whose slogan was "Let's Free Siberia from the Caucasus Mafia."[7]

Although the existence of the ethnic criminal network is a fact, there is no reason to consider this network the cause of the criminalization of Russian society. Moreover, statistical studies show that the "specific share" of the criminal element among migrants is in general lower than that among the "indigenous" population.[8] It is also characteristic, and has been noted by sociologists, that indigenous residents cite "enterprise and social mobility of newcomers" as the main irritating factor.[9] This irritation with the competition of migrants in the labor market, legitimate though it may be, overlaps with stereotypes of the "ethnic Mafia," thus turning these stereotypes into myths which are then propagated by the mass media. Mass layoffs in Russia were not caused by competition from immigrants, at least as far as it is possible to see from official statistics. Still, migrants became subject to racist hatred, and sometimes even pogrom-style attacks, such as those taking place in November 2001 in the Tsaritsyn Market in which three people were killed and several dozen wounded.

As early as the forties, scientists studying totalitarian regimes noted that there is a direct connection between the disintegration of social ties and the increasing popularity of fascist ideas. In this sense the degree of advancement of the extreme xenophobic movements is in inverse proportion to the degree of social solidarity and level of organization of society. Russia, at the beginning of the nineties, provided yet another example confirming this theory. New nationalistic movements were characterized not only by anti-Semitism, which is typical of the extreme right, but also by a growing hostility toward Muslims, "individuals from the Caucasus," blacks, and foreigners in general.

During the early nineties the so-called "fifth item" was removed first from questionnaires and later from passports as well. This item served to describe the "nationality" (ethnic origin) of the citizen. This question was closely related to discrimination against Jews and representatives of some other nationalities attempting to enter prestigious educational establishments and obtain jobs. Elimination of the "fifth item," however, caused the dissatisfaction of a number of ethnic groups (for example, nationalities populating the Far North Regions) for whom their national or ethnic identification served as the basis of preferential treatment during Soviet times. Therefore, having declared the principle of formal civil equality, in practice the Russian government faced a complex and tangled web of relationships between nations.

Although Jews were barred from being promoted to political and economic positions of the highest level during the postwar period of Soviet history, anti-Semitism was officially condemned, as it contradicted the principle of "friendship of the peoples." The changes that occurred in the eighties put an end to official discrimination, but at the same time gave rise to the dissemination of ideas that had been condemned earlier. Cessation of discrimination against the Jews during the reform years led to the Jewish community becoming considerably more visible not only in the spheres of science and culture—characteristic throughout the period of the Soviet regime—but also in politics, business, and the mass media. This fact was used to fuel anti-Semitic propaganda, the dissemination of which was yet another side effect of democratic developments during the late eighties to early nineties.

The demographic crisis of the Russian population became another reason for the nationalism of the nineties. This crisis commenced back in Soviet times, but was further exacerbated by neo-liberal reforms. Birthrate decline was a natural consequence of urbanization. Since by the middle of the twentieth century, the majority of Russians had migrated to major cities and urbanized ethnic minorities had become Russified, declining birthrates among city dwellers were perceived as a demographic decline of Russians. In the nineties, the birthrate decline was accompanied by a dramatic increase in mortality due to the deterioration of medical care, local military conflicts, the rising crime rate, unemployment, and the extreme poverty of the population.

Ethnic Tensions Seen Through the Looking Glass of Sociology

Russian sociologists have varying opinions regarding the issue of how widely spread racial antipathy and ethnic enmity are in society at large. I. N. Gavrilova, in her analysis of interethnic relations in Moscow, comes to the following conclusion: "Our level of tolerance (both at the state level and in everyday life) is considerably higher than in many other former Soviet Union republics, even when one does not take into account the situation in the Baltic countries. . . ."[10]

Another well-known sociologist, G. L. Kertman, is of a different opinion. By analyzing the results of social surveys, he discovers that conclusions with regard to the "ethnic tolerance" of Russian society are based on answers people give to generic, declarative questions. In other words, if an individual is asked about his attitude to racist or anti-Semitic propaganda in principle, the overwhelming majority state their negative attitude. However, as soon as the sociologist moves to specific issues (for example, "What do you think about Jews, Azerbaijanis, black nations, and others?"), a significant number of respondents who condemned racism in principle may nonetheless make various racist or anti-Semitic comments.

Only 18 percent of respondents support the idea of formally restricting the rights of "aliens" in Russia. However, twice as many people spoke in favor of restricting access for "non-Russians" to positions in the government, introducing all sorts of election participation quotas and qualifications for them, prohibiting access to certain jobs, and so on. "Therefore, we clearly observe a glaring contradiction: A considerable number of respondents speak in favor of equal rights for 'aliens' and in favor of restricting their access to governing authorities, which means 'deprivation of rights,'" notes Kertman.[11] Other sociologists have a similar view of the situation. For example, a study performed by Zinaida Sikevich in a number of Russian cities shows that frequently respondents, while denying the existence of mass animosity towards national minorities in the country, at the same time admit "a *personal* feeling of dislike toward one or several nationalities."[12]

According to Kertman, there is a rather widely spread understanding of the impropriety of showing open aggressive nationalism and of the inadmissibility of practicing generic discrimination on the basis of ethnicity. However, this understanding (partially "atavistic," dating back to traditional Soviet ideas of "friendship of the nations," and partially a newly acquired one in the context of liberal and democratic notions regarding human rights) overlaps with other ideas prevailing or gaining strength in the society. While generic concepts of "political correctness" require that the rights of all citizens be respected, the "spirit of the times"—particularly after the second war started in Chechnya—justifies racial hatred by relating it closely to such ideas as patriotism, love for one's country, need for order, and even with the need to protect the "law-based state"—in this case, to protect it from "wild nations," which, as far as the respondents think, are constitutionally unable to abide by the law. Under these circumstances, ideas concerning the "clash of civilization" acquire an openly racist tinge in the mass conscience, since they enable one to combine a declarative adherence to liberal (i.e., "Western" and "Christian") values and an animosity toward ethnic minorities. This form of nationalism or racism is the most common found among the educated. "Therefore, a widely accepted idea that nationalistic views are more common among the uneducated strata of the population is not well-founded," notes Kertman. Contrary to one's expectations, "highly educated members of the public are prone to nationalistic views even more than others among the population."[13] Specifically, one-quarter of respondents with a higher educational background supported the thesis of inherent superiority of some nations over others. In other groups of the population, those views prevailed among one-fifth of respondents. In a similar manner, sociology does not support the hypothesis stating that young adults who grew up in a situation of prevailing liberal ideology and market economy show a higher level of internationalism. The surveys indicate that exactly the opposite is true. Young adults who have not been through the "Soviet training" but have actively faced competition among different ethnic groups "tend to absorb nationalistic terminology easier, and identify themselves with it."[14]

In conclusion, Kertman notes that "firm" internationalists comprise about 40 to 45 percent of the total population. At the same time there is a rather high proportion—about 15 percent—of consistently and openly racist individuals, who are ready to proclaim their principles even at the level of general declarations, unabashed by the fact that such opinions contradict the official framework of good manners and even the law of the country. About as many of the residents of Russia are inconsistent or undecided racists, who could be called "undecided internationalists".

The resulting picture is not at all trouble free. The presence of a "grassroots nationalism" (or racism) provides fertile soil for the growth of political organizations of this type. In turn, the success enjoyed by those organizations and their ability to look respectable leads to making racial prejudice a legitimate and unifying trend in the community. Politicians, frequently guided by simple opportunism, try to use those trends to improve their ratings. The most dangerous thing is that this not only occurs with second-rate political figures, but with leading political figures as well, and within the official mass media. As an example of the latter, we can look at a daily evening television program: "However" ("*Odnako*") which is shown on the First National Channel, ORT, traditionally considered to be a mouthpiece of the Kremlin. *Odnako's* anchors, Mikhail Leontiev and Maxim Sokolov, regularly call Chechnya a nation of bandits, complain about the Arabs who forced the French out of Paris, and so on. Even though Russian legislation includes provisions stating that propaganda of interethnic animosity is a criminal offense, there were no attempts to take the program off the air, let alone to begin criminal proceedings against its authors. At the same time the authorities show markedly less tolerance when representatives of the opposition are involved. In particular, General Albert Makashov, a member of the Communist faction of Parliament (CPRF) was threatened with court proceedings for an anti-Semitic statement, and he was able to avoid prosecution only due to his parliamentary immunity.

This "inconsistency" on the part of the authorities is perceived by society at large as a signal of sorts, which enables one to make a distinction as to which forms of racism are "permissible" or "not permissible." In particular, racist statements aimed at residents of the Caucasus or at Muslims are perceived as more "permissible" and "acceptable" than statements of the same type aimed at Armenians, Jews, Germans, and others.

From Yeltsin to Putin

Beginning in 1992, the Russian government began seeking its own approach to the "national issue." The first step in this direction came in the form of agreements between the central and regional governments, which were signed by Boris Yeltsin and the presidents of the autonomous administrative entities. In the course of this process, ethnic republics were able to bargain for special powers by threatening to separate if they did not get what they wanted. The most acute conflict flared up between Moscow and Tatarstan, with the latter announcing that it was a "sovereign republic" and "subject to international laws." Negotiations between Moscow and Kazan resulted in the transformation of Tatar sovereignty into the right to independently resolve issues related to privatization within the territory of this autonomous entity, which was granted to the local elite. However, the separation threat was perceived quite seriously, considering the overall situation, which included disintegration of the Soviet Union in 1991 and military action in Chechnya. The heads of the republics did not want real secession; however, in the early nineties they used it as a bargaining chip, which tended to yield significant compromises on the part of the central authorities.

Agreements of this type led to the formation of regional ethnocratic regimes in Kalmykia, Bashkiria, Tatarstan, and Yakutia. The specific features of those regimes included not so much cultural domination of the "title nation" as much as the unrestrained power of the ruling bureaucratic clan, which tended to be formed on the basis of ethnicity and sometimes just on basis of family connections.

Similar developments could be observed also in the autonomous republics of the Northern Caucasus. In Russia, privatization of state property was assumed to be a way of dividing the Soviet inheritance among bureaucratic clans, which had been spawned by the very same Soviet system. Inevitably, this process of dividing up property resulted in "political capitalism," where the position of a group in business is inseparable from its influence in politics. Georgy Derlugian writes: "The system, based on 'political capitalism' and a shadow economy, suffers from chronic instability. It is too dependent on personal connections, informal arrangements, and bureaucratic intrigues. In post-Soviet conditions it incorporated crime and violence along with mobilization of mass protests. In the Caucasus, where power is significantly dependent on outside contacts in Moscow, where it is entangled with ethnicity, and where all this complex, historically shaped configuration is inevitably rich in contradiction and weak spots, political and economic competition surface as sudden, and frequently violent events, whose reasons frequently remain mysterious both for observers and even for ground-level participants."[15]

These political conditions formed an authoritarian political system that included oppression of the press, falsification of election results, keeping political opponents under surveillance, and so on. The issues of cultural assertion by the "title nation" of autonomy receded further and further away from being a priority. Specifically, the leadership of Tatarstan expressed no interest whatsoever in the issue of developing Tatar culture outside the republic and did not render any noticeable assistance to Tatar schools, cultural centers, or national communities. The only thing the leadership of the Republic did was arrange to supply textbooks in the Tartar language for schools of neighboring regions (and even those had to be paid for by the recipients). Meanwhile, the majority of Tartars in Russia continues to reside outside Tatarstan. For example, in Moscow and the Moscow region, the Tartar population (including mixed marriages) numbers half a million people, during the first half of the nineties the share of Tartars in the population of the capital grew from 1.8 to 2.9 percent.[16]

Agreements between the central authorities and the autonomous republics aggravated ethnically Russian republics, who pointed out to Moscow (and rightly so) that such actions were undermining the Federation, given that, without equality between the regions, there can be no equality among the citizens. However, in the early nineties Russian elite groups did not pay much attention to those problems. By the late nineties, however, an opposite tendency emerged. The world view of Russian elite groups shifted from being cosmopolitan to being nationalistic. While in the beginning of the decade, liberal "Westernophilia" was supposed to provide a reason for dismantling the old Soviet framework, privatization, and opening the market, by the end of Yeltsin's stay in power new proprietors became more and more conservative, aiming first of all to make their social position legitimate through ideas of "national unity," "strong power," and "consolidation."

The war in Chechnya became an important milestone in the development of national relationships within Russia. Both the first and the second Chechen campaigns were caused, first of all, by internal controversy among elite groups in Russia, but they had far-reaching ramifications for society as a whole. Of all the autonomous formations within Russia, it was Chechnya, led by its President Dzhohar Dudayev, that went furthest toward becoming a sovereign entity. However, this does not mean that the Chechen government completely rejected the idea of negotiating the independence of the republic with Moscow. Grozny offered to negotiate several times and indicated that it was ready to compromise. In 1991 Russia, withdrew its troops from the republic, held a referendum on the 1993 Constitution there, and did not attempt to force Chechnya to sign the Federation Treaty; on that basis one can say that it recognized Chechen independence de facto. On top of that, the independence of Chechnya was based on the same documents that stipulated establishment of the independence of the Russian Federation. As Russia denounced the agreement of 1922 that held together the Soviet Union, it automatically granted the autonomous entities the right to choose again whether they wished to continue and stay within the state being formed anew, or to leave it. (This is the procedure outlined in the Union Agreement itself in case it was to be denounced.) While Tatarstan's position was ambiguous, Chechnya chose independence but did not close the doors on further negotiations with the central government.

The attack of the Russian army against Chechnya in 1994 cannot be explained by fear of the uncontrollable disintegration of Russia. By the mid-nineties the Federation Treaty had been signed, and there was obviously no threat of this kind. By that time Yeltsin's rating was extremely low, presidential elections were looming ahead, and a small victorious war should have strengthened the president's position. However, the opposite occurred: The war turned into a series of shameful failures for the Russian army. In 1996 Yeltsin won the elections through the unleashing of a massive anti-Communist campaign in tandem with falsification of election results, which were most obvious specifically in the ethnic autonomous regions, where customary authoritarian practices were applied.

Immediately after the elections, a truce was reached with Chechnya and the way was open for legal recognition of the republic. However, a new government crisis in Moscow led to another exacerbation of the situation in the Caucasus. The second war in Chechnya became part of the process of the transfer of power in the Kremlin from Boris Yeltsin to Vladimir Putin.

Unlike the first military campaign in Chechnya, the second one was accompanied by a massive campaign of anti-Chechen propaganda in the press and on television. This led to a situation when racist and xenophobic positions gained acceptance in the media. In military terms, the second war was not much more successful than the first one. The promise was made to suppress military resistance in the Chechen Republic by March of 2000 (when the presidential elections were to be held), and it continued basically at the same level two years later. However, the second war in Chechnya was considerably more cruel toward the civil population, and resulted in the almost complete destruction of Grozny; it forced at least one-third of the population to leave the republic.

Another consequence of no less importance was not only allowing racism to become legitimate in society, but the pronounced tolerance of the leadership with regard to racism and the "Greater Russian" nationalism. Arbitrary police action toward "individuals from the Caucasus" was now justified by wartime necessity and fear of terrorism. The ideas set forth by the opposition in the early and middle nineties now gained considerable official support, and now the social content of nationalism had changed. It was no longer the ideology of the lumpen masses; on the contrary, to a growing degree nationalism was infiltrating the conscience of the respectable bourgeois elite. This could not but draw protests from part of the liberal intelligentsia, who defended the ideas of traditional "anti-imperial support for the West." However, this group of society was becoming more and more isolated.

When Vladimir Putin came to power in 2000, nationalistic and "neo-imperial" ideas gained the status of official state ideology. The project for national integration, put together by those close to the new president, envisaged creating a more strict centralized system and asserting the priority role of the Russian nation as defined in the traditional imperial and orthodox sense.

The first step down this road took the form of tightening the laws on citizenship. This was followed by the growing role of the Orthodox Church: The Orthodox patriarch was the only one among all religious leaders who sanctified the transfer of power from Yeltsin to Putin. The slogans of the day were "Orthodox spirituality" and "Eurasian approach," interpreted as specific value systems that distinguished Russians from others. Those values included loyalty to the authoritarian central government and rejection of the cultural seductions of the liberal West, not including, of course, the principles of the liberal capitalist economy.

It is no surprise that national minorities immediately perceived a threat. The problem of Islam became especially acute, particularly after the terrorist attacks on September 11, 2001, in the United States.

Prospects

In the middle of the nineties, when the "Great Russian" nationalism had not yet gained official status, the liberal intelligentsia agreed with the defenders of Soviet tradition that ideas of racial or ethnic priority represented a threat to the mere existence of Russia as a multinational state. Possibilities for the integration of national minorities into a unified Russian society are directly dependent on the extent to which the prevailing political and cultural environment is favorable to the groups in question. The more aggressive the state becomes toward minorities, the more minorities reject the state and the stronger is their ethnic solidarity. At the same time, in 1999–2000 we saw not only a tightening of state policy toward ethnic minorities, but also a crisis of ethnic nationalism in the autonomous republics. While during the first half of the nineties, slogans reflecting the ethnic nationalism of minorities fit within the general "anti-imperial" rhetoric of "democracy," in 1999–2000 they contradicted one another. On the other hand, the ethnic clans in regional bureaucracies had attained their goals and were interested in successful interaction with the Moscow elite. Simultaneously, the majority of the population in the autonomous entities felt a growing resentment against the ruling bureaucratic clans and were growing more and more disappointed with the slogans of "ethnic revival."

As a result, the new course taken by Moscow in the area of national policy did not meet serious resistance, either from above or from below. Under the circumstances it was not ethnic nationalism but internationalism that served as an alternative to the "Great Russian" nationalism. Attempts to organize internationalist democratic movements started in the summer of 2000. The most noticeable one was the Movement in Support of Civil Rights, founded at the initiative of the Chechen community. Despite the considerable role played by Chechens, the movement kept underscoring that it was not an ethnic one, but rather an internationally oriented movement for human rights protection, aimed at functioning throughout the territory of Russia and supporting the interests of all oppressed groups, including cultural, religious, ethnic, and social groups. Another example is the emergence of "internationalist societies," which brought together migrants from the Northern Caucasus not on the basis of ethnic background, but rather on the basis of their regional affiliation, thus protecting the interests of Russian and Chechen refugees from Grozny, for example.

In conclusion one may say that in modern Russia ethnic connection may play the role of either bringing people together or tearing them apart. Which tendency prevails depends both on the policy of the country and society's reaction to that policy.

After the Soviet Union crumbled and the single political entity that was inherited from the Russian Empire itself disintegrated, issues pertaining to national identity and ethnic relationships have to be given fresh thought. In the end, we will have to answer questions not only regarding how to build relationships between "Russians" and other nations residing in Russia, but also questions concerning how "Russians" themselves are to be defined. If, as a result of this transformation, we arrive at an inclusive understanding of Russian ethnic identity, it is quite possible that the country will transform itself into an interethnic "melting pot" in which a considerable proportion of minorities will be integrated into a continuously self-renewing and inclusive Russian nation. It was this "inclusiveness" that was repeatedly mentioned by the Russian philosophers of the nineteenth century. Not only migrants from the former Soviet republics, but new immigrants as well are quite capable of recognizing themselves as part of Russia—not only as equal citizens of the country and full-fledged members of society, but also as individuals contributing to the history and culture of the Russian nation. This, of course, would not equal total assimilation and the rejection of their inherent traditions, since those traditions may become an important source for enriching Russian culture.

This democratic perspective is opposed by a strategy of state development based on the narrow definition of the nation as a union of Eastern Orthodox Christian Slavs, transforming all other residents of the country into second-rate citizens who are subjects of the Empire. As such, the Russian state will, on the one hand, be unable and unwilling to assimilate its ethnic minorities, and, on the other, will consider them an alien and dangerous element, a potential enemy from within. Under this condition, the Russian nation will inevitably fall prey to its own policy. What we are facing is not a choice between the strategy of a "melting pot" or a "prison for the nations," but rather a choice between the preservation and development of society, or the ruin thereof.

Notes

1. Zinaida Sikevich, "Ethnic Hostility in the Mass Consciousness of Russians," in G. Vitkovskaya and A. Malashenko, eds., *Intolerance in Russia. Phobias, Old and New*: Moscow Carnegie Center 1999), p. 111.

2. Vitkovskaya and Malashenko, *Intolerance in Russia*, p. 169.

3. T.T. Timofeyev, Yu. S. Oganisyan, V. T. Polunin, and A.B. Yarlykov, eds., *Problems of National Relations under Conditions of Globalization* (Moscow: GUMDN, 2001), pp. 84–85.

4. See *Moscow Industry Newspaper*, 12–18 April 2001.

5. See *Population of Russia, 1999. Seventh Annual Demographic Report* (Moscow, 2000), p. 132.

6. Georgy Derlugian, "The Chechen Revolution and Chechen History," in D.E. Furman, ed. *Chechnya and Russia: Societies and States,* (Moscow, "Politinform-Talburi," 1999), p. 209.

7. Vitkovskaya and Malashenko, *Intolerance in Russia*, p. 128.

8. Ibid., p. 160.

9. Ibid., p. 110.

10. Timofeyev, et al., *Problems of National Relations Under Conditions of Globalization*, p. 79.

11. Ibid., p. 138.

12. Vitkovskaya and Malashenko, *Intolerance in Russia*, p. 105.

13. Timofeyev, et al., *Problems of National Relations under Conditions of Globalization*, pp. 139, 140.

14. Vitkovskaya and Malashenko, *Intolerance in Russia*, p. 111.

15. G. Derlugian, *Chechnya and Russia: Societies and States*, p. 216.

16. *Moscow in Figures: Annual Statistical Compilation*, (Moscow: 1990), p. 26; and *Moscow in Figures: Annual Statistical Compilation* (Moscow: 1996), p. 12.

5

Family and Children During the Economic Transition

Natalia Rimashevskaya

The family is a core "cell" of the social organism, a basic socioeconomic unit of society. In addition to procreation—the physical and social reproduction of the population—the family determines the quality of life and the qualitative characteristics of each citizen, including his or her health potential and education, living conditions and balanced diet, fair and equal gender relations, and participation in public life, as well as his or her dignity and security.

Types of Russian Families

Russian researchers distinguish three basic types of monogamous families in Russia: patriarchal or traditional, child-centered or modern, and spouse-centered or post-modern.[1] These three types coexist and form a wide array of models. However, they emerged in a certain historical sequence.

In a patriarchal family—the most archaic type—the man dominates; he is the head of the family. The woman obeys the man, and the children obey the parents. The husband's superior position is based on the fact that the family's economic resources are concentrated in his hands and also on the custom that the man makes the principal decisions. This is where the rigid division between men's and women's roles originates. Usually, families of this type have many members. They embrace two or three generations as well as collateral relatives. The authority of family members depends on a member's sex and age. The parents have absolute power; the old enjoy the most respect; and children's upbringing is authoritative in nature.

The turn of the twentieth century saw active women's emancipation processes, which led to a relative equality in the relations between spouses. Simultaneously, the ideas of social emancipation of children gained popularity. This resulted in the emergence of a new family type, the child-centered family, where all adult members attributed special importance to the child's well-being, upbringing, and education, and where enormous efforts were made to keep marriages intact mainly in the interest of the children. The need to control the time and frequency of conception appeared, the reproductive period became restricted, and the concept of family planning developed. The child-centered family displayed an increase in the monetary and spiritual care of children. Simultaneously, new gender and intergenerational relations formed.

According to S.I. Golod, the child-centered family has three models, which are determined by the nature of the relationship between parents and children. In the first subtype, the "authoritarian family," the older generation typically dominates. The child is often merely a tool to bolster parents' self-assurance. In the "ambivalent family"—the second subtype—the relationship between parents and children reflects the nature of the relationship between the parents, which can be either warm or cold. The third subtype, the "quasi-autonomous family," is a transition from pure child-centeredness to prioritizing the child's autonomous development.

The victory of the principle of women's equality and an increase in women's economic and social status, coupled with the growing popularity of the idea that children should be given more autonomy, led to the formation of the spouse-centered, or post-modern, family. In this type of family the egalitarian relationship between spouses dominates. Stability of the marriage depends on the couple's desires, interests, and the quality of the marriage.

Privacy and autonomy of each family member are typical qualities of this type of family. "Autonomy," Golod writes, "manifests itself in that the interests of both the husband and wife are more diverse than the interests of the family as a whole, while each spouse's needs and circles exceed the bounds of the marriage. The couple's emotional aspirations are regulated not so much by customs and traditions, as by psychological features, moral principles, and esthetic ideals."[2] The main values of the family are determined primarily by the relationship between the spouses, and the relationship between the parents and children is second in order of importance. There is no obvious head in the post-modern family. Roles vary depending on the situation. The emotional side of relationships comes to the forefront.

In the context of the post-modern family there develops the "nontraditional" family, which is different from classical monogamy. Two types of "nontraditional" families need to be mentioned: single-parent families and alternative marriages. The former can be divided into two groups: families of widowed or divorced individuals and single-mother families. Single-mother families form as a consequence of a birth out of wedlock. Alternative marriages also have two subtypes: unmarried couples residing together and reconstructed families (where at least one of the parents is a step-parent).

The categories of families mentioned above have many models; and the spectrum of the subtypes will inevitably broaden, and the number of families of the classical nuclear type will shrink.

Family Make-up in Russia

A 1996 U.S.-Russian study carried out in Moscow and in rural areas in the Pskov and Saratov regions was devoted largely to exploring marital quality in the context of Russian society's transition to a market economy. The study focused on gender attitudes of spouses, household task division, decision-making in marriages, perceptions of marital quality, divorce considerations, and verbal and physical abuse. Despite the fact that the social transformation in Russia has generated some changes in social roles and in values and mindsets, the patriarchal family remains the dominant type.

In light of the family typology considered in this paper, some structural features of the Russian family might be of interest. The U.S.-Russian project showed that family units in which unmarried couples were living together make up 5.9 percent of all marriages in Moscow, 6.4 percent in the Pskov region, and 7.6 percent in the Saratov region.[3]

The study registered intensive growth in the proportion of births that occurred out of wedlock. Before 1985, the percentage of births out of wedlock hovered at about 10 percent; after 1985 it rose rapidly; and in 2000 it reached 28 percent.[4] In recent years, the number of illegitimate children has been growing steadily. Society should not ignore this, given that birthrates in Russia are extremely low. In rural areas, the percentage of births out of wedlock is somewhat higher (30 percent). In some areas, it is over 50 percent. For instance, in the Komi-Permyak Autonomous Region it is 62.7 percent, in the Chukotka Autonomous Region 53.5 percent, and in the Republic of Tuva 58.0 percent.[5]

Immediately following World War II, the proportion of out-of-wedlock children in Russia totaled 24 percent, i.e., almost one-fourth of all newborns. At that time, in the war-torn country, which lost an enormous number of young men, it was understandable. With each passing year, the percentage of children born out of wedlock dropped. It was 17 percent in 1955, 13 percent in 1960, and reached 10 percent in 1968. From the late 1960s to the mid-1980s, this indicator stabilized at about 11 percent. After this, it started to grow again. In the 1990s, the growth rate in out-of-wedlock children was very high, and the absolute number of births to unmarried women became very significant. In 1997, it exceeded 300,000; in 2000, the number of births to married women was 912,500, while 354,300 babies were born out of wedlock. On average, over 40 percent of illegitimate newborns are recognized by their fathers.[6]

Russian statistics differentiate among three categories of newly born babies:

Children of married parents;

Children born out of wedlock, when both parents jointly file for a birth certificate, and cases in which paternity has been established by a court decision;

Children with only the mother filing for a birth certificate, children given up by their mothers immediately following birth and registered by application from obstetrics services and children's homes, as well as abandoned babies whose mothers are unidentified.

The reasons behind the increase in births out of wedlock depend to a large degree on the age group to which the mother belongs. Very young women give birth to illegitimate children mainly because of low awareness of contraception at the beginning of their sex lives. Pregnancies of women under 20 years of age are often accidental and unwanted. For women older than 20 there are many different reasons, one of which may be that single mothers receive child-support payments.

The percentage of single-parent families as compared to the total number of families remains almost unchanged over time—one-fifth (around 20 percent). In accordance with the typology used in this chapter, this group includes both families of widowed and divorced individuals and single-mother families, i.e., families where the parent is unmarried or is no longer married.

The former type results from widowhood and divorce. According to A.G. Volkov's calculations, very few individuals over 75 years of age in Russia are married. Twenty-three percent of all marriages end because the wife dies, 53 percent end due to the death of the husband, and the remaining 24 percent end in divorce.[7]

Statistics show an overall trend toward a decline in the average number of children under 18 years per family, as well as a reduction in the percentage of two-parent families and families with more than two children. According to the 1989 census data, there were 23.5 million families with children in Russia in 1989, or 57.5 percent of all families. The majority of families with children (51 percent) had one child; the proportion of families with two children was 39 percent. Only 9.8 percent of families had more than two children. The 1994 microcensus data indicated that this trend became more prominent as the birthrate declined. The share of one-child families grew to 54 percent; the proportion of families with two children dropped to 37 percent; and only 9.4 percent of families had more than two children (total = 100.4 percent due to rounding). Over this period, the number of children per one hundred families fell from 163 to 160.[8]

A similar trend was registered by the U.S.-Russian study of 1996. Its results showed that 11.7 percent of all families in Moscow, 23.7 percent in rural areas of the Pskov region, and 12.8 percent in the villages in the Saratov region did not have children. Among Moscow families, 40.5 percent had one child, as did 44.2 percent in the Pskov region, and 46.5 percent in the Saratov region. Families with more than two children numbered 6 percent of Moscow's families, 7.3 percent of those in the Pskov region, and 15.1 percent in the Saratov region.[9]

It needs to be stressed that in the period from 1988 to 1997, 5.2 million children lived in families with divorced parents. This number grew by an additional million in the period from 1997–1999.[10]

If we consider not only families, but also households in general, taking into account those individuals who live alone, we will see the following picture. There are 40 million families and 50 million households in Russia today, and they may be divided into five general categories:

> One-person households, of which there are two types, each equally common: elderly individuals and young people. The former is composed predominantly of women, as the discrepancy in the life expectancy between men and women is 12 to 13 years in favor of women. The share of one-person households equals one-fifth (20 percent) of all households.

> Married couples with children living with them, i.e., families comprising two generations. The majority of households (52 percent) belong to this category.

> Married couples with no children living with them or one-generation families. The majority of families in this group are young couples in the period of family formation. However, about one-half of households in this category are old couples and couples with children living separately.

> Single-parent families with children (embracing two generations) or with children and parents (embracing three generations). This segment represents almost one-eighth (13 percent) of the overall number of households.

> Three-generation families of married couples with children. Their share is small, only about 1.2 percent.

Russia has seen a clear trend toward a smaller-sized family and household, following a similar process in Western Europe. For instance, in Germany at the beginning of the twentieth century, big families were considered the norm; 44 percent of households at that time had at least five members. At the end of the twentieth century, in 1997, cohabitation of several generations became quite infrequent: almost two-thirds of all households (68 percent) consisted of one or two individuals. The German Federal Statistics Office forecasts that in 2015, 37 percent of households will be one-person households.[11]

It is interesting that the distribution of family types in Germany is similar to that of Russia today. Single-parent families make up 13 percent of all families in Germany; married couples without children make up 43 percent; the number of married couples with one child is 20 percent, with two children 18 percent, and with three or more children 6 percent.[12]

When looking at families as households, it is important to mention the "financial" relations among generations. Of all new families—couples who have been married for 5–10 years—only one-half are living independently and separately, while the other half cohabitate with the parents of one of the spouses and/or other relatives. One-fifth (19 percent) of new families have joint budgets with parents of the spouses and/or other relatives. Over half (59 percent) of new families receive financial help from parents and other relatives. However, among three-generation families, the older generation enjoys financial independence in a small group of families (about 2 percent).

Families differ not only in terms of relations within them and among their members. The age of the family is another very important factor. Being a "living" organism, the family goes through independent phases of formation, development, and death. However, unlike other living creatures, the disappearance of a family is usually its simultaneous transformation into a different, subsidiary form. This process determines the family life cycle.

In the core of the family development and life cycle lie the demographic changes related predominantly to procreation. Another contributing factor is change in the social status of individual family members, which eventually creates economic dynamics. Thereby, three aspects of family development can be identified: demographic, social, and economic. All three are highly interdependent. The family life cycle has three phases: the period of "growth," the period of "maturity" or "flourishing," and that of "extinction." Although the three family development aspects internally interconnect, each of them has its own "benchmark points," which are determined by changes in family life. Therefore, it is no accident that the "age" of a family, which is calculated from the time the family forms, is an extremely important element in family analysis and description.

Over the full family development cycle there occurs the so-called "inflection" point, which is typical for all three aspects mentioned. It falls in the seventeenth to nineteenth year in the development cycle and practically coincides with the time when children start leaving home, which is the period that determines the start of a new cycle. At the same time, it coincides with the moment when children finish the first stage in their education.

A certain wavelike pattern characterizes family development and its life cycle. It divides the progression of the cycle into two segments. One segment is the area in which the family income level is falling, as monetary wealth decreases in comparison with the initial level, registered when the family forms, i.e., when the couple gets married. In turn, this area has its own point in time (or "saddle" point) when income reaches its minimum. It falls approximately in the fourteenth year in the family's life. This is usually followed by slow growth as the family comes out of a period of falling income and into a period of growing income. Here the income is higher than at the outset of the family's life. This period ends with a new intensive drop in monetary wealth. There is a certain symmetry among the different stages in the family development and life cycle, suggesting that rigid social mechanisms are at play here.[13]

Marital Relations During the Market Transition

The socioeconomic changes that fell upon Russian society at the end of the twentieth century—and most intensely in 1992—were unprecedented in depth and influence. Reforms "from above" resulted in a crisis in all aspects of public life for society as a whole as well as at the level of the family and the individual. The radical changes affected the country's politics and economy, the structure of the state, interethnic relations, the population, and the social sphere.

The situation of the family in Russia is clearly related to trends of marriage and divorce. Statistical data indicate that the overall marriage rate has a clear downward trend, which changes only insignificantly over time. In 1960, the overall marriage rate amounted to 12.5 percent, while in 2000 it was down twofold, totaling 6.2 percent. Such a decline manifested itself in the total number of officially registered marriages: 1.5 million in 1960 and only 0.9 million in 2000.[14] Additionally, the divorce rate has steadily increased with minor vacillations. In 1960, the overall divorce rate was 1.5 percent, while in 2000 it reached 4.3 percent, i.e., it increased three times.

The matrimonial behavior of the population formed under the influence of many different socioeconomic and sociopsychological factors.[15] A drop in the number of divorces after that number reached its highest level in 1979 is in part the result of a considerable reduction in the number of marriages, a trend that started in 1984. This is because one-third of all divorces occur in young couples, i.e., those who have been married for less than five years. A decline in the divorce rate is to some extent also related to the fact that a divorce during a social and economic crisis inevitably leads to lower living standards for the majority of families with underage children, as a divorce deprives a family of one parent.

Several principal factors explain the trend toward lower marriage rates, which became evident in the second half of 1980 and worsened by the late 1990s. Firstly, partner cohabitation has become increasingly popular among young people. Often, couples living together do not get married even if they start having children. Others reside together before marriage, a practice that is becoming more widespread as a temporary, but often indispensable step on the way toward the legal registration of an emotionally and psychologically viable relationship. Second, people are getting married at an increasingly older age, after each member of the couple attains stable social status. According to Goskomstat data from 1960, over one-half of men (53 percent) entered into marriage at the age of 18 to 24, while in 2000 this share dropped to 45 percent. Similarly, in 1960, 63 percent of women married when they were between the ages of 18 and 24, and in 2000, this number decreased to 57 percent.[16] Third, an overall decline in the economic status of the population, a growth in unemployment, especially among young people, and a drop in living standards force people to get married later rather than earlier. A lower number of young people at the most common age for marriage also contributes to this phenomenon.

Starting in the early 1980s, women have been filing for divorce more often than men. Today, women initiate over 70 percent of all divorces. The main reason for this is the increase in women's social status, which includes education, professional skills, professional standing, and economic independence. The younger the couple, the more likely it is to reject a patriarchal relationship in favor of egalitarianism in the family.[17]

Explanations of the higher divorce rate are more complicated. Socioeconomic changes have had a contradictory effect on the divorce rate. In general, the atmosphere of tension and stress becomes more widespread with an increased striving to survive, thus breaking down close relationships and contributing to higher divorce rates. A dramatic decline in the social status of different strata of the population may easily have spurred conflicts between spouses, as various sociological studies have shown.[18] An increase in unemployment has also led to tension and instability within families. The freedom to move and travel, along with the availability of new emigrant-based labor markets, has contributed to family destabilization. The spread of alcoholism following the restrictions of the mid-1980s was another factor adding to family conflicts. Importantly, liberalization of divorce regulations has affected the increase in the divorce rate.

Another factor that bears consideration is the effect that the introduction of a multiplicity of values has had on marital stability; a new liberal ideology provides opportunities to attain individual freedom and hence facilitates the revival of ideas of sexual equality that may cause tension in a marriage. Hierarchical relations between spouses and their roles in the family remain unchanged or have been moving toward greater polarization, according to some recent research. Women are becoming less competitive in the labor market because of the increasing responsibility they bear in their private lives. Under the Soviet system, women were protected by policies supporting their work outside the home, including day-care centers, summer camps, child benefits, as well as cheap dry cleaning, shoe repair, and other similar services. The loss of such support and the increased burden on women's lives may contribute to marital breakups.

Radical changes in housing policy have contributed to changes in patterns of marriage and divorce. The on-going housing privatization, the emergence of an active housing market, and the fact that the government can no longer guarantee housing to all Russian citizens have all had a contradictory effect on matrimonial behavior in Russia. The December 1992 Goskomstat survey of new families showed that half of them lived on less than 50 square feet per person, while 9.1 percent of families resided in dormitories. Despite these poor conditions, the number of couples who get married in order to solve their housing problems is falling. On the other hand, the number of divorces that formerly may not have occurred because it was impossible to buy housing is on the rise. Where housing considerations may have prevented divorces in the past, they do not necessarily do so today.

On the other hand, certain factors that have grown out of the current situation have served to counterbalance the sources of instability mentioned above. For one, the lower standards of living of the majority of the population have forced many families to unite their resources to face misfortunes. Also, the formation of family businesses has proven a source of family unity and thus a new force against divorce.

Despite its destabilization, the Russian family has the potential to play a key role in the development and strengthening of a stable middle class in Russia. It can also assist in Russia's revival if the state pursues a social policy of supporting the family and promoting the integral role of women in the market economy. With the emergence of other aspects of democracy, the innovations needed may become more attainable.

The History of Reforms and the Family

The economic reforms that began in 1992 have aggravated the socioeconomic status of the majority of the Russian population. The "shock therapy" of the early 1990s lowered people's incomes and simultaneously expropriated practically all of their savings. The year 1992 also saw the beginning of a destruction of the social infrastructure, which led to partial abolition of free health care, education, and cultural services, as well as the stable provision of housing and utilities services.

The second decisive phase of economic reforms took place with voucher privatization, which transferred public property into private hands. In practice, this meant that a narrow group of officials within and close to the state government took over public property. The population gained no benefit from these reforms, but rather ended up with a piece of paper called a "voucher," which proved to be useless.

The next stage of reforms involved a "large-scale" state property redistribution under the so-called "loans-for-shares program." As a result, major Russian industrial enterprises producing export commodities became the private property of a small group of people. The enterprises were sold for prices intentionally much lower than what they were really worth, which led to the emergence of a clan of oligarchs.

Simultaneously, all sorts of "games" went on in the financial sector: MMM and other pyramid schemes, the ruble denomination, and state regulation of the exchange rate. The overall population suffered losses all over again, while a small group of people grew wealthier. The series of state economic undertakings ended with the Kiriyenko default of August 17, 1998, and Russians were thrown back to 1992. Everything that they had saved over the preceding seven years was expropriated "from above." The system of holding back wages, pensions, and benefits, which is called an "effective" method for fighting inflation, is in fact a means of crediting the state at the expense of an impoverished population. These transformation processes dramatically influenced all aspects of life in Russian society. They produced five urgent social problems each carrying implications for children and young people. First, wages, pensions, and other payments dropped drastically, two to two-and-a-half times annually. The minimum wage still totals only 20 percent of the subsistence level, resulting in an increase in poverty, as outlined below.

The second problem is the social polarization of Russian society, which led to the emergence of "two Russias," opposite in terms of the patterns of behavior, preferences, and values of the people who represent them. Two standards of living formed, each having its own income level and consumption structures, as well as its own set of prices for and selection of goods and services. The representatives of the "two Russias" speak two different languages and understand each other poorly. This is dangerous also because the political elite "lives" in the country of the rich and very rich. According to experts, the standard of living in one of the "two Russias" is 100 times higher than that in the other ($30 a month for the poor, and $3,000 for the rich). Therefore, the average living standard indicators may be very misleading.

This social polarization leads to a sustainable stratification of society and destabilizes the situation in the country, negatively affecting children and young people.

The third problem is emerging poverty in Russia. In the second half of 2001, the subsistence level was just slightly over 1,500 rubles (or $50). According to the most optimistic estimations, about 30 percent of the population, or 44 million people, live below this extremely feeble line.[19] About half of the total number of the poor are children and young people under 30. One-third of the poor become so because of low wages, wage arrears, and unemployment. The second third is impoverished due to low pension payments. The last third is the group that has traditionally been low-income: single mothers, families with more than two children, and disabled individuals. Poverty, unemployment, economic and social instability, hopes that never come true, and collapse of plans for the future intensify marginalization of the population. Exclusion results in the formation of a large stratum of paupers, which is also a consequence of downward social mobility. Our estimates show that 10 percent of the urban population can be described as the "social bottom," which includes about 1.3 million street children.[20]

The fourth problem is high unemployment, a "sword of Damocles" of sorts for the majority of working people. There are about 6 million unemployed among the economically active population in Russia.[21] The young generation, individuals in preretirement age, former army servicemen, those employed in the military-industrial sector, immigrants, forced migrants, and women are the most vulnerable groups.

Finally, the fifth problem is the deterioration of social protection mechanisms and the social infrastructure, most importantly social insurance, pensions, free health care, education, and housing and utilities systems. Special polling of residents of Cherepovets, a town in the Vologda region, in September-November 2001, indicated that people's attitudes toward higher consumer services tariffs remain fairly critical. Over 60 percent of respondents said that it would have been better if the reforms were introduced more gradually, while about one-fourth considered the reforms unnecessary. The main reason for such opinions is the decline in well-being of the majority of the population.[22]

The Family in the Emerging Economic System

Family economics have played an important role in the survival of Russians who have been drawn into the roaring whirlpool of economic changes. Families have mobilized internal resources and reserves, using every possible means, from accumulating a stockpile of food products to relying entirely on a family garden. The family appears to be the most fundamental element in guaranteeing physical survival in the context of a dramatic decline in monthly incomes.

Functioning as a psychological refuge, the family today appears to be an "island of stability," given that a significant part of society has few or no social reference points. In a time of growing estrangement, mutual mistrust, aggressiveness, and pessimism, the family—identified with the home one grew up in—becomes a buffer against conflicting and polarized forces within society. The family helps to solve pressing issues for those in social risk groups with few resources at their disposal, including disabled individuals, alcoholics, drug addicts, unemployed people, refugees, and ex-convicts.

The family remains unquestionably and universally valuable, transmitting cultural heritage, ethnic traditions, and ethical norms; its importance grows today not only for each individual in particular, but for Russia as a whole. In a context in which social networks are breaking down and the market economy's civic relations are only in the early stages of formation, the family becomes an integrating element. The role of an individual's identification with his or her family grows hand in hand with the process of market relations' institutionalization.

The family is a powerful social institution. Thousands of invisible ties connect it to the economy, social structure, state government, and cultural institutions. Changes in society are bound to affect the family, its composition, stability, functions, and development. The family and society relate to each other in such a way that when the role of society weakens, the role of the family strengthens. Hence, lower economic activity in the realm of social production has led to an increase in the role of the family's economic function, which has blossomed with privatization and market relations. The collapse of state paternalism, which formerly determined an individual's entire life paradigm from birth to death, has resulted directly in higher family sovereignty and individual independence. A good case in point is the fact that the private residential housing market grew in response to the drastic decline in housing provided to families by the state.

During the Soviet period, the family's role in the economy was significantly limited by the state and reduced virtually to zero. The family had no economic functions. Private property was nonexistent, and there was only a limited possibility of possessing personal property.

The family's economic role increased during the transition to a market-oriented society for three reasons. The first factor was institutional reorganization of housing. Russia underwent large-scale privatization, and over 50 percent of all residential housing was privatized. A full-fledged housing market formed. Mortgage credits to build and buy housing were introduced. Without housing privatization it would have been impossible for families to become sovereign, as the state provision of free housing to citizens (albeit on average 10 years after a citizen applied for it) was actually the primary manifestation of state paternalism. Only with private housing could a family feel economically free, gain a new social status, and become a player in the market economy.

The second factor was unemployment and underemployment, which produced the development of home-based, family-owned, and individually-owned businesses. Women were focused mainly on solving their families' survival problems, while men were actively looking for their niche in the market.

The third factor—active family involvement in the consumer segment of the economy—arose from the radical reduction in living standards and higher prices for goods and services at the same time that family incomes went down. This situation forced the family to provide for its own social services to cover the gaps in the state social infrastructure.

In particular, there was an almost 50 percent reduction in the number of various child-care establishments. Budget financing was cut, monetary resources to maintain children's organizations disappeared, and the cost of child-care services increased. However, as family incomes were going down, families were forced to stop using these services, and the full burden of the everyday care of children shifted to mothers. This burden was aggravated by a growth in unemployment, forcing a significant portion of the economically active population to leave the social production market.

Family participation in the economy assumed four principal forms. The first kind of family economic activity was self-employment, a phenomenon that first appeared in the second half of the 1980s. A typical example of this type of economic activity was the so-called *chelnoki* (duffel-bag traders), who during Soviet times were viewed as nothing but *spekulianty*, i.e., those who illegally resell goods to take advantage of varying prices. In the 1990s, *chelnoki* formed the basis of small business, thereby laying the foundation for the development of the middle class. This type of activity also embraces children doing ancillary work for street traders, as well as students and elderly people involved in street commerce. Self-employed individuals often offer private housekeeping, sociocultural, and educational services.

The second type of household economic activity is the family business. This includes families involved in some sort of cottage industry. A typical example is families working in farmyards, who are important contributors to the current revitalization of rural areas. Initially, family entrepreneurship assumed the form of cooperatives, which were legalized in early 1987 when the Council of Ministers of the former USSR approved tentative charters of cooperatives for producing consumer goods and providing food, dry cleaning, shoe repair, and other similar services to the population. Recent years saw the emergence of family firms and businesses, as well as family farms. A large proportion of family entrepreneurs deals in trade or provides middleman services.

The third type of family economic activity is credit and financial transactions. Individual family members open bank accounts, buy shares, and receive loans. This type of activity greatly depends on fluctuations in the financial markets.

The fourth form is the leasing of property, residential areas, country houses, vehicles, garages, various sorts of equipment, agricultural machinery, and trucks. This type of economic activity existed during the Soviet period but was considered illegal.

Transformations in the Russian Family

Changes in socioeconomic conditions in Russia have greatly influenced the status of various groups of families. The in-depth transformation of civilization cannot but greatly affect all aspects of life, including the institution of the family, the central element in any society. The transition to the market economy has fundamentally changed not only the structure and typology, but also the functions and roles, of the family, its development cycles, and family relationships, generating a new spectrum of interconnected phenomena at the microlevel of life in Russia. These changes have particular bearing on three areas of Russian family life.

First, the relationship between the family and the government has changed. In keeping with an idea originating with the neoliberals, Russians today think that the state continues to exert a paternalistic influence on the Russian family, just as it did during the Soviet period. "The Soviet way of life," one neoliberal writes, "practically eradicated the stimuli to individual activity and initiative and weakened the natural ability of a human being to protect himself, including in the social sphere."[23] At the same time, according to Russian liberals, it is unrealistic to expect any help "from above" today. In actuality, this interpretation of the relationship between the family and the state is at best a myth. More precisely it is an unsuccessful attempt to justify the state's helplessness in a crisis situation, during which it is supposed to fulfill its "social contract" obligations particularly well. The authorities have practically stopped guaranteeing the minimum wage and pension that would correspond to the subsistence level. They can no longer honor and enforce wage agreements, and consequently the state and businesses are incurring considerable payroll debts.[24] The state guarantees neither free health care nor education. In this context, it is precisely the state that—not for paternalistic reasons, but rather to fulfill its intrinsic functions—is responsible for establishing and guaranteeing the rules by which not only the average, but also the minimum, wage would be sufficient to provide for the population's basic needs for reproduction of the population and a quality work force. By way of stark comparison, the International Pact on Economic, Social, and Cultural Rights (IPESCR) defines the right to work thusly: Work should give the worker and his family sufficient income to provide for nutrition, clothing, and housing, as well as a continuous improvement in living standards;[25] ILO Convention No. 122 makes similar statements.

When wages drop to levels "lower than minimum" and 40 percent of workers earn less than necessary to sustain a subsistence standard of living, leaving a full one-third of the population (and two-thirds of pensioners), concerned about how to survive physically it is hard to talk about state paternalism. The population and the state today cannot help having opposing interests. Moreover, it would be appropriate, rather than to talk about state paternalism, to suggest that the people are helping the government by being patient. On the contrary, if and when wages provide people with a normal consumer-goods basket, access to insurance against standard risks, and vital consumer services, then we could talk about the problem of state paternalism; but, if this happens, state paternalism would have no reason to exist.

The second issue is the boundless expansion of economic functions of the family during the societal transition to the market economy. The family displays maximum initiative. It proves daily and in real terms that it needs sovereignty and independence. On the surface, everything looks relatively good, but in actuality, the expansion of the family's economic role has led to the weakening of its educational, cultural, and even reproductive functions. If we incorporate into our calculations regarding compensation levels the fact that one-fifth of all workers have two or more jobs,[26] we will be once again misguided, as we would not take into consideration the number of hours people actually work per day. According to our data, some people work 70-hour weeks.[27] Out of these conditions come higher numbers of abandoned newborns and homeless children, as well as the development of asocial behavior in all groups of the population.

The third issue is related to changes in relationships within families in the context of the liberal market economy. It is well known that during the Soviet era, relations inside the family were becoming increasingly egalitarian. Despite the fact—or possibly thanks to it—that women bore a "double burden," as both mothers and workers, their social status within a family was rapidly establishing itself and growing. Today, during the founding of market relations, which produce increasing unemployment and mass poverty, and the formation of the labor market, the female work force has become less competitive and is considered "second rate." This phenomenon not only has affected the social production sector of the economy, but has also exerted a strong influence on family relationships, both between spouses and between parents and children. Having lost their social status, women have given up their status in their private lives as well. Egalitarian relations are being pushed into the background, and we are witnessing a revival of the patriarchal type of family relationship. However, the progress women made in the period from the 1950s to 1980s in smoothing gender asymmetry is impossible to reverse, leading to a natural growth in tension within families, and permanent conflict, destabilization, violence, and discrimination in the family.

The Russian Family and Current Reforms

Obviously, such phenomena cannot but influence the dynamics of demographic reproduction and the quality of the population. It is no accident that we register lower health indicators, growing mortality rates, a higher incidence of disease (especially in women), poorer health in each consecutive generation, depopulation, and a decrease in quality indicators in general. This is one of Russian society's core problems.

Based on what has been said, one important, possibly well-known, conclusion needs to be drawn. Given their profound effect, the social reforms that Russian society is starting to adopt cannot help but affect the family and its functions. Future and current social reforms must necessarily be viewed in the light of their influence on the family, its internal relations, and its functions in society.

First of all this relates to pension reform. Thirty-eight million Russian pensioners can be somewhat equally divided into two groups. One group is made up of pensioners themselves, single and married retirees living by themselves. The other group is mixed families, where pensioners live together with working relatives. The latter group is worse off financially. Two-thirds of mixed families have incomes below the subsistence level, as there are two negative factors in play here: low pension payments and even lower wages. To a considerable extent, this situation resulted from the fact that the pension system reforms had been launched before the country restructured the system of payment for work. The contradiction resulting from this policy is unjustifiable.

Families and households suffer even more severely from housing and utilities reforms. The authorities strive to raise prices for housing and utilities services to 100 percent of the cost of their production without ensuring a corresponding increase in the incomes of the majority of the population. At present, almost one-third of Russians already fail to pay housing fees. The increased tariffs will not bring the expected results, but will only generate additional social tension.

A similar situation is currently developing in the health care system. By interfering with health care, the market makes it increasingly harder for the least-provided-for citizens to obtain medical services. One-third of poor families cannot afford hospitalization and medications, the prices of which are constantly increasing.

The concept of tuition, which is being gradually introduced into Russian education, also creates obstacles for children from low-income families. Half of the parents in such families have no confidence that they will be able to provide their children with professional skills.

All of the above lead us to the conclusion that the social policy currently in the development stage or already partially implemented must take into account the polarization in the population's living standards, because each individual is equally valuable to society.

Women and Children in the Period of Family Transformation

Russia's main resource is its people, its specific demographic genofund, as attested to in Pitirim Sorokin's eloquent and well-argued article "Sovremennoe Sostoianie Rossii" (Russia's Contemporary Condition).[28] In the period from 1914 to 1921, the country suffered enormous quantitative losses (21 million people), but qualitative damage is always more harmful. "The fate of any society depends primarily on the qualities of its members," Sorokin writes. "A society composed of idiots and talentless people will never prosper. If you give a group of devils an outstanding constitution, you would not create a great society. It works the other way around as well: A society made up of talented and strong-willed people will inevitably create more elaborate forms of cohabitation." He continues, "Thorough study of the rise and fall of entire nations shows that one of the principal reasons for these transformations was precisely dramatic changes in the quality of their populations." In Sorokin's opinion, only the talent of the Russian ancestors allowed them to establish a mighty state and a number of great universal values. In this light, children's health is of paramount importance, as children determine the future of a country.

All over the world women bear the majority of the responsibility for raising children because they give birth and feed babies in the first months of their lives. In a patriarchal society, there is the understanding that babies need a mother's care, but not that they also need close emotional contact with a father. Meantime, the belief that parenthood should be balanced is becoming increasingly popular in today's Russia. However, our research indicates that in practice the overwhelming proportion of child-caring duties is still carried out by women. The distribution of duties between parents testifies to this.[29]

These studies show that in today's Russia an "absent father" is becoming a common phenomenon. More than ever before, men are concerned with breadwinning. Under the pressure of economic reforms, accompanied with inflation and unemployment, married men are forced to work extra hours to maintain their families' standards of living. At the same time, husbands today are required to more fully participate in family life. Men are starting to notice the collapse of the traditional order. The existing differences in views on roles in the family create the potential for conflict. The phenomenon of the Russian grandmother caring for children is becoming a thing of the past as a result of the degradation of the pension system and the necessity to continue to work after retirement.

The family institutional crisis manifests itself primarily in the family's increasing failure to fulfill one of its primary societal functions: procreation (i.e., giving birth and raising and supporting children). The family is the social institution that provides children with their first social experiences, and the way parents raise a child directly affects that child's development as an individual.

The difficulties experienced by the majority of children in Russia can be traced to the breakdown of Communist values, which prevailed for many decades, which were imbibed as though with their mothers' milk, and which were acted upon from a very early age. The new social orientations have yet to form, and there is a lack of clear moral and ethical norms and principles serving as mechanisms to regulate social relations. Existing in this vacuum is especially difficult for those who have not yet found themselves a "guiding star."

In crisis situations, it is generally true that vulnerable groups such as children, the elderly, the disabled, and the ill suffer the most, and Russia is certainly experiencing a crisis today. Research indicates that the situation of children has become extremely complicated; the same is true of the relationship between children and their parents. The problems arise prior to birth, as can be seen in the high number of abortions in Russia. In 1995, for each 100 births there were 74 abortions.[30] Note that this is happening when the birthrate in Russia, already very low, is on the decline. In 1992, the overall birthrate totaled 10.7 per 1000 population, while in 2000 it was only 8.7.[31]

"For children," Pitirim Sorokin writes, "a mother's love is a vital necessity. Deprived of love's warmth, children weaken and die as quickly as they would from infections, famine, or inappropriate diet."[32] He continues, "the therapeutic power of love is especially important in prevention of and curing mental and moral disorders. . . . Insufficient love in childhood usually results in moral and mental illness."[33] "Unwanted, unloved, and neglected children who were deprived of the blessing of love in early childhood die early or grow up stunted."[34]

The most dramatic fact today is the decline in children's health. Only two-thirds of children are born healthy, while only 30 percent of newborns can be called absolutely healthy. Children that enter the world today are less healthy than those born in the past. This is confirmed by the correlation between lower health indicators for women, first and foremost pregnant women, and higher numbers of births of unhealthy children. In 1998, 38.6 percent of all pregnant women had anemia, and 34.1 percent of children were born diseased. In the period from 1990 to 1999, the share of childbearing women with anemia grew 3.1 times, while the proportion of infants born with health disorders increased 2.8 times. Russia has a high infant mortality rate. The average rate for the country overall in 2000 totaled 15.3 per 1000 live births. However, in some regions this indicator in 1999 was as much as 2.5 times higher. This was the case in the Evenk Autonomous region (40.3), the Altai Republic (28.5), Chukotka Autonomous Region (26.9), and Amur region (28.8).

Children start suffering from chronic diseases at very early ages. To a considerable degree, this is linked to the fact that children are born with weakened health, and, as they grow, so does their weakening health. Therefore, it is no wonder that children's mortality rate (ages 0 to 4) in the 1990s vacillated around 21–22 per 1000 live births.[36] Health indicators for teenagers are low as well. Twenty percent of children of preschool age and 50 percent of adolescents have chronic diseases. Only 5 percent of grade school and high school graduates are absolutely healthy. Two of every three conscripts cannot serve in the army for objective reasons such as health. All of the above can potentially lead to a long-term decrease in the quality of the nation's human capital, as an unhealthy generation cannot produce a healthy one. As of January 1, 1999, the total number of disabled children reached 600,000.[35] The most significant health losses are incurred when a person is a child or teenager. While in the past the majority of health problems occurred in old age, now they are more common among the young. This is a reversal of the natural order, in which an individual loses health gradually with age.

There is a high incidence of mental disorders among adolescents. In 1999, 140,500 teenagers, 64 percent of whom were mentally retarded (had oligophrenia), were under dispensary supervision. On top of that, as of the beginning of 2000, 90,800 adolescents were receiving counseling from psychiatrists.

Tuberculosis has spread widely among children and young people. In 1999, the rate of tuberculosis was 18.3 cases for every 100,000 children under the age of 14. An increase in alcoholism and other types of substance abuse among children is also very disturbing. In 1995–1998, the number of teenagers who were diagnosed with alcoholism for the first time increased 2.1 times, with drug addiction increasing 3.8 times, and toxic substance abuse growing almost 6.6 times. In 1998, 9.6 and 195.8 out of every 100,000 children and adolescents, respectively, were diagnosed with syphilis. In addition, the incidence rate among girls was 3.2 times higher than among boys, and 1.6 times higher than among the total population.[37]

The level of educational services received by children is also on the decline, due largely to the fact that education is no longer mandatory. Therefore, it should not be surprising that about 2 percent of children of school age do not attend school, while a significant share of children have entered the labor market, thus replacing education, and are now working at various jobs from dishwashing to posting ads and other notices. The issue of working street children is becoming increasingly urgent, and springs from the problem of homeless and neglected children in general. Research concerning working street children in St. Petersburg shows that the number of such children under the age of 13 in the city totals 40,000–50,000. These children are working for predominantly economic reasons, such as the desire to buy food, help the family, simply "survive," and earn money to buy drugs. Some of these children are forced to work by someone else. On average, children work about 6 hours a day and earn from 10 to 200 rubles daily.[38] The Institute for Socioeconomic Studies of Population at the Russian Academy of Sciences estimates that there are 1.3 million children living on the street in Russia today.[39]

Research indicates that an individual receipt of an education that provides knowledge and skills greatly depends on the educational level in the family, and on the other hand is directly correlated with income, the level of self-identification, and so forth. However, the upsurge of unemployment in Russia in the first half of the 1990s led to an overall deterioration in professional skills and a loss of appreciation for the value of knowledge.

Very negative trends have been registered in the relations between children and parents who have lost their jobs or have lower wages. At the same time, parents are also treating children unfairly and lack an understanding of ways to approach such issues as a crisis in relationships with their children, increased alienation of children, the development of egocentric attitudes, and a lack of restrictions. In the Novosibirsk region, over 10,000 children are being raised in state institutions, although 90 percent of them have parents; 11,500 children live in families that belong to risk groups; and 3,500 have the "social status" of street children.[40] The longer hardships last, the more difficult it is to return an individual to normal life. Also, the number of children abandoned not only at birth, but also during the first few years of life, has grown.

The family has always been a child's early socialization medium. However different men's and women's roles are, in many cultures the family prepares a child for being an adult. In families young people learn about gender roles and the division of household duties. However, social changes are increasingly shifting this responsibility to the system of education, peers, and the media.

Cases in which children are deprived of housing and personal possessions are on the rise, along with those in which the family situation forces children to run away from home. According to I.I. Grebesheva, the director general of the Russian Family Planning Association, "the tragedy in the Russian demographic situation is that low birthrates and high incidence of abortion are accompanied by an increase in the number of murders of newborns and in growing social orphancy. . . . The number of orphans is currently 3 times higher than it was in the last year of World War II."[41]

According to various sources, the total number of street children in Russia is either 2 to 3 million or 1.5 to 2 million. Sources say that the following conditions force children to go to live on the street:

> A child is an orphan; his/her parents are dead or absent. In most cases these are children in single-parent families, where the father abandons his parental duties before the child is born.

> A child is a "social orphan." This happens when a court order takes parental rights away from a parent, parents refuse to fulfill parental functions (they receive prison terms or act asocially), or the family does not have the income to support a child.

> A child experiences physical abuse.

The high numbers of street children have drawn increased attention from the executive and legislative branches of government. In June 1999, a federal law "On the System of Prevention of Child Neglect and Juvenile Delinquency" was adopted. It helped to increase the effectiveness of efforts to protect the rights and legal interests of children who need state support.

Several principal focus areas were identified to prevent the number of street children from increasing:

1. expand the number of family placement options for orphans;
2. place children in the care of guardians;
3. increase the number of family-type orphanages and foster homes;

4. organize special closed educational establishments, and
5. establish a network of entertainment, educational, and health institutions.[42]

One of the most urgent issues is to socialize young people, who are the main driving force of development, transformation, economic growth, and technical progress. In the meantime, this social group displays an intensive growth in stratification, trends toward poverty, and other negative factors. It remains the most explosive of all groups. It has many demands, but the means to satisfy them are very limited. On the one hand, young peoples' abilities to adapt to the new socioeconomic environment have turned out to be higher than expected, but on the other hand, dissatisfaction with their own condition results in the emergence of such an "unhealthy" reaction as passive protest. Instead of a social explosion, we have seen social degradation, which is more dangerous for Russia's development in the long run than a social explosion. Unemployment, low wages, and the low prestige of work requiring complicated skills create an "explosive mixture" of all-out nihilism among the young generation, which in its own way "romanticizes" such asocial behaviors as drug addiction, vandalism, and crime.

Negative social factors pile up on top of one another, multiplying their effect on demographic processes. With precision comparable to that of a natural experiment, we can conclude that the new conditions in Russia listed above are the social price of reforms, and that the price has turned out to be so high that it calls into question whether the Russian genofund will be preserved.

Notes

1. S.I. Golod, *Sem'ia i brak: Istoriko-sotsiologicheskii analiz* [Family and Marriage: A Historical and Sociological Analysis] (Petropolis: St. Petersburg, 1999), 92.
2. S.I. Golod, *Sem'ia i brak*, 181.
3. Dana Vannoy, Natalia Rimashevskaya, et al., *Marriages in Russia: Couples During the Economic Transition* (Westport, Connecticut; London: Praeger, 1999), 36–37.
4. Goskomstat, *Demograficheskii ezhegodnik Rossii* [Russian Demographic Yearbook] (Moscow: Goskomstat, 2001), 150.
5. Goskomstat, *Demograficheskii ezhegodnik Rossii*, 155, 157, 159.
6. http://www.polit.ru/printable/453814.html.
7. A.G. Volkov, *Sem'ia—ob"ekt demografii* [The Family as the Subject of Demography] (Moscow: Mysl', 1986), 193.
8. Goskomstat, *Sem'ia v Rossii* [The Family in Russia] (Moscow: Goskomstat, 1996), 42.
9. Dana Vannoy, Natalia Rimashevskaya, et al., *Marriages in Russia*, 36.
10. O.I. Antonova, *O polozhenii detei v Rossiiskoi Federatsii. Gosudarstvennii doklad* [On the Situation of Children in the Russian Federation. State Report] [Moscow, 2000], 6.

11. *Deutschland* 2, 1999, 39.

12. *Deutschland* 4, 2001, 22.

13. For more detailed results of the study of family development cycles see Natalia Rimashevskaya, "Zhiznennii tsikl sem'i" [Family Life Cycle] in *Demografiia i sotsiologiia. Bednost': vzgliad uchenykh na problem*, ed., Natalia Rimashevskaya (Moscow: ISESP RAS, 1994), 122–149.

14. Goskomstat, *Demograficheskii ezhegodnik Rossii* [Russian Demographic Yearbook] (Moscow: Goskomstat, 2001), 119.

15. A detailed analysis of marriage and divorce trends in Russia can be found in the article by A.A Avdeyev, "Braki i razvody v Rossii" [Marriages and Divorces in Russia], *Narodonaseleniye*, February 1998/January 1999.

16. Goskomstat, *Demograficheskii ezhegodnik Rossii* [Russian Demographic Yearbook] (Moscow: Gomkomstat, 2001), 130–131.

17. Natalia Rimashevskaya, ed., *Zhenshchina, Muzhchina, Sem'ia v Rossii: posledniaia tret' XXveka. Proekt "Taganrog"* [The Woman, the Man, and the Family in Russia: Last Third of the Twentieth Century Project "Taganrog"] (Moscow: ISESP RAS, 2001).

18. See, for example, Natalia Rimashevskaya, ed., *Family Well-Being and Health. Project "Taganrog—3.5"* (Moscow: ISESP RAS, 1998), 183.

19. Goskomstat *Sotsial'no-ekonomicheskoe polozhenie Rossii* [The Russian Socioeconomic Situation], 9 (Moscow: Goskomstat, 2001), 208.

20. Natalia Rimashevskaya, "Obednenie naseleniia Rossii i 'sotsial'noe dno': resul'tat spetsial'nogo issledovaniia" [The Impoverishment of the Russian Population and the "Social Bottom": Results of a Special Survey], in *Narodonaseleniye* 2 (1999).

21. Goskomstat, *Sotsia'lno-ekonomicheskoe polozhenie Rossii* [The Russian Socioeconomic Situation], 9 (Moscow: Goskomstat, 2001), 208.

22. *Monitoring obshchestvennogo mneniia. Ekspress-informatsiia 24* [Public Opinion Monitoring. Express Information. 24], Vologda Science Coordination Center, TsEMI RAS, November 2001.

23. E. Gontmakher, "Sotsial'naia politika v Rossii: Evoliutsiia 90–kh i novyi start" [Social Policy in Russia. The Nineties Evolution and a New Start], *Pro et Contra*, Summer 2001.

24. Goskomstat, *Sotsial'no-ekonomicheskoe polozhenie Rossii* [The Russian Socioeconomic Situation], 9 (Moscow: Goskomstat, 2001), 202.

25. UN Secretary General Report, *Improvement of Social Protection and Reduction of Vulnerability in Globalization*, UN Economic and Social Council. Social Development Commission, Session 39, 13–23 February 2001, 5.

26. *Rossia-99. Sotsial'no-demograficheskaia situatsiia* [Russia-99. Sociodemographic Situation] (Moscow: ISESP RAS, 2000), 126–127.

27. Natalia Rimashevskaya, ed., *Family Well-Being and Health. Project "Taganrog–3.5"* (Moscow: ISESP RAS, 1998), 185.

28. Pitirim Sorokin, "Sovremennoe sostoianie Rossii" [Russia's Contemporary Condition], *Novy Mir* 4–5, 1992.

29. Vannoy, Rimashevskaya, et al., *Marriages in Russia*, 87.

30. Goskomstat of Russia, *Sem'ia v Rossii* [Family in Russia] (Moscow: Goskomstat, 1996), 179.

31. Goskomstat, *Demograficheskii ezhegodnik Rossii* [Russian Demographic Yearbook] (Moscow: Goskomstat, 2001), 55.

32. P.A. Sorokin, *Glavnye tendentsii nashego vremeni* [The Main Trends of Our Time], (Moscow: Nauka, 1997), 265.

33. Sorokin, *Glavnye tendentsii nashego vremeni*, 266.

34. Sorokin, *Glavnye tendentsii nashego vremeni*, 271.

35. Goskomstat, *Sotsial'noe polozhenie i uroven'zhizni naseleniia Rossii* [Social Conditions and Living Standards of the Russian Population], (Moscow: Goskomstat, 1999), 208.

36. Russian Labor Ministry, *Statisticheskie dannye, kharakterizuiushchiesia polozheniem detei v Rossiiskoi Federatsii* [Statistics on the Condition of Children in the Russian Federation] Moscow, 2000.

37. Goskomstat, *Statisticheskii biulleten'* [Statistical Bulletin], 1(75) (Moscow: Goskomstat, 2001), 124.

38. International Labor Organization, *Analiz polozheniia rabotaiushchikh ulichnykh detei v Sankt-Peterburge* [An Analysis of the Condition of Working Street Children in St. Petersburg], St. Petersburg, 2000, 5–7.

39. N.M. Rimashevskaya, "Obednenie naseleniia Rossii i 'sotsial'noe dno,'" 6–26.

40. S.I. Pykhtin and L.M. Zobreva, *Sotsial'naia podderzhka sem'i v Novosibirskoi oblasti v sovremennykh sotsial'no-ekonomicheskikh usloviiakh* [Social Support for the Family in the Novosibirsk Region under Current Socioeconomic Conditions], materials from the Second "World of Family" Congress, Moscow, 2001, 30.

41. I.I. Grebesheva, *Otechestvennoe roditel'stvo: sotsial'nye problemy* [Parenthood in Russia: Social Problems], materials from the Second "World of Family" Congress, Moscow, 2001, 50.

42. The Federal Assembly of the Russian Federation, O*n Ministry of Education Measures for the Prevention of Child Neglect and Juvenile Delinquency*, Moscow, October 2001.

6

Social Shocks, Social
Confidence, and Health

Richard Rose

Men and women are social animals.[1] Social medicine postulates that better
social conditions make for the better health of individuals, while the health
of people living in what is colloquially called a "sick" society suffers.[2]
Emile Durkheim went so far as to argue that negative changes in social
conditions are a major cause of suicide. However, people die as individuals, and clinical medicine looks for causes of mortality in the physical circumstances of individuals. Although the biomedical and the social
approaches to health may stress contrasting influences, they are not necessarily contradictory. People who have major physical disabilities can have
trouble fitting into society, and poor people may have a diet that is bad for
their physical health.

Social influences on health have a collective impact; if the air or water of a
city is polluted, then every urban resident is affected. The transformation of the
Soviet Union into the Russian Federation is an extreme example of a collective
shock for every citizen, repudiating abruptly institutions that people had been
accustomed to for almost all their lives and causing the pervasive transformation of both the polity and the economy. However, within every given social
context there are variations in the health of individuals affected by social shocks.

Why is it that some people remain relatively healthy in the face of transformation while others become less healthy? The simple clinical answer—
because they are younger—is inadequate. Age-specific mortality rates show
that causes of avoidable death have often risen in Russia since the breakup of
the Soviet Union.[3] Relying on explanations of poor health or avoidable mortality based on heavy smoking or drinking begs another question. Why do
some Russians drink themselves into an early grave or become nicotine addicts while others do not? What is the missing link between social conditions

and individual health that determines why some Russians enjoy a healthier and longer life than others?

Insofar as shocks of transformation affect everyone in society, they predict an undifferentiated response, or one in which the health of everyone deteriorates. There can even be a tendency toward equalization of members of society, if those who were formerly better off suffer most from the collapse of the system in which they had prospered. Monocausal theories of social disintegration causing widespread deterioration in health treat individuals as passive objects of society. Such a reductionist model of human behavior allows no room for individual responses to be mediated by specific circumstances, by an individual's particular social context, or by actions that individuals take in response to shocks.

Shocks of transformation are but one element in a multicausal model of health. While shocks are pervasively felt throughout society, their effects are mediated by many intervening variables that require a multivariate model for a satisfactory explanation. Shocks are best understood as challenges to which individuals respond, some maintaining their health while others experience a deterioration in theirs. In order to remain healthy or survive in challenging circumstances, individuals must adapt. The ways in which people adapt are heavily influenced by their socioeconomic resources and by individually internalized predispositions. For example, more educated persons are likely to have more resources for maintaining themselves, those with a healthy diet are in better physical shape to cope with challenges. The effects of social integration are ambiguous. Russians who strongly identified with the Communist regime were more shocked by the collapse of their normative system, but the great majority of Russians were not ideological Communists, and many welcomed some of the changes that have accompanied the transformation, such as great gains in personal freedom.[4]

This chapter links social and individual circumstances in order to show the conditions under which, as well as the extent to which, social shocks cause bad health and social confidence protects people against the stress of social shocks. Social confidence is here defined as the belief held by an individual in the ability to control what happens to his or her life. Confidence is social in that it refers to an individual's ability not only to achieve such personal goals as learning to play the piano, but also that person's capacity to respond successfully to unexpected challenges from abrupt changes in institutions of society. Yet confidence is also an individual attribute, for it must be internalized by a person as a consequence of interactions in society. From the perspective of social psychology, interaction with others is critical, but from the perspective of accounting for health, it is the individual's internalization of a positive attitude that is most important.

The Shock of Transformation

The development of an individual, with all its implications for his or her health, occurs within a social setting. This is evident in such situations as those in which individuals pursue bodybuilding activities as part of a group; for example, President Putin became skilled in judo as a result of training he received at a *Trud* sports club. The influence of a social setting is also evident when young people take up smoking in emulation of older friends.

Socialization describes the process by which individuals learn behavior that allows them to fit into their society. Socialization theories emphasize the dependence individuals have on pre existing norms of behavior to which they are introduced in the home, at school, by peer groups, and at work. With little or no explicit awareness, individuals take for granted the norms and practices of their society, whether that society be a market economy, a nonmarket command economy, or an economy without money altogether. Through socialization, individuals gain a measure of confidence in dealing with routine challenges, as well as with those that are out of the ordinary.

In every society, some individuals are misfits who do not meet society's expectations. Emile Durkheim distinguished three different forms of failed socialization. The first he labeled egoistic failure, in which an individual's failings lead to detachment from conventional social relations. Secondly, there is altruism, in which an individual so identifies with a group that there is a willingness to sacrifice one's life in situations such as war or for a religious cause. Thirdly, there is anomie, in which the shock of rapid change in the social order deprives individuals of the norms that guide how they are expected to act. Change can be negative, such as military defeat and occupation, or positive, such as rapid economic growth. Whereas egoistic alienation happens because an individual fails to meet stable social standards, anomie is the result of a society failing to maintain social norms. Durkheim argued that the strains of having to "learn greater self-control" because of the breakdown in established social norms creates "intolerable suffering."[5]

The treble transformation of the Soviet Union into the Russian Federation is a textbook example of the disruption of the macrostructures of society on a scale sufficient to produce a pervasive sense of anomie. Even though the Communist system was far from successful in its attempt to indoctrinate the ethos of the new Soviet man, socialization in the Soviet Union was an intensive process in which political and economic values were very explicit. The justification for these values collapsed with the fall of the party-state. And the new rulers of the Russian Federation did not seek to promote a new ideology with new norms to live by, as happens when an individual experiences a religious conversion. Instead, there was an ideological vacuum: President

Yeltsin emphasized getting rid of the past more than he focused on promoting a new system of democracy and markets. Likewise, President Putin has distanced himself from endorsing a clear set of norms. Each has done what Durkheim predicted would cause anomie, namely, leaving individuals to decide for themselves what sort of social norms to live by.

The Soviet state broke up into 15 independent states. Instead of dominating a population of almost a quarter billion Soviet citizens, plus more than 100 million people in the Warsaw Pact countries of Central and Eastern Europe, Russia became an independent state with 100 million fewer citizens and much less international standing. The breakup has left many Russian households with relatives living in what has become a foreign country, such as Ukraine or Kazahkstan. The implosion of a nonmarket economy affected the everyday activities of individuals as workers, raising fears of unemployment and causing nonpayment of wages to people nominally employed, and consumers have cumulatively experienced many thousands of percent in price inflation. Learning how to cope with a market economy was an unprecedented experience for nearly every post-Soviet citizen. The freedom gained by their new system of government has been used by Russians to express distrust of their new institutions.

The evaluation of the impact of shocks on Russian health has been heavily dependent on epidemiological studies using aggregate official statistics, especially statistics of early and avoidable mortality among men. Ecological inference requires the projection onto those who are alive at the end of a time period those conditions identified as having caused the deaths of a small percentage of the population during the time period in question. Projections are generalized from relatively small numbers of age- and gender-specific causes of death with a low incidence.[6] Problems of ecological inference are especially great in a Russian context. Deficiencies in health statistics were chronic during the Soviet Union,[7] thus raising questions about the validity of any attempt to make long-term trend analyses from Soviet times to current conditions. Official statistics showed male life expectancy actually falling by two years from the time Leonid Brezhnev entered office in 1964 to 1982, while male life expectancy was rising in advanced capitalist countries.[8] Statistical abnormalities have persisted since. Male life expectancy was reported to have fallen by 3.1 years from 1992 to 1993, a change so great as to suggest a major statistical adjustment in a time series.[9]

While the shock of transformation has been felt by every Russian resident, responses have been differentiated. Differentiation has occurred in the economy too, as some people have prospered while others have become poorer; in the polity, as some public officials have gained power while others have lost power; and in social life, as openness to the "far abroad" (that is, Europe and the

United States) has been welcomed by some while shunned by others. Aggregate statistics do not identify the individuals who are above average, the other side of a story in which many are heading to an early death.

Individual-level data can be obtained by clinical methods or by survey methods; the two sources are complementary. Clinical evidence provides biomedical measures of health. However, evidence from hospitals and clinics tends to underrepresent healthy persons who do not consult doctors. Moreover, biomedical measures do not show an individual's psychological state or social relations, two elements critical in determining whether individuals can maintain their health in response to transformation. Sample surveys can represent the whole of the national population, healthy as well as unhealthy. Surveys can also collect copious sociological and attitudinal data and, as a proxy for biomedical evidence, self-reported data about smoking and drinking, as well as self-assessments of physical and mental health.

The following pages analyze data from the ninth New Russia Barometer (NRB) survey of the Centre for the Study of Public Policy, University of Strathclyde, a representative nationwide survey designed by the author and fielded by VTsIOM (the Russian Center for Public Opinion Research). A total of 1,600 adults age 18 and upward were interviewed in a multistage probability sample with 160 primary sampling units.[10] Interviewing occurred in April 2000, half a generation after Mikhail Gorbachev had started the process that has transformed Russian society. If individuals were permanently scarred by the shocks of transformation, this would be evident by the time of the interview. However, if individuals are capable of adapting when challenged by such shocks, this too would come out.

Social Confidence

In the literal sense, everyone in Russia today has had to either reconcile him or herself to the transformation of society, emigrate, or die. The question is not *whether* Russians have responded but *how* they have responded to shocks that have been anomic in scale. To obtain an overall picture, the April 2000 NRB asked: *How have the big changes since Soviet times affected you?* More than three-quarters of respondents gave replies indicating that they were adapting to life in new circumstances. The largest group (42 percent) had already adapted, 30 percent reported they were trying to adapt, and 8 percent of relatively older Russians said they were living as before without noticing changes. A total of 20 percent said they were unable to adjust to the big changes since Soviet times; this group was disproportionately over the age of 60.

From other questions about changes in economic conditions and social status, it is evident that the process of adjustment has involved significant downward social mobility. Moreover, the great majority of people continue to face at least occasional disturbances in their everyday lives, and few think they live in a society that is "normal," a term connoting much the same to Russians as to Westerners.[11] However, difficulties are intermittent rather than chronic. When Russians are asked whether during the past year they have ever had to go without food, heating, electricity, or clothing they really needed, the median respondent reports that this happens rarely, and only 3 percent say they often do without all these basic necessities.

In response to social shocks, individual Russians have fallen back on skills developed during Soviet times to cope with an economy that created frequent shortages and a regime that formerly subjected people to intrusive ideological mobilization or even terror.[12] In the face of novel problems, individuals have shown resilience, bouncing back from difficulties, on some Sundays doing without meat and at other times enjoying a big meal, either with produce from their dacha or food bought with wages that were finally paid.[13] More than that, a growing number of Russians have gained materially. The NRB survey found that in spring 2000, 83 percent of households had a color television set, 35 percent a videocassette recorder, and 16 percent a car, while only 15 percent had none of these popular consumer durables.

The Extent of Confidence

Transformation has been a learning process for individual Russians. People have first had to learn how to adapt to new conditions of life, and some have been able to learn better than others. Individuals have also learned the extent to which they can or cannot meet unforeseen and unprecedented challenges, and in so doing, have gained or lost confidence in their capacity to control their own lives.

To measure the extent to which individuals have social confidence, the NBR surveys use a question initially developed for the study of social medicine in the United States:[14] *Some people feel they have complete control over their lives, while others feel that what they do has no real effect on what happens to them. How about yourself?* Respondents are asked to place themselves on a ten-point scale in which 1 represents no control at all and 10 represents a great deal of control over what happens. The implications for health are substantial. If people are fatalists, they may not take precautions to avoid accidents that might happen at work or while driving a car, assuming "what will be, will be," whereas individuals who feel that their own actions control what happens to them may protect their health by limiting drinking, not smoking, and exercising.

Like social capital, the measure of control here deals with social relationships, but it differs from the indicators that Robert Putnam uses, such as

Figure 6.1 **Wide Dispersion of Social Confidence in Russia**

Question: *Some people feel they have complete control over their lives, while others feel that what they do has no real effect on what happens to them. How about yourself? On this scale of 1 to 10, where would you place the control you have over the way your life turns out?*

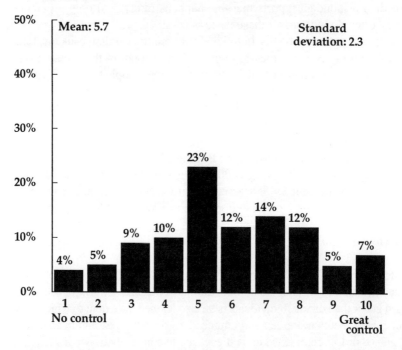

Source: Centre for the Study of Public Policy, University of Strathclyde, *New Russia Barometer, IX.* Fieldwork by VTsIOM, 14-18 April 2000. Number of respondents: 1,600.

membership in organizations, involvement in informal social networks, and trust in other people.[15] Statistics about organizational membership say nothing about an individual's capacity to influence what happens within it, and that ability is likely to be very limited when preferences of members are aggregated at the national level, as is done with trade unions, political parties, and joint stock companies. Involvement in informal groups suggests a degree of collective interest, but leaves open whether individuals who belong to groups are better able to cope when on their own. Trust in other people is the opposite of social confidence, which is about *trust in oneself when dealing with other people.* In a society in which other people are trusted to cooperate, then self-confidence may be the complement of confidence in

Figure 6.2 **Social Confidence in Post-Communist Countries Compared**

Question: *Some people feel they have completely free choice and control over their lives, while others feel that what they do has no real effect on what happens to them. How about yourself? Where would you place yourself on this scale of choice and control over the way your life turns out?*

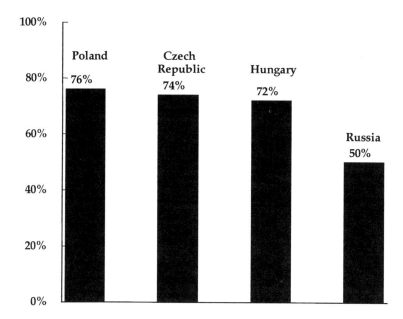

Source: As in Figure 6.1 plus Paul Lazarsfeld Society, *New Democracies Barometer*, survey, 1998. Number of respondents in Czech Republic and in Hungary, 1,017; Poland, 1,141.

others. But in Russia there is widespread distrust of other people and of major institutions of state and society.[16] For an individual to be confident when dealing with an untrustworthy, inimical, and potentially threatening situation is a very positive statement of that person's confidence.

Russians distribute themselves very broadly, from great control to fatalism (see Figure 6.1). While 23 percent placed themselves at 5, the psychological midpoint of the scale, 28 percent placed themselves at the fatalist end of the scale between 1 and 4, while 49 percent were on the confident end. The mean score of 5.7 shows that, notwithstanding the extreme challenges of treble transformation, most Russians have maintained a degree of confidence in the face of adversity. However, the standard deviation of 2.3 produces a relatively large coefficient of variation (.40), emphasizing the wide dispersion of Russians in terms of social confidence.

The level of social confidence in Russia is substantially lower than in the post-Communist countries of Central and Eastern Europe. In the Czech Republic, Hungary, and Poland, three-quarters show positive self-confidence in their ability to exercise control over their lives, half again the proportion in Russia (see Figure 6.2). This is consistent with the shock of transformation being negative in Russia, whereas in Central Europe large majorities greeted transformation as liberation from oppressive domination by Moscow. Russian social confidence is lower still by comparison with the United States. In the World Values Survey, 85 percent of Americans felt positively about their own social control, compared to 50 percent of respondents in the NRB. Moreover, the mean score of 7.6 for American social confidence with a standard deviation of 1.9 shows widespread consistency in the confidence of Americans to control their own lives.[17]

Accounting for Variations in Confidence

While transformation affects every Russian, contrary to Durkheim's prediction there is no uniformity in individual responses. To account for variation, we should not concentrate on a single set of determinants, whether individual or social. Social confidence ought to reflect both sets of influences. Multiple regression analysis is an appropriate method for determining which particular individual attributes and social conditions are significant, net of the influence of others.

The NRB IX survey contains multiple indicators of potential influences on social confidence. Two types of individual attributes are often hypothesized:

1. Biological characteristics such as gender; and
2. Human capital indicators such as education.

An alternative approach hypothesizes the importance of social influences to include:

1. Macrolevel shocks of transformation with causes outside the control of individuals, such as not being paid wages when due;
2. Social integration insulating individuals from the effects of transformation in society as a whole, such as involvement in village life; and
3. Health-specific behavior, such as smoking or not smoking.

When sixteen different indicators are entered in a multiple regression analysis, in total they explain 12.4 percent of the variance in the confidence that

Table 6.1

Influences on Social Confidence (Dependent variable: Control of life)

Variable	b (decimals omitted)	BETA
Biological		
Age	−01	−11
Female	n.s.	n.s.
Human capital		
Education	07	08
Household income	n.s.	n.s.
Subjective social status	n.s.	n.s.
Transformation shock		
Doing without necessities	−10	−11
Economic situation better before	−13	−08
Problems getting paid	−27	−05
Adapted to big changes	−25	09
Social integration		
Town size	−16	−10
Divorced	−42	05
Widowed	−47	−07
Pride in Russian citizenship	15	05
Someone to rely on if ill	n.s.	n.s.
Trust most people	n.s.	n.s.
Attend church services	n.s.	n.s.

Source: New Russia Barometer IX, 2000. For details of independent variables, see Appendix. For the dependent variable, see Figure 6.1.
Variance explained: adjusted R^2 12.4%.
n.s.: Not significant at the <.05 level.

Russians have in controlling what happens in their lives (see Table 6.1). Of these measures, ten are statistically significant at the <.05 level. On the other hand, six theoretically important influences, such as household income and subjective status, fail to register statistical significance.[18]

All four measures of the shock of transformation are statistically significant. Social confidence is lower among individuals who subjectively perceive their household's economic situation as being better before perestroika. Two current material indicators of the effects of transformation are also significant. People who occasionally, sometimes, or often go without basic necessities such as food are less likely to feel in control of their lives, as are Russians who have had their wages or pension paid late or not at all in the past year. While economic well-being does not increase social confidence, doing without necessities lowers it.

Face-to-face social integration can occur independently of the stability or transformation of society as a whole. In his analysis of anomie, Durkheim took marriage as central for social integration, and divorce or widowhood as conditions conducive to producing anomie. Among Russians, marriage remains the norm, but the NRB found that 8 percent of respondents were divorced and 13 percent, mostly older women, were widowed. In each instance, net of everything else, individuals deprived of a spouse after having been married were significantly less likely to consider that they controlled their lives.

The maintenance of individual pride in being a Russian citizen is a classic Durkheimian indicator of social solidarity, and 80 percent say they are somewhat or definitely proud to be a Russian citizen. Pride differs little between ethnic Russians and nonethnic citizens. Empirically, this is a significant counterweight to a deterioration in material conditions. But contrary to theories of social capital, there is no significant influence on social confidence from having a social network that can be relied on when ill, fellow church members to offer support, or trust in most people. Being embedded in village or small-town life, where face-to-face relations are stronger than in large cities, actually depresses social confidence, a wry commentary on the social consequences of the collectivization of agriculture.

Individual attributes, both biological and human capital, have a limited influence on social confidence. Neither subjective social status nor household income,[19] conventional indicators of human capital in Western societies, affect an individual's sense of controlling his or her life. While older people are less likely to feel in command of their lives, more educated people are more likely to feel a sense of social confidence.

Social Confidence and Health

The basic hypothesis here is that social confidence, that is, an individual's capacity to control what happens, leads to better health, reflecting the old ideal of *mens sana in corpore sano* (a sound mind in a sound body). However, the two are not necessarily found together; elderly people in bad physical health, for example, can be in good spirits emotionally, and young people in good physical health can be emotionally mixed-up. Hence, the following will consider separately the influence of social confidence on physical health and mental health. Given the *prima facie* importance of biological influences on physical health, social confidence ought to be more important in determining mental health.

Physical Health

The NRB uses a standard question to assess physical health:

Over the past twelve months would you say that your physical health has been:

Excellent	4 percent
Good	33 percent
Average	38 percent
Poor	15 percent
Very poor	10 percent

Replies correlate strongly with alternative indicators of Russian health, such as being able to carry out normal activities without physical constraints or illness.

A regression analysis of influences on physical health shows an unusually good fit, explaining 32.6 percent of the variance. Ten independent variables are statistically significant and ten are not (see Table 6.2). It is hardly surprising that age is the single most important influence on physical health. Net of its effect, women are also more likely to report that their health is below average. However, this association arises from the fact that older men are underrepresented in the Russian sample because men born before the Second World War are more likely to be dead.

Both the shock of transformation and social confidence are important influences on physical health, but they operate in opposite directions. Individuals who often do without food, clothing, or heat and electricity are likely to be less healthy. However, individuals who feel they can control what happens in their lives and have adapted to big changes in Russian society are more likely to have better physical health.

Human capital has a bigger positive influence on physical health than does social integration. Consistent with findings in social medicine in Western societies, Russians who have more education and a higher subjective social status are more likely to be healthy. Income is an insignificant influence on health. By contrast, five of the seven indicators of social integration fail to register significance. Trust in people, a key indicator in Putnam's definition of social capital, fails to be significant, and membership in organizations is so unimportant—90 percent of Russians do not belong to any one of a number of organizations—that the question was not even asked in the ninth NRB. Divorce or widowhood, important in Durkheim's theory of anomic suicide, likewise lack statistical significance. Pride in Russian citizenship and having someone to look after you when ill are just barely statistically significant.

Table 6.2

Influences on Physical Health

Variable	b (decimals omitted)	BETA
Biological		
Age	−17	−30
Female	−20	−10
Human capital		
Education	04	09
Household income	n.s.	n.s.
Subjective social status	05	10
Transformation shock		
Doing without necessities	05	−11
Economic situation better before	n.s.	n.s.
Problems getting paid	n.s.	n.s.
Social confidence		
Control	05	12
Adapted to big changes	11	08
Social integration		
Town size	n.s.	n.s.
Divorced	n.s.	n.s.
Widowed	n.s.	n.s.
Pride in Russian citizenship	07	05
Someone to rely on if ill	05	05
Trust most people	n.s.	n.s.
Attend church services	n.s.	n.s.
Health-specific behavior		
Extent of drinking	03	07
Smokes	n.s.	n.s.
Diet-conscious	n.s.	n.s.

Source: New Russia Barometer IX, 2000. For details of independent variables, see Appendix.
Variance explained: adjusted R^2 32.6%.

Health-specific behaviors are of little importance: smokers do not report worse physical health than others, and Russians who believe that their diet affects their health are not in better condition. The positive sign for the relation between drinking and physical health—net of other influences, those who drink more tend to be a little more healthy—is an artifact of more drinking among young men in good health. For many, drinking appears to be an activity undertaken in youth but which lessens upon settling down with family and an occupation. Among the population as a whole, half of the respondents report drinking less than once a month and even among those who report drinking more often, the median is inclined to take a drink once a week. It is the minority who do not moderate their drinking and die for reasons associated with their alcohol consumption.[20] This suggests that alcohol-related causes of death, such as cirrhosis of the liver, result from causes that should be generalized to the majority with caution.

The combination of plus and minus signs for Beta coefficients emphasizes that determinants of health push in opposite directions. Aging leads to a worsening of health just as greater social confidence can lead to improved health. However, the two sets are not equal in their impact.[21] A significant influence with a low b value will have little impact; for example, deterioration in a family's economic situation is likely to reduce health by only 0.13 on a five-point scale for physical health. Since physical and mental health are measured on five-point scales, an impact of half a point or more represents a significant step up or down from having average health.

The impact of biological influences on physical health is substantial; in statistical terms, net of other influences the physical health of a person age 65 would be 0.8 lower on the 5-point scale than that of a person age 18. To a large extent, human capital can offset the impact of biological aging. After controlling for age, the physical health of persons with the highest subjective social status and level of education on average is almost three-quarters of a point higher than persons with the least education and lowest social status.

If an individual is high in social confidence, this more than offsets the impact on physical health of the shocks of societal transformation. Russians who are highest in controlling their life and have already adapted to change are likely to rate their health almost half a point (0.47) higher than those who are lowest. By contrast, those who are highest on the doing-without scale are likely to rate their physical health lower by 0.36 of a point. Social integration also raises physical health; people who are very proud of their Russian citizenship and definitely have someone to rely on when ill rate their health more than a third of a point higher than those lowest on both indicators. After discounting the negative effects of transformation shock, the positive effects of social confidence and social integration together raise physical health half a point.

Mental Health

The standard question for measuring emotional health in the NRB is:

Over the past twelve months, would you say your emotional health has been:

Excellent	3	percent
Good	34	percent
Average	43	percent
Poor	13	percent
Very poor	7	percent

Table 6.3

Influences on Emotional Health

Variable	b (decimals omitted)	BETA
Biological		
Age	−01	−19
Female	−11	−06
Human capital		
Education	n.s.	n.s.
Household income	n.s.	n.s.
Subjective social status	04	08
Transformation shock		
Doing without necessities	−07	−17
Economic situation better before	−04	−06
Problems getting paid	n.s.	n.s.
Social confidence		
Control	05	11
Adapted to big changes	07	08
Social integration		
Town size	n.s.	n.s.
Divorced	n.s.	n.s.
Widowed	15	06
Pride in Russian citizenship	11	09
Someone to rely on if ill	12	13
Trust most people	04	06
Attend church services	n.s.	n.s.
Health-specific behavior		
Extent of drinking	03	06
Smokes	n.s.	n.s.
Diet-conscious	n.s.	n.s.

Source: New Russia Barometer IX, 2000. For details of independent variables, see Appendix.
Variance explained: adjusted R^2 21.6%.

Although the distribution of emotional health in the population is very similar to that for physical health, the correlation between the two (0.50) is far from complete, and determinants of emotional health are not the same as those for physical health.

Altogether, the regression model can account for 21.6 percent of the variation in emotional health (see Table 6.3). A total of twelve indicators register a statistically significant influence. While individual attributes are significant for emotional health, their influence is less than for physical health. For example, the Beta for the relationship of age and emotional health is −18, compared to −30 for physical health. While subjective social status remains significant for emotional health, education does not.

The shocks of transformation and social confidence are similar in influence but opposite in direction. Russians who are more often doing without necessities are more likely to worry and have poor emotional health. Interestingly, the degree of doing without has a greater influence on emotional health than on physical health (a Beta of –17 as against –11). Whereas a decline in a family's economic situation since before perestroika has no influence on physical health, it does have a small but significant influence on emotional health. A sense of controlling one's life and adaptation to transformation are significant causes of better emotional health.

Having someone to look after you when ill and trust in other people are significant for emotional health but not for physical health. Pride in citizenship is an indicator of social integration significant for both forms of health. An anomaly in Durkheim's terms is that those who are widowed are more likely to be in good emotional health, net of other influences. Health-specific behaviors are not significant for emotional health, except for drinking, a statistical relationship arrived at after controlling for other influences.

Social influences have the largest impact on emotional health, and positive social conditions have more than twice the impact of the negative shock of transformation. Being highest on control and adaptation to change is likely to raise emotional health by 0.43 of a point. The emotional health of individuals who definitely have someone to look after them when ill, who are very proud of their Russian citizenship, and who rate highest in trust in other people is altogether likely to be three-fifths of a point higher than for those at the other extreme of these distributions.

A Causal Model of Health in Response to Social Shocks

A causal model of health should be parsimonious, omitting influences that are not significant statistically. In the foregoing regression analyses, 7 of the 20 hypothesized influences had an insignificant relationship to both physical and emotional health. Two referred to material conditions, household income and having problems in getting paid; three were social integration measures: church attendance, town size, and divorce; and two were health-specific measures of behavior, smoking and diet consciousness. In addition, some influences were only marginally or inconsistently significant.

While parsimonious, a causal model should not be monocausal, as is the case with reductionist attempts to explain the decline in Russian health as a response to the shock of transformation. In the above regression analyses, eight influences register as a significant influence on both physical and emotional health: both biological measures, age and gender; both social-confidence measures, control and adaptability; one measure of social shock, doing without necessities; one measure of human capital, subjective social status; and

Figure 6.3   **A Causal Model of Health in Response to Transformation**

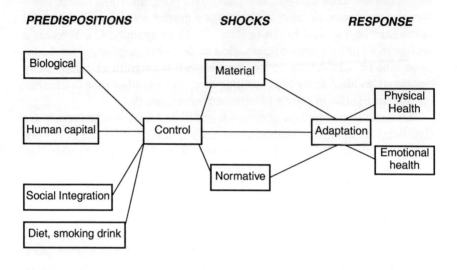

PREDISPOSITIONS   *SHOCKS*   *RESPONSE*

two indicators of social integration, pride in citizenship and having someone to rely on when ill.

The causal model in Figure 6.3 summarizes the sequence of influences that cumulatively determine physical and emotional health. Individual predispositions created by socialization in Soviet society are the starting point for evaluating the impact of transformation. Before the fall of the Soviet Union, a Russian of the median adult age (40) would have had his or her biological circumstances fixed, as well as a pattern of diet, smoking, and drinking. By midlife, each individual would also have a stock of educational capital and have reached an income and occupational plateau. Each adult would also have achieved a greater or lesser degree of integration into Soviet society. Since Russians differed in their predispositions when transformation began, including their sense of social confidence, the material and normative shocks of the collapse of the Soviet Union differentiated the way in which individuals responded, with some adapting readily, others continuing to try, and still others giving up.[22]

For the sake of clarity, Figure 6.3 shows the relation between influences as linear; in fact, there are substantial feedbacks. For example, shocks of transformation can alter an individual's previously fixed social status or revalue an individual's educational capital. Teachers of English will see the demand for their services rise, while teachers of Marxist-Leninist principles will be less in demand.

The model of health in transformation incorporates the significance of macrosocietal changes that have been stressed in epidemiological analysis, while also taking into account variations in individual predispositions and response. It goes beyond the biomedical concern with physical causes of death to consider how some people maintain their health while others depress aggregate statistics of life expectancy and increase the number of avoidable deaths. The shocks of transformation test the capacity of individuals to control what happens to them and adapt. Ironically, in order to understand the impact of social shocks, we must turn to data about individuals.

Notes

1. This chapter is an outgrowth of work undertaken as part of the European-Commission-funded project on Living Conditions, Life Styles, and Health in the Commonwealth of Independent States, organized by the Institute of Advanced Studies, Vienna, and the author's project on Coping with Organizations: Social Capital Networks in Russia, supported by the Leverhulme Trust.

2. Robert M. Kaplan, "Promoting Wellness: Biomedical versus Wellness Models," in *Promoting Human Wellness: New Frontiers for Research, Practice, and Policy*, eds., Margaret Schneider Jamner and Daniel Stokols (Berkeley: University of California Press, 2000), 44–77. Cf. Richard Rose, *The Impact of Social Capital on Health* (Glasgow: University of Strathclyde Studies in Public Policy No. 358, 2001).

3. See *A Decade of Transition: Regional Report* (Florence: Unicef Innocenti Research Centre, 2001), statistical annex 4.

4. For the views of Russians in response to transformation, see Richard Rose and Neil Munro, *Elections without Order: Russia's Challenge to Vladimir Putin* (New York: Cambridge University Press, 2002), chapters 3, 9, and 10.

5. Emile Durkheim, *Suicide: A Study in Sociology* (London: Routledge, 1952; translation), 252.

6. See Martin McKee and Duncan Hunter, "Mortality League Tables: Do They Inform or Mislead?," *Quality in Health Care* 4 (1995), 5–12.

7. Barbara A. Anderson and Brian D. Silver, "Infant Mortality in the Soviet Union: Regional Differences and Measurement Issues," *Population and Development Review* 12 (1986): 705–738; cf. France Meslé, Vladimir Shkolnikov, and Jacques Vallin, "Mortality by Cause in the USSR in 1970–1987," *European Journal of Population*, 8 (1992), 281–308.

8. See Irene A. Boutenko and Kirill E. Razlogov, *Recent Social Trends in Russia, 1960–1995* (Montreal: McGill-Queen's University Press, 1997), 9.

9. See Vladimir G. Treml, "Problems with Soviet Statistics: Past and Present," *in Defense Conversion, Economic Reforms and the Outlook for the Russian and Ukrainian Economies*, eds. Charles Wolf Jr. and Henry S. Rowen (New York, 1994), 19–37. For an analysis that takes official statistics at face value, see Timothy Heleniak, "Economic Transition and Demographic Change in Russia, 1989–1995," *Post-Soviet Geography* 7 (1995), 446–458.

10. For full details of the sample, the questionnaire, and answers subdivided by age, see Richard Rose, *Russia Elects a President: New Russia Barometer IX* (Glasgow: University of Strathclyde Studies in Public Policy No. 330, 2000). The questionnaire can also be consulted at www.cspp.strath.ac.uk.

11. See the discussion in Rose and Munro, *Elections without Order*, chapter 10.

12. Cf. Vladimir Shlapentokh, *Public and Private Life of the Soviet People* (New York: Oxford University Press, 1989) and Alina Ledeneva, *Russia's Economy of Favours* (Cambridge: Cambridge University Press, 1998).

13. For a detailed elaboration of these concepts, see Richard Rose, "Adaptation, Resilience and Destitution," *Problems of Post-Communism*, 42, 6 (1995), 52–61.

14. S.L. Syme, "Control and Health," in A. Steptoe and A. Appels, eds., *Stress, Personal Control, and Health* (New York: John Wiley, 1989), pp. 3–18.

15. See Robert Putnam, "Democracy in America at Century's End," in *Democracy's Victory and Crisis*, ed. Axel Hadenius (New York: Cambridge University Press, 1997), 31.

16. William Mishler and Richard Rose, "What Are the Origins of Political Trust? Testing Institutional and Cultural Theories in Post-Communist Societies," *Comparative Political Studies* 34, 1 (2001), 30–62.

17. Ronald Inglehart, Miguel Basanez, and Alejandro Moreno, *Human Values and Beliefs: A Cross-Cultural Sourcebook* (Ann Arbor: University of Michigan Press, 1998), variable 95.

18. Preliminary regression runs tried out alternative measures of income and transformation shock and social integration; those that were consistently insignificant here and in Tables 6.2 and 6.3 are omitted for the sake of clarity and parsimony.

19. An alternative measure of material well-being, the number of consumer durables in a household, was also found to be without influence on an individual's social confidence.

20. The NRB surveys identify four groups: nondrinkers, occasional drinkers, moderate drinkers, and a small group of self-punishing heavy drinkers. In the ninth New Russia Barometer survey, 14 percent said they had a drinking binge at least once a month; 26 percent occasionally; and 60 percent had not had a drinking binge in the last year.

21. Impact is measured by multiplying unstandardized (b) coefficients by the arithmetic difference in the range of values for each statistically significant independent variable. For example, net of all other influences, the impact of destitution (b value –0.046) on a scale with a 9-point gap between never doing without to often doing without three basic needs reduces physical health by 0.41 (.046 x 9) units. In calculating impact, the b values reported in Tables 6.2 and 6.3 are carried out to two significant digits before multiplication. For details of the range of variables, see the Appendix.

22. A middle-aged Soviet citizen will have developed a greater or lesser sense of control of events prior to the collapse of the Soviet Union. Subsequent events, including success in adapting to transformation, may modify that sense of control but do not create it from scratch. This is shown statistically in Table 6.1 on page 107 by a Beta of .07 for the influence of adaptation on control. Nor is control a synonym for adaptation, for a separate regression, not reported here, gives a Beta of .08 for its current influence on adaptation.

Appendix

Indicators for Regression Analyses

	Minimum	Maximum	Mean	Std Dev
Physical health	1 Very poor	5 Excellent	3.05	1.01
Emotional health	1 Very poor	5 Excellent	3.15	0.93
Control of life	1 No control	10 Full control	5.70	2.28
Age	18	80	45	17
Female	0 Male	1 Female	0.54	0.50
Education	1 Elementary or less	10>1 Higher education degree	5.05	2.58
Total monthly household income	200	8000	1970	1492
Subjective social status	1 Lowest	10 Highest	4.96	2.18
Doing without necessities	0 Never deprived	9 Often in all 3	4.08	2.41
Problems getting paid	1 No problems	2 Has problems	1.42	0.49
Household economic situation worse now	1 Much better now	5 Much worse now	3.55	1.38
Adaptation to big changes	1 Never	3 Already adapted	2.30	0.78
Town size	1 <10,000	5 > million	2.83	1.51
Attendance at religious services	1 Never	5 ≥ once/week	1.80	1.00
Trust most people	1 No trust at all	7 Complete trust	4.99	1.56
Pride in Russian citizenship	1 Not at all proud	4 Very proud	3.08	0.79
Someone to rely on if ill	1 Definitely not	4 Definitely yes	2.51	1.03
Divorced	0 No	1 Yes	0.08	0.28
Widowed	0 No	1 Yes	0.13	0.33
Smokes	0 No	1 Yes	0.36	0.48
Extent of drinking	1 Never	7 ≥ 2 times/week	3.78	1.98
Own health reflects diet	0 No	1 Yes	0.50	0.50

Source: *New Russia Barometer IX*, 2000. November of cases: 1,600.

7

When Crime-Fighting Fails
The Case of Russia

Stephen Handelman

Why has a genuine crime-fighting culture failed to take root in Russia? This may seem a strange priority with which to be concerned after ten years of dramatic political and economic change. But it is another way of asking why the promise of justice, an essential part of Russia's original democratic revolution, has lagged behind the state's other extraordinary transformations. Of course, Russia has the basic tools a modern state needs to preserve law and order—a powerful police force, a criminal code administered by an active court system, even the repeatedly expressed will by the two post-Communist administrations of Boris Yeltsin and Vladimir Putin to make public safety and clean government a national priority. Yet the underlying commitment to a transparent society, one in which justice is administered impartially at every level—the hallmark of crime-fighting cultures in Western democracies—has fallen far short of the state's rhetoric.

Instead, particularly with the accession of Putin and his pledge to create a "dictatorship of the law," the Russian state seems poised to fall back on Soviet-style methods of authoritarian policing and rigid security-oriented policies. This, it must be said, appears to have the support of a majority of Russians themselves, who tell pollsters they are prepared to give up some of the privileges and freedoms gained since the fall of the Soviet Union if it means their families will be safer and that bureaucratic venality can be contained.[1] Considering the waves of crime and corruption that have swept over the country like an ice storm over the past decade, it seems a rational choice. And it has long been clear that, without concerted government action to stem lawlessness, the future economic and political stability of the Russian state—its entire hopes of transformation, in fact—are at risk.

There are no easy answers about what went wrong, about whether it is still possible to construct an alternative approach, or even whether it is desirable to try (in many respects, the choice has already been made). It is worth noting that other nations of the former Soviet bloc have had mixed success in tackling crime and in developing "democratic" crime-fighting cultures; even those with more solidly legalistic traditions, such as the Czech Republic, have seen increases over the past several years in drug trafficking, addiction, and corruption. Arguably, they will never be able to get their own problems under control unless Russia grapples with its disease successfully, since the former hub of the Soviet empire remains an important breeding ground for the smuggling, organized criminal activity, and financial machinations that affect its neighbors. But it is useful nevertheless to explore the nature of post-Communist criminality in Russia, as well as the environment in which criminality has festered in order to find some signposts for the future.

Crime in Russia

Crime has been the most vivid failure of the post-Communist experiment. It has led to widespread disillusionment with "capitalism" as Russians have understood it, and with the notion of democracy itself. For most of the last century, Russians lived in a society in which few civilians carried guns, where the streets were safe, where personal security was guaranteed (as long as one posed no political threat to the state), and in which any signs of ostentatious wealth were carefully hidden behind Party dachas.

The adjustment in the last decade has been traumatic. While some Russians have prospered, most have not. And the predictable economic problems have been compounded by visible loss of personal security and trust in authorities. Perhaps the most telling loss is that of the sense of community that sustained Russia through civil war, foreign invasion, economic catastrophe, and political repression: the sense that neighbors, for good or ill, were looking after one another. Law and authorities played little part in these feelings of security, since few people had any experience or confidence in a heavily politicized system of legal norms. Revealingly, polls continue to show that a majority of Russian citizens (certainly those in their 40s and older), when given a choice, prefer their lives before 1991 to their lives afterward.[2]

This is not to say that important strides have not been made. In keeping with his election promises, Putin has forced through long-awaited reforms to the criminal procedure code and the court system, made an effort to tackle government corruption (though his critics say it is a selective effort) with a newly invigorated auditors' commission, and eliminated some of the leading oligopolies of wealth. Business regulations have become more consistent, bankruptcy laws have been tightened, new tax laws for businesses are aimed at cutting off the flow of capital flight from the country, and the Duma is working on a code to protect private property. Russia's economic recovery since the financial crash of 1998 has also made things more stable. These elements of crime-fighting, motivated at least in part by concerns about foreign investment, have been praiseworthy.

Nevertheless, making Russia safe for foreign investment cannot be the prime goal of public security policies, and it is clear that Putin and other Russian leaders are acutely aware that they need to do much more. Russians of all social and economic sectors have reason to feel impatient. Street crime, including rape, theft, and common assault, is worsening again, after an initial improvement in the late 1990s. Russia's homicide rate in 2001 was second only to South Africa's, and "mafiya-related" crimes (which are not further defined) increased by 83 percent over the previous year.[3] Russians continue to tell pollsters that personal security is higher than anything else on their list of concerns. And they are demonstrating that in practice, with large-scale purchasing of guns for personal use. The problem of private gun ownership has gotten to be so serious in St. Petersburg that municipal authorities have instituted a Western-style "buy-back" program for firearms.

Violence is part of the uncomfortable backdrop of everyday life in many Russian regions. A too-frequent Russian scene of the 1990s was one in which gunmen emerged from a crowded urban street, shot their victim, then escaped while dozens of horrified witnesses looked on. Usually, a gun was left at the scene by the killer, a telltale Mafiya calling card. While the visible violence of the Mafiya has abated (most of the turf wars between groups have ended), it still impacts ordinary life in strange and sometimes comic ways. Last July, in one widely reported case, a contract killer advertised on the Internet offering "assisted death, possibly without the agreement of the patient." He was later arrested.

Drug use is as much a key indicator of social deterioration as violence. The number of cases involving illegal drug possession in Russia increased 1,200 percent over the last decade, with the largest increase occurring among those under 20. According to official estimates, 2.5 million Russians—mainly under the age of 30—are addicts. And this is probably far below the actual number. Narcotics-related crimes increased by 4.5 percent between January and September 2001 over the same period the previous year. Drugs are increasingly easy to get.[4] According to one report, there are some 2,000 discotheques and nightclubs in Moscow where everything from Afghan heroin to Colombian cocaine is available for sale. A further troubling statistic: almost 20 percent of Russian draftees admit to using some form of drugs. The problem is as serious in the regions as it is in the large urban centers. In Kaliningrad, according to official statistics, close to 30 percent of the city's two million inhabitants are drug addicts.[5]

The growing drug phenomenon is partly a sign of the influence of organized crime groups who have become involved in the trade after initially steering away from it. Russian police estimate that the narcotics trade brings in some $1 billion a year, citing that 12,000 drug-related crimes were committed last year by organized gangs. Drug-trafficking networks that extend from Central Asia and the Caucasus to the Baltics and the Pacific coast have made Russia a pivotal hub for international traffickers. Putin has called mounting drug use a "national security problem."

It is certainly that—but it is also an indictment of the country's social and economic policies. Repeatedly, over the decade, Russian analysts (and even Western observers) have predicted that the crime problem will begin to dissipate once Russia achieves a more "normal" life. Russian oligarchs point out that it has been impossible to succeed in business over the past decade without breaking laws. Russian crime bosses say the same thing, insisting that their children will be perfectly prepared to live in a lawful environment—once the right laws are passed. And they are backed up by academic studies which suggest that Russia's breakdown of law and order is similar to the experience of "transitional states" elsewhere. That is undoubtedly true, but the problem of crime is hard to separate from the specific failings of the post-Communist Russian regime to deliver on its promises of a better life. And the most vivid illustration of this is the continuing power and influence of the Russian Mafiya.

The Russian "Mafiya" and Organized Crime

For at least two centuries, Russian criminal organizations have occupied a unique place in Russian society. Operating on the margins of national life, they served as a kind of pressure release valve for both the Czarist and Communist states. The phrase that they used to collectively describe themselves since the early twentieth century—"thieves' world" (*vorovskoi mir*)—is especially revealing. They inhabit a world of their own, with its own paramilitary hierarchies, codes of behavior, and jargon, that exists apart from the mainstream. This world is by no means benign. It attracts killers and psychopaths as well as ordinary thieves, social misfits, and rebels. But it also provides a space for activities unregulated by the state, for a kind of freedom unavailable anywhere else. (This is one reason many veteran Mafiya bosses today consider themselves the "real" dissidents of Soviet society.) The fact that the "thieves' world" survived the collapse of the Soviet Union, while most other institutions of the Communist state did not, was a testament to its cohesion.

Few could have predicted, however, the shift of these groups from the margins of Russian life to its very center, following the collapse. Today, the "thieves' world" ethos, approach, and organizational abilities penetrate most aspects of Russian politics, the economy, and the bureaucracy. This is not quite the same as suggesting that the "Mafiya runs Russia," or, as many do, that Russia has become a Mafiya state. Actually, many of the original Soviet-era gangs have disappeared or changed radically as the post-Communist economy has grown more sophisticated. But the "thieves' world's" ability to impose a sense of order proved a virtue in a society that had increasing reason to be distrustful of the unpredictability and inequities of the "new" capitalism.

There is a precedent for this in other societies. Organized crime served similar functions as a buffer and an interpreter for the strange new world encountered by immigrant communities in the United States. Today, many Russians may likewise see themselves as "immigrants" from the old order. For them, the traditional Mafiya godfather, or *vor,* provides a buffer against the predatory chaos of the new state, in which once-feared institutions like the Communist Party and the KGB have reinvented themselves and become part of the "Wild East" capitalism. Where law and legality have little resonance, Mafiya organizations can be associated with protection and security rather than with lawbreaking, with resistance to arbitrary government authorities rather than with undermining social order. One could in fact argue that these ex-outlaw groups represent what's left of the social capital inherited from the Soviet period.

If the sources of social capital are in those networks that provide cohesion, mutual trust, predictability, and security, then the Mafiya provides that in full. Where it once worked for its members against the larger society, it now works for large sections of Russian society, in small towns and regions across Russia, against capitalists and bureaucrats. Another group with the potential and ambition to play that role is the Orthodox Church (although it was seriously compromised during the Communist era), and it is no accident that many leading Mafiya bosses identify strongly with the church and are prominent supporters of charities across Russia. Through the 1990s, the "cult" of the gangland crime boss who protected the poor and outwitted the powerful was celebrated in popular songs and folk myths. Moscow street children tell interviewers they see the criminal world as a way out of their own traps. Ordinary people who are not directly affected by the Mafiya's protection rackets or extortion see them as little different than their own lives of petty scams and manipulations of authority which they learned through the Communist era.

Needless to say, the actual criminality of the Mafiya is sometimes ignored. People who are more aware of street crimes and rapes than with protection rackets consider the Mafiya as providing some order in their neighborhoods. Businesses, which cannot depend on the state to enforce laws and contracts, are similarly drawn (voluntarily at first, then by force) to the "roofs" offered them by Mafiya bosses.

The principal challenge of Russian governments is therefore not to eliminate the Mafiya, but to make it unnecessary. The government, put on the defensive, has repeatedly concentrated on numbers when it has announced progress in its "wars on crime"—number of gangsters arrested, number of Mafiya bosses killed—while allowing the environment that perpetuated criminality and disrespect for law to continue. There is still no sense that Russian officialdom understands this point. In a country where it is not uncommon to hear stories about children dying on an operating table because hospitals can't pay for electricity, the Mafiya can portray itself as the protector of the ordinary Russian citizen from the depredations of the state. It is safe to say that when these economic and social issues are tackled, the Mafiya will be pushed back into the margins again.

Meanwhile, however, organized crime has already penetrated vast areas of the economy and politics. The profile of Russian crime groups has not changed substantially in a decade. According to the Internal Affairs Ministry (MVD), there are over 3,500 organized criminal groups, with some 5,500 members. At least 20 of these groups span regions. Collectively, they control up to 60 percent of state-run enterprises and up to 50 percent of private-sector business. A third of the country's banks are connected with them in some way, either through direct ownership or in providing a source of money-laundered cash.

They have also moved into politics. There was already a substantial presence of mob-connected deputies in the Duma, but this phenomenon has spread to the regions as well. Fifty of the 252 candidates for seats in the Primorsky Krai regional council last December were reportedly "connected to criminal structures." And politicians have found themselves targets of Mafiya violence. The most vivid example, perhaps, is Said Amirov, the wheelchair-bound mayor of Makhachkala in Dagestan, who survived the fourteenth attempt on his life last year after grenade launchers were fired on his motorcade.[6]

The targets of contract killings map the steady expansion of the shadow cartels into key, vulnerable areas of Russian life. In the mid-1990s, many of the most prominent victims were bankers, entrepreneurs, and veteran Mafiya godfathers. A representative sampling of some of the high-profile "hits" during the last four months of 2001 suggests the close alliance between municipal and regional bureaucrats, those responsible for the maintenance of civic and business life, and criminal networks:

Leonid Oblonsky, first deputy prefect of Moscow's Zelenograd District, in charge of retail and wholesale businesses: shot to death July 24;

Valery Maslakov, head of a defense-related company in Bolshoi Kamen that resells metal and processes nuclear waste from decommissioned nuclear submarines: murdered mid-September;

Sergei Balashov, deputy prefect of Moscow's Western District, in charge of construction projects: shot to death November 2;

Nikolai Tolstykh, director of the Krasnokamenskaya coal mine in the Kuzbass: shot November 7;

Sergei Brusnitsyn, owner of four St. Petersburg stores: shot November 21;

Leonid Bochkov, head of the Nakhodka Port Authority: shot November 26.

In any country, such a sustained round of targeted killings would trigger outrage and suspicion, and certainly a government probe into the origins. But the Russian official reaction has been almost phlegmatic. Commenting on the murder of Leonid Oblonsky, Moscow Mayor Yuri Luzhkov suggested that the victim was probably killed as a result of his "refusal to give certain opportunities to some organization."

In fact, it is increasingly unlikely that "traditional" Mafiya groups such as those responsible for the bloody open warfare in the early part of the decade are responsible for these deaths. The existence of sophisticated cartels comprising government officials, security and police organs, and powerful business "authorities" (who have the ability to hire Mafiya members or former police and military officers to do their killing for them) has become increasingly visible on the Russian landscape. These cartels have amassed the economic power and military muscle to take over huge sectors of the economy, such as the oil industry, coal mining, and timber production, and thus to control entire regions. Their power is closer to that wielded by the old Party bosses than the traditional godfathers of the "thieves' world."

Not surprisingly, most Russians feel powerless to do anything about this. A murky world in which unseen forces control life is hardly a new experience for Russians. But combined with post-Communist alienation, it introduces a particular paralysis to the citizens of New Russia. A study done by the Kennan Institute in 2001 on the growing problem of homeless children found most Russians appalled by the phenomenon but persuaded there was little they could do about it. This apathy, reported Clementine Fujimura, an associate professor at the U.S. Naval Academy and an author of the study, "is a reflection of that ingrained reluctance to get involved."[7] Such cynicism, distrust, and fear—while some might consider it a culture in its own right—indicates a disconnectedness with the aims of the larger society. It is not only a clear result of the criminalization of Russian life, but an explanation for the failure to mount a genuine grassroots battle against the most visible element of that criminalization: corruption.

Corruption in Russia

Corruption has become the most self-acknowledged problem of Russian democracy. Russian officialdom uses apocalyptic terms to describe it. It threatens Russia's security "at least as much as terrorism does," says Prosecutor General Vladimir Ustinov. And that opinion is ratified by outside commentary: "Corruption is not just a collection of criminal activities in Russia; it is a perverse system of governance," said Transparency International last year, after ranking Russia near the top of the 91 states included in its annual corruption perception survey.[8] It now costs the Russian government an estimated $15 billion a year in direct and indirect tax losses. The worse it seems, however, the more it becomes an excuse to do nothing. If everyone "knows" that Russia is corrupt, everyone also "knows" there's nothing that can be done about it.

According to one survey last year, 75 percent of all Russian officials take bribes. But another survey found that only 25 percent of citizens admitted to giving them.[9] Such surveys are at best only impressionistic glimpses into Russian society, but they suggest that tolerance for petty larceny, scams, and swindles is widespread. This is in part a holdover from the Soviet era, when private "hustling"—from illegally selling vegetables grown in a private garden to bartering parts siphoned from an assembly line for favors—was an accepted form of survival. It is also a testament to the failure of national institutions to deal with the demands of the new economy.

Andrei Illarionov, one of Putin's economic advisers, recently went on national TV to display a chart documenting more than 500 steps that were necessary to start a business—each step of which required the payment of a "gratuity" or small fee. Putin has dramatically reduced the number of business activities that require government licensing (from 2,000 to 100) and thus narrowed the scope for petty corruption. But the general sense of protection from extortionate government demands is not yet there. Small wonder that so many shopkeepers and entrepreneurs freely hand over a portion of their income to criminal racketeers whose terms of trade are, while more brutal, somewhat clearer. "There is essentially a state racket at work," said Aleksandr Ioffe, cochair of the Russian Entrepreneurial Organizations Union, a lobby group. According to Ioffe, the government crackdown on outright bribery has only siphoned the mandatory "gift-giving" into other forms, such as being forced to buy fire extinguishers from a firm favored by officials.[10]

There's little point in going to the police. Over 10,000 officers have been put on trial since the beginning of the year, of whom 2,700 have been sued for corruption. While this seems a substantial figure, the MVD forces number nearly 2 million. And the problem, as evidenced by police officers themselves, is much wider. A *Novaya Gazeta* poll found that almost half of all militia officers think their commanders are more concerned about enriching themselves than maintaining law and order. The same level of distrust for police is clear among ordinary Russians. In November, nearly 51 percent registered distrust. Deputy MVD minister Yevgeny Solovev conceded the point: "Criminals now consider acquiring protection from the Interior Ministry as often as from the criminal world."[11]

The next step up the law enforcement ladder—the courts—is even more problematic. They are "corrupt almost to the point of absolute inadequacy," complained Anatoly Chubais, a former prime minister who now heads UES, the national energy company. Chubais said such corruption halts reforms, discourages investments, and prevents economic growth.[12] It also adds to the sense of powerlessness.

The economy still isn't really free, as evidenced by the continued use of the black and gray economies, the Soviet artifacts that enabled the state planned economy to keep going long after its usefulness. Some estimates put the shadow economy at as much as 40 percent of Russia's gross domestic product. In any case, it is clearly this economy in which most citizens participate and survive. Earning wages that are largely useless to cope with normal market prices, Russians barter, scrape, and manipulate the system as they always have. Moscow's 174 private markets alone were responsible for an estimated $5.6 billion in shadow earnings last year, much of it earned by small private traders and businessmen.[13] The Putin government has made some valiant efforts to get some of this money back into the official economy, for example, by instituting a 13 percent flat income tax (the lowest in Europe). But the arcane regulations and high taxes imposed elsewhere in the chain still defeat hopes of developing a genuine free-market environment. At the higher end of the economic scale, entrepreneurs continue to send an estimated $20 billion a year out of the country to avoid taxes and other government scrutiny.[14]

Why have such good-faith attempts failed so far? For one thing, there are few visible penalties applied. Only 14 federal and regional deputies, 302 bankers, 21 state officials, and 15 judges were charged with misappropriation of funds or other corruption-related charges last year in what one assumes is anything but a representative proportion of the real problem. But a more cogent explanation is that the government's anticorruption campaigns, like its anticrime campaigns, are perceived as selective. Officials at lower levels are more likely to get charged than those at higher levels, and grafting individuals at the top will be ignored unless there is some political utility to moving them out of the way.

Corruption has always been a 'family' affair in Russia. It is often harnessed to political ends. Putin wasted little time after entering office in cracking down on Boris Berezovsky and Vladimir Gusinsky, two of the country's most powerful oligarchs. But other powerful financial groups with arguably as many skeletons in their closets have been left alone. The campaign was seen by Russian observers as an attempt by Putin allies to root out powerful members of Yeltsin's circle, with the idea that my "corrupt" oligarch is better than yours. This philosophy can be applied to the crackdown launched last fall on several senior ministers and top bureaucrats on corruption charges. "What is happening now is not about fighting corruption," observed Dmitri Pinsker of the *Russia Journal* in November, in a fairly typical comment:

> and the Prosecutor General's Office is not motivated by a purely economic or legal interest in the people it is investigating. This is about a new carve-up of assets and power. It is also about the new people in the Kremlin—the Petersburg Chekists, allies, former classmates, and colleagues of Putin—expanding their sphere of influence at the expense of the waning "Family" that once held a monopoly on key political decisions.[15]

While due account must be paid to the Russian polemical style of journalism, it is hard to avoid seeing anticorruption campaigns as a subset of the struggle between political rivals or, as Russians like to put it, rival "clans," which in turn saps much of the government's energy. "Russia is a Byzantine country," says Boris Nemtsov, a former deputy prime minister and now leader of the Union of Right Forces: "The under-the-carpet struggle is for it the meaning of life."[16] The hidden wink in that statement explains volumes about the general cynicism of Russian citizens toward the crime-fighting credentials of their government and their consequent apathy toward the measures that may be applied.

Law Enforcement

Why in fact should the government be interested in generating the kind of grassroots crime-fighting culture that has enabled the West to face up to the excesses of capitalism? Instruments like the Racketeering Influenced and Corrupt Organization Act (RICO) and the Witness Protection Program, which were introduced relatively recently in the U.S. and have become potent weapons in breaking up organized crime, were only possible through a sustained level of trust in the government's ability to deliver protection and act on the information it received.

The clearest sign of distrust is that, for all the dizzying statistics Russian law enforcement authorities parade regularly about their "successes" in bringing gangsters to book and breaking up corrupt conspiracies, their credibility is open to question. In 2001, for example, Russian authorities announced convicting 14,000 "leaders and active participants of organized crime groups."[17] This is, of course, nearly three times as many Mafiya members as are in existence, according to other government figures; and if it were added to the thousands of announced arrests of gangsters over the previous ten years, one would have to assume that either there were no criminals left in Russia by now, or that they were multiplying at a scientifically miraculous rate. Of course, the truth is that most of those arrested are minor hoodlums and crooks who bear only a vague connection to structures of organized crime in business and government. Meanwhile, most of the high-profile killings and assassinations of leading businessmen, bankers, politicians, journalists, and government officials over the past decade remain unsolved.

The level of trust in Russian society is already worn by a decade of what it considers economic betrayal. It is no surprise to find that various "secret" organizations—networks of law enforcement and intelligence officials—have grown up as a parallel to official government security organs to root out corruption. One such organization claimed to have as many as 8,000 members in 2000, but remained vague about its activities.[18] The kind of citizen empowerment (or even regional empowerment) that Russian leaders have historically been wary of giving is clearly still far in the distance. Yet ironically some of the new government's tough measures may create the space for exactly that to happen, even as these measures demonstrably increase the government's power over the nation's economic and civic life.

One reason to hope for such empowerment can be found in the ambiguous approach of Putin himself. Although his reform instincts are inseparable from his interest in asserting the supremacy of the state (in keeping with his KGB background), the president has also displayed populist tendencies. He has openly talked about increasing the salaries of civil servants and police to reduce the motives for graft and embezzlement, and at the same time he has displayed interest in cutting down the enormous security and military bureaucracies that are a decided holdover from the Soviet era. Just as notably, he has encouraged the strengthening of "civil society," even going so far as to encourage a conference attended by thousands of nongovernmental organizations in Moscow in the winter of 2001.

The press is another key embattled area of Russian society that has received mixed signals from the Putin government. While the president has played a powerful role in eliminating some key TV networks that have been publicly critical (nominally as part of his attempt to go after oligarchs who have fallen from favor), the press is still recognized by the government as being one of the few trusted institutions of Russian society. Last year, the MVD actually gave an award to a journalist for exposing corruption in its midst. Aleksandr Knishstein of Moskovsky Komsomolets won the award for his exposé of a police general who ran a major kickback operation inside the anticorruption crime directorate. The general, of course, happened to be associated with Yeltsin-era officials, but nevertheless it was a significant recognition of the press's ability to command the debate.[19]

The Putin government's new laws reforming the criminal procedure code and the judicial system will also have a far-reaching impact, particularly in increasing popular involvement in the legal system. Beginning in January 2003, jury trials were to be mandatory for all cases of "dangerous crimes" like rape or murder around the country. As of 2002, only 9 of Russia's 89 regions employed juries. The power of prosecutors to determine which cases come to trial, to appoint defense lawyers, and to order search-and-arrest warrants—all features of the authoritarian Soviet system—will be sharply curtailed. And a large step has been taken toward the independence of judges and defense lawyers. The reforms are "a very important stage in the process of modernizing our state," argued Putin. And, despite criticism that they still do not go far enough to reduce arbitrary government prosecutions, he is right.

Yet it took nearly five years, and some ten attempts just to get the current legislation through. It remains to be seen whether the new laws on the books will be enforced with any greater impartiality than the existing Russian laws. Moreover, the government's evident interest in creating a new legal landscape is compromised by its own renewed obsession with security. Last year, the Putin government announced it would return to the Soviet practice of classifying key regulations related to the security of the state.

What remains missing is a legal culture in which all citizens feel they have an equal interest in obeying the law. "We still live by customs rather than laws," Moscow mayor Yuri Luzhkov has said. The "customs" he referred to did not need to be spelled out: a few Russians with power, privilege, and connections can get away with things that ordinary Russians cannot. Other Russians point out that projects to strengthen civil society, such as the government's Civic Forum, have little future unless a powerful middle class emerges. But the current environment of lawlessness, mistrust, and unpredictability will not encourage Russia's nascent middle class to assert itself. In the absence of a genuine civil society in Russia, there will be little impetus for the creation of a crime-fighting culture. But a crime-fighting culture is also crucial to the creation of a civil society. It is within these tragic paradoxes that Russia must sort out its uncertain future.

Notes

1. See *Izvestia*, 4 December 2001. One sample opinion poll, conducted by the All-Russian Public Opinion Research Center, showed that "personal security" was Russians' primary concern.

2. A 1991 survey cited by James L. Gibson of Washington University in St. Louis in the April-June 2001 issue of *Post-Soviet Affairs* found 71 percent in favor of the pre-perestroika political system, compared to 38 percent who favored the current system. The survey was conducted by Richard Rose of the University of Strathclyde (Scotland). Gibson concludes: "Many people may be in favor of democratic freedoms, other things being equal, but not consider them adequate compensation for all the other things that they have lost in the post-Soviet transition. The Brezhnev-era system may be preferred for reasons that have no necessary connection with democracy or the lack of it—e.g., because it provided stability and security." A more recent poll, conducted by ROMIR-Gallup International on 1 January 2002, found 55.1 percent of Russians, in a survey sample of 2,000 respondents, preferred "life before the reforms launched in 1991 to their present-day life." Reported by *Interfax*, 6 January 2002.

3. "Contract Killings Remain a Regular Occurrence in Moscow," *Jamestown Foundation Monitor*, 3 December 2001.

4. Figures on drug use from several sources: for the 2.5 million figure, see report on the International Conference on the Anti-Drug War in Saratov, 6 September 2001, quoted in *Johnson's Russia List* #5429, Center for Defense Information, Washington, D.C., 7 September 2001. Academician Tatyana Dmitrieva of the Russian Academy of Medical Science, quoted in *Radio Free Europe/Radio Liberty (RFE/RL) Newsline*, 10 July 2001, gives a slightly larger estimate of 3 million drug users, and notes the number has increased 1,200 percent over the last decade. But this figure only underscores the paucity of such statistics in the Soviet era. For increase in narcotics-related crimes in 2001, see *Interfax (Russian News Agency)*, 30 October 2001.

5. For the discotheque and Kaliningrad figures, see "The Moscow Connection," *Cali El Pais* (Colombia), 29 November 2001. For draftees, see report of a special meeting of the Russian Security Council, *RFE/RL Newsline*, 1 October 2001, vol. 5, no. 185.

6. See *Jamestown Foundation Monitor*, 3 December 2001, for Primorski Krai figure. Amirov story reported in *RFE/RL Crime and Corruption Watch*, 16 November 2001, vol. 1, no. 3.

7. "*Empowering through Victimization: Moscow's Homeless Children,*" lecture at the Kennan Institute of the Woodrow Wilson International Center for Scholars, Washington, D.C., 25 October 2001, cited in *Johnson's Russia List # 5557*, 20 November 2001.

8. *Global Corruption Report 2001*, *Regional Report on Commonwealth of Independent States*, Transparency International, 114. For tax loss figure, see *RFE/RL Crime and Corruption Watch*, 16 November 2001.

9. Reported in *Kommersant-Vlast*, 30 October 2001.

10. Sharon LaFraniere, "Putin Targeting All Who 'Feed Off' Small Business," *Washington Post*, 29 December 2001.

11. Trial figures and Solovev quote reported by *Izvestia* and ORT Television, 26 November 2001, cited in *RFE/RL*, 26 November 2001, vol. 5, no. 222. Militia poll

figures from survey commissioned by *Novaya Gazeta*, Oct. 29, 2001, reported in *RFE/RL*, 1 November 2001, vol. 5, no. 208.

12. Interview with Anatoly Chubais, *Profil (Moscow)* 44, November 2001, cited in *Johnson's Russia List #5572*, 29 November 2001.

13. Mikhail Fradkov, director of the Federal Tax Police, quoted in *Kommersant-Vlast*, 20 November 2001. For estimate of private market turnover, see *Interfax-Moscow*, 18 July 2001.

14. See *Kommersant-Vlast*, 30 October 2001.

15. "A Fight against Corruption or a Witch-Hunt?" *The Russia Journal*, 2–8 November 2001, cited in *Johnson's Russia List #5523*, 3 November 2001.

16. See *Jamestown Foundation Monitor*, 29 November 2001.

17. *Kommersant-Vlast*, 20 November 2001.

18. Reported in *Versiya Weekly* 43, cited in *RFE/RL*, 16 November 2001, vol. 5, no. 218. The group presented the vague idea of working to "revive trust" in police. One member said the group has already been contacted "by businesspeople who have problems with enforcement agencies and the underworld."

19. Knishstein won the award for his exposé of MVD Lt. Gen. Aleksandr Orlov, a senior aide to then-Interior Minister Vladimir Rushailo, and the head of the ministry's anticorruption unit. Orlov subsequently fled to Israel to avoid charges in the case.

8

The Gender Dimension of Social Capital in Russia

The Novosibirsk Case

Tatyana V. Barchunova

"Hardly anyone is 'average'"
Robert Putnam

The subject of this chapter is the gender dimension of social capital in Russia.[1] The only seemingly possible way to cope with this subject is to follow the notorious instructions received by a hero in *The Pickwick Papers,* by Charles Dickens: A journalist assigned the task of writing a paper on Chinese metaphysics was advised by his senior colleague to analyze the *Encyclopaedia Britannica* articles "China," and "Metaphysics" and combine them into one. In order to approach the subject at hand, it would be necessary to combine at least three articles—"Gender," "Social capital," and "Russia." Unfortunately, this strategy will not work here, making an alternative approach necessary.

In the first section of this chapter I will try to show why the combination strategy will not work. In the second section I will attempt to outline the research surrounding the gender dimension of social capital in Russia, which I will refer to as "communal gender." Finally, I will show the preliminary results of an analysis of communal gender in one particular region of Russia, the city of Novosibirsk.

Approaching Gender, Social Capital, and Russia

Mechanically combining the three subjects of gender, social capital, and Russia is impossible. The combination of "social capital" and "gender" is difficult for at least two reasons. First, each of these concepts is based on a different type of social relation. Social capital is conceptually grounded in the ideas of connectedness, networking, trust, and civic involvement. The core idea here is communal initiatives of a primarily non-hierarchical type. Even if the goal of self-organization is, for example, to eliminate crime, alliance and cohesion are emphasized as the instruments to cope with this social problem. Gender studies very often focus on the same class of social issues (e.g., violence) as do those concerned with social capital. Although the social and political project related to gender studies is aimed at equality, civic involvement, and solidarity, gender theory is grounded in concepts of domination, power, and hierarchy. Gender studies deal with one particular aspect of power and domination, the domination of one sex over the other.[2] The emphasis in gender studies on oppression and discrimination on the basis of sex has led critics of gender theory and its feminist background to label some trends in gender theory as "victim (gender) feminism."[3]

The second reason that makes it difficult to combine what has been done in gender studies with the research on social capital is that most of the gender studies in and of the Communist and post-Communist countries were dealing with *representations* of gender, while the study of social capital is aimed at the research of *practices* of participation and involvement. In other words, gender theorists borrowed the social constructionist approach to gender in understanding gender as a "social construct" rather than as a process of "social construction."

The combination of "gender" and "Russia" is slightly less complicated and has been explored over time. Sociologists who started to study the Russian gender system at the beginning of the 1990s borrowed methodology and conceptual frameworks from Western scholars, but went further when they adopted the conceptual framework of gender theory in reconstructing historical versions of the traditional Russian gender system, its modification under socialism, and its recent transformations in post-Socialist countries. One of the most important advancements during the past decade was the notion of a "gender contract" under socialism and its modifications under transformation. Elena Zdravomyslova and Anna Temkina have termed this type of gender relations the "working mother" gender contract.[4]

One of the driving forces of the gender analysis that culminated in the formulation of this concept was the following question: Was the October Revolution aimed at the liberation of women in Russia from male dictatorship and has it succeeded in this liberation, or did "socialism" turn out to be another stage of their patriarchal slavery?[4] The answer to this question defined the Soviet gender contract not as a contract between females and males but as a contract between females and the socialist state.[5] The agenda of the October

Revolution was not to liberate women from male dictatorship but to suppress the interests of all individuals regardless of gender and make them subservient to the state.[6] The concept of contract, borrowed from liberal theory, was redefined as an "antagonistic relation between a female individual and the state," and as a side effect, eliminated other genders as an object of analysis. In this respect, gender studies in Russia repeat the evolution of gender studies in the West. The recent studies of men and men's culture in Russia, however, can be integrated into the study of social capital in Russia only to a limited extent since the key concepts of the Russian masculinity studies are failure, crisis, and narcissism,[7] which seem to be inconsistent with the concepts of social capital analysis that emphasize ideas such as connectedness and participation.

Combining "gender" and "social capital" with "Russia" does not seem to be valid either. Although trivial elsewhere, it bears mentioning here that social capital in Russia varies from one region to another. Therefore, to combine the three elements we need to specify the region and the period to which we are referring. From this point of view, researchers looking at Russian social capital are in an unfavorable position compared to those who study social capital in the West. For instance, Robert Putnam, in his research of the social capital in the United States, could use all sorts of indices, including such indices as the dynamic of playing card purchases over several decades.[8]

The relevant systematic long-term evidence on Russia is not available. The researcher has to be either very resourceful in using all sorts of indirect data, or in using only very general indices which may lead to questionable conclusions. For instance, measuring social capital in Russia with the use of a civic community index and comparing units as big as regions led Christopher Marsh to the conclusion that a "large non-Russian, indigenous population" may be a factor in "lack of attributes associated with a civic community."[9] Since Marsh sees a direct correlation between civic community development and social capital, it looks as though—according to him—the high percentage of the non-Russian population is inconsistent with social capital growth and it is only the Russian population that has a special ability to invest in social capital. The project of the analysis of the gender dimension of social capital in Russia comparable to the projects of Putnam in his large-scale quantitative analysis of Italy or the United States does not seem to be realistic for many reasons, including the lack of data.

The only realistic way to study the gender dimension of social capital in Russia today is to look at particular social bonds in particular regions. It does not necessarily mean that the differences between regions are so substantial that no generalizations are valid, but at this stage of exploration it makes more sense to focus the analysis rather than to overgeneralize.

Also, when it comes to the analysis of social bonding in Russia today, it becomes quite evident that large-scale, all-Russia organizations are nonexistent or very rare, even when speaking about political parties. For instance, most of the nongovernmental organizations (NGOs) in Novosibirsk are micronetworks of people who used to be friends, relatives, or coworkers before they started their organizations. There is no direct correlation between the number of members in the network and the complexity of their projects. For instance, one of the most famous nongovernmental projects in Novosibirsk and the Novosibirsk Oblast was the construction in 2001 of a road from the Sovetskii region of Novosibirsk to one of the summer colonies and the arrangement of public transportation to this summer colony. The core group planning the project consisted of only two members, providing roughly 700,000 dacha owners access to their lots via this road.

In summary, the difficulties in the mechanical combination of "gender contract," "social capital," and "Russia," lead me to split the concept of social capital into local "communities of practice," and thus, my goal is to analyze "communal gender," or more precisely, the gender dimension of particular communities of practice.

Communities of Practice

The concept of the community of practice was designed by two British experts in the theory of learning, Jean Lave and Etienne Wenger.[10] The crucial traits of the community of practice, according to Wenger, are: mutual engagement, i.e., essentially regular interaction; a joint negotiated enterprise; a shared goal and the practice involved in achieving that goal; a shared repertoire of negotiable resources accumulated over time, including specialized terminology and linguistic routines, and resources like pictures, tapes, gestures, and meals.[11] In other words, we can speak of at least two components of communities of practice: doing something, and what Wenger calls the negotiation of the meaning of this doing.

One of the most important dimensions of the concept of communities of practice is that "membership in a community of practice is acquired as the result of a process of learning."[12] It is this conjunction of learning and doing that makes the community of practice concept appropriate for the analysis of the so-called transformation period in Russia. Now that "the old employment system of secure, lifetime jobs with predictable advancement and stable pay is dead"[13] and the current social dynamic demands new labor as well as new recreation skills, the concept that unites both learning and doing seems to be particularly appropriate for analyzing social processes. In communities of practice, the process of learning is facilitated through interaction and communication between its members.

It is interesting that often the members of communities of practice realize that efficient operation is impossible without acquiring new knowledge and skills. Thus, at one of the Fairs of Novosibirsk for nongovernmental organizations (November 2001, Sovetskii region), Elena Nikitina, the leader of the group of young disabled people "NAMI," said in her presentation that the group had to do surveys to analyze the problems and needs of young disabled people in order to be efficient in their mutual support groups.

This idea of a conjunction of learning and doing in community development was successfully realized by Sarah K. Lindemann-Komarova. She started a regional Civic Initiatives Support Center in Novosibirsk and a Krasnoyarsk Center for Community Partnerships ("Sotrudnichestvo"). She is part of a group that initiated the so-called "fairs" of nongovernmental organizations and formulated the concept of these extended presentations of nongovernmental initiatives to stimulate cooperation between government, business, and NGOs. In her book, *Community-School Foundations: Mechanisms for Creating Social Partnerships and Local Philanthropy,*[14] which offers a detailed description of the operation of community foundations and guidelines for creation of such foundations, Lindemann-Komarova gives extensive instructions on how to do research to identify community needs. However, as I will show below, the learning component of communities of practice cannot be reduced only to sociological research. It covers acquisition of new skills and knowledge in the process of the operation of the community of practice.

By way of illustration, one of my colleagues, 25-year-old Dasha Odinikova-is a Ph.D. candidate in Russian literature, and she is also a member of a community of practice centered around the amateur theatre known as "Intrigue." She said in her interview that through doing theatre she had learned plenty of management skills she would have never acquired otherwise, rather than referring to the more obvious skills that one might learn from such involvement, such as learning to speak in front of a large audience.

Another colleague, 32–year-old psychologist Vladimir Yanushko, was even more categorical in stressing the learning mechanism of doing. Together with his partners from the psychological center *Rodnik,* that or "Spring," he started a community of practice that is aimed at the self-organization and self-help of teenagers. The members of this community are professional psychologists, members of municipal and oblast administration youth committees, adolescent children, and their parents. Professional psychologists teach teenagers basic, practical psychology at special training sessions which include role-playing games, and then their pupils share their knowledge and skills with their peers. *Rodnik* now has a network of more than thirty adolescent volunteers, both boys and girls—who work in summer camps and during the academic year. Vladimir says that reading and didactic education are important for him, but he achieves the most substantial professional growth through the training sessions he performs for his students.

The model of agency within communities of practice is an alternative to the "adaptation" paradigm. The adaptation paradigm transforms social agents into passive objects of social and economic transformations and views them as marginal to the "mainstream" social reality, made up, in this view, by governmental social policy. Thus, the concept of community of practice is relevant to both social research and to the construction of the collective identity of those social agents who are solving important social problems but feel marginalized. This feeling of marginalization was expressed, for instance, by Natalia Baranova, one of the presenters at the Civic Forum meeting of nongovernmental, nonprofit organizations in Novosibirsk (November 2001): "Unfortunately, *all this* third sector, all its groups during the last years had virtually no influence on politics in Russia and outside Russia. The third sector, so to say, has lived its own life, solving and sometimes, very successfully, solving problems while *remaining outside current national and regional politics*" (italics added).

It is very hard to build a strict dichotomous classification of communities of practice; even the distinction between professional and nonprofessional groups can be relative when confronted with the central characteristics of an actual community of practice. Communities of practice can be constituted by registered or nonregistered nongovernmental organizations. However, there are registered groups that cannot be identified as communities of practice and vice versa; the lack of an institutionalized form does not necessarily indicate the absence of a community of practice. For instance, a group of sauna-goers might constitute a stable community of practice. However, I have not heard of any such community being registered.

I will concentrate on associations that consider themselves nonprofit organizations, though for many of them their services and activities are their major material resource, and often, the only one. Sometimes, nonprofit and for-profit activities are very closely entwined as a result of being performed by the same people. An illustration of such a case can be found in the activities of Nadezhda Latrigina, a beauty-salon owner in Novosibirsk. She uses the telephone line of her business as a crisis line for battered women and their children; likewise, she uses the flyers promoting her crisis line to advertise the beauty salon. For those who are not familiar with the problem of space in Novosibirsk, this intermingling of services might seem unusual, to say the least; but for those who understand the local situation, having one workplace for two businesses would hardly seem strange.

Role-Playing Games as Communities of Practice

There are over 2,000 registered NGOs in Novosibirsk and Novosibirsk Oblast.
Some of the ostensibly new organizations are not actually new, since they are
related to the associations or types of practices that existed before 1985. A
good example of such communities of practice is the network of mostly young
people involved in role-playing games. The games were started at the beginning of the 1990s by the activists within the clubs of science fiction fans that
existed long before that. According to estimates of respondents Yevgeny
Korshunov (26 years old) and Svetlana Dzhemileva (29) who belong to the
first generation of one of these communities of practice in Novosibirsk, there
are about 10,000 members throughout Russia. Yevgeny said in his interview
that there is even an idea to start a political party on the basis of this network.
Many members of these communities have acquired through role-playing games
many of the skills necessary for political activity. Yevgeny argues that up to 15
percent of the support groups of those running for elections in Russia have
consultants who have obtained all their business and management skills through
role-playing games or were somehow affiliated with these communities.

A role-playing game is both learning and doing. The doing component
consists of a number of joint endeavors such as assembling the team; constructing the game site; making accessories such as maps, costumes, and so
on; arranging training sessions; and fund-raising for game and travel expenses. The communities are made up of all kinds of artisans: those who
make shoes and armor and others who can sew. Professions are normally
gendered, but they are all considered equally valuable and allow individual
masters to make money by producing the necessary accessories for the games.

The learning part consists of several components.[15] Every participant is supposed to get familiar with the literary text that constitutes the structure of the
game. It might be a science fiction book, a fantasy book, or an Indian or Scan-
dinavian epic story; it might be an episode from the Bible or from modern
history such as World War II. The worlds of the games comprise elaborate
rituals that have to be either carefully constructed or strictly followed.[16] For
instance, if the game involves Christian prayers, they have to be learned and
recited by heart. In addition, the costumes and other accessories produced by
players are researched to fit historical designs or descriptions, and any conventional replacements are negotiated. The cognitive part also covers acquisition
of such emotional "skills" as the ability to face defeat and victory.

The construction of meaning, or rationalization, of these communities of
practice is an important and sophisticated activity. The members of these
communities say that role-playing games attract them because of the opportunities for personal growth, and the acquisition of communication compe-

tence, survival mechanisms, strategic planning skills, and simulation methods. According to Yevgeny Korshunov, a person who gets involved in the game movement cannot get out of it since it becomes "your social network, your environment, and the subject of conversations."

However, the negotiation of meaning seems to be a serious problem for these communities. According to my respondents, the major problem here is that not all the participants share the same motivations for participating. There is a fringe category of participants who seem to be only consumers, not caring about the game as such and treating it as a pastime, and thus ruining the game world. According to Yevgeny Korshunov and materials in Svetlana Dzhemileva's archives, the game communities within the larger Russian network vary in terms of types of organization and approaches to the construction and reconstruction of the game worlds. Some of them deal on a regular basis with local authorities, municipal schools, and extracurricular programs. There are even communities that offer their services to municipal entertainment programs.

The level of self-organization of these groups reveals the high intensity of their networking both before the games, in the form of elaborate training programs and communication systems including electronic and nonelectronic means, and during the games, through safety rules and drug control, medical care in emergency cases, and strict distribution of roles and functions. There might be 400 participants in a game.

The game community, in turn, constitutes just a part of the network of other communities of practice. One other part is the nongovernmental Museum of the Sun, which is a museum for the cultural artifacts of sun cults. The museum arranges solstice celebrations and has other programs. The game community helps the museum to arrange its performances, while the museum shares its space with the community. The game community is also connected to youth amateur and professional theaters and psychological communities who use role-playing games as training instruments.

The systems of metaphysics and ethics constructed and followed by members of game communities, according to Natalia Beletskaya, a Ph.D. candidate in philosophy, deserve special analysis and comparison with such sophisticated systems of thought as gnosticism.[17] Both men and women are involved in the construction of the metaphysical system guiding this community.

The Gender Dimension of Communities of Practice

The gender dimension of communities of practice, as well as the effect of the new communities of practice on gender stereotyping, are discussed in this section. This research is based on the following sources: participant observation of micronetworks in Novosibirsk as a member of two nongovernmental organizations and several noninstitutionalized communities of practice; the archives of nongovernmental associations;[18] in-depth interviews with members of various communities of practice; and secondary evidence such as local media, databases on the nongovernmental, nonprofit organizations in Novosibirsk and Novosibirsk Oblast compiled by the Siberian Center for Civic Initiatives Support, and printed materials on the communities of practice in Siberia, e.g., the above-mentioned book on community schools by Sarah K. Lindemann-Komarova.[19]

Role-playing groups grew out of science fiction clubs, which in the past were predominantly male but have evolved into mixed groups. They attract plenty of young people of both sexes, since they provide a place for intergender communication. Now, ten years later, the groups integrate families with children who were born to the first members of the communities.

The gender structure of these communities of practice is not simple. The gender asymmetry can be reproduced here through the scenarios of historical games in which major functions are performed by high-ranking persons like "kings" and their advisers. But there is a significant emotional "function" within the community that is performed solely by women. The worlds of the games usually include a land of the dead, which players enter as the result of war, a fight, or some other disaster. In the interval between "death" and taking on another role, a player stays in the land of the dead. Says Yevgeny Korshunov: "Though the land of the dead is not real (*igrushechnaia*), getting there can be serious moral stress, especially if one 'dies in a fight.' There are people who are very good at mitigation of this critical condition. . . . Usually, those who are responsible for helping people in this situation are women. This is considered to be the 'hard female burden.'"[20]

The asymmetry of positions of power being played primarily by men is offset by a greater gender balance in opportunities available for young women to be game designers or "masters." Apparently, female masters change the whole understanding of what a game should look like. Says female master Tatyana Kulakova, a 31 year old who supervises teenagers and instructs role-playing games at a neighborhood youth club: "For me a game is primarily a joint creative effort (*sotvorchestvo*). This is not what I invent and make others to do as I want. What is important for me is what comes out of what we are doing together! . . . The interaction with the players is the primary thing for me, and the other is an opportunity to see the world from someone else's point of view."

The notion of a game's value lying in its interactive nature is a recent trend in this particular community, differing from the original idea based on winning or losing. "We have come up with what are called image games, where what is important is how you feel yourself in the world (*mirooshchushchenie*), how you play the role. It is not important if you won or not. The most essential thing is that your kingdom behave consistently.[21] For instance, if your kingdom is peaceful and promotes peace it should not suddenly destroy the other kingdom! And if you are aggressive, you should not sit and shake with fever only because the enemy is twice as big as you are!" This new understanding of the goals of the game allows, according to this female master, many new young people to get involved.

The Novosibirsk game community has close connections with other groups both in Siberia and beyond the region. Some of them interact with educational institutions as well as with municipal and oblast governments. The level of self-organization and the ramifications of this whole network contradict the popular opinion that the individualistic ideals of capitalism have ruined the networks that existed under socialism. In the case of game communities, networks that existed before the transition have been reinforced. They seem to have given more social space to young women than their forebears.

New Communities of Practice

Let us now look at the communities of practice that have started during the transition. One of the interesting qualities that these groups have in common is their fast dynamic; even relatively new groups, such as associations of families with many children, have changed their strategies and styles of operation. As Galina Deineko (47 years old), the head of the Yeltsovka association, says in her interview, in the beginning of the 1990s all their activities were regulated: "Everything was regulated (*normirovano*), including the activities of social organizations. Our activity was mostly material. We were distributing various goods. Even when I was in the hospital I ran out to buy a jumpsuit outfit for my daughter because I knew by the time I needed it they would probably not offer it to me." At that time the major activists of the association were recruited from trade agencies, since they had access to goods.

Since the distribution system has come to an end, what Deineko calls the "idcology" of their programs (which is in fact what Etienne Wenger calls the "meaning") has changed, as have the distribution programs, although both are still are involved in material support. According to Deineko, the most important thing now is "moral and emotional support which is based on principles that do not change. Any person who is involved in social work has to follow principles that do not change every year, or even every ten years. There are some things which have to be invariant even for a hundred years. . . . Many people inquire why we need the association of the families with many children when we have social security offices. . . . They don't understand that moral principles cannot be supported by administrative structures; they can be supported only by those who are vitally interested in them." A good illustration of the changes in their policy can be seen in their activities during the transition from the distribution of the housing economy to the market economy in this area. Says Galina, "Before the transition, the government was supposed to provide housing. . . . This was supposed to happen during the early stages of transition as well. But the government acted, as if (*kak by*) they were not supposed to provide housing any more; they have immediately disavowed. They managed to arrange it in such a way that before the private sector had been formed as more or less stable, they had absolutely disavowed their responsibility." Because of this unexpected change, people became lost and desperate; they did not know what to do. The Yeltsovka association did not know how to cope with the problem either, since its members were not involved in the construction projects. However, as Galina says, "they were working with people, calming them down, trying to explain the situation. . . . You have to spend hours, days, and nights just to listen and explain what happened, that the state that was supposed to provide housing does not exist any more."

The changes Galina speaks about have also had an impact on the gender dimension of their activities. She says that when their association was started, their clients were guided by a "male ideology." Though sometimes their nominal clients were women with many children, there were "men who stood behind them." They were enchanted by the word "association." Says Galina, "It was a new word and they thought that it meant circulation of funds, that there were capitalists there, and capital . . . and values. Everything is accumulated in there. Go and grab!" Finally the men stepped back, and now her association deals mostly with women. For them, one of the most important values is to be respected by the community. And if they receive something from the association, they consider it to be a sign of respect.

The major point of their current ideology, says Galina, is that "we have to take care of ourselves. . . . It is hard but there is no other way out." Her model of the relationship between the state and the family seems to fit the model of classical liberalism. She stresses, "The state should not touch the family. The state should not touch it by any means." The major project of the association is called the "Field." The project is aimed at "self-supply" of vegetables, primarily potatoes. The learning component of the project is essential. The activists of the organization spread new technologies of growing potatoes, arrange seminars, and provide special seed supplies. They deal with the Agricultural Academy of Novosibirsk and other scientific institutions. The Yeltsovka association constitutes a case of a new and dynamic community of practice with an explicit ideological component. What still needs to be analyzed in this case is the process of the negotiation of meaning.

The typology of professional communities of practice has changed substantially under the transition with the emergence of such professions as brokers, distributors, and trade agents, including multilevel marketing agents selling dietary supplements, cosmetics, and other products. These professions did not exist in the distribution system, and they demand not only new skills but also new approaches, even if they had prototypes under socialism. These occupations are typical communities of practice, since in many cases the people who join them have limited time or opportunities to get special professional training before they actually start their professional careers, or the professional training they get at school is not sufficient, and therefore they have to build their skills and acquire the appropriate knowledge during the process of doing the job. In many cases, the activities of the new members of the communities constitute what will be later accepted as the norms and the know-how of the community.

The emergence and growth of new communities of practice has a subversive effect on gender stereotypes. Even when we are dealing with "feminized" activities like shopping, tourism, multilevel marketing, and so on, the traditional stereotype of male innovators and female supporters of the tradition does not make sense. The emergence of new communities of practice undermines this stereotypical distinction. However, undermining this stereotype is not a simple, one-way process. Thus, the representation of women involved in new adventurous occupations can be positive as in the novel by E. Domenikova and A. Sokolov, *The New Russian Lady*[22] but it can also be extremely negative as in the novel by Novosibirsk writer Irina Ulyanina *All Girls Love the Rich*.[23]

Another example of the subversive effect of new communities of practice on gender stereotyping can be seen in the sphere of technology. There is a very widespread stereotype that this is a male sphere. In several schools in Novosibirsk there are quite a number of communities aimed at the application of new educational technologies. A good example of these communities of practice are internet-based projects like the International Education and Research Networking Project in schools # 5, # 162, and classical school # 3. Both students and teachers are involved in these communities. The students are both girls and boys; however, most Russian schoolteachers are women. Therefore, their participation in the internet-based projects at schools subverts the common gender stereotype of the male-dominated technology sphere. The other important aspect of this kind of community of practice is that very often the students are more advanced computer users than their teachers. In this case, the traditional school roles change, and the relationships between students and teachers become less authoritarian. The educational component of these communities of practice is enormous and includes a wide spectrum of skills such as creative writing (in native and foreign languages), drawing, programming, as well as communicative competence. The cooperative spirit of the Internet project was explained by one of the participants in the project using the metaphor of the family, which is not insignificant since the notion of family seems to be the only secular symbolic resource not burdened by political and religious connotations.

Most of the members of small communities of practice get involved in community projects because of the alienation of the majority of the population from larger scale social and economic politics. In Novosibirsk Oblast, big politics is a gendered enterprise. Recently, for the second time, not a single woman was elected to the oblast deputies' council. The core group of the council is a sort of directors' body consisting of heads of enterprises. In the year 2001, the number of representatives of political parties decreased compared to the previous council. This means that for another four years there will be no women in legislative power in the region.

The major conflicts in Novosibirsk Oblast related to the redistribution of property are also gendered. Although the majority of the participants in this conflict are men, the region does not lack politically and socially active women. These women follow alternative strategies of economic and social politics, and their strategies vary. The alternative women's directors' body has founded a branch of the Women of Russia political movement. The social status of its leaders is quite similar to the social status of the deputies of the oblast deputies' council. They are directors of educational and medical institutions and top managers of business enterprises. They aim to represent the interests of their employees.

While there are opportunities, however limited, for women to get involved in local politics, most women of the region solve their problems through communities of practice aimed at dealing with the various critical situations they and their families are facing. A member of a community foundation from the Siberian city of Omsk says: "You watch TV and you see strikes, terrorist acts, blood, and slaughter. You come to a school and you see people inspired by good. Here the enthusiasts work. Long ago I wanted to say: 'Let's work together.' My husband asks me: 'Can you really do anything?'"[24] The answer to this seemingly rhetorical question is: "Yes, of course." Small communities are confronted with a variety of problems, including disability, alcoholism, drug addiction, forced migration, domestic violence, and unemployment. The learning component in dealing with these cases enhances many relevant skills and forms of knowledge, such as psychology, medicine, law, and management. The construction of meaning in terms of both learning and doing is essential because of the need to cope with the stresses of the situations and the intensity of the community work. Many of the centers or contact telephones for these communities of practice are located at members' homes, making the work particularly intense; for instance, many disabled people are working as home dispatchers for their organizations.

Some activists have to deal with emergency situations twenty-four hours a day and get their whole families involved. One such case was described by respondent Irina Ostanina (40 years old), the head of "The Helping Hand" (*Ruka pomoshi*) association, which deals with forced migrants. She and her family are migrants from Kazakhstan. When they first started their association—which is now a close group of three women (a computer programmer, a systems designer, and an accountant for a government transportation authority)—Irina had to use her home telephone as the association's contact telephone. The rationalization of this use of a personal resource is understandable, and without the phone line, providing emergency services to the migrants would have been impossible, but locating the association in her home caused a great deal of trouble for her and her family. She says, "I think that to help your neighbor is something your soul wants." Her justification of what she and her partners are doing is very similar to that described by Galina Deineko: The scarcity of governmental resources and the emotional support the government cannot provide make it necessary for communities to work on their own behalf. Irina says, "My partners are inspired by this idea that we need to help people to stand on their own two feet (*vstat' na noggin*). For if we don't take care of them, who will? The government does not have resources, even the migration department does not have them. They are very limited in their resources—they record them, they give them credits. But when someone is depressed and cries and comes to us to share his story, we can tell him: 'Don't lose your heart—we have had even more complicated cases.' We give him advice. Then he comes back or calls back and says: 'You know, I talked to you and I have changed my attitude toward life.'" Irina plans to start a network that aims to bring previous migrants who have successful businesses into contact with more recent migrants who are still needy. She does not consider this begging, but rather thinks that participants from each group will obtain reciprocal advantages. Her group has good contacts with various German agencies who sponsor their endeavors.

On the face of it, the communal gender of groups like The Helping Hand in Novosibirsk is primarily female. However, women's programs like this are often either backed by male experts or rely on consulting with males as experts in their fields. This is true of such groups as The Helping Hand, which has young male lawyers as volunteer consultants; Women Together, which has a male commercial director; the Women's Humanitarian Foundation, which was inspired by a male psychologist; and the breast-cancer prevention group *Vera*, which hires male consultants and gets family members of both sexes involved.

At the institutional level, these groups classify themselves as women's groups for such purposes as applying for grants. However, as communities of practice, they are gender-mixed. The notion of the mixed communal gender can be expressed in the rationalization of the performance of the organization. Thus, Larissa Cherepanova, the leader of Women Together, has expressed the integration of the group members as follows: "We are not only a 'Women Together With Women' group. We are also a 'Women Together With Men' association."

The communities of practice that are the most varied in terms of gender composition are, presumably, the Novosibirsk youth communities that focus on being an alternative to mass culture. Some of these groups are centered around homosexual cafés and other public places where, according to Tatyana Maximova's research,[25] both gay and heterosexual young people come together. Additionally, the Novosibirsk homosexual arena is less segregated into separate gay and lesbian groups than the one in Moscow. There are no institutionalized gay rights associations in Novosibirsk, but when the initial group formed to register a gay rights association, it was made up of both heterosexual and homosexual young people.

The Construction of Meaning in Communities of Practice

It is very easy to fall into generalizations when considering the functions of different genders in different communities: Women do managerial work, while men perform as professionals. However common this distribution of roles, it is not universal by any means. At this stage of my research, I can say that at least one function in these communities of practice is not gendered: the function of the construction and negotiation of meaning within the community. The meaning of the community's particular practice, even when expressed by an individual member of the community, can be constructed and communicated to other members by a person of any gender. The construction of meaning can be carried out through use of a metaphor, a parable, a symbol, or a tale. Seamstress Olga Sherbakova in designing clothing looks for the "sounds of clearness." Ceramicist Liudmila Levina (55 years old) thinks that the only way a person can get out of the vicious cycle of disasters is to "sculpture oneself."

The construction of meaning may take the form of a sophisticated metaphysical system with all sorts of sources, such as Christianity, humanism, parapsychology, natural science, and so forth, combined into all manner of unusual and interesting systems. One of the most common concepts of these metaphysical systems is energetics *(energetica)*, a sort of contemporary phlogiston, which is used to explain efficiency or the lack thereof in communication.

The construction of meaning is an important source of vitality for communities of practice, since without this sometimes esoteric justification of their practices, the agency of community members could easily be blocked by the vicissitudes that inevitably accompany hardships such as breast cancer, drug addiction, tuberculosis, and domestic violence.

In order to illustrate my thesis, let me give an example of a conjunction between an esoteric meaning construction and the very rational and organized activities in one of the most critical areas of social policy in Novosibirsk: housing. In one district in Novosibirsk, the community of practice aimed at constructing affordable municipal housing is centered around the local NGO known as the "Peace Cultures." One would expect that an NGO with such a name would be involved in antiwar campaigns and other pacifist activities. However, the leader of the group, Liubov Pupchik, is focused on the affordable housing problem. Liubov has been a leader since her secondary school years. She used to lead 2000 Komsomol members at a large plant in Novosibirsk. She studied engineering at the local Technical College and worked for the Governmental Housing Office. In 1991 she graduated from the Academy of Labor and Social Relations (the former Trade Union Movement School in Moscow). She ran in elections in Novosibirsk Oblast and Novosibirsk City for the Deputies Councils and seems to be extremely enthusiastic about what she is doing. She has integrated a number of professional building contractors and architects in the endeavors of the group to formulate the sanitary norms of housing for Novosibirsk and to start a series of construction projects aimed at solving the housing problem. She initiated an agreement between the plant Reinforced Concrete Production # 7, the Kirov district steamshop, the ElSib (turbine production) Plant, the Peace Cultures group, and the Kirov district administration to start the construction of housing in the district, arranging several roundtable discussions on the subject in which professional builders participated along with administration officers and college professors.

The connection between Pupchik's management of this project and her concept of world and peace may not be readily clear. She holds that her efficiency as a manager grows out of her special vision of social problems: "All inhabitants of the Earth are embodied creatures from the other planets and everyone has to realize that he or she is coming from a different planet. The only way to be creative and not to be destructive is to realize that you are different from the others and why you are different from the others. . . . The key to peace, harmony, and efficiency is the awareness of this difference.

The lack of awareness implies conflict and even murder. All human beings are privileged because, as embodied in protein bodies, they can exchange information. The exchange of information guarantees the further development of the civilization and peace." She sees her identity through the mission of connecting people.

The series of roundtables on housing were not the only ones in which she participated. After her trip to the United States in 2001 as a member of a group of women leaders, she participated in a series of roundtable discussions arranged by two other enthusiasts, Natalia Demidova and Natalia Filimonova (from the department for social policy of the municipal government), on the position of women in Novosibirsk. These roundtable discussions included activists from nongovernmental organizations (medical, educational, political, and so on), and the goal of these discussions was to compile a municipal program for the improvement of the position of women. Pupchik was one of the connecting links between the government and nongovernmental communities, putting into action her experience of combining knowledge and doing.

Summary

The goal of this research was to examine the gender dimension of social capital in Russia. In order to do this research I had to identify the adequate conceptual tools and design a program that would help avoid empty overgeneralizations.

I have proceeded from the hypothesis that social capital in Russia is "dispersed" rather than "concentrated." Connectedness and trust unite *small* groups of social agents solving their *particular* problems. Therefore, I needed a concept that would express both the idea of social bonding and would be operational in the research of those small networks. The notion of "communities of practice" developed by J. Lave and E. Wenger proved to be well-suited to this task. Being the alternative to the adaptation paradigm, it is a reliable methodological tool that can be used to overcome the dualism of social reality and agency. The communities of practice *are* the social reality rather than the adaptational techniques *to* the social reality, be it projects of psychological support and self-organization of adolescents, role-playing games, or nongovernmental migration mutual-support groups. This notion is important in attempting to demarginalize those who have constructed marginalized identities under transformation.

The explanatory force of the concept of the community of practice is due to its three essential components: doing, learning, and negotiation of meaning. In most cases, the conjunction of the learning and doing components is easily identified. However, the negotiation of meaning in many cases is barely apparent. My preliminary conclusion is that group negotiation of meaning is less common than individual construction of meaning. It may also be true that the process of negotiation of meaning is hard to trace without participant observation.

My research has revealed that social capital in Russia—in particular, in Novosibirsk—is more "concentrated" than expected, since small communities can be related to one another in any number of ways: as partners, as owners of facilities, or as human resources (e.g., when one community recruits new members from the others).

In my analysis of the gender dimension of communities of practice, I introduce the phrase "communal gender." The history of gender studies has developed as the analysis of relations of power and domination. The analysis of the Russian gender system has culminated in the notion of the so-called gender contract "working mother," which stressed the domination of the state over one gender (women). This notion has eliminated the other gender as the object of research. Recent studies in masculinity aim in part to restore the balance, but the fact that they concentrate on aspects of masculinity such as failure, crisis, and narcissism re-creates asymmetries and makes for an awkward fit with the social cohesion framework. The concept of "communal gender" attempts to stress the cohesive element of gender relations. However, this approach does not invalidate an analysis of gender stratification and gender conflicts in the communities of practice.

Questions such as: "Which gender is communal?" and "What are gender relations in communities of practices?" have no straightforward answers. However, I can make some preliminary comments on these issues.

The negotiation or construction of meaning in the communities of practice that I have analyzed does not seem to be gendered. Both genders participate in the construction of meaning. Without this rationalization, the agency of the members of the communities of practice would have been blocked. The extension of the learning constituent of the communities of practice under transition is subversive for gender stereotypes since new skills and knowledge are acquired by both males and females.

The communal gender is sometimes different from the "institutional" gender. While a nongovernmental organization can be identified as a women's group, the actual community of practice can be mixed. The larger role women play in nongovernmental associations compensates for the lack of women in "big" governmental politics. The role of women in government grows, though, with the growth of the significance of symbolic capital.

Communal gender is dynamic. It can change, as my analysis of some communities has shown (e.g., the case of the Yeltsovka association).

Further research will be aimed at extending the description of communities of practice to other types of associations, such as those centered around bodily practices (e.g., nudists, cold-water hygiene practitioners, and other health-care groups); ethnic associations; religious and spiritual practices; self-governing grassroots organizations; politically engaged groups; and such multidimensional groups as dacha communities. We are also interested in the leadership dynamic of both mixed and single-sex groups and institutionalized organizations. A special question to be confronted here is: Do volunteer associations of people tend to have charismatic, totalitarian, or democratic leaders? Our further research will also be aimed at the symbolic resources that the communities of practice accumulate.

There is much to understand about communal gender. For instance, is there any impact on gender composition of communities as the result of Western funding and access to other resources.

This research on communities of practice has left many unanswered questions. In keeping with the concept of combining knowing and doing, one of those questions might be: To what extent can research *on* social capital be an investment *in* social capital?

Notes

1. I would like to express my gratitude to my colleagues Ruslan Assadov, Natalia Beletskaya, Tatyana Maximova, and Tatyana Polishuk, and to all my respondents who were eager to share with me their networking experiences, for their support in this adventurous project. I am thankful to my partners at the Summer Program of the Central European University (Budapest 2001)—Deborah Cameron, Juliet Langman, and Louise Vasvari—who exposed me to the concept of the community of practice, and also to Kate Schecter, Judy Twigg, Jane Secor, and John Connell for providing me with relevant reading materials.

2. The core of American historian Joan Scott's classical definition of gender "rests on an integral connection between two propositions: Gender is a constitutive element of social relationship based on perceived differences between the sexes, and gender is a primary way of signifying relationships of power." Joan Scott, "Gender: A Useful Category of Historical Analysis," in *Gender and the Politics of History* (New York: Columbia University Press, 1999).

3. Naomi Wolf, *Fire with Fire* (New York: Random House, 1993); see also: *Third Wave Agenda: Being Feminist, Doing Feminism*, eds. Leslie Heywood and Jennifer Drake (Minneapolis: University of Minnesota Press, 1997), 8–13, 49–50, 63–64, 66–69, 134–39, 141–47.

4. Irina Tartakovskaya, "Gendernye aspekty transformatsii" (unpublished).

5. Irina Tartakovskaya, "Gendernye aspekty transformatsii"; Tatyana Barchunova, "The Selfish Gender: The Reproduction of Gender Asymmetry in Gender Studies," *Studies in East European Thought* 55: vol. 1 (March 2003), pp. 3–25.

6. Irina Tartakovskaya, "Gendernye aspekty transformatsii."

7. See, for instance: Sergei Oushakine, "Vidimost' muzhestvennosti," in

Zhenshchina ne sushchestvuet; sovremennye issledovaniia polovogo razlichiia, ed. Irina Aristarkhova (Syktyvkar: Syktyvkarskii Universitet, 1999), 116–131; Marina Kiblitskaya, "'Once We Were Kings': Male Experiences of Loss of Status at Work in Post-Communist Russia," in *Gender, State and Society in Soviet and Post-Soviet Russia*, ed. S. Ashwin (London: Routledge, 2000), 90–105; Elena Zdravomyslova and Anna Temkina, "Die Krise der Maennlichkeit im Alltagsdiskurs. Wandel der Geschlechterordnung in Russland," *Berliner Debatte Initial* 12 (2001):4, 78–90; Irina Tartakovskaya, "'Nesostoiavshaiasia maskulinnost' kak tip povedeniia na rynke truda," (forthcoming).

8. Robert D. Putnam, *Bowling Alone: The Collapse and Revival of American Community* (New York: Simon and Schuster, 2000), 102 ff.

9. Christopher Marsh, "Social Capital and Democracy in Russia," *Communist and Post-Communist Studies* 33: (2000): 192.

10. Jean Lave and Etienne Wenger, *Situated Learning: Legitimate Peripheral Participation* (Cambridge, England: Cambridge University Press, 1991); Etienne Wenger, *Communities of Practice* (Cambridge and New York: Cambridge University Press, 1998).

11. Etienne Wenger, *Communities of Practice*, 76.

12. Janet Holmes and Miriam Meyerhoff, "The Community of Practice: Theories and Methodologies in Language and Gender Research," *Language in Society* 28 (1999): 179.

13. Peter Cappelli, cited in Robert D. Putnam, *Bowling Alone*, 88. Peter Cappelli describes the situation in terms of Western countries, but the same is true of the situation in Russia.

14. Sarah K. Lindemann-Komarova, *Obshchestvennye shkol' nye fondy: mekhanizm sozdaniia sotsial' nogo partnerstva i mestnoi filantropii* (Krasnoyarsk: Tsentr "Sotrudnichestvo na mestnom urovne," 2001), 160.

15. See, for instance: A. Yermolaev, T. Borshevskaya, Yu. Lazarev, and others, *Obuchaiushchie aspekty rolevykh igr* (Kazan: Assotsiatsia fantastiki i rolevykh igr, 1995).

16. "Rolevye igry i ikh pravila" (Kemerovo). A manuscript guide from Svetlana Dzhemileva's archive, 16.

17. Oral communication to the author.

18. *Obshchestvennye ob"edineniia Sibirskogo regiona. Negosudarstvennye, nekommercheskie, nepoliticheskie obshchestvennye organizatsii, deistvuiushchie na territorii Sibirskogo regiona*, izdanie 3, tom I (Novosikirsk: Obshchestvennye organizatsii Sibirskogo regiona, 2001).

19. Lindemann-Komarova, *Obshchestvennye shkol' nye fondy*, 160.

20. Author's interview with Korshunov in Novosibirsk, October 23, 2001.

21. That is, game scenario and design.

22. Ekaterina Domenikova and Andrei Sokolov, *Novaia russkaia ledi* (Moscow: Vagrius, 1999).

23. Irina Ul'anina, *Vse devushki liubiat bogatykh* (Novosibirsk: Mangazeia, 1999).

24. Cited by Sarah K. Lindemann-Komarova, *Obshchestvennye shkol' nye fondy*, 61.

25. Oral presentation, 1999.

9

Religion and Spirituality as Factors Affecting Social Cohesion in Contemporary Russia

Tatyana Matsuk

Do religion and spirituality facilitate growth in social cohesion in today's multiethnic and multifaith Russia? Do they help to establish civil society in Russia, as they did at one point in the United States? These questions are not easy to answer. On the one hand, the post-Soviet period immediately following Gorbachev's perestroika became an era of true freedom of worship, unique in Russian history. However, on the other hand, freedom of worship was supported only by incomplete legislation and was used by those who wanted to make as much money from it as possible. Many felt depressed and confused, and all types of "fishers of men" tried to profit from this. As a result, instead of social cohesion, we saw growing atomization of society. After ten years of Yeltsin's reforms, Russia has gotten nowhere close to having a functioning civil society, or one in which social initiative originates from the bottom. On the contrary, the state is striving once again to take control of all aspects of the lives of its subjects, including their ideological and religious preferences; a number of the "traditional" religions are using the state to fight against their competition and to receive all sorts of benefits. Today, when religious extremism is growing in the world, these trends are exceptionally dangerous, particularly in a country whose entire history has been one in which the lack of freedom has been ever-present.

Sources of Religious Extremism in Russia

After Islamic fanatics carried out the terrorist attack on the U.S. on September 11, 2001, religion, and especially extreme religious movements, came to the forefront. Twenty million people in Russia consider themselves Muslims, and the propaganda of politically radical Islamic groups is often successful among them. There are extremist Nazi and ultra-Nazi movements within Orthodox Christian groups and "new" pre-Christian Pagans. Extremist ideas attract primarily young people; because of this, any study of problems relating to religion must start with the highly alarming phenomenon of extremism.

Extremism in modern Russia is mainly rooted not in religion or spiritual life, but in the country's socioeconomic and political problems and history. Examples of this can be seen in a number of different Russian contexts.

Portraying the war in Chechnya as a fight against international terrorism, Russian authorities pretend to be forgetting that the Chechens and a number of other mountain-dwelling ethnic groups—who live in clans and have original cultures and blood-feud traditions—were annexed to the Russian empire by force after a fifty-year colonial war. This was followed by repeated rebellions by the famished people suppressed by punitive forces, and their deportation from their own territories during Stalinist repressions. Naturally, Chechens and the so-called Cherkess tribes, which were deported from the Caucasus in the nineteenth century, never forgot this. Their descendants now living in Turkey, Syria, and other Eastern countries finance Chechen militants, while Imam Shamil's militant Islam—in whose name he fought against Russia for thirty years—now forms the basis of the radical movement known in Russia as Wahhabism. There is nothing surprising in the emergence of separatist and even radical sentiments in Tatarstan either, as people there still remember Ivan Grozny's campaigns against Kazan.

Long before the breakup of the USSR, some parts of the North Caucasus experienced latent unemployment that led to a growth in the number of crimes. In the late 1980s, a Moscow taxi driver told me about the unusual cruelty of the so-called Chechen mafia. Today, after two Chechen wars, a ruined infrastructure, hundreds of refugees, and virtually nonexistent industrial production not only in Chechnya but also in adjacent multiethnic Dagestan, the socioeconomic condition of the majority of the population is simply disastrous. There are no jobs. According to Yevgeny Kiselev, the anchor of the television program "Itogi," in the Urus-Martan region of Chechnya, an area that is reflective of the situation in Chechnya as a whole, there are 100,000 able-bodied individuals but only 5,000 jobs.[1]

The peaceful population continues to suffer at the hands of federal troops, representatives of various clans are fighting for power, and young people fail to see a future or ideals for themselves in their everyday lives. They can easily follow anyone that offers them any sort of purposeful existence or even merely a means of existence. Radical Islam is becoming a manifestation of people's dissatisfaction with their way of life, and the war becomes an occupation that puts bread on the table and gives a purpose to life.

The well-off and better-educated young residents of Muslim regions go to mosques where traditional Islam is preached. However, this is no guarantee that they would not become radicals if presented with an opportunity. Studies of the social composition of antiglobalist, Islamic, and other extremist movements indicate that prosperity does not prevent many people from experiencing dissatisfaction when those around them are socially underprivileged and disenfranchised. It is exactly the desire to do something about the unfair world order that often incites them to radical views and actions. Unable to find civilized solutions to problems, they look for enemies to fight against. This is particularly true in Russia, where the developments of the last decade were hardly fair to the Russian population at large; plenty of confidence artists were ready to take advantage of social problems and of people's spiritual quests.

Any extremist movement comprises people with a particular psyche who are inclined toward religious fanaticism. However, religion is a particular manifestation rather than the essence of the mindsets and strivings of those inclined toward fanaticism. This mindset is often quite simplistic.

Regardless of whether young ethnic Slavs with pro-Nazi and ultra-Nazi views call themselves skinheads, Satanists, or supporters of the organization "Russian National Unity," radical Orthodox, or neopagan movements, those who carry out pogroms against people from the Caucasus at markets, set synagogues on fire, desecrate Jewish cemeteries, and beat up people from different races or ethnic groups are the products of socioeconomic problems in a society in which social dislocation results in hooliganism and aggressiveness. According to Deputy Justice Minister Vladimir Vasiliev, 394,000 juveniles are currently registered with the police in Russia, and 123,000 of them have only an elementary-school education. Of the 10,000 minors registered with the Moscow police, 7,500 have no education or opportunities to get an education or a job. One hundred thousand parents are registered with the police because they fail to properly take care of their children.[2]

The situation of homeless children is even worse. According to various data, there are from one to three million street children in Russia. Feeling unsafe around grown-ups, these children flock together or join a group where they feel strong and needed; they do not care about the beliefs or ideology of the group.

Youngsters, the unemployed, elderly, poor, and ill, those with no immediate family, those deprived of their usual living environment, living standards, or sense of life, and those without social safety networks become the breeding ground for the development of the so-called "destructive cults." These pretend to be civic, health, or religious/charitable organizations that in actuality cater only to the interests of their leaderships and strip their victims of the last of what they have. The most dangerous of such organizations have been branches of the Japanese Aum Shinrikyo and Ukrainian White Brotherhood, which have recruited a large number of teenagers.

Although the manifestations of extremism pose obvious threats to Russian society and impede its social capital growth, they do not help to answer the question of whether religion is a source of social cohesion in contemporary Russia. The influence of extremist groups will decrease as socioeconomic problems become less acute, but the relationship between society, the state, and religious entities will remain urgent. Depending on the makeup of religious groups, religion will positively or negatively affect social cohesion. Unfortunately, September 11 and the consequent fight against terrorism may have given statesmen a green light to curtail civil liberties, primarily in the realm of freedom of worship—trends that began to take shape in Russia several years ago.

Freedom of Worship in Russia's History: The Relationship Between Church and State

Russia is a multiethnic country; however, after it adopted Christianity, it experienced a virtual lack of freedom of worship for a thousand years. All reforms, including those concerning religion, were carried out by state rulers without taking into account people's feelings, desires, or preferences.

Russia's Christianization was accompanied by shouts and wails, as people could not accept the desecration of their idols. The Russian population continued to mark pagan holidays, some of which had to be "Christianized." Patriarch Nikon's reforms seemed to change rites very insignificantly, but they led to the Old Believer movement, which essentially opposed the strengthening of the state's influence on all aspects of life.

In accordance with its doctrine, under which the head of state was God's representative on Earth, the Russian Orthodox Church (ROC) and the monarchy shared a relationship of mutual support, a so-called "symbiosis." The Church consecrated the tsar's authority, thus sanctioning all of his actions, while the authorities guaranteed that the Church would enjoy prosperity comparable to that of a large feudal landowner, along with a virtual ideological monopoly. When the Church attempted to hinder Peter the Great's reforms, he simply transformed it into a part of the state apparatus.

The Russian empire was forced to endure Islam, but only to a certain degree; it confined Jews to the Pale of Settlement and persecuted Old Believers and all sorts of other sects that emerged as a reaction to the absolute state authority and were the beginnings of civil society. It repressed and persecuted such groups as the Molokans, Dukhobors, and Khlysts, in particular for their pacifist views and many of these groups then emigrated to Canada. Writer Leo Tolstoy, who did not recognize the Church as an institution, was excommunicated. Under the pressures of the First Russian Revolution of 1905, Russians were formally endowed with freedom of conscience. The foundation of the Union of Russian People immediately followed and it launched Jewish pogroms. The Pale of Settlement began to disappear only in 1915 when German troops came to territories populated by Jews. The number of university placements varied for people belonging to different faiths.

Soviet authorities formally separated church from state, first flirting with "religious minorities" and inviting emigrants to return, and later repressing them along with the Orthodox clergy. The new universal "belief" in the Communist paradise on Earth and the domination of militant atheism were thus established. The state's claim of freedom of worship was fraudulent. The Church patriarchs who agreed to collaborate with the state became part of the nomenklatura, and according to multiple pieces in the post-Soviet press, many of them also worked as KGB agents.[3]

Religion enjoyed relatively more freedom only during the Second World War, during which time the Church collected donations to secure victory in the war; likewise, the state's goal at the time was to do everything possible to unite people and raise their spirits. Also during this time, the Soviet Union signed a number of international agreements on human rights.

Russians continued to mark some religious holidays, but overall the atheist propaganda was successful. I count two possible reasons for this. First, Russia was witnessing a considerable decrease in the popularity of religion as early as the second part of the nineteenth century. According to contemporaries, "the majority of believers went to church and confessed once a year during Lent," and church life "went virtually unnoticed by both the laity and the clergy."[4]

Second, the Bolsheviks managed to replace in people's consciousness one ideology with another, and these were analogous in many ways. They replaced Orthodoxy with Marxism and Leninism, autocracy with party leadership headed by a secretary general, and the Russian national idea with the motto "People and party are one and the same!"

True and full freedom of worship emerged in Russia only in 1990 when the RSFSR Law on Freedom of Religion was passed. Lawyers and human rights activists highly praised the legislation. In 1993, an article on freedom of conscience was added to the constitution. The collapse of the dominating official ideology spurred spiritual quests. All religions were legalized, and all became active and started engaging in charitable activities. Organizations connected to "over fifty various religious movements were registered in the country. Among these, many were previously nonexistent, illegal, or had operated underground, such as Jehovah's Witnesses, the True Orthodox Church, charismatic churches, Mormons, the Bah'a'i Faith, the Assyrian Church, Hinduism, Tantrism, Paganism, shamanism, Zoroastrianism, the Bohemian religion, and so forth. The Russian Orthodox Free Church was permitted to function. . . . The law allowed religious groups to own or rent places of worship and other property either received from the state or acquired in some other way."[5] As of October 1, 1997, "the State Registry of Religious Organizations listed a total of 16,017 religious organizations."[6] This situation might have encouraged growth in social cohesion and social capital, but only if Russia had truly been experiencing a transition to an economically free civic society.

In actuality things turned out to be very different. Those who wanted to use the enormous amount of spiritual and related resources that had been left totally unmanaged for private gain, also used freedom and legislative gaps in the country to take control over all aspects of life. Politicians, adventurers, and con men who poured into Russia as if it were a new Klondike also tried to take advantage of people's confusion. Meanwhile, instead of comprehensively assisting those who suffered as a result of reforms, the clergy was concerned primarily with retaining its piece of the property pie and securing the maximum number of rights, perks, material goods, and power.

It became obvious that the previously dominant religions, first and foremost of which is the ROC, might be pushed into the background. Only four months after the 1991 coup, according to the radio station "Svoboda" ("Freedom"), the Moscow patriarchy launched its attempts to persuade President Boris Yeltsin to adopt a new law on restricting the activities of foreign missionaries from all "nontraditional" religions on Russia's territory.[7]

Yurii Rozenbaum, a doctor of law and a professor, commented:

> Being effective on the whole, the Law on Freedom of Religion is not devoid . . . of flaws and has certain gaps. . . .Usually in such cases, additions and changes are introduced to the law without amending its concept and structure and the meaning of its provisions. However, this approach does not suit those who for the last several years have been trying to repeal the law. Who are they and why do they do this? . . . As it happens, the opposition to the law says almost nothing about the reasons—political, economic, legal, and so forth—why it wants to replace it. It is impossible to take seriously statements by some deputies of the Russian State Duma and the so-called "faith advocates" that a new law has to put an end to the operation of the majority of "sects" allegedly infringing upon citizens' rights. It is unfortunate that the law is being drafted by people unaware of Article 143 of the Criminal Code on the "Foundation of an Association that Infringes on the Individual and Rights of Citizens." If such an organization is

detected, its founders, leaders, and active participants can be made criminally liable and even imprisoned. . . . Obviously, no civic organization, state body, private entity, or individual has the right to carry out unlawful activities. This is an axiom. . . . The problem is that some religious confessions in their constant rivalry with others fail to compete effectively in promoting their faiths, especially today, in the context of complete spiritual and religious freedom. Having ceased to count on themselves, they now hope that the state will assist them and enforce laws that stop or limit activities of other religions, and in particular those groups that have close affiliates abroad and enjoy their support. Changes in religious life in any country, growth in popularity of some faiths and decrease in that of others, and emergence of new religious movements, are all historically and socially inevitable phenomena, and it is pointless and even dangerous to fight against or regulate them. . . . It is absolutely unacceptable for the law to divide religious organizations (and consequently citizens) into privileged, traditional, nontraditional, tolerable, less tolerable, and intolerable, a priori prohibited, or something else. Analysis indicates that all legislative proposals currently in the works have essentially been developed for a single purpose: to restrict activities by some religions in order to create a favorable environment for others.[8]

Nonetheless, in 1994, regional authorities started adopting unconstitutional laws that limited the activities of "nontraditional" religions. Consultative councils on "totalitarian sects" are emerging, consisting primarily of representatives of religions from which these sects split at some point, as well as students of religion-turned-experts on so-called "scientific atheism." Rehabilitation centers for victims of "destructive cults" are also being founded with the participation, or under the auspices, of the ROC, with "rehabilitation" here meaning primarily reorientation from an "incorrect" belief to a "correct" one.[9]

Despite opposition on the part of legal experts, scientists, and human rights activists, the State Duma passed a new Federal Law on Freedom of Conscience and Religious Associations, which entered into force on October 1, 1997. This was followed by a new registration of religious groups, a tool the authorities had previously tested on businesses and civic organizations and that they used to liquidate entities that they considered "excessively" free or failing to perfectly comply with their rules. Many organizations faced troubles during reregistration, and in two cases, the Constitutional Court had to intervene. Some groups, e.g., Jehovah's Witnesses and the Moscow office of the Salvation Army, were never allowed to reregister. Legal experts still fail to agree on whether the rejection received by the Salvation Army was lawful. The fundamental problem is that unregistered religious organizations have no right to own property, carry out charitable acts, or engage in publishing;

the inability to conduct these activities makes the presence of the Salvation Army in Russia pointless.

The law contains a preamble that ascribes a "special role" to certain "traditional" faiths to the detriment of the "nontraditional." It introduces a 15-year residence requirement, without which a religious organization cannot be registered as a legal entity. The law also includes a provision under which "the right of a person to freedom of worship and religion can be restricted for purposes of the country's defense and to guarantee its security."[10] It seems that this may be just the beginning of an attack against freedom of worship.

Despite the fact that the Russian Federation has been declared a secular state in which all religions have equal rights, the Russian government clearly favors the ROC. All the so-called power ministries have agreements with it.[11] Yurii Rozenbaum states:

> We frequently see that religious rites and ceremonies accompany official state events, such as inaugurations, openings for state establishments and companies, and so forth. There are an increasing number of cases in which the state renders financial assistance to some religious organizations by way of direct and indirect subsidies from the state budget—in other words, out of taxpayer money. The authorities are assigning some religious organizations state functions, for example, they make them responsible for transferring places of worship and cult articles to believers and carrying out educational work in the army and penitentiary and public educational establishments. We see more and more often that certain state bodies and religious institutions merge their efforts to solve federal issues.[12]

At the same time, officials routinely discriminate against not only new religious movements, but also Catholics and Protestants. These groups face resistance even when they approach authorities "about a sale or lease of land or property, not to mention free transfer; whereas simultaneously the Moscow patriarchy is receiving huge plots of land and buildings."[13] Patriarch Alexis II has proposed to the executive authorities that some land that belonged to the ROC before the Bolshevik Revolution be given back to it,[14] Russian universities offer majors in theology, and the authorities are considering whether to introduce the study of "traditional" religions in grade and high schools.

Through its official representative Vsevolod Chaplin, the Moscow patriarchy explicitly states that it prefers the European system of relationships between church and state to the American system, although we know from history that it is the American model that fosters the rapid development of civil society and lawful state in a country with multiple religions. Kremlin political strategist Gleb Pavlovsky shares this point of view: "I believe that the American model is interesting to learn. However, it would not work in Russia. It emerged when a great number of religious dissidents came to an enormous territory, ousted and killed off the native population—the Indians—and created a secular state, which was prohibited from ever intervening with religion. The majority of people came to America in search of religious freedom. In Russia, we are building a new state on the territory previously ruled by an ideology that had trampled down the religious and private life of the old Russia. So we cannot be compared to Indians who set out to restore their civilization: this is nowhere close to the American experience!"[15]

Pavlovsky also supports the full restitution of the ROC's property, and he believes that the Church made a fatal mistake in the early 1990s: It gave the state the right to evaluate itself and choose its state building strategies . . . Our nation is the Russian civilization. Russian enlightenment can build on nothing but Eastern Christianity. As such and only as such we are European."[16] These views underpin the amendments to the 1997 law currently being developed by the authorities, which will even further restrict activities carried out by "nontraditional" religious groups, and in particular deprive them of the opportunity to register "as civic organizations (religious, cultural, educational, and so on)."[17]

The concept of relations between church and state based on the criterion of traditionalism is being discussed, along with the need to form a state body in charge of religion. Sergei Buryanov is of the opinion that it is easy to find those who orchestrate this if one reviews the analytical note on the state of affairs in the Moscow patriarchy compiled by the presidential administration. According to it, "the dominating trend in internal church life in recent years has been a gradual but steady strengthening of conservative and traditional forces. These forces simultaneously carry an implicit charge of state patriotism. These trends can be relied on in drafting the new concept of relations between church and state."[18]

Obviously, this position gives the ruling "elite" not only support from the "traditional" clergy, but also an opportunity, if not to establish a single ideology once again, then at least to keep in check the population distributed among the major religions and give privileged jobs to former ideologists of scientific atheism.

If we look at the most recent statements of ROC hierarchs at the December 2001 World Russian National Council—visited by statesmen and politicians of all types, from President Putin to Gennady Zyuganov, the leader of the ostensibly opposition Communist Party—the ROC, as it seems, aims at restoring its influence to levels higher than what it enjoyed before Peter the Great became tsar, when after the collapse of Byzantium, Moscow was pronounced the "Third Rome, and there will not be a fourth." The ROC's hopes to achieve this are possibly connected to the fact that Vladimir Putin has became a true Christian believer. In addition, according to the weekly publication *Versiya* (Version), his confessor, Archimandrite Tikhon, is not only the father superior of the Sretensky Monastery in Moscow, which is considered the main ideological center of the Russian Orthodox Church, but also an adherent of Orthodox fundamentalism.[19]

The overall feeling is that the relationship between the state and the religions of its choice, the "most equal" among these equals being the ROC, is returning back to the "symbiosis." Since the people, and not God, choose the president, the church to which he belongs may be tempted to try to control him, although some of its representatives claim that they will cooperate with state officials only as long as civil society is not established in the country.

However, I would not say that the current situation in Russia in the realm of church-state relations and freedom of worship encourages the establishment of a civil society, nor does it assist in improving the social cohesion of the population or the desire to show initiative from below in this multiethnic country.

Religion and Society: Interfaith and Intrafaith Relations

Religion, faith, and spirituality are all broad concepts that can be defined and interpreted differently. In addition, Russian citizens often identify their religious affiliation with the religion fitting with the way of life and ethnic culture of which they consider themselves a part. For this reason, public opinion surveys do not provide a clear picture of how many people in Russia are religious and what their religious preferences are.

An opinion poll carried out by the Russian Independent Institute of Social and National Problems in February–May 2000 at the request of the Friedrich Ebert Foundation indicated that 42 percent of respondents considered themselves believers, 28 percent nonbelievers, and 30 percent said that they were unsure or indifferent. Just under 70 percent showed that they belonged to various, mostly "traditional," religions. Among those individuals who called themselves believers, only 69.5 percent said that they believed in God.[20]

The survey also showed that women and the elderly, the uneducated, and low-income respondents were more likely to be believers; this group also included those dissatisfied with the results of market reforms, those welcoming social equality ideas, and those in passive opposition to the new regime. These people are quite conservative, and their views and preferences are in many respects similar to those of an average Soviet citizen. As for their attitudes to the country's history in the twentieth century, the believers are most unhappy about the Gorbachev perestroika, despite the fact that freedom of worship became a reality precisely at that time. Only 14.5 percent of them think that it is necessary to cultivate sincere belief in God in children. In comparison with nonbelievers, they ascribe more importance to moral and ethical values: 94.6 percent believe that an individual has to pursue a clear conscience and spiritual health.

These researchers have arrived at the conclusion that a contemporary Russian believer is a person with particular moral principles and values rather than a deeply religious individual. Other sociologists have reached similar conclusions, all noting a trend toward noninstitutional religiosity. People often simply have a need for support—including support "from on high"—and the feeling that they are once again standing on firm ground. The public's attitude to the church is another clear indicator of this. Mikhail Tul'sky has said the following:

> Two superficially opposite trends currently coexist in the religious life of contemporary Russian society. On the one hand, the church is one of the most respected social institutions, and the majority of Russians have positive feelings about religion. . . .Of all churches and religions operating in Russia, the Russian Orthodox Church and Russian Orthodoxy are considered to be the most natural choice by 80 percent of respondents. However, the actual size of the ROC's congregation is many times smaller than this. On the other hand, here is the second, completely opposite, trend in the development of Russia's religious life: . . . 6–10 percent of Russians go to church at least once a month. Only this portion of the country's population can be considered the real ROC congregation, because going to church 2–3 times a year is not a religious rite, but rather a visit to a "museum."
>
> . . .Why do 95 million Russians who consider the ROC their natural choice of religion not participate in church life? The answer to this question is simple: In their view, the ROC is the traditional church of their ancestors, which has almost nothing to do with contemporary life. Various sociological surveys indicate that in the period from 1994 to 2000, there was a fairly steady trend toward a slow decrease in the popularity and authority of the Church in the eyes of the people. According to a poll conducted by the Center for Market Conditions Research in August 1998, 29 percent of Russians believed that the ROC had strengthened its position through its close relations with the authorities, and not by getting closer to people. 15.4 percent stated that the Church's friendship with the state is "ruining its reputation." The overly close relationship between the Church and authorities is the main reason that Russians do not trust the ROC.
>
> A survey carried out by the Public Opinion Fund on January 22–23, 2000, confirms this result. The study showed that people are mainly dissatisfied with the patriarch because he is dependent on the authorities. "He is a politician and he works for the top leadership and dances to its tune," some individuals said in response to an open-ended question.[21]

Currently, the Russian "elite," comprising primarily the former Communist nomenklatura, considers it good form to show that it is religious. However, very often this looks like an unconcealed demonstration of something that does not exist. Many people get baptized and become members of religions for pragmatic reasons, such as a desire to cure a disease or to get free food or assistance, or even a comfortable job. Some simply do not want to take a chance in case "the afterlife really exists."

Sincere believers are those who come to religion after going through serious life shocks. However, in my experience, former Soviet activists who fought for Communism and have now become fervent supporters of a religious faith make up a large proportion of neophytes. It is possible that these people have a particular psyche that needs to have someone to follow and something to fight for. Unfortunately, such people are inclined to work for the power ministries. For others, religion has become simply a refuge and a justification for their egoism. Asked for help, these people say, "Everyone has a cross to bear. God challenges us in accordance to how much we can bear."

The adoption of the new Law on the Freedom of Conscience and Religious Associations in Russia, which caused a stir abroad, went practically unnoticed by the majority of Russians, who are concerned with their everyday survival. However, the new policy has already made itself felt. Here is what has been happening in the Arkhangelsk Region: "In the early 1990s, the majority of religious organizations, which at the time were only forming, were busy with their internal problems and did not pay much attention to their competitors. In the mid-1990s, they started to oppose the Russian Orthodox Church and all other churches, mainly the Protestant Church. The mass media began to publish unprofessional pieces, which insulted believers' feelings and infringed upon their honor and dignity as well as upon the business reputation of religious groups. Even though open conflicts were avoided, the atmosphere of mutual mistrust, isolation, and 'concealed' confrontation became an intrinsic part of inter-religious relations."[22]

"Virtually all human rights activists talk about a growth in religious intolerance in society, which went as far as an attempted public burning of Adventists in Buynaksk. Frequently this is incited by the state's actions."[23] "Traditional" and "nontraditional" cults accuse each other of commercialization, destructive influence, interfering with peoples' mental states, stripping believers of their money and possessions, and so forth. In addition, journalistic reports indicate that such accusations may be valid.

Muslims fear close relations between church and state, as these might push Islam to the background. They are concerned about the possible growth in anti-Islamic sentiments in the context of the "fight against international terrorism." Jews are also worried, as propaganda of state-imposed anti-

Semitism by a number of Orthodox parishes continues to increase.[24] The stance of the Moscow patriarchy on the Catholic Church, and Alexis II's negative reaction to the Pope's visits to former Soviet territory—which the ROC views as its traditional sphere of influence—have become notorious.

As regards the situation within particular faiths, none of the "traditional" groups in Russia can call themselves united. Newspapers and radio stations repeatedly talk about this. The most united of all are communities tradition-ally persecuted first by the tsarist and later the Soviet regimes: the Old Be-lievers and the Baptists. In general, in Russian history, the Old Believer movement played the role that reformation played in the West. It produced the majority of merchants, industrialists, and patrons, who were actively in-volved in charities and even provided revolutionaries with funding. People living in Old Believer communities are used to working hard and helping one another. However, the influence of the Old Believers and the Baptists in the country has so far been insignificant. Used to being on the defensive, groups often develop a particular attitude toward the outside world, distance themselves from everything "alien," and rarely change their way of life. It is also often hard to leave such communities.

In conclusion, I should say that in today's Russia, religion is not a factor contributing to social cohesion and the accumulation of social capital.

Spirituality as a Source of Social Capital

In Western culture, the term "spirituality" typically refers to religious con-sciousness. In contemporary Russia, this concept has a broader meaning: Spirituality is defined as that which concerns the spirit as opposed to matter. A fine illustration of the Russian understanding of the word appears in a ballad "Blagoslovliaiu vas, lesa" ("I bless you, Woods") by Pyotr Tchaikovsky, based on lyrics by Alexei Tolstoy. The lyrics are from a poem with a reli-gious plot, but the ballad does not give this impression. It is a hymn of praise that a deeply spiritual person sings to everything that surrounds him: nature, people, and the heavens. Such a person cannot pursue destruction, as he perceives the world around him as a part of himself. Being poor, he is always rich. He realizes that giving can bring more pleasure than taking. He is a creator whose life is full of meaning. And it does not matter whether he recognizes any religious doctrine or not.

In any case, spirituality is about the high ethical nature inherent in every human being. It opposes basic instincts; restricts and ennobles carnal de-sires; and makes people strive for and create goodness and beauty, literally and figuratively break away from the Earth, help a neighbor and ask for nothing in return, endure suffering with courage, and even sacrifice life (and only their own!). Believers think that these things come from God. In their view, spirituality is communication with God and His reflection in a human being. A nonreligious person has a different explanation for the source of spirituality. But do their world outlooks prevent them from understanding one another and acting on the same moral principles?

Russia's diverse, harsh, and rich physical environment generates creative and very decent personalities, as well as a collective urge. No ideology foisted from above will strip Russians of these qualities. There are highly spiritual people ready to help a neighbor at any time and work with others for a common benefit among representatives of all sorts of faiths, as well as among atheists and agnostics. I have always been able to find subjects to talk to them about and avoid discussing their personal choices. As long as there are a certain number of such people, Russia has a future, regardless of the doctrines its authorities try to impose. It is a real concern, however, that living conditions in Russia over the last decade are leading to a situation in which this kind of person may be becoming nonexistent.

I fully identify with legal and human rights experts who believe that their task is to make sure that freedom of worship evolves into the right to belong to no religion, having a different, not necessarily a religious, world outlook with the ability and freedom to preach it, without breaking the law securing the rights of others.

"A human being is a creature that overcomes its limitations and strives for the transcendent," Nikolai Berdyaev wrote.[25] People are social creatures by their very nature. If the state ceases to constantly unite people from above, out of necessity they will unite from below. The task of the state is to not disturb this process, to avoid foisting on society any single philosophy or faith, and to allow the development of high spirituality, which is fundamentally present in each individual. But it seems that, at the moment, Russia lacks even a hint that these ideas can become reality.

Conclusion

In the context of harsh socioeconomic conditions in Russia, trends toward closer relations between the Russian Orthodox Church and the state have started to take shape. This can lead to the relations characterized as "symbiosis" and based on elements of Orthodox fundamentalism, as well as to attempts at establishing a single ideology in the country. The popularity and authority of the Church with the majority of Russians who historically consider themselves Orthodox Christians grew dramatically at the beginning of the reform period, but is diminishing today. We are witnessing a crisis of traditional religiosity, as the authorities increase their disfavor of nontraditional religions. There is tension in relations between religious groups, as well as a lack of unity inside these groups. Such constitutional rights and principles as freedom of worship and a secular state are being violated. Twenty million Russian Muslims, Jews, and other "religious minorities"—including "traditional" believers—are concerned about their futures. Socioeconomic difficulties and the war in Chechnya generate extremist sentiments. Society's atomization is on the rise. The state-controlled mass media and the media that consider themselves democratic are trying to make the public think that normal people in a normal country have to be concerned primarily with problems within their families. Obviously, in this context, religion cannot encourage growth in social cohesion and the accumulation of social capital in Russia.

Social cohesion and social capital originate in spirituality defined as the presence of a higher spirit in people. The Russian physical environment that calls on people to help one another and be creative facilitates spirituality. Despite the fact that in recent years the majority of people were forced to concentrate mainly on their physical survival, I do not think that the "mysterious Russian soul" has changed significantly.

Market economies, democracy, and civil society can exist in very different cultures; compare, for example, the U.S. and Japan. To preserve and grow social capital we need to make sure that the state does not take control of the people. We can achieve this by insisting that legislation be perfected so that it protects the rights of each citizen—including the right to have his or her own beliefs and world outlook—rather than the interests of secular and religious elites.

Notes

1. "Itogi," NTV television network, 9 December 2001.
2. "Vremena," ORT television network, 11 November 2001.
3. See, for example, Yaropolk Kalitka on the life of Patriarch Alexis II: Yaropolk Kalitka, "Alexis II: zhizn' za sem'iu pechatiami," in *Sobesednik* 27 (1996): 18–19.
4. Oleg Kling, "Filosofskie rassuzhdeniia nakanune revolutsii," *NG-Religii*, 26 December 2001, 1–2.
5. Yurii Rozenbaum, "Osvobozhdennaia sovest'," *Nezavisimaya Gazeta*, 16 April 1996.
6. V. I. Korolev, "O khode registratsii i pereregistratsii religioznykh organizatsii," *Zakonodatel'stvo o svobode sovesti i pravoprimenitel'naia praktika v sfere ego deistviia*, Seminar materials, Moscow, November-December 2001, 12–18.
7. "S khristianskoi tochki zreniia," Radio station "Svoboda," 27 August 2001.
8. Yurii Rozenbaum, "Osvobozhdennaia sovest'."
9. See, for example, Sergei Buryanov, "Svoboda sovesti v Rossiiskoi nauke, zakonodatel'stve i pravoprimenenii," *Pravo i Politika* 7 (2001): 26–37. See also a package of documents on "sects" compiled under the patronage of the Moscow City

Duma, Transcript and Statement from the Conference "Destructive Cults in Moscow. Religious Anonymity. Specific Aspects of Problem Resolution," Moscow, 1 June 2001.

10. Yevgeny Komarov, "Zakon 'O svobode . . .' podvel pod nei chertu," *Novye Izvestia*, 2 February 2001.

11. S.A. Buryanov, "Gosudarstvennaia politika Rossiiskoi Federatsii v sfere svobody sovesti na rubezhe tysiacheletiiu," *Pravo i Politika* 1 (2000): 80–87.

12. Yurii Rozenbaum, "Osvobozhdennaia sovest'."

13. S.A. Buryanov, "Gosudarstvennaia politika v Rossiiskoi Federatsii."

14. Anna Zakatnova, "Tserkov' dobavit pravitel'stvu golovnoi boli," *Nezavisimaya Gazeta*, 24 August 2001.

15. Maxim Shevchenko, "Eshche raz o voinakh myshei i liagushek," *NG-Religii*, 26 December 2001, 1,4.

16. Ibid.

17. S.A. Buryanov, "Svoboda sovesti v kontekste problem formirovaniia grazhdanskogo obshchestva v Rossii," *Zakonodatel'stvo o svobode sovesti i pravoprimenitel'naia praktika v sfere ego deistvii*, (Moscow: Institute for the Study of Religion and Law, 2001), 134–139.

18. Ibid.

19. Dmitrii Pavlovich, "Kremlevskaia pop-politika," *Versiya*, 20 November 2001, 10–11.

20. Ye.S. Elbakyan and S.V. Medvedko, "Sotsial'nyi proekt sovremennogo rossiiskogo veruiushchego: obshchie chert," *Zakonodatel'stvo o svobode sovesti i pravoprimenitel'naia praktika v sfere ego deistviia*, Moscow, 2001, 151–168.

21. Mikhail Tul'sky, "Rol' tserkvi v zhizni rossiiskogo obshchestva," *NG-Religii*, 9 August 2000, 3.

22. G.Ye. Gudim-Levkovich, "Religioznaia situatsiia v Arkhangelskoi oblasti v kontse 20 veka," *Zakonodatel'stvo o svobode sovesti i pravoprimenitel'naia praktika v sfere ego deistviia*, Moscow, 2001, 109–126.

23. Alla Astakhova, "Verish'—ne verish'" *Segodnya*, 7 February 2001.

24. See, for example, Andrei Zolotov, "'Protocols of Zion' Puts Church in Hot Water," *The Moscow Times*, 14 January 2002.

25. Nicolai Berdyaev, "Sud'ba Rossii," Moscow, 1990, 242.

10

Social Capital in Russia's Regions

Judyth L. Twigg

Russian society is highly diverse. Any study of social capital and social cohesion in Russia must acknowledge that their quality and scope will vary significantly across eleven time zones. This chapter disaggregates the study of social capital in Russia at the regional level, asking the following questions: Which Russian regions possess the "most" social capital? Which have the least? How do these measurements vary over time? Why do these spatial and temporal differentials exist? And, perhaps most importantly, how are they significant?

Measuring Russian Social Capital

The operationalization and measurement of social capital is daunting in any context. Scholars attempting to apply the concept of social capital in the West—where it originated and where it has demonstrated the most significance—have encountered significant disagreement and controversy. The application of this conceptual tool to the Russian case treads an even more perilous intellectual and practical minefield. It is not immediately obvious that social capital, as currently defined in the Western scholarly literature, is an appropriate construct for use in a non-Western society. Furthermore, the lack of comparable data for Russia, as compared to most Western countries, on such key social capital–related variables as informal group membership and interpersonal trust, presents significant measurement challenges.

Yet at this early stage of post-Soviet Russia's social and political development, these conceptual objections should not be construed as prohibitive. Rather, they should serve as guidelines for due methodological rigor and interpretive caution. In the abstract, however, there is little reason to believe that the basic premise behind the utility of social capital—that relationships among persons, groups, and communities that foster trust and facilitate action can contribute to a society's personal, political, and economic health—cannot be an idea potentially as powerful for Russia as for any other country in the world.

A substantial literature on the significance of social capital in Russia has evolved since the late 1990s. That literature demonstrates a meaningful and positive impact of social capital in Russia, in terms of health, democratic development, and just plain "getting things done." This chapter, however, is less concerned with the sources and impacts of social capital than it is with how social capital in Russia has been measured, and how those previous measurement techniques might be applied more comprehensively to Russia's regions. The vast majority of studies of social capital analyze or compare countries at the national level. As Petro[1] has argued, however, social capital very probably originates and adheres much more significantly within smaller localities. After all, it is at the level of the community, or even more locally within small community-based groups, that people form the associations and amorphous bonds of trust that are said to be the hallmark of social capital and social cohesion. Kennedy, Kawachi, and Brainerd agree, with findings on the relationship between social capital and health suggesting that "the proximally experienced social context is more significant to health than the general national economic and social context."[2]

Kennedy, Kawachi, and Brainerd consolidate three variables into their operationalization of social capital—trust or mistrust in government, quality of work relations, and civic engagement in politics—and derive their data entirely from surveys conducted by the All-Russian Center for Public Opinion Research.[3] Rose employs more in-depth survey data (the New Russia Barometer survey) to measure social capital in terms of Russians' self-reported involvement in formal and informal networks.[4] Marsh closely follows Putnam's lead in constructing a "civic community index" based on election and referendum turnout, newspaper publishing, and membership in clubs and association.[5] Petro also uses associational activity, together with economic prosperity and trust in government, as indicators of the presence of social capital.[6]

As rich as these works are in their demonstration of the significance of social capital in the Russian case, few have yet taken, in a comprehensive manner, the basic initial step of measuring which regions enjoy more, and which regions less, social capital.[7] The methodological challenges of measuring social capital in all of Russia's regions are profound. First, the direction of the causal arrows is generally unclear. In Petro's formulation, for example, is it economic prosperity that has engendered the presence of social capital, or vice versa? The same question could be asked of virtually every subindicator of social capital, as Putnam's "virtuous" or "vicious" cycles of social capital clearly indicate a circular relationship between variables. Fortunately, for this study, which seeks only to measure the comparative degree of social capital in each region, the point is moot. Indeed, the motivation behind the somewhat limited aspiration of this chapter stems singularly from this methodological point. If the purpose were broader, to assess the sources or the consequences of social capital in relation to other variables such as individual-level health, economic growth, or democratization, then of course great caution would have to be exercised in the construction of the Social Capital Index and other variable indices in order to avoid specification. Since the end game here, however, is merely the construction of a Social Capital Index, then any and all possible contributors to, and indicators of, social capital can be considered for inclusion, resulting ultimately in a more comprehensive and robust (although admittedly exploratory) comparative measurement tool.

Another concern in measuring regional social capital is the fact that Russia's 89 regions themselves are not homogenous. Each region, with very few exceptions, sports an array of rural and urban landscapes, relatively economically prosperous and less prosperous areas, and more or less mutually trusting and socially engaged populations. Ideally, relevant data would be available to incorporate indicators of social capital at the subregional level into an index that could compare not only region with region, but also variations within regions, including urban/rural and other further disaggregated settings. Unfortunately, those data are not forthcoming. In fact, the available data set is inadequate in some instances even for comprehensive comparative study at the regional level; for example, the vast majority of nationwide survey data sets do not contain a sufficiently large sample from each region to construct a statistically complete list of all 89 regions, or even all 78 ethnic republics, oblasts, and krais (including Moscow and St. Petersburg, and eliminating the autonomous okrugs and oblast).[8] In other words, any regional construction of a social capital measurement must be interpreted with the assumption that the aggregate measurement masks significant within-region variation.

Operationalization and Measurement of Social Capital in Russia's Regions

With these caveats in mind, a Social Capital Index for Russia's regions can be constructed. As indicated earlier, this index will be inclusive of a wide array of potential contributors to social capital, since the goal is merely a ranking of regions rather than a statistical comparison of this index with any other variable or index. Ten variables are included here, all of them derived from data in the Russian State Committee for Statistics annual publication *Regiony Rossii*,[9] with the exception of voter turnout (from the East-West Institute's handbook *The Republics and Regions of the Russian Federation*)[10] and civic association (from the Web site of Civil Society International).[11] This section will outline the way the ten variables are constructed and then present the top ten and bottom ten regions as they rank on each individual variable.[12] Rankings are presented for three different years— 1993, 1996, 1999—to illustrate changes, if any, during the first decade of the post-Soviet era.

Communications

One of the key aspects of social capital is networking, the ability of people to communicate with one another. A wide variety of indicators carry the potential to measure this ability. Most accessible in the Russian context are data on the percentage of households with telephones. Because data are only available separately for urban and rural households, the communications variable in the Social Capital Index is constructed as a weighted average, as follows:

> *Rank [Communications] = Rank [(percentage of households in a region that are urban)(percentage of urban households that have telephones) + (percentage of households in a region that are rural)(percentage of rural households that have telephones)]*

Crime

Trust is the most commonly cited factor in the conceptualization of social capital. Unfortunately, because of the limitations of survey data (as described above) for a ranking involving each region, trust cannot be included here in a direct, self-described measurement of individual feelings and assessments. A useful proxy indicator for trust at a base level, however, is crime. People will trust one another, and their society as a whole, if they feel safe in their own homes and on their neighborhood streets. Again, the precise operationalization of the crime indicator is derived from available data:

> *Rank [Crime] = Rank {Inverse Rank [Overall per capita registered crime rate] + Inverse Rank [Per capita murder and attempted murder rate]}*

Table 10.1

Regional Rankings—Communications

1993	1996	1999
top ten		
1 Moscow City	Moscow City	Moscow City
2 St. Petersburg	St. Petersburg	St. Petersburg
3 Magadan	Magadan	Kamchatka
4 Kalmykia	Kamchatka	Tomsk
5 North Ossetia	Kalmykia	Komi
6 Komi	Komi	Kalmykia
7 Murmansk	Karachaevo-Cherkessia	North Ossetia
8 Karachaevo-Cherkessia	Sakha/Yakutia	Arkhangelsk
9 Leningrad City	Leningrad City	Karachaevo-Cherkessia
10 Sakha/Yakutia	Murmansk	Murmansk
bottom ten		
1 Tatarstan	Dagestan	Dagestan
2 Bryansk	Tver	Chita
3 Irkutsk	Chita	Bryansk
4 Tver	Bryansk	Tyva
5 Chita	Kaliningrad	Kursk
6 Ulyanovsk	Irkutsk	Tver
7 Dagestan	Penza	Vladimir
8 Penza	Vladimir	Amur
9 Krasnoyarsk	Tatarstan	Irkutsk
10 Kaliningrad	Krasnoyarsk	Penza

For this and the other "bottom ten" tables, the 76th ranking region is listed first, so the table reads from the bottom up, or from worst to tenth-worst on the specified variable.

Table 10.2

Regional Rankings—Crime

1993	1996	1999
top ten		
1 Dagestan	Kabardino-Balkaria	Dagestan
2 Moscow City	Belgorod	Kabardino-Balkaria
3 Kabardino-Balkaria	Karachaevo-Cherkessia	Moscow City
4 Penza	Orel	Belgorod
5 Voronezh	Adygea	Bashkortostan
6 Bashkortostan	Lipetsk	Penza
7 Karachaevo-Cherkessia	Penza	Lipetsk
8 Belgorod	Kostromo	Voronezh
9 Moscow Oblast	Kalmykia	Tambov
10 Ulyanovsk	Murmansk	Kursk
bottom ten		
1 Primorski Krai	Perm	Irkutsk
2 Sakhalin	Primorski Krai	Khabarovsk
3 Tyva	Khabarovsk	Buryatia
4 Tomsk	Sverdlovsk	Perm
5 Novosibirsk	Irkutsk	Kurgan
6 Leningrad Oblast	Krasnoyarsk	Sakhalin
7 Khabarovsk	Tyumen	Tyva
8 Karelia	Novosibirsk	Primorskii Krai
9 Pskov	Chita	Chita
10 Kaliningrad	Buryatia	Leningrad Oblast

Table 10.3

Regional Rankings—Culture

1993	1996	1999
top ten		
1 Tyva	Moscow City	St. Petersburg
2 Orel	St. Petersburg	Moscow
3 Mary El	Mary El	Yaroslavl
4 Mordovia	Yaroslavl	Mary El
5 Moscow City	Volgograd	Karelia
6 Chuvash	Ivanov	Pskov
7 Kaliningrad	Nizhny Novgorod	Tver
8 St. Petersburg	Samara	Kostromo
9 Novgorod	Mordovia	Kaliningrad
10 Ivanov	Kirov	Saratov
bottom ten		
1 Moscow Oblast	Dagestan	Dagestan
2 Dagestan	Adygea	Chita
3 Chita	Moscow Oblast	Adygea
4 Altai rep	Altai rep	Tyumen
5 Kar-Cher	Kab-Balk	Amur
6 Rostov	Tyva	Orenburg
7 Novosibirsk	Kamachatka	Altai Krai
8 Kab-Balk	Buryatia	Moscow Oblast
9 Krasnodar	Novosibirsk	Magadan
10 Tyumen	Chita	Altai rep

Culture

Another type of networking measurement is the availability of public space for people to network, to meet face-to-face outside the workplace. Theaters, museums, and libraries provide public meeting places of this type. Moreover, Stolle and Rochon have found that participation in cultural affairs correlates highly with generalized trust within a society.[13] In conjunction with these public networks, the publication of books and newspapers in a region signifies important engagement with public affairs and society.

> *Rank [Culture] = Rank {Rank [Per capita attendance at theaters in the region] + Rank [Per capita attendance at museums in the region] + Rank [Number of available library books, per capita] + Rank [Per capita publication of newspapers in the region] + Rank [Per capita publication of books and brochures in the region]}*

Table 10.4

Regional Rankings—Civic Engagement

2001

top ten
1 Moscow
2 St. Petersburg
3 Nizhny Novgorod
4 Krasnodar
5 Primorski Krai
6 Samara
7 Sverdlovsk
8 Khabarovsk
9 Chelyabinsk
10 Irkutsk

Table 10.5

Regional Rankings—Political Engagement

1993	1996	1999
top ten		
1 Karachaevo-Cherkessia	Bashkortostan	Kabardino-Balkaria
2 Pskov	Belgorod	Dagestan
3 Belgorod	Kalmykia	Mordovia
4 Gorno-Altai	Rostov	Tatarstan
5 Ryazan	Pskov	Bashkortostan
6 Bryansk	Penza	Gorno-Altai
7 Orel	Tver	Orel
8 Smolensk	Gorno-Altai	Tyva
9 Kursk	Kurgan	Saratov
10 Tambov	Orel	Yaroslavl
bottom ten		
1 Tatarstan	Murmansk	Leningrad Oblast
2 Kamchatka	Kamchatka	Sverdlovsk
3 Udmurtia	St. Petersburg	Sakhalin
4 Khakhassia	Komi	North Ossetia
5 Perm	Irkutsk	St. Petersburg
6 Tomsk	Sakhalin	Irkutsk
7 Khabarovsk	Sverdlovsk	Kemerovo
8 Mary El	Buryatia	Krasnoyarsk
9 Magadan	Udmurtia	Chuvash
10 Komi	Chita	Kaliningrad

Civic Engagement

Traditionally, the level of involvement in civic associations is one of the standard measurements of social capital. Again, the limitations of survey data prohibit a wholly accurate presentation of self-reported involvement in such associations. But data are available for the raw numbers of nongovernmental organizations present in each region and registered with a primary international repository of such information, Civil Society International (CSI). More than any other category, these rankings must be viewed with caution, since the NGOs represented in this list are by definition skewed toward those with significant international ties or exposure. Also, many regions are not included in CSI's listing. For this reason, a tentative "top ten" is listed here, but a "bottom ten" is impossible to construct. Also, data are only available for the present (2001).

Rank [Civic engagement] = Rank [Number of NGOs listed on CSI's Web site]

Political Engagement

In most standard measurements of political engagement and its relationship to civil society, voter turnout is the primary indicator. Statistics are taken from the 1993 and 1999 parliamentary elections and the 1996 presidential election.

Rank [Political engagement] = Rank [Voter turnout for the relevant year]

Family

Another measure of trust can be derived from the stability and strength of family relationships. Presumably, if families form a core of predictability and trust, then those habits have the potential to extend outward more broadly to society as a whole. The family variable is derived as follows:

Rank [Family] = Rank {Rank [Marriage rate] + Inverse Rank [Divorce rate]}

Work

People's trust in society and in one another can also stem from their workplace experiences. Faith in the stability of one's job can cascade into trust that society will meet other expectations as well; conversely, job instability is likely to

Table 10.6

Regional Rankings—Family

1993	1996	1999
top ten		
1 Gorno-Altai	Dagestan	Gorno-Altai
2 Bashkortostan	Kabardino-Balkaria	Chuvash
3 Dagestan	Mordovia	Dagestan
4 Mordovia	Bashkortostan	Tambov
5 Orenburg	Orenburg	Orel
6 Penza	Penza	Kurgan
7 Tambov	North Ossetia	Chita
8 Stavropol	Tambov	Altai Krai
9 Orel	Ryazan	Penza
10 Adygea	Orel	Kursk
bottom ten		
1 Sakhalin	Komi	Khabarovsk
2 Karelia	Karelia	Leningrad Oblast
3 Leningrad Oblast	Khabarovsk	Primorski Krai
4 Novgorod	Magadan	Karelia
5 Kamchatka	Sverdlovsk	Sverdlovsk
6 Tver	Primorski Krai	Pskov
7 Murmansk	Pskov	Sakhalin
8 Pskov	Krasnoyarsk	Novgorod
9 Ivanov	Novgorod	Smolensk
10 Khabarovsk	Sakhalin	Nizhny Novgorod

Table 10.7

Regional Rankings—Work

1993	1996	1999
top ten		
1 Orenburg	Orenburg	Moscow City
2 Tatarstan	Tver	St. Petersburg
3 Kursk	Moscow City	Yaroslavl
4 Sakha/Yakutia	Ryazan	Samara
5 Tver	Tatarstan	Nizhny Novgorod
6 Tula	Belgorod	Kaluga
7 Vologda	Lipetsk	Tula
8 Bashkortostan	Sakha/Yakutia	Moscow Oblast
9 Belgorod	Kemerovo	Leningrad Oblast
10 Voronezh	Tula	Volgograd
bottom ten		
1 Dagestan	North Ossetia	Tyva
2 Kabardino-Balkaria	Dagestan	Kabardino-Balkaria
3 Karachaevo-Cherkessia	Karachaevo-Cherkessia	North Ossetia
4 Gorno-Altai	Tyva	Kalmykia
5 Kalmykia	Kabardino-Balkaria	Chita
6 Ivanov	Ivanov	Bryansk
7 Kostromo	Chita	Dagestan
8 Sakhalin	Penza	Arkhangelsk
9 St. Petersburg	Murmansk	Murmansk
10 Adygea	Buryatia	Mordovia

produce frustration and resentment against society as a whole. The Social Capital Index for work therefore takes into account employment statistics, with the obvious caveat that these official statistics mask a considerable amount of both hidden (shadow economy) employment and hidden unemployment. The official statistics, however, do capture work in steady jobs rather than the shadow economy's perhaps lucrative but also probably unstable and short-term offerings. For the purposes, therefore, of measuring contributions to social capital, official unemployment statistics may be adequate.

Rank [Work] = Inverse Rank [Unemployment rate]

Health

Healthy people are more likely to feel positively about themselves and about the society in which they live. Even those in good health who see large numbers of their family members and coworkers ill and dying are apt to question the legitimacy of their societal structures. Furthermore, a significant body of research has shown that positive levels of social capital contribute to good health, making health indicators an effective proxy for social capital. The health indicator here is derived from both ends of the life span: infant mortality and life expectancy.

Rank [Health] = Rank {Inverse Rank [Infant mortality] + Rank [Life expectancy]}

Safety Net

The cohesiveness between different economic strata of a society might serve as another measure of its social capital. The larger the gap between rich and poor, the more a society might be expected to display significant fissures. Even in a situation where some small percentage of the population has become unusually rich, those social fissures might be mitigated if a sufficiently robust safety net were constructed as a floor below which the poorest of the poor are not allowed to fall. In Russia, data are readily available to measure the percentage of the population in each region whose income falls beneath a region-specific subsistence minimum income.

Rank [Safety net] = Inverse rank [Percentage of population with incomes below subsistence minimum]

Table 10.8

Regional Rankings—Health

1993	1996	1999
top ten		
1 Karachaevo-Cherkessia	Mordovia	Adygea
2 Penza	St. Petersburg	Moscow City
3 Voronezh	Belgorod	St. Petersburg
4 Mordovia	Moscow City	Murmansk
5 Samara	Voronezh	Belgorod
6 Chuvash	Adygea	Tatarstan
7 Belgorod	Penza	Krasnodar
8 Kursk	Mary El	Tyumen
9 Kaluga	Vladimir	Mordovia
10 Vladimir	Kalmykia	Omsk
bottom ten		
1 Tyva	Tyva	Tyva
2 Gorno-Altai	Altai Krai	Gorno-Altai
3 Irkutsk	Khakhassia	Chita
4 Krasnoyarsk	Amur	Itkursk
5 Tomsk	Primorskii krai	Krasnoyarsk
6 Khakhassia	Chita	Kemerovo
7 Chita	Magadan	Amur
8 Kemerovo	Krasnoyarsk	Khakhassia
9 Kamchatka	Kemerovo	Ivanov
10 Kurgan	Pskov	Buryatia

Table 10.9

Regional Rankings—Safety Net

1993	1996	1999
top ten		
1 Tyumen	Ulyanovsk	Tyumen
2 Moscow City	Tyumen	Murmansk
3 Belgorod	Tula	Komi
4 Kemerovo	Moscow City	Moscow City
5 Ulyanovsk	Lipetsk	Samara
6 Tula	Novgorod	Novgorod
7 Gorno-Altai	Belgorod	Tatarstan
8 Tatarstan	Murmansk	Krasnoyarsk
9 Orel	Bryansk	Rostov
10 Kaluga	Nizhny Novgorod	Perm
bottom ten		
1 Tyva	Tyva	Chita
2 Amur	Amur	Tyva
3 Adygea	Orenburg	Kalmykia
4 Orenburg	Adygea	Mary El
5 Kalmykia	Kalmykia	Penza
6 Kabardino-Balkaria	Kabardino-Balkaria	Chuvash
7 Stavropol	Stavropol	Mordovia
8 Tambov	Tambov	Tver
9 Kurgan	Kurgan	Ivanov
10 Buryatia	North Ossetia	Karachaevo-Cherkessia

Institutions of Higher Education

It would be inappropriate to assume that more highly educated people are more capable of building the networks and internalizing the trust inherent in social capital. The presence of educational institutions in a given region, however, provides another set of meeting spaces where interpersonal networking can take place. Colleges and universities also tend to sponsor lectures, seminars, and other events open to the public that can serve as incubators of social capital.

> *Rank [Higher education] = Rank [Per capita number of students enrolled at institutions of higher education in the region]*

Table 10.10

Regional Rankings—Higher Education

1993	1996	1999
top ten		
1 Moscow City	Moscow City	Moscow City
2 St. Petersburg	St. Petersburg	St. Petersburg
3 Tomsk	Tomsk	Tomsk
4 North Ossetia	North Ossetia	Novosibirsk
5 Novosibirsk	Novosibirsk	Adygea
6 Mordovia	Mordovia	Khabarovsk
7 Khabarovsk	Khabarovsk	North Ossetia
8 Voronezh	Gorno-Altai	Orel
9 Samara	Adygea	Mordovia
10 Ivanov	Orel	Ivanov
bottom ten		
1 Leningrad Oblast	Leningrad Oblast	Leningrad Oblast
2 Kursk	Sakhalin	Sakhalin
3 Sakhalin	Murmansk	Kaluga
4 Murmansk	Chita	Tyva
5 Sakha/Yakutia	Vladimir	Smolensk
6 Chita	Smolensk	Tula
7 Kamchatka	Kaluga	Komi
8 Vladimir	Tula	Murmansk
9 Komi	Kirov	Krasnodar
10 Tyva	Krasnodar	Tver

Social Capital Index

With these ten variables, an overall Social Capital Index can be constructed. The particular contours of the index could be drawn in a variety of different ways, with variables weighted depending on judgments about their relative importance and legitimacy in the production of social capital. For these admittedly preliminary purposes, however, the index is composed of a simple unweighted average of the ranks of each of the constituent variables.

> *Rank [Social Capital Index] = Rank {Rank [Communications] + Rank [Crime] + Rank [Culture] + Rank [Civic engagement] + Rank [Political engagement] + Rank [Family] + Rank [Work] + Rank [Health] + Rank [Safety net] + Rank [Higher education]}*

By nature of the statistical techniques used here, of course, none of these rankings measures the quantitative distance between the "best" and "worst" within Russia. Without some sense of scale, it is impossible to detect just how much more social capital Moscow possessed than Chita in 1999, for example, according to these measures. Illustrative graphs for some of the component indicators of social capital can serve to mark the degree to which there is indeed a substantial gap between the top-ranked and bottom-ranked regions on these scales. For five randomly selected statistics—infant mortality, marriage rate, voter turnout, unemployment rate, and poverty rate—Figures 10.1 through 10.5 show the top three and bottom three Russian regions, along with analogous figures for the United States, for purposes of international comparison. The indicators for the United States show a more positive contribution to social capital, with the U.S. average besting even the top Russian region, in every category except voter turnout. For this crucial measurement of civic engagement, citizen involvement is lower on average in the U.S. than in even the lowest-ranking Russian region.

Interpretation of Regional Rankings

The first question that must be asked of any study of this type is whether the operationalization of the key variables is meaningful. In this case, the issue is whether the Social Capital Index is measuring something unique, as it is tempting to look at the constituent variables—indeed, at the overall concept of social capital itself—and suspect that the index is simply rewarding the more urban, wealthy regions. To test this hypothesis, the index rankings can be correlated with regional statistics for wealth (gross regional product and average per capita household expenditures) and for the per-

Table 10.11

Regional Rankings—Social Capital Index

1993	1996	1999
top fifteen		
1 Orel	Moscow City	Moscow City
2 Belgorod	Orel	St. Petersburg
3 Voronezh	Belgorod	Voronezh
4 Moscow City	Tatarstan	Belgorod
5 Samara	Omsk	Tatarstan
6 Mordovia	Voronezh	Orel
7 Kursk	St. Petersburg	Samara
8 Tula	Kalmykia	Rostov
9 Bashkortostan	Mordovia	Novosibirsk
10 Kaluga	Lipetsk	Mordovia
11 Chuvash	Bashkortostan	Bashkortostan
12 Ulyanovsk	Samara	Yaroslavl
13 Penza	Ryazan	Saratov
14 Tatarstan	Ulyanovsk	Lipetsk
15 Tambov	Yaroslavl	Omsk
bottom fifteen		
1 Chita	Chita	Chita
2 Sakhalin	Tyva	Tyva
3 Leningrad Oblast	Primorski Krai	Buryatia
4 Tyva	Irkutsk	Khakhassia
5 Perm	Khakhassia	Kemerovo
6 Tomsk	Buryatia	Sakhalin
7 Chelyabinsk	Khabarovsk	Leningrad Oblast
8 Irkutsk	Arkhangelsk	Amur
9 Primorski Krai	Perm	Smolensk
10 Kamchatka	Sakhalin	Vladimir
11 Khabarovsk	Amur	Irkutsk
12 Tyumen	Magadan	Ivanov
13 Astrakhan	Komi	Kurgan
14 Krasnodar	Pskov	Tver
15 Amur	Sverdlovsk	Perm

Fifteen rather than ten regions are listed in the "top fifteen" and "bottom fifteen" tables, for a more complete assessment of the "best" and "worst" regions. Also, for 1993 and 1996, only nine of the ten variables are calculated in the overall index, since statistics for Civic Engagement (numbers of NGOs) are not available for those years. Finally, it should be noted that 2001 data for Civic Engagement are incorporated into the last column together with 1999 indicators for all other variables.

centage of the regional population that lives in urban areas (see Table 10.12, on page 185). It is important to stress that the intent here is not to discover correlation or causality for its own sake, but merely to explore the possibility of spurious correlation of the Social Capital Index with its constituent variables.

These findings are somewhat surprising. First of all, there is not a consistent, across-the-board relationship between wealth and social capital. Be-

Figure 10.1 **Infant Mortality, United States (1998) and Selected Russian Regions (1999)**

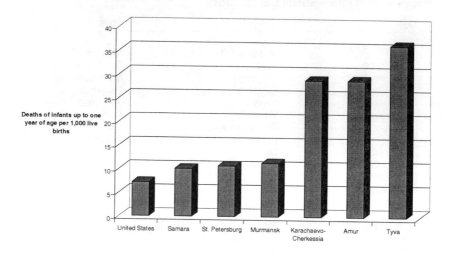

Figure 10.2 **Marriage Rate, United States (1998) and Selected Russian Regions (1999)**

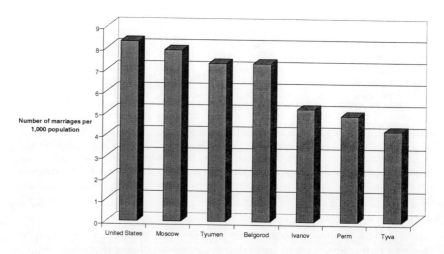

Figure 10.3 **Voter Turnout, United States and Selected Russian Regions
(1996 presidential elections)**

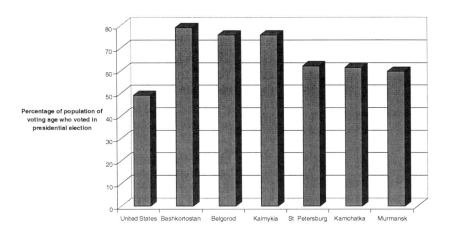

Figure 10.4   **Unemployment Rate, United States (1998)
and Selected Russian Regions (1999)**

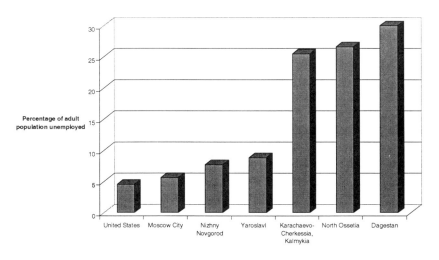

Figure 10.5 **Poverty Rates, United States (1998) and Selected Russian Regions (1999)**

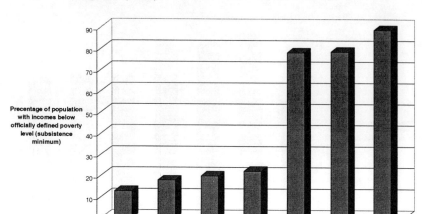

cause the Social Capital Index is measured by rank, the highest value for that variable indicates the presence of the least amount of social capital, so that for 1993 the presence of a positive statistical relationship suggests that the wealthier regions enjoyed the lesser stores of social capital. Similarly, for 1993 and 1996, these correlations suggest that more rural rather than urban regions scored higher in the measure of overall social capital. That relationship seems to disappear by 1999, although a more intuitively obvious relationship—a positive correlation between at least one measure of wealth and social capital—appears for the first time in the most recent year.

In addition, there is no statistically significant relationship between the percentage of a region's population that is ethnic Russian, and that region's ranking on the Social Capital Index. This finding contradicts Marsh, who claims that "non-Russian, indigenous populations . . . may be a factor in explaining their conspicuous lack of attributes associated with a civic community."[14] Instead, this study suggests that non-Russian populations within Russia may indeed be capable of building and benefiting from social capital, perhaps both within their own ethnic communities and between themselves and their ethnic Russian neighbors—a potentially fruitful direction for further study.

A careful look at the rankings for the indicators comprising the Social Capital Index also reveals that there is sometimes remarkable inconsistency in the lists of "top" regions and "bottom" regions. Some regions that rank in the top ten on some indicators simultaneously rank in the bottom ten on others. For example, Dagestan appears in the highest ranks on crime and the family, but near the bottom for communications and culture. Similarly, Kabardino-Balkaria

Table 10.12

Interpretation of Regional Rankings

	% Population that is urban (for relevant year)	Gross regional product (for relevant year)	Average per capita household expenditures (for relevant year)	% Population that is Russian, 1989
1993 Social capital index rankings	0.273*	0.250*	0.311**	−0.094
1996 Social capital index rankings	0.239*	0.118	0.108	−0.072
1999 Social capital index rankings	−0.060	−0.118	−0.273*	−0.048

[i]1989 is the last year for which accurate ethnicity figures by region are available. Presumably these data will be updated when fall 2002 census figures become available.

[ii]Spearman's rho is used here, since one of the variables is entirely composed of rankings.

*Correlation is significant at the .05 level.

**Correlation is significant at the .01 level.

scores well on political engagement, the family, and crime, but very poorly on culture, unemployment, and the safety net. Even St. Petersburg, which comes out near the top of the list for most indicators, scores very low on voter turn-out. This inconsistency may point to a profound flaw within the concept of social capital itself—the components used to construct it are so dissimilar that it is, by definition, a concept too artificial to be meaningful—or, more likely, social capital is such a complex notion that the instruments used to measure it must range sufficiently broadly to capture all of its nuances.

Another set of significant observations about the regional Social Capital Index rankings relates to the variation—or lack thereof—across the decade under study. Over half of the top fifteen regions are consistently present in that top tier for all three years: Orel, Belgorod, Voronezh, Moscow City, Samara, Mordovia, Bashkortostan, and Tatarstan. Another four are present in both 1996 and 1999—Omsk, St. Petersburg, Lipetsk, and Yaroslavl—with Ulyanovsk on the list in 1993 and 1996. The same consistency, although to a lesser degree, prevails in the "bottom fifteen." Six regions hold the dubious distinction of making that list all three times (Chita, Sakhalin, Tyva, Perm, Irkutsk, and Amur), with five others (Leningrad Oblast, Primorski Krai, Khabarovsk, Khakhassia, and Buryatia) present for two out of three.

The geography of these rankings is also remarkable (see Table 10.13). Virtually every region in the top fifteen rankings for at least two of the three studied years is located in European Russia, from the central, north-west, or Volga regions (Bashkortostan in the Urals and Omsk in Western Siberia are the exceptions). Similarly, almost every region consistently rank-ing in the bottom fifteen is in either Siberia or the Far East, with the excep-tion of Perm (Urals) and Leningrad Oblast (northwest). These observations lead to a suspicion that a correlation between sheer distance from Moscow and Social Capital Index ranking would produce a statistically significant result—a suspicion that is confirmed by the data. Perhaps this relationship stems from the higher population densities in the European part of Russia, or perhaps from some other factor—but again, these preliminary observa-tions suggest potential avenues for further research.

Within the entire list of regions, 19 changed ranks significantly during the 1990s (defined as a shift of 25 or more rank places within or across the three years studied). St. Petersburg, Saratov, Rostov, Udmurtia, Chelyabinsk, Novosibirsk, Tomsk, Tyumen, and Kamchatka all rose to notably higher rankings over time, while Bryansk, Vladimir, Kaluga, Ryazan, Smolensk, Tula, Kursk, Kemerovo, Buryatia, and Sakha/Yakutia all fell precipitously down on the list. Again, geography seems relevant, as most of the rising regions are from the eastern part of the country, while those with social capi-tal in sharp decline are primarily from the central macroregions. Perhaps this

Table 10.13

Geography of Regional Rankings

	1993 Social Capital Index	1996 Social Capital Index	1999 Social Capital Index
Regional capital's distance from Moscow	0.561*	0.493*	0.302*

*Correlation is significant at the .05 level.

qualitative observation, together with the statistical analysis revealing a steadily declining correlation between distance from the capital and Social Capital Index during the years under study, suggests a tentative move toward convergence and a diminution of the country's east-west divide.

Finally, an examination of the particular economic and political characteristics of the regions at the top and bottom of the social capital rankings seems to offer little of explanatory value. Both within the top fifteen and within the bottom fifteen, the regions vary significantly in terms of the political party represented by their governors; the stability and quality of gubernatorial leadership; endowment with natural resources; regional leadership attitudes toward foreign investment, market-oriented economic reforms, and the need for policies aimed at maintaining an effective social safety net; and relations with Moscow. For example, one of the "surprises" of the top social capital ranks, Orel, has a strong governor in Yegor Stroev, who has worked hard to construct an effective balance between market reforms and social protection. It is tempting to attribute Orel's high scores in this study, despite it being a relatively financially and resource-poor region without a favorable investment climate, to Stroev's leadership, and to suspect that effective and stable leadership might emerge as a factor accounting for significant stores of social capital in "surprising" places across the country. Similarly authoritative and talented leaders have been in place in Samara and, of course, Moscow. Yet several other of the high-ranking regions, in particular Omsk, Mordovia, and Voronezh, have been plagued with governors and other regional executives accused of chronic mismanagement and/or corruption. In other words, there is nothing of obvious political or policy significance at the regional level to explain where any particular region might rank on the Social Capital Index scale.

In other words, it is entirely possible that this Social Capital Index does indeed capture something inherent within the populations of these regions, something beyond the scope of state policies or any other official statistic. The extensive literature on social capital in developed societies reveals that social capital can produce, over time, an array of benefits, ranging from health to wealth to effective democracy. As policy-makers and international investors look at Russia and wonder where the "best bets" for the future may lie within that country, it may be fruitful for them to take a second look at the regions with high levels of present-day social capital. That quality, even in currently poor and underdeveloped regions, could serve as a crystal ball for potential development in many spheres.

Notes

1. Nicolai N. Petro, "Creating Social Capital in Russia: The Novgorod Model," *World Development* 29 (2001): 229–244.

2. Bruce Kennedy, Ichiro Kawachi, and Elizabeth Brainerd, "The Role of Social Capital in the Russian Mortality Crisis," *World Development* 26 (1998): 2037.

3. Kennedy, Kawachi, and Brainerd, "The Role of Social Capital in the Russian Mortality Crisis," p. 2031.

4. Richard Rose, "How Much Does Social Capital Add to Individual Health? A Survey Study of Russians," *Social Science and Medicine* 51 (2000): 1421–1435.

5. Christopher Marsh, "Social Capital and Democracy in Russia," *Communist and Post-Communist Studies* 33 (2000): 183–199; Christopher Marsh and Nikolas K. Gvosdev, eds., *Civil Society and the Search for Justice in Russia* (Lanham, MD: Lexington Books, 2002); Robert D. Putnam, *Making Democracy Work: Civic Traditions in Modern Italy* (Princeton, NJ: Princeton University Press, 1993).

6. Petro, "Creating Social Capital in Russia," pp. 230–231.

7. Marsh's pioneering study (2000) has done so, as a first step toward discerning the link between social capital and democracy in Russia. He uses only three variables—voter turnout, newspaper publishing, and membership in clubs and cultural associations—to construct a "civic community index."

8. As Rose (2000, p. 1425) points out, the vast majority of survey data used for the measurement of social capital are less than satisfying methodologically, since they generally involve survey questions designed for other purposes and subsequently "retrofitted" by other scholars constructing social capital indicators.

9. *Regiony Rossii* (Moscow: Goskomstat, 1998, 1999, 2000).

10. Robert W. Orttung, ed., *The Republics and Regions of the Russian Federation: A Guide to Politics, Policies, and Leaders* (Armonk, NY: M.E. Sharpe, 2000).

11. Civil Society International, http://www.civilsoc.org.

12. Because of limited availability of data from some areas, and the need when calculating ranks to maintain consistency of data availability across all cases, only 76 of the 89 regions are included in the study. Excluded are Chechnya and Ingushetia, the Jewish Autonomous Oblast, and the ten autonomous okrugs.

13. D. Stolle and T.R. Rochon, "Are All Associations Alike? Member Diversity, Associational Type, and the Creation of Social Capital," *American Behavioral Scientist* 42 (1998): 47–65.

14. Marsh, "Social Capital and Democracy in Russia."

11

Breaching the Soviet Social Contract

Post-Soviet Social Policy Development in Ulyanovsk and Samara Oblasts

Andrew Konitzer-Smirnov

Across the territory of the newly established Russian Federation, the period spanning late 1991 to early 1992 exhibited rapid changes in the structures of regional governance.[1] During this period, the Yeltsin regime appointed new heads of administration to Russia's oblasts and krais, granting them the responsibilities of regional executive power within a federal system only recently dominated by a tightly centralized state apparatus. Charged with maintaining the welfare, integration, and health of their regions during a period of tremendous social and economic upheaval, the new heads of administration faced the daunting task of providing services and opportunities for their citizens as the federal government and state-owned enterprises rapidly shed their social responsibilities. The previous Soviet-era social contract had collapsed, leaving regional economies both more independent and more exposed.[2] This new era challenged the inexperienced governors to adapt to a policy-making environment in which the governments of federal subjects were suddenly required to strike a balance between extremely scarce resources and the provision of a minimal level of social and health services.[3] Responses varied on a rough continuum ranging from attempts to maintain substantial elements of the Soviet social contract to efforts to rapidly destroy the old system and rebuild social services and health care provision along the lines of various Western models. Regional executives' choices yielded important ramifications for the health, welfare, and cohesion of societies in all the federal subjects.

This chapter examines how the administrations of the two neighboring regions of Samara and Ulyanovsk responded to these challenges and the ramifications of their policy choices for the welfare and cohesion of their societies. It demonstrates not only the degree to which post-Soviet social policies could vary from region to region, but also how such choices impacted the structure and intensity of divisions between various "haves" and "have-nots" in society. The results of this analysis have important implications for the types of policies chosen, as well as for the study of social cohesion and social capital in Russia. With regard to policy choice, the analysis demonstrates that attempts to preserve elements of the previous Soviet social contract (and thereby the bases for Soviet-era social cohesion) face nearly insurmountable challenges in a federation marked by increasingly free inter-regional competition for capital and other economic factors. For the study of social cohesion and capital in Russia, the analysis presents another warning to researchers and analysts who speak of these issues in terms of "Russian" conditions. As in many countries of the world, variations in these factors are often as strong between federal subunits as between sovereign states, and any examination of this topic must thereby acknowledge regional diversity.

Social Cohesion, Social Welfare, and Health

As with many other recently popularized terms like "globalization," "institutions," and "culture," the concept of social cohesion has nearly as many meanings as applications.[4] Past discussions of this concept demonstrate a confusing conceptual intermingling between social *cohesion* and social *capital* (thereby obfuscating both concepts), little agreement over the causal relationship between economic performance and cohesion (is cohesion endogenous, exogenous, or both?), and definitional challenges regarding who is "cohering" around which particular issue(s), institution(s), or set of values.[5] Since it is not the function of this chapter to provide a detailed treatment of these conceptual issues, I will simply define in as clear terms as possible the conceptual framework for this particular treatment of the social cohesion issue.

The research of Jo Ritzen, William Easterly, and Michael Woolcock provides a useful starting point for framing the present analysis.[6] Drawing from the work of these authors, the present study defines a cohesive society as one in which most individuals from various social groups have access to economic opportunities and social services. This is a "minimalist" definition of social cohesion that essentially treats cohesion as the absence of exclusion from these services and opportunities. I justify this choice of definitions on the grounds that the first task in the development of social cohesion is to ensure that all social actors "have a place at the table" within a given society. With these minimal conditions satisfied, the development of "higher order" social cohesion (here defined as trust and cooperation among individuals) may proceed through the growth of social organizations and other civic activities.[7]

Having thus defined social cohesion, the next issue focuses upon how groups in contemporary Russia's subnational settings are included and excluded from economic opportunities and social services. Here I take a rather statist approach to the issue of social cohesion. Starting from the widely held conception that the Soviet Union was at base a state-dominated system with a very weak civil society, the burden for any significant social transformation necessarily falls upon the new state institutions themselves. As indicated in the preceding paragraph, an initial step in developing the barest minimum of social cohesion in the post-Soviet setting involves the inclusion of different social groups into emerging economic and social institutions. For regional administrations, this task involves striking a balance between the provision of social services and ample work opportunities, and assuring that no single socioeconomic group suffers a distinct disadvantage in its attempts to gain access to these services and opportunities. In the post-Soviet setting, where the centralized economy no longer determines the distribution of economic activities, this implies that administrations must create the conditions to attract capital while still extracting the necessary tax revenues and other resources to maintain adequate social services.[8]

Successful inclusion, defined here as the effective and "reasonable" distribution (to borrow Ritzen, Easterly, and Woolcock's terminology) of social services and equal access to economic activities, yields two minimal forms of cohesion. First, social groups respond to the state's effectiveness in guaranteeing social services and promoting economic opportunities by cohering around increasing levels of trust in state institutions. Second, in a more Parsonian sense of the term "cohesion," society coalesces around an acceptance of the particular societal division of labor that provides benefits for the broadest spectrum of groups.

Guided by this framework, the remainder of this chapter examines the different approaches of the administrations in Samara and Ulyanovsk Oblasts to solving the socioeconomic challenges of the post-Soviet era. While I based the choice of these oblasts in part upon my previous familiarity with Samara, they nonetheless offer an interesting and useful two-case comparison. The regions' proximity, comparable economic structures (at least in the early 1990s), and equivalent levels of urbanization allow one to hold a number of factors constant and thereby assess the effects of each administration's respective policies.[9]

I start first with an examination of the two approaches, demonstrating how Ulyanovsk attempted to preserve elements of previous state-society relations while Samara undertook efforts to transform them. Following this assessment, I present a tentative analysis of the relative success of these two systems in creating social cohesion by examining variation in support across social groups differentiated by income, age, education, gender, urbanization, and employment status.

To Preserve or Dismantle?

Ulyanovsk and Samara are neighboring regions situated along the Volga River in the southern European portion of Russia. According to the most recent data (1999), Samara has a population of 3,294,000 situated on 53.6 thousand square kilometers of territory. Approximately 80 percent of the region's population lives in urban settlements, and manufacturing constitutes the largest economic sector, employing 27.5 percent of the working population. The region historically maintained a reputation for its aerospace and weapons factories, the AvtoVAZ auto plant (the largest auto producer in Russia, supplying roughly 75 percent of all domestic auto production), chemical production, and oil and gas extraction and refinement. However, by 2000, the aerospace and weapons-production industry was a mere shadow of its former self, and machine production related to the AvtoVAZ plant remained the primary foundation of the economy.[10]

Though smaller and slightly less urbanized, Ulyanovsk Oblast nonetheless reflects many of the same characteristics as its neighbor. According to data from 1999, Ulyanovsk has a population of 1,463,200 situated on 37.2 thousand square kilometers of territory. Urban settlements are home to 73.1 percent of the population, and, as in Samara, manufacturing provides the largest source of employment, employing 29.1 percent of the working population. Like its neighbor, Ulyanovsk is also recognized for its aerospace, weapons, and automobile manufacturing (the UAZ auto plant). While both weapons and aircraft production have decreased in importance, Ulyanovsk's Aviastar aircraft production plant is still relatively active (among other projects, this plant produces the gigantic "Ruslan" cargo plane). In terms of other types of production, Ulyanovsk is less well endowed than its neighbor with regard to oil and gas production, but maintains some chemical production. Construction companies also play a large role in the regional economy.[11]

Throughout the 1990s, the Samara and Ulyanovsk administrations exhibited a remarkable contrast in leadership styles, ideology, and bases for legitimacy.[12] To frame the approaches in terms of their relationship to the Soviet social contract, Ulyanovsk's governor, Yuri Goriachev, took his appointed office in 1992 with promises to shelter the region's population from the perceived ravages of Gaidar's reforms through a slow retreat from the remnants of the old social contract.[13] In neighboring Samara, Governor Konstantin Titov promoted the rapid dismantling of the remnants of the old social guarantees and the restructuring of the region's economic and social service sectors.

Both the policies themselves and the means by which each administration legitimated them attracted initial supporters from specific sectors of society. Goriachev's paternal style appealed to pensioners and the workers and directors of the region's aging military and agricultural enterprises—those individuals expected to be most harmed by the economic and political changes underway in other portions of the federation. The governor's promise to provide protection against "*urrah* democrats" (those perceived as democratic zealots, many of whom lived and worked in the capital city of Ulyanovsk and later provided the nucleus of the governor's opposition), shock-therapy liberals, and criminals gained him solid support as a "defender" of the oblast.

One of the Ulyanovsk administration's first actions was to offset the effects of the price liberalization that so drastically affected the lives of Russian citizens during the winter of 1992. To accomplish this, the oblast concluded contracts with firms that had been transferred into the hands of individuals drawn from, or allying themselves with, the governor's ruling clique.[14] Through barter and partially monetarized exchanges, these firms provided food and other essential goods to consumers at some of the lowest prices in the Russian Federation.[15] In another practice reminiscent of the centralized economy, firms in the region provided many goods and services directly to projects and activities undertaken by the oblast social-services department. Agricultural enterprises also played a key role in this process. In what at least one analyst saw as an effective answer to the Russian agricultural crisis,[16] the Ulyanovsk Oblast administration created a system of *tovarnii kredit*,[17] whereby farmers and farm enterprises could receive materials like seed, fertilizer, tractor parts, fuel, and lubricants in exchange for selling portions of their harvest to the administration at below-market prices.[18]

In neighboring Samara, Konstantin Titov's administration undertook a very different approach to dealing with the challenges of the post-Soviet era. In the initial stages of reform, oblast authorities took little action to shield Samara's citizenry from the negative effects of price liberalization and the breakdown of central planning. The Titov administration, building its support among local industrialists in the energy and banking sector, small and medium *biznesmeni*, and other working-age citizens and students not tied to weapons production and other traditional industries, sought to overcome the difficulties of the post-Soviet economy by promoting new business growth and encouraging outside investment. A perusal of regional press accounts from the early 1990s indicates that Titov treated economic restructuring and liberalization as a near imperative—the only means to escape Russia's current socioeconomic woes.

Such policies succeeded in attracting a comparatively large amount of outside investment (including foreign capital) to the region and drove the steady development of new forms of economic activity that gradually offset the worst effects of the decline of the region's military-industrial and aerospace complex. Throughout the second half of the 1990s, Samara consistently appeared among the top ten regions in a variety of economic performance measures. In terms of finance, by 1996, Samara was an established "donor" region,[19] and after 1998 the region boasted one of the few balanced regional-level budgets in the federation.

An examination of wage dynamics in the two regions provides perhaps the most succinct means to assess the immediate and long-term effects of these alternative socioeconomic policies upon citizens' standard of living. In the early 1990s, a comparison of average wages taken as a percentage of each region's respective minimum cost of living (*prozhitochnyi minimum*) indicated that workers' incomes, while lower in absolute terms in Ulyanovsk than in Samara, yielded substantially greater purchasing power (at least in terms of basic goods) in the former region. Such results stemmed primarily from the Goriachev administration's complex of price supports and other social guarantees. Ulyanovsk maintained this margin over its neighbor until roughly 1995–1996 when increasing wages in Samara, along with the collapse of many social guarantees in Ulyanovsk, gave Samara's workers comparatively greater purchasing power. After 1996, standard of living measures for Samara's working population continued to pull steadily away from comparable measures in Ulyanovsk.[20]

In the long term, the Goriachev administration's attempts to retain elements of the Soviet system in a single region cast Ulyanovsk into a type of limbo between what the regional state institutions continued to promise and the reality of inadequate budgetary flows, inefficient public services, and a sputtering regional economy. As the 1990s continued, the preexisting economic structures continued to deteriorate while new capital investment sought out better business climates in other regions. In addition to the negative impact of these developments on budget revenues, the population itself suffered from stagnant wages that could not keep up with steadily creeping prices.

In terms of social-and health-sector finance, this led to the *de facto* devolution of state services to the private and nonprofit sectors at the same time, as the administration's continued adherence to paternalism left both sectors woefully underdeveloped to handle these new responsibilities. Unlike in Samara, where the administration encouraged the development of paid medical services and viable NGOs for the provision of organization of social services, Ulyanovsk had few such entities or institutions to take up the state's often involuntarily divested responsibilities. In the end, the burden fell directly upon a citizenry who, partly because of the regional administration's economic policies, lacked the means to cope with these new demands.[21] The dismal state of the private and nonprofit sector meant that those who sought nonstate services found few providers. Even those who could afford their own care and assistance were often forced to use the same services as those who were by necessity reliant on the state, thus perpetuating unnecessary burdens on the system and further reducing the resources available to the rest of society.

To borrow Mustard's formulation, the Samara Oblast administration struck a more effective balance between development in the "real economy" and the provision of health and social services. Oblast authorities made efforts to enhance the investment climate and attract business with openly liberal development policies. At the same time, the administration reduced costs in the social and health sectors and promoted the development of private and nonprofit sector alternatives for the state's divested responsibilities. The result was a comparatively more efficient and self-sustaining system. Greater economic performance produced the budget revenues necessary to finance the region's leaner social-and health-services sectors and resulted in the more or less full provision of those goods and services that the state continued to guarantee. Simply put, Samara's administration promised less than its counterparts in Ulyanovsk, but due to a combination of the above factors, actually delivered more.

Having provided this general comparison between each region's socioeconomic policies, the following two sections examine in detail the developments in the regions' health-and social-services sectors. In the course of this examination, I indicate how reforms in these sectors resulted in the exclusion and inclusion of various social groups with resulting variation in the levels of social cohesion across oblasts.

Health Care

The chairman of the Ulyanovsk Oblast Committee for Health Care summarized the Goriachev administration's approach to health care by saying that, "In medicine you need a strong vertical administration."[22] Interviews with representatives from the oblast branch of "ROSNO" (*Rossiiskoe strakhovoe narodnoe obshestvo*—a federation-wide health insurance company) indicated that, from 1992–1996, this "vertical administration" essentially meant ignoring the implementation of the Russian mandatory health insurance system and financing regional health institutions in much the same manner as was done prior to 1992. Only workers received insurance policies, while the administration covered costs for the remaining population's health services through direct payments from the oblast budget. For the most part, authorities perpetuated the Soviet-era practice of distributing finances based on an accounting system that largely ignored the actual provision of services. Many institutions continued to receive fixed budget funds based primarily on their physical size.[23]

While this "business as usual" approach (i.e., no insurance policies) helped promote the administration's paternal and conservative image, it produced chaos in the oblast health care system. Hospitals and clinics received compensation in sums that bore little or no relation to the actual services provided. Aside from a number of "star institutions" that the administration kept well financed, organizations were chronically short of supplies, and doctors (aside from the head doctors who often pocketed a large sum of the finances for themselves) suffered from chronic wage arrears and underpayment. Furthermore, receiving medical services outside of one's own region, while a problem even for those with insurance policies, was nearly impossible for those citizens of Ulyanovsk who had no policy at all.

The actual structure of the region's Soviet-era health care system also remained largely intact. While private care and the practice of performing paid services at state health institutions developed in some other regions, similar institutions and practices were slow to take root in Ulyanovsk. Whether because of the administration's egalitarianism or the regime's desire to maintain centralized control over as many aspects of regional life as possible (both explanations frequently arose in interviews), health care in Ulyanovsk remained a largely state-financed sector. One particularly well-publicized example of the administration's interference in the development of paid services involved a private dentist office in the center of Ulyanovsk city. During the governor's weekly "*selektornyi*,"[24] the head of the oblast department of health presented a report regarding some suspicious and potentially illegal activities surrounding the clinic. Apparently dissatisfied with the report, Goriachev himself implored the head of department to "dig deeper" and went on to say that this clinic "for people with stuffed wallets" had received its property for a suspiciously low price (a jab both at the clinic and the city administration), acquired a great deal of "very expensive equipment," and seemed to work far shorter hours than "the rest of us."[25]

Centralization brought additional problems, as sizeable funds passed under the control of individuals subject to very little public oversight. In 1995, an investigation by federal authorities resulted in a shake-up at the region's Territorial Fund for Mandatory Medical Insurance (TFOMS), with charges ranging from mere incompetence to fraud and embezzlement. At the time, Bank "Novyi" and Bank "Simbirsk" served as depositories for regional insurance funds. Bank "Novyi" entered bankruptcy in 1995 and was unable to return both the deposited funds and any interest accrued on the deposit between November 1994 and April 1995 (for a total loss to the oblast of a little more than 2.4 billion 1995 rubles). Bank "Simbirsk" also experienced trouble, paying only 5.7 percent of the interest accrued between October 1994 and April 1995, for a total debt of a little more than 581 million 1995 rubles. Other aspects of the report cited extremely high wages for personnel at the insurance fund, payments to local firms of sums disproportionate to the services and goods provided, and the use of insurance money to cover services and facilities that lay outside the federally mandated responsibilities of the regional health insurance system.[26]

Such a scandal was symptomatic of far-reaching transparency and accounting problems within the system. As interviews with ROSNO representatives indicated, even after regional authorities formally brought the insurance system into line with the federal standards of 1995–1996, the region's medical system finances remained a mystery. ROSNO's director, Vasily Babushkin, summarized the situation saying: "Ask a nurse, ask a doctor, ask an administrator—no one knows how much is paid, who receives the money, and where the money goes."[27] Some estimates indicated that insurance covered roughly 20–30 percent of all health-sector costs, but even a local expert on Russian medical insurance could not offer precise numbers.[28]

Conditions in Samara Oblast differed even before the collapse of the Soviet Union. Samara (then known as Kuybyshev) was among a select group of territories chosen for the implementation of the Council of Ministers' experimental "new economic mechanism" (NEM).[29] This experiment primarily focused on a new system of accounting and finance for the territories' health care systems. Instead of the traditional Soviet method of apportioning funds based on the size of an institution's staff and number of beds, the NEM focused on the number of patients visiting the institution and the actual costs of services provided. Personnel received wages according to the services they performed rather than receiving the fixed payments typical of the existing system. This change in accounting standards directed more attention to cost savings. Moving away from the "more is better" attitude that seemed to grip nearly all aspects of Soviet society, regional health organizations focused on reducing unnecessary capacity, and increasing outpatient and preventative treatment. According to one source, across the time spanning the implementation of these reforms and the end of the Soviet era, the number of unnecessary hospitalizations fell by 13.7 percent, the average length of stay in hospitals by 7.2 percent, and calls for emergency services by 12.6 percent.[30]

The NEM never expanded into other regions, and the experiment ended with the collapse of the Soviet Union in 1991. Nonetheless, members of the current oblast administration attribute some of the lessons learned during that period to the subsequent course of reforms in this sector.[31] Following approval of the legislative basis for Russia's new system of mandatory free health care,[32] Samara Oblast was one of the first in the federation to implement Russia's mandatory free health care system (established by gubernatorial decree on December 13, 1993).[33] As stipulated in federal law, citizens received insurance policies to cover the expense of treatment in their districts' clinics and hospitals. Unlike the Ulyanovsk case, those who were not receiving wages acquired policies from an insurance company that won a periodic tender to provide health insurance for the unemployed. Oblast budgetary funds covered the costs of these policies, paying the insurance company in much the same way as a private firm would.

However, even with the health insurance system's implementation, the existing regional health care structure demanded far more financial resources than the system could provide. Early in the reform process, oblast officials recognized the need to reduce system costs through the development and expansion of paid services, reduction of excess capacity, introduction of outpatient treatment and "day clinics," and training of general-practice doctors.

General-practice doctors helped reduce costs by breaking away from the hyper-specialization of the Soviet era. Rather than visiting several specialists in order to diagnose and treat even the simplest problems, patients visit a general-practice doctor who either treats their ailments or refers them to an appropriate specialist. This institution saves time and resources for both patients and the medical system as a whole. Drawing in part from experiences in various international exchanges, regional health specialists established a department in the Samara State Medical University for the training of general-practice doctors. In 2000, four years after the establishment of the department, the region hosted one-third (535) of the 1,500 general-practice doctors working in the Russian Federation.

Outpatient treatment and day clinics also played an important role in reducing unnecessary and costly inpatient treatment.[34] In addition to establishing a growing set of such clinics, medical authorities built incentives into the system in the form of wage supplements drawn from a portion of the savings, in order to encourage doctors to opt for less expensive outpatient clinics.[35] By 2000, 1,379 (39 percent) of the oblast's 3,509 beds stood in outpatient clinics, and 19.1 percent of all patients received outpatient treatment. To compare with federal trends, the 81,310 patients who received outpatient care in Samara during 2000 accounted for a full 10 percent of the patients receiving such treatment in the entire federation.

Some of the results of Samara's cost-saving measures are evident in the following figures. From 1988 to 2000, the number of beds for inpatient treatment in the oblast fell from 124.3 per 10,000 individuals to 85.7. This reduction resulted in the more efficient use of existing resources, and the average number of days per year in which each bed was occupied rose from 300 in 1988 to 313 in 2000. Increasing focus on outpatient treatment resulted in a reduction of the number of hospitalizations (inpatient) from 247 per 1000 individuals in 1988 to only 186 in 2000. Finally, the average number of days to treat an inpatient fell from 14.7 in 1988 to 13.3 in 2000.[36]

Other positive effects of restructuring are evident in Samara's pharmaceutical market. Throughout the 1990s, many regional governments in Russia, including Ulyanovsk, ostensibly sought to guarantee lower prices for consumers by setting price controls on medicines. Samara Oblast authorities deregulated the regional pharmaceutical market after 1992. While initial problems arose with price gouging, false advertising, and quality control, after 1995 the regional pharmaceutical department took a more active role in monitoring the market and providing consumer information. The department published a bimonthly magazine called *Pharmacy and Medicine* that included data on prices for different medicines across the region and information and telephone numbers for consumers interested in knowing more about specific products. By providing such consumer information, the pharmaceutical department forced local companies to focus on product quality and lower costs as a means to attract customers. As a result, in 2000, the average retail prices in Samara were 2 percent lower than the national average (wholesale prices were 19 percent lower). In addition to the cost benefits, deregulation also resulted in a substantially wider variety of medicines in Samara's pharmacies than were available in other regions.[37]

A brief comparison of the total health expenditures of Samara and Ulyanovsk provides a more objective illustration of the functioning of each region's health care system (see Table 11.1). For both 1998 and 2000, the portion of Samara's consolidated budget devoted to health care was roughly 15 percent. In neighboring Ulyanovsk, health care consumed over 22 percent of the total budget in 1998 and nearly 30 percent in 2000. Two factors account for these outcomes. First, as noted in the table, Samara enjoyed significantly higher budget revenues during both years. However, another factor contributing to this outcome was the greater inefficiency of Ulyanovsk's health care system. A breakdown of the total expenditures illustrates this point. Expenditures for wages to "personnel" (defined below) accounted for between 1.5 percent and 1.6 percent of the total health budget in Samara. In Ulyanovsk, the same category consumed nearly a third of all health budget expenditures during both years.[38] Similar differences persisted across other categories, with the exception of new construction and equipment purchases, which drew either an equivalent percentage of both regions' budgets or a larger portion of Samara's.

Table 11.1

Comparison of Health Care Budgets

	Samara 1998		Ulyanovsk 1998		Samara 2000		Ulyanovsk 2000	
	% Total exp.[a]	Rubles per capita	% Total exp.[a]	Rubles per capita	% Total exp.[a]	Rubles per capita	% Total exp.[a]	Rubles per capita
Total budget expenditures	—	2,864.90	—	1,536.-1	—	3,563.81	—	1,872.41
Total health expenditures	15.59	446.74	22.44	334.63	14.65	522.02	29.71	556.39
Including:								
Personnel	1.5	6.75	31.2	107.53	1.6	8.28	31.9	177.28
Supplies	0.4	1.97	15.6	53.85	0.5	2.42	18.0	100.32
Food	0.2	1.01	9.0	31.05	0.3	1.79	7.9	43.76
Equipment	1.7	7.75	2.5	8.55	1.6	8.29	1.6	8.82
Construction	8.3	37.29	8.3	28.39	8.4	43.85	5.8	32.43
"Other"	87.7	391.97	33.3	114.37	87.6	457.40	34.8	193.77

[a] Figures in the "Total health expenditures" row indicate the percentage of total budget expenditures devoted to health care. For health care budget items (all rows below "Including"), the figures indicate the percentage of total health care expenditures devoted to each item.

These marked disparities indicate another significant difference between the two regions' health care finance policies. Samara's health care budget demonstrates the oblast's implementation of a "single channel" health care finance system. To remind the reader, according to the normative scheme for health insurance provision in the regions, insurance companies are to cover the costs of both the employed and unemployed, with the oblast budget making payments for the policies of the latter group; the vast majority of financing passes through the Territorial Obligatory Health Insurance Fund (TFOMS). The volume of budget finances falling into Samara's "other category" represents the portion of budget funds diverted to cover policies for the nonworking sector of the population, as well as underpayment by enterprises for their workers' policies. In accordance with federal laws, TFOMS funds cover most wages, medicine, food, and supplies. Ulyanovsk's budget represents the type of partially institutionalized "dual channel" system existing in many regions. The Ulyanovsk TFOMS covers a portion of both the employed and unemployed, but the oblast budget pays for only a portion of the policies for the latter. At the same time, a portion of the payments for practitioners' and administrators' wages, medicine, supplies, and food pass directly from the oblast budget to regional medical institutions. The dual channel system results in additional waste from the added bureaucratic costs, redundancy, and questionable accounting procedures. As in many other regions of the country, such a system remains in place partly as a result of a bureaucracy seeking to maintain both itself and its control over health expenditures.[39]

What implications did the variation in health policies and their outcomes have for levels of social cohesion in Samara and Ulyanovsk? The Samara administration's restructuring efforts created a system that, in addition to providing overall higher-quality services, better served the needs of individuals from different social groups.[40] Oblast authorities provided the full range of federal government-mandated services alongside higher-quality, paid services. This approach not only offered consumers more choice, but it alleviated the state-funded system of the unnecessary burden of providing medical goods and services for individuals who could afford to pay for it themselves. As the result of both higher revenues and greater cost efficiency, the oblast health system also could focus on health programs for a broader set of social groups, including the elderly, young mothers, and children. Finally, as demonstrated in the following section, savings in the health sphere left more budget money for other social-cohesion-promoting state responsibilities like social services.[41]

Ulyanovsk's health policy, while initially promoted as a means to preserve many of the old system's comprehensive guarantees, resulted in a system that perhaps best served the elderly. The Goriachev administration's form of egalitarianism meant that all were subject to equally poor care, diminished further by the added burden of supporting individuals who would otherwise opt for paid services.[42] Furthermore, the overall inefficiency of maintaining a "dual system" of medical finance increased the drain on the oblast's available resources, promoted graft, and lowered the general quality of regional health care. While the final result did not necessarily privilege the elderly (who were subject to the same poor care as others), it did offer the rest of society services inferior to those it might otherwise have enjoyed through extensive restructuring of the health sector.[43]

Social Programs

The situation surrounding the social sphere in Ulyanovsk Oblast echoed some of the problems within the region's health care system. Throughout the 1990s, and in accordance with the Goriachev administration's "slow transition to the market," the administration continued to direct much of the region's budget toward the payment of energy, transport, and food subsidies. These untargeted programs essentially wasted resources on individuals who could otherwise afford to pay and thus reduced the finances available to provide quality goods and services for the needy.[44]

In the absence of "real" money, the administration resorted to barter and an extensive network of volunteer organizations.[45] With regard to barter, various firms provided essential goods like medicine and food, UAZ sent vehicles directly from the plant to social service institutions, and construction firms contributed materials for the construction of facilities. In some instances, barter met the needs of both local firms and the regional government. However, the demonetarization of the system contributed to the region's budget revenue problems and left decision-makers with the constant headache of converting bartered goods into resources proper to the task in question—UAZ's jeeps and vans are only so fungible.

The situation with volunteer organizations deserves special note as it raises some broader questions about using social organizations as proxies for social capital and challenges particular understandings of what constitutes a "thriving" nongovernmental sector. The dominance of the terms "social organizations" and "clubs" in any discussion of Ulyanovsk's "third sector" was indicative of the extent to which these organizations were essentially remnants of the Brezhnev era. Information on these organizations was very scarce, and Ulyanovsk Oblast rarely appeared on outside lists of NGOs participating in various interregional activities. Interviews with leaders of other Volga-region NGOs indicated that social organizations in Ulyanovsk were either shells of old Soviet organizations or were so closely tied to various government institutions or political figures that they essentially acted as arms of the regional government (and were hence subject to charges of politicization similar to those directed against the health care sector). Furthermore, the region's organizations suffered from a lack of funds and rarely rated a mention in terms of national and international grant competitions. Summarizing the situation, Sergei Agapov of the Povolzhe Historical, Ecological, and Economic Association stated that Goriachev simply failed to promote the conditions for a thriving nongovernmental sector because of the continued emphasis on paternalism and the state.[46]

Such factors challenge some of the attempts to operationalize social capital and cohesion by examining official data for the number of social organizations operating in a region.[47] Organizations differ not only in their goals (sports clubs, guilds, religious organizations, charities, and so forth) but also in their quality. One hundred underfunded, state-dependent, five-member organizations probably offer less for the development of social capital than fifty larger financially and politically independent organizations. Moreover, the legal and institutional environment within which these organizations operate may also have a strong impact on their effectiveness as bearers of social capital. Further, more detailed, case-study-based investigations of these issues are necessary in order to understand how conditions vary from region to region and what effects various types of organizations have upon post-Soviet regional societies.

Returning to the topic of social services, the Goriachev administration's bid for the support of the elderly population resulted in a relatively advantageous position for this sector of society. Interviews with social services staff members and the head of the Ulyanovsk city social-services department indicated a marked emphasis on programs oriented toward pensioners and invalids. In addition to a host of clubs and activities, the oblast hosted a unique system of spas and sanatoriums for the elderly, veterans, and invalids. Individuals could visit these establishments, take part in social activities, and receive various nontraditional treatments. However, indications of the region's dire financial straits appeared even around these monuments to regional social policy. Whereas nontraditional treatments are oftentimes regarded as supplementary to more traditional methods, the head of the city social-services department indicated, "we need to use nontraditional methods because we lack the money for anything else. If we can't afford to treat or cure ailments, we at least try to make the elderly feel comfortable and happy."[48]

If the region focused a significant portion of its scarce resources on the elderly, one could not say the same for the young. Child welfare, an area for which regions bore complete financial responsibility, was subject to chronic arrears and underpayment (see a comparison of child welfare expenditures in Table 11.2). Throughout the decade, the oblast administration had attempted to offset insufficient cash payments through practices of barter and payments in kind. This might include reductions in apartment fees or free essential goods and services from local firms to the neediest families. Nonetheless, arrears steadily increased. In March of 2000, the administration claimed that it would begin steady payments starting with dues owed from the previous month. However, in practice this once again applied only to the most needy families—single parent households, invalid and underage parents, and large families in which the per member income dropped below that of the current poverty level (608 rubles and 63 kopeks). At the time, there were 250,000 children in the oblast who were eligible for child welfare payments, and the oblast's new plan would not cover anywhere near this number.[49]

The performance of Samara's social service sector (see Table 11.2 for a comparison of budget expenditures) returns us to the importance of balancing economic performance and public goods provision. For most of the 1990s, Samara's administration consistently met its obligations in terms of unemployment and child welfare payments, while guaranteeing pensions and gradually expanding the set of additional social services. Although efficiency gains wrought by the administration's avoidance of such untargeted programs as high subsidies to the energy, housing, and transportation sectors partly assisted in achieving these outcomes, interviews with oblast administration officials consistently pointed to a more mundane contributing factor: higher budget revenues resulting from better economic performance. Samara's focus on new business development, while initially yielding detrimental residual effects on social welfare in the form of unemployment in traditional sectors and an overall higher cost of living, eventually produced sufficient financial resources to ensure that the administration met its social service obligations (hence the significant margin of Samara's overall social service expenditures over Ulyanovsk's). By the end of the 1990s, the Samara administration had the basic provision of services in the region under sufficient control to begin implementing such programs as the provision of access ramps for the handicapped, programs that other cash-strapped administrations could not even begin to consider.[50]

As in the case of regional health care, the Samara administration also sought to improve the provision of social services by promoting the development of services and goods provided in the nongovernmental sector. According to an oblast administration report, there were 3,292 social organizations operating in Samara Oblast in 2000, a large portion of which focused on social services of various sorts.[51] Conditions in the region were favorable to the development of third-sector organizations. The oblast administration passed the law "Charity Activities in Samara Oblast," which made NGOs

Table 11.2

Comparison of Social Policy Budgets

	Samara 1998		Ulyanovsk 1998		Samara 2000		Ulyanovsk 2000	
	% Total exp.[a]	Rubles per capita	% Total exp.[a]	Rubles per capita	% Total exp.[a]	Rubles per capita	% Total exp.[a]	Rubles per capita
Total social service expenditures	10.6	302.71	7.4	113.69	13.7	488.19	6.1	113.27
Including:								
Soc. servant wages	8.0	24.13	7.0	7.95	6.6	32.35	10.1	11.40
Medical products	0.5	1.50	0.2	0.27	0.6	2.75	0.1	0.09
Food	3.0	9.05	4.5	5.07	2.2	10.79	7.0	7.96
Equipment	1.5	4.60	0.1	0.07	0.5	2.65	0.0	0.00
Construction	0.9	2.56	0.5	0.55	0.8	4.06	0.5	0.57
Child welfare	47.3	143.15	43.6	49.57	19.1	93.39	40.1	45.55

[a]Figures in the "Total social service expenditures" row indicate the percentage of total budget expenditures devoted to social services. For the social service budget items (all rows below "Including"), the figures indicate the percentage of total social services expenditures devoted to each item. For total budget expenditures see Table 11.1.

and other social organizations in the region exempt from certain forms of taxation, formed a council to coordinate the efforts of NGOs and government officials, and set up the "Governor's Fund for the Support of Social Initiatives" to coordinate and support social activities. Samara also featured the Povolzhe Historical, Ecological, and Economic Association, a sort of clearinghouse for NGOs that provided administrative, legal, and research assistance for NGOs throughout the Volga region. Finally, the region hosted a number of seminars, conferences, festivals, and grant competitions for NGOs and other social organizations.[52] The development of these organizations and their coordination with the regional social service agencies assisted in reducing costs, providing better coordination of programs, and strengthening the regional nongovernmental sector.

Perhaps the most publicized example of the Samara administration's success in balancing economic development with public goods provision came in the autumn of 1999 when Governor Titov challenged federal authorities over the size of regional pensions. The scandal initiated from the federal government's failure to implement the 1997 federal law "Of the procedures for calculating and increasing state pensions" (from 21 July 1997) which required an increase in the coefficient between the state minimal pension and the official average wage from .525 to .7. Despite this legislation, the federal government continued to pay out pensions at the previous, lower coefficient of .525.[53] On October 13, 1999, Governor Titov delivered a decree which stated that pensions in Samara would be paid according to the .7 coefficient and that the extra funds needed to finance this increase would be drawn from surplus payments into the region's pension fund.[54] This decree drew an immediate response from the general procurator who stated that the oblast administration had no right to redistribute federal resources. A very public confrontation ensued after which the governor conceded to federal authorities and stopped drawing money from Samara's pension fund surplus. Nonetheless, the oblast continued to pay out pensions according to the .7 coefficient with additional funds drawn directly from the regional budget.[55]

Titov's struggle with the federal government was probably noisier than necessary.[56] Pensioners received their monthly payments according to the lower coefficient for nearly two years, and the Samara administration only took action on the eve of a Titov's ill-fated 2000 presidential bid. Even so, it had its intended effect—increasing the governor's popularity among a sector of society that traditionally opposed the type of reforms that the administration undertook over the past several years. Furthermore, while nothing could save Titov's bid for the presidency in March of 2000, increased support among pensioners played an important role in his reelection to the governorship in

July.[57] The fact that financial constraints prevented Ulyanovsk's administration from even contemplating a similar move is yet another indication that the Samara administration had struck a better balance between pro-growth policies in the economic sphere and the provision of public services.

As with their health care sectors, the varying approaches to social service provision in Samara and Ulyanovsk Oblasts had important implications for social cohesion. The Goriachev administration's focus on the elderly resulted in the exclusion of most other sectors of society from both social services and economic opportunities. Students, workers in nontraditional firms, small and medium-sized business owners, children, and parents all bore the brunt of policies that drew excessive resources from an economy starved of investment and new business development. Nonpensioners not only suffered from the lack of opportunities in the region, but they were also the first to lose social service benefits when budgets fell short. As the economic situation in the region stagnated, even the "privileged" groups suffered from heating crises, infrastructural breakdowns, and shortages of goods.

In Samara, the population suffered an initial jump in prices, reductions in job opportunities, and a decrease in public good provision, but by the end of the 1990s, nearly every social group in the region enjoyed better living standards than in neighboring Ulyanovsk.[58] Steadily improving wages and job opportunities benefited the working-age population, and increasing budget revenues allowed for the provision of social services on a level that exceeded that of even the Goriachev administration's early years. By avoiding the untargeted social programs undertaken in Ulyanovsk, the Samara administration achieved greater success in implementing a social division of labor that provided jobs for working age individuals and adequate tax revenues for a more efficient and viable social service sector.

Engendering Trust?

Returning to the social cohesion framework discussed above, if broad-based access to social services and economic opportunities increases social cohesion, one might expect to see marked variation in the distribution of support for regional socioeconomic and political institutions across different social groups in the two oblasts. In the limited space remaining, I present a brief examination of this proposition using survey data gathered prior to each region's 2000 gubernatorial elections and demonstrate how support for regional institutions was distributed across a set of social cleavages.[59] In the absence of more precise measures, I use support for the executive as a proxy for institutional support. I justify this choice on the grounds that regional politics is a very personalized matter in which individual governors embody

Table 11.3

Social Cleavage-Based Regime Support: Samara and Ulyanovsk Oblasts, 2000

	Samara $N = 2029$ $e^{\wedge}\beta$ [a]		Ulyanovsk $N = 1571$ $e^{\wedge}\beta$ [a]	
Age	0.94	(0.03)	1.17***	(0.06)
Pensioner	1.48**	(0.14)	2.00***	(0.18)
Student	0.86	(0.19)	1.30	(0.57)
Unemployed	1.15	(0.20)	0.71	(0.33)
Female	1.36***	(0.09)	1.55**	(0.12)
Rural	-1[b]		1.34*	(0.14)
Education	0.98	(0.03)	0.80***	(0.05)
Personal material status	1.44***	(0.06)	1.37***	(0.07)
LR X^2	57.56***		209.12***	
McFadden's R^2	0.02		0.11	

Notes:

[a]Designates the odds ratio for each independent variable. These are interpreted by subtracting 1 from the given value and interpreting the difference as the percent change in odds that the event (support for the candidate) will occur given a one-unit increase in the indicator. Hence, for "age" a one-unit shift from a lower age category to a higher would yield a 6 percent decrease in the odds of supporting Titov and a 17 percent increase in the odds of supporting Goriachev.

[b]While the Samara survey included only respondents from the capital city, we can nonetheless gain a grasp of an urban/rural cleavage in Samara Oblast by looking at the distribution of votes in the 2000 gubernatorial election. On average, Titov captured 57.26 percent of the vote in rural districts. This compares to 54.80 percent in smaller cities, 51.67 percent in the districts of Toliatti (Samara's second largest city and the site of the giant AvtoVAZ automobile plant), and 50.14% in the capital city of Samara. These figures suggest that support varied little from city to countryside.

*p < .05 **p < .01 ***p < .001

a broader set of policies, institutions, and ideological approaches to governance (the governor of Samara is not simply "Konstantin Titov," but a "promarket democrat," a "neoliberal reformer," and so on).

I use a logistic regression model including age, employment status (a categorical variable), gender, education, and personal material status as predictors for incumbent support. Because I am examining whether greater inclusion of various social groups yielded broader-based support and trust in the regime, I expect the socioeconomic predictors to account for the most variation in government support in that region where access to services and economic opportunities was most unevenly distributed. To take age as an example, a distribution of public goods across all age groups would yield more equal support across the different age categories and make this variable a poor predictor of regime support. However, a regime that focuses its efforts more on the elderly would create a situation in which one could better predict support for the candidate by looking at the respondent's age. Table 11.3 presents the results of the models.[60]

I draw the reader's attention to the most indicative results. First, McFadden's pseudo-R^2 measure indicates that this set of cleavages provides much more explanatory power in the Ulyanovsk case than in Samara. A glance at the levels of significance for each of the predictors provides some indication as to why this is so. Excluding the urban rural measure that was absent in the Samara model, five of the eight social cleavage measures were significant in the Ulyanovsk case as opposed to only three in Samara. Hence, whereas the uneven distribution of public goods in the Ulyanovsk case yielded a situation at the end of the 1990s in which an observer could predict incumbent support based largely upon an individual's placement within certain social groups, one could not say the same for Samara. Even in the case of pensioners—generally considered to be opponents of the types of reforms touted by the Titov administration— the administration's attempt to boost pension payments, and better guarantees of social services apparently garnered support, with pensioners actually 49 percent more likely to support the administration than workers (the baseline category for this variable). Support for the Samara administration was significantly more broad-based than in Ulyanovsk.[61]

Conclusion

Developments in Samara and Ulyanovsk offer an indication of the degree to which the breakdown of the social and health service sectors could vary from region to region and how these outcomes affected the level of cohesiveness in the regional social milieu. Better quality, more broadly distributed public goods and employment opportunities in Samara created wide-based political support for an outwardly liberal regime. In Ulyanovsk, the administration's rhetoric of social guarantees and protection from the ravages of the market conflicted with the realities of the region's bloated and poorly managed health and social sectors. The elderly population received the most benefits, while the remaining groups in society suffered from insufficient state support and inadequate means to substitute such goods and services in the private and civil sector. Rather than maintaining the state-nurtured social cohesion of the Soviet era, the Ulyanovsk administration created a system that alienated the educated, young, and working-age sectors of society—the very groups responsible for supporting the main beneficiaries of the system: pensioners.

Nonetheless, this study does not conclude with an endorsement for the indiscriminate application of the "Samara model" to other Russian regions. In many ways, Samara's reforms occurred in a rarified environment that would prove difficult to duplicate in many other regions. Somewhat ironically, Samara's liberal reforms were in part supported by the AvtoVAZ plant in Togliatti (a colossal "gift" of Soviet centralized planning), and the extensive gas pipelines and refineries that occupy the region. AvtoVAZ produces nearly three-quarters of Russia's domestic automobiles and accounted for roughly 2 percent of all the taxes collected in the Russian Federation in 1999.[62] While the firm is also a major tax holdout, the factory itself, along with the hundreds of local enterprises related to it, provides a large and relatively steady source of tax revenues for the oblast administration. Samara also enjoys natural resources in the form of oil and gas and a substantial transport and refining infrastructure. Most members of the administration with whom I spoke indicated that these preexisting factors contributed greatly to the oblast's success in restructuring the social and health sectors. Tax revenues played an especially important role in the social sector, both guaranteeing steady child welfare payments and allowing the governor to supplement pensions.[63]

With these points in mind, I conclude this chapter on a cautionary note. As the Ulyanovsk case indicated, the realities of post-Soviet interregional factor flows and the disintegration of the centralized economy defy attempts by any single region to carve out a sanctuary from even Russia's nascent market forces. In the absence of a strong natural resource base, state-heavy approaches like those in Ulyanovsk are probably doomed to fail as new business development is stunted and tax revenues fail to meet the demands of the unreformed social-and health-services sectors.[64] However, the success of the Samara approach was due in no small part to the presence of a solid preexisting economic base yielding both a more wealthy society and higher budget revenues. One might speak of "virtuous circles" in which social cohesion yields better economic performance that in turn creates even greater cohesion. Nevertheless, questions remain as to where these circles begin and whether societies can create and maintain such cohesion in the absence of adequate economic resources.

Notes

1. Materials for this analysis were collected during a year of field research in Samara and Ulyanovsk from August 2000 to August 2001. Financial assistance for this research was provided by an Institute of International Education (IIE) Professional Development Fellowship and the ACTR/ACCELS Regional Scholar Exchange Program. I wish to thank all the members of the Study Group on Social Cohesion for their comments on earlier versions of this manuscript. Special thanks also go to Lidia Goverdovskaya, Igor Yegorov, and Valentin Bazhanov for arranging contacts with

regional officials in Samara and Ulyanovsk. The points expressed in this chapter are my own and do not necessarily represent the positions of IIE, ACTR/ACCELS, or the Carnegie Corporation.

2. For details about the Soviet social contract see Linda Cook, *The Soviet Social Contract and Why It Failed: Welfare Policy and Workers' Politics from Brezhnev to Yeltsin* (Cambridge, MA: Harvard University Press, 1993).

3. However, as some works on federal fiscal relations have shown, the budget constraints on regional administrations were still much "softer" than those in other advanced industrial federations. See Daniel Treisman, "The Politics of Soft Credit in Russia," *Europe-Asia Studies*, 47 (1995): 949–976; Darrell Slider, "Russia's Market-Distorting Federalism," *Post-Soviet Geography and Economics*, 38 (1997): 445–460.

4. For a brief history of social cohesion and differentiation/integration theories see Ian Gough and Gunnard Olofsson, "Introduction," in *Capitalism and Social Cohesion*, eds., Ian Gough and Gunnard Olofsson (New York: St. Martin's Press, 1999) 1–10.

5. This "list of woes" excludes a whole set of additional problems concerning issues of measurement and testing.

6. Jo Ritzen, William Easterly, and Michael Woolcock, "On 'Good' Politicians and 'Bad' Policies: Social Cohesion, Institutions, and Growth," *World Bank Policy Research Working Papers* (Washington DC: World Bank, 2000).

7. Without widespread social and economic inclusion, the development of social organizations and strengthening of group identities may actually detract from social cohesion as various "in-groups" coalesce into "crony" networks (or worse)—excluding "out groups" and deepening social divisions. For more on the relationship between organizational social capital and exclusion see M. Levi, "Social Capital and Unsocial Capital," *Politics and Society*, 24 (1996): 45–55; D. Stolle and T.R. Rochon, "Are All Associations Alike? Member Diversity, Associational Type, and the Creation of Social Capital," *American Behavioral Scientist*, 42 (1998): 47–65. Gaddy and Ickes provide an argument for the detrimental effects of certain types of inter-elite "relational capital" on the Russian economy in C. Gaddy, and B.W. Ickes, "An Accounting Model of the Virtual Economy," *Post-Soviet Geography and Economics*, 40 (1999): 79–97.

8. In this instance I wish to focus particularly on the importance of balancing primary wealth creation in what Mustard refers to as the "real economy" with the provision of public goods like social services and health care. An emphasis on the latter may affect the former by resulting in underinvestment and driving capital and other economic factors to other regions. The subsequent downturn in economic activity not only hurts the working sector of society, but also results in the eventual deterioration of public goods provision as tax revenues decline. On the other hand, underinvestment in public goods provision creates a situation in which nonworking sectors of society (pensioners, students, children, and invalids) are "excluded." See Fraser Mustard, "Health, Health Care, and Social Cohesion," October 1998 (1 December 2001), *http://www.robarts.yorku.ca/pdf/apd_mustard.pdf*; R.G. Evans, "Health Care as a Threat to Health: Defense, Opulence, and the Social Environment," *Daedalus* 4 (1994): 2; R.G. Evans and G.L. Stoddart, "Producing Health, Consuming Health Care," *Canadian Institute for the Advanced Research of Population Health Working Paper*, 6 (1990).

9. In earlier discussions about Ulyanovsk, a number of commentators from outside the region indicated that the oblast was mainly "rural" and therefore was a poor match for Samara. However, as indicated in the brief description of the regions below, such statements reflect a peculiar misperception about the region that probably results

in part from its relatively recent and rapid urbanization (mainly after the 1940s, with rapid acceleration in the late 1960s and early 1970s). A consistent characteristic of interviews with officials and other individuals who had recently arrived in the region was shock over the extent of urbanization, coupled with curiosity over the region's "rural" misnomer.

10. Samara Oblast Committee of State Statistics, *Samarskaia Oblast-99: Statisticheskii sbornik* (Samara: Samara Oblast Committee of State Statistics, 2000).

11. Ulyanovsk Oblast Committee of State Statistics, *Ekonomicheskoe polozhenie Ul'ianvoskoi Oblasti v 1999 godu* (Ulyanovsk: Ulyanovsk Oblast Committee of State Statistics, 2000).

12. Materials for this section were gathered from regional press materials, interviews, and other sources in Samara and Ulyanovsk. Arbakhan Magamedov's contribution to Hokkaido University's "Regionii Rossii: Khronika i rukovoditeli" provided a useful guide for navigating post-Soviet events in Ulyanovsk. See, A. Magamedov, "Khronika politicheskii sobytii," in *Regionii Rossii: Khronika i rukovoditeli. Tom 6: Nizhegorodskaia oblast, Ul'ianovskaia oblast*, eds. K. Matsuzato and A. Shatilov (Sapporo: Hokkaido University Slavic Research Center, 1999).

13. I emphasize the term "remnants" to denote the degree to which the social guarantees undergirding the Soviet social contract had deteriorated even prior to the collapse of the Soviet Union. Once again, see Cook, *The Soviet Social Contract and Why It Failed*.

14. Ulyanovskkhlebtorg (the regional bread monopoly) provides one of the clearest examples of this type of collusion. In a unique chapter in the history of Russian privatization, the region's entire bread industry was "privatized" into a single joint stock company that held a monopoly over all bread production in the region. In exchange, the firm supplied inexpensive bread to the population that, despite promises of full subsidization, was only partially financed by the oblast administration (Oleg Samartsev, interview with author, Ulyanovsk City, Ulyanovsk, 3 November 2000).

15. The Soviet coupon system also continued to operate for a number of goods and good categories until at least 1996.

16. Robert McIntyre, "Regional Stabilization under Transitional Period Conditions in Russia: Price Controls, Regional Trade Barriers and Other Local-level Measures," *Europe-Asia Studies*, 50 (1998): 859–871.

17. Literally, "goods credit."

18. Igor Yegorov, series of interviews with author, Ulyanovsk City, Ulyanovsk, Autumn 2000.

19. A donor region is one whose contributions to the federal budget are in excess of the federal funds returned to the region. In 1996, only nine regions of Russia's eighty-nine were official "donors." See Avtandil Tsuladze, "Tri pravitel'stva—tri istochnika protivorichii," *Segodnya Online*, 28 June 2000. (10 December 2001). http://www.7days.ru/w3s.nsf/Archive/2000_164_polit_text_culadze1.html.

20. See Goskomstat Rossii, *Regionii Rossii: 2000* (Moscow: Goskomstat, 2000) and Goskomstat Rossii, *Regionii Rossii: 1998* (Moscow: Goskomstat, 1998).

21. In effect, what was occurring in Ulyanovsk was what the European Commission termed "negative convergence." Certain disadvantaged groups in society (such as the elderly and rural populations) benefited at the expense of a growth in opportunities and support for other members of society. As the European Commission report states, "cohesion is concerned with increasing economic growth and new opportunities . . . for disadvantaged social groups and does not imply a reduction in either growth or jobs for others." See European Commission, "First Report on Economic

and Social Cohesion" (Luxembourg: Office for Official Publications of the European Communities, 1996): 14–15.

22. M. Radova, "Za Zdorov'e!: 'V meditsine nuzhna vertikal,'" *Narodnaya Gazeta*, 17 December 1997.

23. This is actually a relatively mild description of Ulyanovsk's post-1992 health finance. Natalia Tutunik, head of ROSNO's voluntary insurance department, indicated that finances were also distributed according to political motives. Medical institutions under head doctors with close ties to Goriachev received more funds than others (Natalia Tutunik, interview with author, tape recording, Ulyanovsk City, Ulyanovsk, 14 July 2001).

24. The *selektornyi* was a program broadcast every Saturday morning during which the governor and members of the administration discussed regional problems, took phone calls from citizens, made policy pronouncements, and publicly attacked challengers. Toward the end of the administration's rule, this paternalistic show became one of the administration's primary instruments for "ruling" the oblast.

25. Gennady Yakimchev, "Aleksandr Nabegaev provali, pervoe zadanie," *Simbirskii Kur'er*, 11 April 2000.

26. L. Makarova, "V poiskakh rastrachennogo. . . ," *Simbirskii Kur'er*, 19 October, 1995.

27. Vasily Babushkin, interview with author, tape recording 12 July 2001.

28. Vasily Gorbunov, interview with author, tape recording, 15 July 2001. Persistent attempts to conduct interviews at the oblast TFOMS were met with rejection.

29. The other territories included Kemerovskaya Oblast and Leningrad City. For more on this system see Judyth Twigg, "Balancing the State and the Market: Russia's Adoption of Obligatory Medical Insurance," *Europe-Asia Studies* 50 (1998): 583–602.

30. N.M. Skuratova, "Dvenadtsatiletnii opyt reformirovaniia sistemy zdravookhraneniia na regional'nom urovne. Rezultaty realizatsii reformy zdravookhraneniia v Samarskoi oblasti. Perspektivy," 4 December 2001. http://www.medlan.samara.ru/reform/skuratova.html.

31. Interview with Rudolf Galkin, "Samarskaia model' mezhdunarodnogo zdravookhraneniia," *Meditsinskaya Gazeta*, 15 March 2000.

32. Russian Federal Law, "Of Medical Insurance for Citizens of the Russian Federation," 28 June 1991.

33. Administratsiia Samaraskoi Oblasti Glavnoe Upravlenie Zdravookhraneniia, *Gosudarstvennyi doklad o sostoianii zdorov'ia naseleniia Samarskoi Oblast za 1994–1998 gody* (Samara: Administratsiia Samaraskoi Oblasti Glavnoe Upravlenie Zdravookhraneniia, 1999): 105.

34. According to Head Doctor Lydia Fedoseeva, rates of unnecessary inpatient treatment in Russian hospitals could reach as high as 30–40 percent. See Lydia Fedoseeva, "VOP na baze mnogoprofil'noi polikliniki," *Meditsinskaya Gazeta*, 13 June 2001.

35. According to Fedoseeva, abuse of this system (i.e., referring patients for outpatient treatment when more intensive care was necessary) was an initial concern among administrators. However, monitoring of referrals and strict punishment for any transgressions have reduced the incentives for such behavior.

36. N.M. Skuratova, "Dvenadtsatiletnii opyt reformirovaniia sistemy zdravookhraneniia na regional'nom urovne. Rezultaty realizatsii reformy zdravookhraneniia v Samarskoi oblasti. Perspektivy." A comparison to 2000 Federal level data is further

illustrative: average number of beds—108.7; average number of days occupied—313; average length of inpatient treatment—15.8 days; and number of hospitalizations per 1000—209.

37. "Lekarstvennyi paradoks," *Meditsinskaya Gazeta*, 13 June 2001. However, the author also noted that the large number of pharmaceutical companies in Samara was a critical factor in this outcome. The absence of similar conditions in other regions might result in higher prices.

38. In per capita terms, expenditures on wages in Ulyanovsk were roughly 16 (1998) to 21 times (2000) greater than in Samara. Per capita budgetary expenditures on medicine in Ulyanovsk were roughly 27 and 41 times greater, and food products drew per capita expenditures of 31 (1998) to 24 (2000) times those of Samara.

39. Mikhail Zasypkin, interview with author, tape recording, Samara, Russia, 26 June 2001. Judyth Twigg also offered assistance in interpreting these figures.

40. However, this is not to say that the region's health care system is entirely without deficiencies. Among other problems, shortages of supplies continue at the level of medical institutions, and services in the countryside have suffered from the closing of some rural clinics and hospitals. My personal observations (as either a patient or accompanying one) also indicate that the practice of unofficial side payments to medical personnel is still very common. As the reader continues, he or she must bear in mind that the Samara case is one of *relative* success in the economic, social service, and health care sectors.

41. Of course merely comparing budget expenditures begs the question as to which system provided *better health*. If one takes into account the greater health risk in Samara oblast (itself partly the result of higher volumes of pollutants resulting from a more active economy), statistics indicate roughly equal outcomes for the two regions, with Samara making particular strides in reducing infant and maternal mortality and improving mothers' health. Nonetheless, the link between choice of health care systems and health outcomes is tenuous at best. For more on the relationship between reforms and health in the Russian Federation see Judyth Twigg, "Russian Health Care Reform at the Regional Level: Status and Impact," *Post-Soviet Geography and Economics* 42 (2001): 202–219.

42. With the exception of the wealthiest who could simply travel to other regions (like Samara) for paid health care.

43. This is another example of the "negative convergence" that marked the Ulyanovsk model.

44. The cost of tickets on Ulyanovsk's transport was largely frozen for much of the 1990s. By the winter of 2001, broken heaters, frozen doors, and complete shutdowns were commonplace on Ulyanovsk city's trolley system. Bread subsidies also remained until the very end of the Goriachev administration. However, the administration sometimes failed to reimburse Ulyanovskkhlebtorg, and the demand for the bread was such that the stores were often without it by midday.

45. According to the regional statistical agency, there were 1,324 social organizations registered in the oblast in 1999. Ulyanovsk Oblast Committee for State Statistics, *Ekonomicheskoe polozhenie Ul'ianovskoi oblasti v 1999 godu* (Ulyanovsk: Ulyanovsk Oblast Committee for State Statistics, 2000): 233.

46. Sergei Agapov, interview with author, Samara City, Samara, 28 April 2001; Irina Zvereva, interview with author, 28 April 2001.

47. For one example, see Christopher Marsh, "Social Capital and Democracy in Russia," *Communist and Post-Communist Studies*, 33 (2000): 183–199. Such works

essentially attempt to apply Robert Putnam's methodologies to Goskomstat data. See Robert Putnam, *Making Democracy Work: Civic Traditions in Modern Italy* (Princeton: Princeton University Press, 1993).

48. Ema Grigoreevna, interview with author, tape recording, Ulyanovsk City, Ulyanovsk, 12 July 2001.

49. Elena Gavrilova, "Destine postorbital tol'ko na bednost'," *Simbirksii Kur'er*, 11 March 2000.

50. Mikhail Zasypkin, interview with author, tape recording, Samara City, Samara, 26 June 2001.

51. The regional state statistical agency actually puts the total number of registered social organizations (by form of property) at 4,001. From 1997–2000, the number of such organizations nearly doubled. Samara Oblast Committee for State Statistics, *Samaraskaia Oblast—99* (Samara: Samara Oblast Committee for State Statistics, 2000): 293.

52. Samara Oblast Administration, "Obshchestvennie organizatsii," 2001. 15 January 2002. http://www.adm.samara.ru/content/14/14/474.

53. Political Section, "Bezproigryshnyi khod. Dazhe esli Moskva dob'etsia otmeny resheniia o pereschete v Samaraskoi oblasti pensii, Konstantin Titov ostanetsia v vyigryshe," *Samarskoe Obozrenie*, 22 November 1999.

54. Decree of the Governor of Samara Oblast, "O merakh realizatsii federalnogo zakona 'O poriadke ischisleniia i uvelicheniia gosudarstvennykh pensii' na territorii Samarskoi oblasti," No. 290, 13 October 1999.

55. This partly accounts for the marked increase and restructuring of Samara's social service expenditures in 2000 (Table 11.2). Particularly, one should note the significant jump in the percentage of expenditures unaccounted for by the mandatory budget items.

56. Igor Valerevich Averkiev, interview with author, Perm City, Perm, 22 June 2001. Regions like Perm had supplemented pensions in a more subtle way by using regional budget funds—the same procedure to which Titov subsequently resorted.

57. Dr. Yevgeny Molevich, interview with author, Samara City, Samara, 15 October 2000. See also, Zoya Andreeva, "Yevgeny Molevich: Titov sam sozdal sebe oppozitsiiu," *Reporter*, 21 July 2000.

58. Official statistics at the end of the decade indicate that Ulyanovsk's pensioners maintained a certain standard of living margin over their counterparts in Samara. However, these figures fail to take into account the consistency with which society was provided with subsidized goods and services and the reliability of pension payments. Such figures only indicated the standard of living of a pensioner who received his or her pension on time and in full and who enjoyed complete access to the entire complex of subsidies in the region— a very rare occurrence.

59. The Ulyanovsk study was an oblast-wide, 1,630-respondent, random survey undertaken in September of 2000 by the Ulyanovsk state Technical University's "Perspektiv" Sociological Laboratory (Valentina Shuvalova, Director). The Samara survey was the third part of a four-stage survey of a 2,099-respondent sample from the city of Samara, undertaken by the Samara Oblast Fund for Social Research in June 2000 (Vladimir Zvonovsky, Director).

60. In the limited space available many of the details of this analysis were omitted. Anyone interested in knowing more about the analysis are encouraged to contact the author at: *ackst8@yahoo.com*.

61. In any event, Titov won the 2000 regional executive election with 51 percent of

the vote. Goriachev received only 24 percent of the regional vote and lost to his opponent, General Vladimir Shamanov.

62. Kondratenko, *Biudzhet Samarskoi Oblast* (Samara: Samarskii Universitet, 1999).

63. Samara also benefited from a unique concentration of foreign investment and other forms of foreign assistance. While most of this resulted from the policies of the administration, changing political agendas in foreign partner-states also played an important role (see Miles Pomper, "Economic Aid Goes Local," *CQ Weekly*, 10 July 1999). In any event, the sheer concentration of programs and the tendency for their self-reproduction created a situation unlikely to be replicated in other regions of the federation, if for no other reason than the inability to concentrate so many programs in eighty-eight other regions.

64. I mention natural resources in this instance because other regions in the Russian Federation (like Tatarstan) have financed Goriachev-style policies with tax revenues drawn from oil, minerals, or other profitable raw materials (thanks to Valentin Bazhanov for raising this point).

12

International Assistance to Russia
Models That Work

Kate Schecter

After ten years of reform efforts in Russia and the former Soviet Union, development organizations are looking back to review programs that have worked and those that have failed to fulfill their promises. The health and social problems facing Russia are overwhelming and appear intractable. Despite millions of dollars in international aid and government efforts to curb these ills, along with some improvement in the economy, infectious diseases continue to spread. Poverty continues to plague the majority of the population, and the general standard of living remains low. Abandoned and homeless children roam the streets of Russia's major cities.[1] Tuberculosis and HIV/AIDS infect all strata of society. Infant and maternal mortality rates remain high. The male mortality crisis, inherited from the Soviet era, continues.[2] The problems are daunting, and no one organization can tackle all of them.

In the early 1990s, large multilateral and bilateral organizations such as the World Bank and USAID worked on policies and legislation from above in the hope that broad reform would affect all segments of the health care system. By the mid-1990s it became evident that the top-down approach of the World Bank was not working and that smaller scale, local initiatives were more successful. The Soros Foundation decided to wrestle with one major issue at a time; it launched a multimillion dollar campaign to prevent and treat tuberculosis and infectious diseases. Smaller American NGOs and bilateral assistance organizations from Western Europe joined the effort, working from the bottom up through local governments or individual institutions. At the beginning of the new century, it has become clear that the bottom-up approach has been far more successful and enduring, but only where the central government is supportive of the grassroots initiative.

How can international aid assist in developing social cohesion in Russia? Numerous obstacles prevent foreign aid from being accepted or used correctly. In Russia, anti-Americanism permeates society, exacerbated by the resentment engendered by debt. Corruption within the government has created a popular perception that all foreign aid money is misused by dishonest politicians or well-paid consultants. Funds disappear, but the debt remains to be paid. In other cases, international assistance has been accepted and used for legitimate projects in Russia; in such cases, when a community feels the positive impact of this assistance, it fosters social cohesion.

International Assistance Strategies and Obstacles

In the desire to implement international aid, organizations often overlook whether or not the issue being addressed is actually the highest priority of those it aims to help. When any organization ignores to what degree the issue is demand-driven and imposes its own agenda on the recipients of its aid, that program is doomed to failure.

For example, the World Bank is often caught in a web of its own requirements and therefore fails to address the most demanding issues of the countries it wants to help. The World Bank always works first with national governments, offering whatever the central government requests; this practice often results in the ultimate rejection of a loan, or worse—the acceptance of a loan followed by waste of the funds acquired and ultimately an unproductive debt. The International Monetary Fund (IMF) faces similar self-imposed constraints. In Russia, the IMF lent far more money than did the World Bank. Rather than addressing the large IMF loans made to Russia for macroeconomic restructuring, this chapter focuses on World Bank lending in the social sectors, specifically in health.

International assistance can be a double-edged sword because it often has unintended negative consequences. Evidence shows that the overall impact of foreign aid has been positive in Russia, except when it fails to address the expectations of the key stakeholders. In a recent report on why health is important for U.S. foreign policy, Jordan Kassalow suggests that debt relief should be tied to specific, measurable objectives in the development of a health care system. Some of these measurable objectives, such as vaccination rates, can be achieved in a relatively short period of time. Other measurable indicators of change in a health care system include the number of physicians trained or retrained in modern, evidence-based practices and reductions in hospital stays and emergency visits. Primary-care clinics that detect and help to control such illnesses as cancer, diabetes, and hypertension also provide improvements that can be measured over time.[3]

Most international agencies other than the World Bank provide grants or technical assistance. Very few organizations provide cash to the recipients. George Soros's Open Society Institute requires that the Russians running a program must generate local funds in order to get matching funds from the Soros Foundation in New York.

The mechanisms and conditions of financial aid differ greatly. The World Bank loans money to central governments, which then distribute the funds to local governments or nongovernmental organizations. Prior to the disbursement of a loan, large grants prepare the recipient country for receiving the loans; before the World Bank gives these preparatory grants, the recipient must guarantee that it will take the loan. Despite these safeguards, loans are not always accepted, even after preparatory grants fund pilot projects and pay for the development of an implementing agency within the recipient country. This occurred in Russia with the TB/AIDS loan which was under preparation for a few years, only to be rejected by the Russian government in 2001.

The World Bank uses a mechanism called "trust funds" to pay for preparatory grants. Western Europe, Canada, and Japan, along with most of the countries that contribute to the World Bank, provide trust funds. Most trust funds require that a consultant from the country in which the trust fund originated provide technical assistance. This can lead to difficult situations, such as when a consultant with no expertise about Russia is tasked with providing advice on how to reform the Russian system.

The most notorious example of this kind of mismatch and "wealthy-nation advice" is the shock-therapy disaster of the early 1990s. The concept of shock therapy was generated by a small group of economists, most of whom were American consultants. It was imposed on the Russian system without appropriate forethought or preparation. The initial policy decision to impose shock therapy led to further economic crises that could have been avoided. Although this particular situation was not part of a World Bank program, the trust fund mechanism sets the stage for just such ill-advised policy recommendations by foreign consultants.[4]

"Donor fatigue" has led to a reassessment of foreign aid. A current debate between the U.S. government and the World Bank focuses on both the amount of aid that is appropriate and the question of debt-relief for the most highly indebted countries of the world.[5] Currently, debt-relief is unavailable to any of the former Soviet states. None of these countries is designated as "highly indebted" because, having been World Bank or IMF loan recipients for less than ten years, none has expended the grace period granted by the World Bank before loan repayment must occur. In addition, per capita income must be below a certain threshold in order for the country to be considered a "highly indebted poor country" and thus qualify for debt relief.

The pitfalls of the World Bank approach have been extensively documented.[6] Four primary criticisms have been made of the World Bank's model of foreign aid. First, the World Bank's strategy lacks focus. Critics argue that the agenda is too large, and that by trying to be the all-encompassing eradicator of poverty, the World Bank has not achieved its goals. In a few cases, there is evidence that loans and the ensuing debt have deepened poverty.[7] This criticism certainly has merit. Numerous World Bank projects were neither focused nor demand-driven and thus ultimately never reached fruition. To its credit, the World Bank has been trying to address emerging issues such as infectious diseases and the AIDS epidemic; such an international, UN-affiliated institution would be roundly criticized if it ignored these critical global crises as they erupted.

Second, the internal structure and mechanisms of World Bank loans are cumbersome and slow. Implementation takes many years. Assessments prior to implementation have ignored or barely addressed the potential impact the project will have on the environment or the political tensions already in place in the country. In a few cases, angry protests have erupted because a project caused more harm than good.[8]

The third criticism is that the "magic bullet" approach to development continues to fail because it assumes that the solution to a host of problems lies in one key factor. World Bank senior economist William Easterly has written a book highly critical of the World Bank's record. He commented in a recent interview, "What strikes you as you look back over the decades is this repeated cycle where we've all thought there was one key factor that would transform poor countries into growth economies. At one point it was family planning. At another, health care or capital investment or 'adjustment loans.' And none of these have had any sustained effect on economic growth."[9]

The fourth criticism addresses the low success rate of World Bank programs. Despite the fact that the mission of the World Bank is to reduce poverty, the correlation between aid, improved living standards, and economic growth is not always clear. African countries, which have received more aid than any other countries over the last fifty years, have shown the least improvement. Yet the World Bank continues to loan money to these countries despite these poor records.

Frustration with the failures of foreign aid over the last decade has led to a concerted campaign to abolish the World Bank and the IMF.[10] An organization called "Fifty Years is Enough," made up partially of former World Bank staff, is directed particularly at the World Bank and its practices. The debate over foreign aid is as old as the practice itself. In the 1950s, soon after WWII, Milton Friedman wrote a convincing essay predicting the problems that would emerge from granting or loaning large amounts of money to developing countries.[11] Much evidence has emerged since Friedman's essay supporting his concerns that foreign aid does not work. Money given directly to central governments has often fallen into the hands of corrupt politicians, thus never reaching its intended recipients. In Russia, millions of dollars disappeared, not only leaving the country in debt, but also exacerbating anti-American and anti-Western sentiments. Friedman argued that money spent on teaching democratization would be wasted; unfortunately, there are many examples of countries that have received millions of dollars in aid, only to become more authoritarian rather than democratic. In order to ensure accountability, loans and grants are often given to central governments who are then supposed to distribute the funds. Often, corrupt governments invest in projects which are the favorite of a particular constituency or politician but have no clear benefit for the population, or, worse yet, the recipient government does not distribute the money at all.

Joseph Stiglitz notes in a recent review of George Soros's book on globalization that the solution is not to abolish the IMF and the World Bank, but rather to make both institutions function better.[12] Soros points out that the "foreign aid market" is inevitably less efficient than the normal market. He also stresses that not all aid can be measured in terms of quantitative data; qualitative results are equally valuable, although much more difficult to gauge. Soros's "open society" concept has operated under this premise from the outset, always stressing the importance of learning new processes and ways of thinking, even if these processes are not always measurable or quantifiable.

The Partnership Model

The failures of international aid are notorious, but aid has had a prolonged and profound positive impact on the standard of living for Russians and other former Soviet peoples. When Communism collapsed in 1991, the American health care establishment responded to the critical needs of the decaying health care systems of the entire region by establishing the American International Health Alliance (AIHA). In 1992, with financing from USAID, leading U.S. health organizations formed consortia with their counterparts in the former Soviet Union and Central and Eastern Europe.

The term "partnership" is widely used. The international donor community uses the term to denote everything from a donor-recipient relationship to two donor organizations cooperating under a memorandum of understanding. The term is nonthreatening, and it blurs the line between donor and recipient, obfuscating monetary transactions that may be a part of the arrangement. Whatever the relationship, partnerships work best when they are well defined from the outset.

AIHA partnerships have evolved over the last decade into a successful model. This discussion will focus primarily on the implementation of the model in the health care sector, but the model itself may be used in a wide variety of contexts. To "level the playing field" and instill as much parity as possible, the AIHA model of partnerships requires a set of basic criteria from the outset.

AIHA partnerships consist of voluntary efforts by doctors and health care workers in the United States who donate their time and experience to train their counterparts. The Russian (or other former Soviet) physicians, nurses, and medical personnel must also be willing to take time to learn how to improve their systems. These are peer-to peer relationships based on the participants' recognition of the expertise that lies on either side of the ocean. Neither side gets paid for their time. Through a rigorous selection process, AIHA pairs medical consortia from U.S. cities with consortia from former Soviet cities. Together the partners hammer out a plan to improve the local health care system. The success of the program rests on the voluntary efforts of hundreds of individuals, donations from numerous institutions in the United States, and thousands of peer-to-peer exchanges. The recipients must obtain local funds for capital repairs, salaries, and all recurrent costs (such as utilities for the clinics or hospitals, reagents for medical equipment, and other types of supplies that must be continually resupplied). One hundred such partnerships have been created throughout the former Soviet Union and Central and Eastern Europe in the last decade.

In the United States, these public-private partnerships have resulted in a tremendous commitment from nongovernmental sources, leveraging over $193 million of in-kind contributions (including more than 157,000 volunteer person-days) since the program's inception. U.S. universities, hospitals, and companies like Eli Lilly and ServiceMaster have donated over $14.8 million in medical and educational supplies and equipment to partner institutions throughout the region. The result is that for every dollar that USAID provides, the partners and corporate donors contribute one-and-a-half dollars. This voluntary effort reveals the wellspring of goodwill and desire to interact on both sides of the Atlantic.

The projects undertaken by partnerships must be demand-driven. A key component of the model is the requirement that partners must conduct a community needs assessment to gauge its most urgent needs and develop a more participatory environment. In order to encourage local groups to develop according to their own needs, U.S. partners are trained to avoid offering a blueprint of how they operate in their own context. Many partnerships develop community boards which help build democracy by providing forums for voicing community concerns.

This approach avoids the consultant model which often operates by sending in a team of experts to train local professionals. The consultant strategy has proven problematic in that it rarely elicits ideas from local stakeholders, nor does it ensure that the initial training will have any lasting effect. These projects often engender resentment and lead to a situation in which the "technical assistance" provided is unsustainable once the consultants leave.

Finally, all partners are required to have an "exit strategy" which involves "graduating" from the process of direct active assistance after four years. Many partners maintain close relations and can seek supplemental grants, but there must be a clear end date for the project from the outset in order to push both sides to achieve their objectives in a reasonable time period. The clear exit strategy, which is part of the initial development of the partnership, avoids the dependency and lack of self-generated funding that has been such a problem with most foreign aid in the past.

The direct result of all of these efforts in the Russian health care sector can be seen in shorter hospital stays, the delivery of more outpatient services, and in turn, the treatment of more patients. Russian and other former Soviet doctors are working with new and improved equipment, and they have exposure, access, and training to utilize new technologies and treatments. They have developed close bonds with their American coworkers over the last decade.

In addition to improvements in health care services and the professional enhancement achieved through the partnership process, participation in these collaborations has resulted in a fundamental shift in the mindsets of those taking part. Through the democratic process of partnering, a number of radical new concepts have become normalized: patients' rights and patient-centered care, and a far more significant role for nurses. Critical thinking and taking initiative to change the system are among the incalculable benefits of the partnership process. Although the partnerships are in public health care institutions where services are officially free, they are introducing concepts of fee-for-service and sliding scales.

In the health sector, AIHA has now sustained its model for a decade in a few cities in Russia. For example, the impact of the partnership between Dubna and La Crosse, Wisconsin, gradually changed the whole Russian city. The original partnership identified diabetes as a serious problem in the community. Since 1993, when the diabetes program started, the Dubna Diabetes Education Center has trained more than 2,500 diabetics and 340 medical practitioners. Insulin use has declined by 30 percent and the average length of hospital stays associated with diabetes-related complications has decreased by half.

The partnership model extended beyond health care partly because a dynamic and progressive mayor caught on to the possibilities for change. He gradually extended some of what they learned through the AIHA partnership into other sectors of Dubna's economy.

An essential element of comprehensive change is reforming the education system so that the new approach can be transferred to the next generation. In Dubna, initial investment in the health sector spread the idea of partnering to the school system and led to an ongoing exchange program with Wisconsin high school students.

One important aspect of education in the AIHA projects has been the establishment of Internet access for Russian partners. One of the early achievements of Soros's Open Society Institutes and the small grants administered by the Soros Foundation was the development of Internet access across Russia. The Soros Foundation administered small grants to dozens of institutions throughout the former Soviet Union and Central and Eastern Europe. These grants allowed students, doctors, and scholars to access the Internet and connect to a vast world of information. Even in the far reaches of Siberia, doctors can "wander through the halls" of an advanced medical library in the United States and search for the most recent protocols and guidelines for treating diseases.

AIHA recognized the importance of the Internet and from the early 1990s made Internet access part of all of their partnerships. To date, 130 "Learning Resource Centers" provide information and communication services to over 85,000 people in the region. Americans can send the most advanced information to their counterparts, and long-distance learning is becoming more common. In addition to creating accessibility through the Internet, AIHA created a separate Web site called "The Eurasia Health Network," which is a library of current health articles translated into Russian. For a number of emerging health issues, such as new protocols for preventing the transmission of HIV/AIDS from mothers to their babies, this is the only Russian-language source available.

The influence of these partnerships can reach beyond the local level. Through local governments and community boards, the partnerships influence multiple levels of government. In order to affect legislation and improve the working conditions of doctors and other health care workers, many of the partnerships have lobbied for reforms at the national level. Once the central government sees the changes occurring at the local level, there is a greater chance of comprehensive national reform. An important lesson that has been learned over the last decade is that working solely from the top-down does not create results, but neither does relying on small pilot projects or grassroots initiatives. The drawback of the partnership approach is that it is small scale and only over time can the changes spread.

Other successful models used elements of the AIHA model to address a particularly urgent issue. A successful project by Doctors of the World in St. Petersburg aimed to address the health needs of street children by opening drop-in clinics throughout the city. The project began with the clinics; it then grew to encompass legal defense of the rights of the homeless children who were being thrown into TB-infested detention centers because the police had no alternative shelters for them. Although the number of street children continues to grow in Russia, the program demonstrated how clinics could help with urgent health issues and how a referral system for indigent children and youth could be created.

The main criticism levied at all these programs is that they are not creating an incentive for recipients to help themselves. George Soros recognized this danger and closed a number of Open Society Institutes because they were unable to remain financially viable. AIHA recognized this risk from the outset; the partnership model strives to create the local capacity to continue the reforms once the partnership is over. The model must be clear from the outset: if the key components are not there, the partnership can become a gift-giving charity operation in danger of falling apart once aid is withdrawn.

The Impact of Foreign Assistance

The terms "sustainable" or "sustainability" are used to argue that a certain approach or tactic is worthy of funding because it will provide lasting benefits. There is no question that sustainable methods do exist; those methods that will leave internal capabilities behind or generate income once foreign aid ceases are sustainable. The concept of sustainability is questionable when it is applied to a large-scale reform effort. Achieving long-lasting effects on a smaller scale can be easier because individuals have more control over financing mechanisms and can directly manage the resources necessary to keep a project going. A good example can be seen in Dubna, where small-scale counseling centers, primary-care clinics, and support groups have sprung up and continue to flourish long after the Americans who first introduced these concepts have left the city. It is a greater challenge to maintain sustainable bureaucracies where there is little individual accountability or personal investment. Large-scale medical equipment and pharmaceutical projects by World Bank loans in the mid-1990s resulted in few tangible benefits, leaving many of those Russians involved in these loans feeling bitter and resentful about the huge debts incurred.

The obvious limitation of the grassroots, small-scale projects is that they are successful in one place but difficult to replicate. "Scaling up" becomes a challenge. The challenge for both the donor agencies and those implementing the project on the ground is moving from model pilot programs to all-encompassing national reform. In Russia, one sector may show improvement or one region may flourish, but without simultaneous legal reform, improvement in the economy, and a national consensus on a strategy for moving forward, any local change will likely be confined to the particular context in which it occurred.

The long-term impact of the "bottom-up" approach can be seen in the shift in mindset toward taking initiative and risk in order to break out of the Soviet system. Some joint ventures and relationships with foreigners that have sprung out of them have now endured for an extended period. The Russian counterpart has not been punished as they might have been a decade ago. When international trade and professional partnerships flourish, they not only improve the market and the quality of services, they build trust and thus create an atmosphere conducive to taking risks.

Another lesson that has been learned over the last decade is that what works on a small scale often cannot be replicated by the government. Change—genuine "successful" change—happens one community at a time. On the other hand, once there is buy-in from participants—change can be rapid. In Russia and Ukraine, smaller communities and individual progressive doctors who were exposed to the Western health care system and given a chance to implement reforms, were quick to change. In the case of child welfare, again, the individuals who have invested time and resources into helping children have seen concrete success stories—but these have happened one child at a time.

Conclusion: Is There a Role for the International Donor Community in Russia in the Future?

The changes taking place in Russia are in their nascent stages. Although there are improvements, health care and health status remain below Western standards. Epidemics continue to plague the general population: AIDS and TB are on the rise. More and more children are orphaned every year, and the problem of street children persists. A new generation of children born to mothers infected with HIV/AIDS or TB will place a severe burden on the already ailing health care system. As health insurance begins to take hold as an alternative mechanism for financing health care, people on the fringe of Russian society will continue to rely on the state to protect them. Russia will continue to have a predominantly centralized and government-sponsored health care system. There will continue to be a need for assistance on many fronts, and the population will continue to expect social welfare benefits from the state. In order to meet these demands, the Russian government will continue to need foreign assistance. Public and private aid will remain essential to the survival of Russia. Partnerships in health care can be models for integrating and democratizing Russian society.

Once Russian citizens actually have a say in reform strategies and implementation, their hopes will be raised for a better standard of living and a more equitable society. Partnerships have led to more cohesive communities, and have broken down many antiforeign and anti-American sentiments. Foreign aid must continue in Russia; the key is to make the aid more responsive to local needs and more effective over the long term. In the Hippocratic tradition of doctors from both the East and West, the main goal must be to first do no harm in the quest to help.

Notes

1. The Russian press covers this problem weekly. For a few examples see *Johnson's Russia List* citations.

2. Jordan S. Kassalow, *Why Health Is Important to U.S. Foreign Policy* (New York: Council on Foreign Relations and the Milbank Memorial Fund, 2001).

3. The Bush administration has been influenced by these arguments about measuring outcomes and has linked the new U.S. aid package to this concept. President Bush announced in his speech at the Inter-American Development Bank in March 2002, "America's support for the World Bank will increase by almost 20 percent over the next three years. We expect the World Bank to insist on reform and results, measured in improvements in people's lives." Mr. Bush announced an increase of the foreign aid budget of 15 percent per year or $5 billion over three years. This is the first large increase in more than a decade. Joseph Kahn and Tim Weiner, "World Leaders Rethinking Strategy on Aid to Poor," *The New York Times*, 18 March 2001.

4. For more on the aid efforts of the early 1990s and the problem of inappropriate or misinformed advice by wealthy donor-nations see Janine R. Wedel, *Collision and Collusion; The Strange Case of Western Aid to Eastern Europe 1989–1998* (New York: St. Martin's Press, 1998).

5. Nancy Birdsall, Allen C. Kelly, and Steven W. Sinding, *Population Matters; Demographic Change, Economic Growth, and Poverty in the Developing World* (New York: Oxford University Press, 2001), and Carol Lancaster, *Transforming Foreign Aid: United States Assistance in the 21st Century* (Institute for International Economics: Washington, D.C., 2000).

6. Jessica Einhorn, "The World Bank's Mission Creep," *Foreign Affairs*, 80 (September/October 2001): 22–35. William Easterly, *The Elusive Quest for Growth: Economists' Adventures and Misadventures in the Tropics* (Boston: MIT Press, 2002).

7. Easterly, ibid.

8. The most notorious controversial projects that have engendered public protests are the Narwan Dam, the Northern Chinese resettlement project, and two oil pipeline projects. An external "inspection panel" reports on these controversial projects, but the reports are not published publicly. The results of the recommendations of the inspection panel are periodically cited in the press.

9. Ken Ringle, "Bank Shot: Writing from the Inside: An Economist Says the World Bank Is Failing its Mission," *The Washington Post*, 20 March 2002.

10. James Harding, "The Anti-Globalization Movement," *The Financial Times*, September 9, 2002.

11. Milton Friedman, *Foreign Economic Aid: Means and Objectives* (Stanford: The Hoover Institution on War, Revolution and Peace, 1995).

12. Joseph Stiglitz, "A Fair Deal for the World," *The New York Review of Books* 49 (23 May 2002): 24–28, in a book review of George Soros, *On Globalization* (New York: Public Affairs, 2002).

13

Can International Cooperation Contribute to Social Cohesion in Russia?

Lessons from the Swedish Experience

Maria Lagus

General Background

The fall of the Berlin Wall in 1989 and the process of change that started in Central and Eastern Europe created a new situation, one that affected Sweden as well as many other countries. The Baltic Sea regained its position as a link between the countries surrounding it and ceased to be a barrier that effectively separated the eastern and western shores. Sweden all of a sudden had a number of new, close neighbors. Contacts had to be developed with countries that had been difficult even to visit before. Businessmen could see a huge new market opening up. National boundaries do not apply in questions concerning the environment, and new possibilities occurred to solve environmental problems by joining efforts across borders.

More than a decade has passed, a decade of "freedom" in Russia. New ties have been established at all levels between Russia, the Russians, and the foreigners who were attracted by developing opportunities for business, cooperation, or simply friendship. Many are disappointed today, both within and outside of Russia, in particular those who thought that the defeat of Communism and the planned economy would automatically lead to democracy and a market economy. Can this disappointment be turned into success?

Many have come to assist Russia on its way to democracy, rule of law, and a market economy that can function well for all its citizens. To what extent can foreign assistance contribute? Examples from Swedish-Russian cooperation projects will be used in search of examples of working strategies toward development of social capital and social cohesion in Russia.

Social capital is defined as the norms, relationships, and institutions that determine the nature and quality of a society's public and private interactions. Social cohesion is the result of effective and abundant social capital. A cohesive society is a society that enjoys a sense of common purpose, shared values, a stable identity, and a widely agreed-upon vision of the future, as well as a framework within which to pursue that vision. In the examples covered here, Swedish support is limited to transfer of know-how and experience through Swedish expertise; i.e., no money was transferred to Russia, and no Russian salaries have been paid.

Swedish-Russian Cooperation

In 1991, the Swedish Parliament decided on support for cooperative programs with countries in Central and Eastern Europe, with a particular focus on the neighbors around the Baltic Sea. For Russia—a huge country compared to Sweden—it was suggested that efforts be concentrated in regions in the northwest, since they were close to Sweden. An important motive behind the decision was to foster peace and stability in the immediate geographical vicinity as a component of general foreign and security policy. Taking geography into consideration, there were of course a number of other implications of this new situation for Swedish society that allowed contacts at all levels: between individuals, between companies, between consumers and producers, and between officials.

If we look at the situation from a bilateral point of view, there was a need to "normalize" the situation in order to develop mutually beneficial neighbor relations in all fields. It seems obvious that personal and institutional relations would effectively contribute to security and stability in the region. It has therefore been a strategic issue from the Swedish standpoint to involve as many different actors as possible on both sides and from all areas of society. Many had no previous experience in international cooperation.

How then were target areas for support and cooperation chosen? An important assumption was that Russia was, in principle, well developed as regards human resources and infrastructure. As a visitor to Sweden from the region expressed in the early 1990s: "You know, we are not underdeveloped but misdeveloped, if anything." In light of this insight, it is important to ask: Which were the most strategic "misdevelopments" in Russia, and how could foreign assistance possibly contribute to positive change?

Target Areas

Four broad target areas for support were set up by the Swedish parliament as a framework for cooperative programs that should aim at:

- promoting common security
- deepening the culture of democracy
- supporting development of a functioning market economy, and
- supporting environmentally sustainable development.

After an evaluation in 1994, "development of a functioning market economy" was reformulated into "socially sustainable economic development." This change was made when it had become evident that the social costs of economic reconstruction in Russia were unacceptably high, with the burden put on the weakest groups in society, i.e., children and the elderly. Not only was it important to alleviate the burden for humane and humanitarian reasons, but also because the drastic worsening of economic conditions and rising poverty would be a threat even to a sound reform policy and to the process of democratization.

Through the wording "culture of democracy," it was stressed that free elections and democratic institutions in themselves are not enough to bring about a stable and an efficiently functioning democratic society. The formal network should be completed by a "culture," defined as all those things that make up democracy, making it into something more than rhetoric. The culture should reflect attitudes and have to do with norms and morals; it should consist not only of the feeling that the opinions of individuals have value, but also of activities of civic society, of free media, and of a political life; and it should give rise to a society in which people feel the willingness to take responsibility for the common welfare and in which they are allowed to do so.

In 1996, the four target areas were supplemented by a decision by the Swedish parliament that equality between women and men should be considered and promoted in *all* Swedish development cooperation financed by the government.

Social Sector Cooperation—An Ideological Dimension

Sweden has had a fairly extensive social security system run by the state, a system that was forced to cut expenses drastically during the 1980s due to severe budget restrictions. The fact that the system had been extensive, together with the need to reduce costs, seems to have created a ground for common understanding in cooperation between Sweden and Russia in the field of social assistance.

With the basic philosophy that Swedish support should be offered in areas where Swedish competence is relevant and competitive, it has been natural to focus on such social support that is organized and distributed by the public sector. There is only very limited experience in Sweden regarding nongovernmental organizations as actors in the field of social security.

Two main functions of Swedish support to Russia can be distinguished:

1) To find efficient ways of distributing limited public resources to those most in need of it;

2) To shift working methods from a medical to a social view. The individual shall thereby be regarded as a capable and responsible subject in society.

There is a huge gap in Russia between the legal responsibilities of the state to support its citizens and the financial resources available to provide the support. Steps have been taken toward structural change and development of social welfare work, utilizing the idea of social support based on need assessment. To this end Sweden has supported a number of pilot projects.

To pave way for a change, advice has been given on a system that can provide information on individual income and other relevant information, as well as on new legislation. Furthermore, projects have been carried out creating open services close to clients, thereby reducing the need for expensive care at institutions. Continuous discussions focusing on attitudes and values in relation to social work have been part of the projects, as have exchanges of experience regarding methodology in care of the elderly and in rehabilitation of children with disabilities. Also, attitudes toward the disabled and prevention of drug abuse among young people have been a focus of discussion.

Effects of Cooperation in the Social Sector

Participants themselves consider the change of attitude of social workers toward their clients to be the most important outcome. The project has succeeded in areas within the control of the project itself and failed where the necessary support (e.g., legislation) was not in place as planned and required.

Efforts at the central level to make use of the new competence, attitudes, and so on, and to formulate new strategies and guidelines on its basis, are of vital importance if anything other than very local effects are to be achieved. In this case, the city government adopted new programs for care of the elderly and for the care of persons with disabilities, with an emphasis on cooperation between social services and health care.

Lessons Learned

In most modern welfare states, programs are financed by taxes as well as contributions (e.g., by individuals and employers). Differences between welfare models with regard to distribution can be described in terms of needs-testing and means-testing of individuals in need of service. Social assistance is in most cases organized and implemented by the public sector, the private sector, or nongovernmental organizations. Normally all of these actors are involved to some degree or another.

The ideological dimension of cooperation between countries in areas of social assistance was discussed at a conference titled "Social work as a tool to promote inclusion, prevention and development in the social cooperation between the European Union and Russia," held in St. Petersburg in May 2001. It was noted that the European Union member states and Russia have much in common, but have each chosen different means of combating social problems. Whereas problems are universal, solutions are often contextual. It should therefore be taken into consideration that international cooperation involves an exchange of ideas that have ideological dimensions.

Russia is confronted with the urgent task of solving its serious social problems in the aftermath of its reform process. Whether it chooses a system of financing or distribution will have far-reaching implications, and this choice needs to be carefully considered. Sharing experience in this field with other countries will hopefully be useful.

Looking at *sources of financing*, there continues to be, on the one hand, a lack of confidence in a state that undermines people's willingness to pay taxes and thereby prevents the establishment of a successfully functioning public social security system. There is, on the other hand, no general alternative, such as an insurance system, to financing.

In terms of *distribution*, the state-owned companies that used to take responsibility for a large part of social security distribution no longer exist. Remaining official structures in the social sector are poorly adjusted to the new requirements and often lack relevant knowledge and working methods.

Private-sector social initiatives have hardly been developed due to the lack of the systems needed for financing and the legal framework for regulating their actions. The tradition of nongovernmental organizations as service providers is weak in Russia. Existing Russian organizations often depend on foreign support for survival and have few prospects for securing alternative financing.

The Culture of Democracy Within a Cultural Context

Russian demands on Sweden for support for democratic development have been weak. It has also been questioned whether it is relevant to offer such support to a country that is formally and by definition democratic, even if its performance still shows deficits. Democracy has been addressed most directly in exchanges between Russian and Swedish journalists and politicians, as well as in the cooperation between nongovernmental organizations in the two countries.

Support for strengthening local self-government in a number of regions has been considered in an effort to indirectly influence democratic development. Swedish support to NGOs was primarily motivated by a belief that an organization made up of members acting for a common purpose would be an excellent school in democracy, thus contributing to a culture of democracy in Russia. Organizations gathering people engaged for the same issue would hopefully stimulate active participation in the development of society; competence in democratic decision-making would be fostered through the need to develop a common view. Swedish democracy was developed in such a way.

Effects of Support for Democratic Development

In particular, projects including journalists and politicians have been well received. Lasting networks between journalists have been established, and a more reader-friendly layout has been developed, along with a dialogue with readers.

Support to local self-government has been successful in that it has created contacts and friendship, as well as contributing to increased knowledge in many areas of local competence. However, the *effects on society* from the support to local self-governments remain limited as long as political stability is lacking and financial resources are not decentralized at the same pace as are responsibilities. Evaluations show that effects on democracy from NGO support were poor.

Even if the cooperating Russian organizations at times had managed to achieve positive results through their activities, it was difficult to notice effects on democratic structures or working methods. One explanation of this might be that Swedish and Russian organizations had different motives for their engagement in cooperation. There had never been any demand from Russian organizations for the kind of support that the Swedes wanted to provide. A more important reason for Russian organizations to engage in international cooperation was that their participation in this work gave them a higher status and more authority in their contacts with officials in Russia. It can be assumed, however, that even if the cooperative projects have not directly influenced the culture of democracy, they might have contributed to pluralism and a stronger platform for the individual.

Lessons Learned

Support aimed at strengthening individuals by helping them believe in the possibility of influencing democracy through their own activities, for example as politicians or journalists, has a good chance of influencing society. Support along the lines of training local officials to use new knowledge to compensate for a lack of resources and political support appears less likely to have far-reaching effects. Discussions between Swedes and Russians have revealed an ambiguity around the concept of democracy, which led to misunderstandings.

In developing a culture of democracy it is natural that a country's historical and cultural heritage play an important role. Respect, knowledge, and understanding from foreign experts and others are therefore important to secure in any cooperative project.

Given the Russian heritage of forced collectivism, it is likely that the Russian people's interest in a common purpose and shared values, i.e., social cohesion, needs to grow out of a strengthened idea of the individual. From a stable individual identity and the enjoyment of personal freedom, the need to voluntarily interact with others may grow.

Whereas the Swedish understanding of democracy is closely linked to the microlevel, that is, to active participation by the individual in social life, the Russian understanding seems to be more linked to the macrolevel or the formal "infrastructure." The Russian political culture builds on a tradition of decision-making based on power rather than authority. Citizens are seen as "subjects" subordinated to a strong ruler, with obligations toward the state but no rights as defined by law. This has contributed to the understanding that the freedom of an individual can occur mainly outside the law. Democracy is commonly understood as either weakness or maybe an act of generosity by authorities, and it is only natural to try to exploit this generosity for personal gain.

Swedish organizations consider that representing many members in a political dialogue with officials is a strength. In contrast, leaders of Russian organizations consider members an impediment to fast results; they also constitute a risk to the unity of the organization if they express different opinions. Russian organizations consequently seek to strengthen their influence or "power" through the status of international links rather than through the authority held by a large number of Russian members.

Swedish organizations' goals of transferring their "grassroots" experiences to their Russian counterparts are at risk of being hampered by Russian law. If interpreted narrowly, a 1995 law forbids the government and its officials to interfere with the activities of nongovernmental organizations and vice versa; this law might hinder attempts by organizations to receive the status of "a body for referral," or it might limit their ability to act as serious and powerful discussion partners with the government.

A Model to Assist Russian People in Need of Help

When considering a model best suited to assisting Russians in need, it is helpful to ask several questions:

1. Is it easier to get fast results through reforming existing structures, or is it more efficient to start from scratch by developing completely new structures, e.g., through the private sector or through non-governmental organizations?
2. How fast can viable local Russian organizations be created and developed into competent actors in the social sector?
3. Is it possible to bring about enough confidence in the state to achieve a willingness to pay taxes so that it can afford to run a social sector system? How fast can an alternative system of financing be put in place?

Swedish experience points at a need to balance shortsighted wishes for immediate results with the time necessary for Russian decision-makers to find and develop a viable system that functions well in its context. Study visits have proven effective. Pilot projects may be useful for testing models as a basis for decision, and results need to be interpreted to suit the Russian context.

Russian organizations often prefer to rely on foreign counterparts and donors instead of trying to cope with their own authorities. The reason for this may understandably be that working with outsiders is a faster way to move toward results. A risk of this relationship is that the foreign partner may play a traditional role of being the strong leader and thus perpetuate a dynamic in which those designated to learn are passive objects rather than active subjects and agents of change.

The reluctance of organizations or private initiatives to involve Russian authorities has much too often led to a situation in which Russian officials are not interested in, and do not feel responsible for, what has been invented or planned for them. Cooperation between public and private initiatives therefore needs to be encouraged by international cooperating partners to make efficient use of limited resources.

Equality Between Women And Men

When approached outside of Sweden, the issue of whether to consider equality between women and men has created a lot of confusion and questioning. The aim of Swedish policy is that women and men, in every important aspect of life, shall have equal rights, equal possibilities, and equal obligations. This aim is supported by international conventions (e.g., the Beijing Declaration) and is hardly questioned by anybody. This issue needs to be addressed in regards to the Russian context in order to explore the extent to which imbalances between the sexes exist, and to determine the degree to which this is a concern for Russian society and a potential issue for foreign donors.

In Russia, as well as in Sweden and many other countries today, women and men formally enjoy "equal rights"; in official rhetoric nobody opposes formal equality. The former Soviet Union was first in the world to guarantee legally supported formal equality between women and men in such areas as the right to education and to employment.

In terms of equality of possibilities and obligations, several questions need to be addressed:

1. What are the expectations of women and men, for example, when it comes to influence and decision-making in society?
2. What expectations are there when it comes to family matters?
3. How are these expectations reflected in the general attitudes and norms prevalent in society?

Swedish support to Russia has been addressing different aspects of gender inequalities found in Russian society. Development of statistics has been supported as a tool for analyzing the actual situation and to reveal possible imbalances. Other types of support came in the form of projects aimed at making the situation better for the disadvantaged gender, along with suggested models for the reform of existing gender roles. When it became evident that women were harder hit than men by unemployment, support was given for strengthening the capacity to develop the competence of unemployed women; this helped put them in a better position to enter the labor market or to start their own business.

Effects and Lessons Learned

Statistics show that poverty is a rising problem in Russia and that poverty is not equally distributed among the population. The main victims are children, but other affected groups are single parents (i.e., mothers) and elderly women.

Furthermore, statistics show that women continue to be disadvantaged in the labor market.

Female unemployment is not due to lack of competence. It is normally not because of a lack of competence that so few women are found in top positions in Russia. The share of women in decision-making bodies seems, however, to increase slowly in most countries, except in Russia and some other countries of the former Soviet Union in which women's share has decreased in recent years.

There are no laws preventing women from being politically active, but there seem to be informal obstacles. One obstacle is the way politics in Russia is carried out, believed by Russian women to be "dirty" and making them feel uneasy. Another obstacle is the attitude shown by men toward women. For example, when asked why women's participation in political life is so limited, many male politicians answered that women must take care of their families. This example brings up some important questions:

1. What prevents Russian men from taking care of their own families?
2. What underlying norms and attitudes does this reflect?
3. Do men feel excluded from family life, and, if so, what does that imply?

According to terrifying figures during the first half of last decade, life expectancy for men decreased dramatically. The reasons behind this seem to have been complex, although mainly of a psychosocial character. Many men, deprived of their jobs and their reason-to-be, seemed to have lost a foothold in the new society that only a few—normally those who already had power or who were young and receptive—managed to take advantage of.

It seems as if the traditional division of labor in Russia means that men take responsibility and monopolize the power over the outer world, i.e., society, whereas women take responsibility and monopolize the power over the inner world, i.e., family matters. In a strict balance of power, equally strong parties tend to protect their preserves and do not let the other party in. As a consequence, men could not rely on a natural refuge in their families when they lost their positions in the new society.

Whatever the reason, there is certainly a gender imbalance that needs attention. Solutions are probably not most efficiently found in general measures, but ought to be sought in analyzing the specific situations of men. Taken as an example, it could be worthwhile to compare the situation of women and men. If women survive better, are there lessons to be learned and applied to the lives of men? And are there lessons to be learned for women from situations in which men fare better than they do?

The Route from Disappointment to Success: Some Suggestions

The primary motivation of all foreign support to Russia must be to strengthen the inherent capacities and the confidence of the people in themselves and in their leaders. The following have been found to be strategic issues for a foreign donor to consider when approaching Russia:

- New leadership attitudes need to be supported;
- Logical links between individuals and structures need to be secured;
- Women are important agents of change and need to be considered as such;
- Donors need to take more *and* less responsibility.

Responsible Behavior Among Donors

It is important to realize and respect that Russia is neither poor nor unable to run its own business. There are, however, problems caused by "misdevelopment." Russia is not in need of new "big daddies"—either Russian or foreign—modeled after its tsars and dictators. Instead, Russia and its people need to trust and rely on the country's own enormous capacity and potential. It also needs leaders that respect and rely on the capacity of the people.

Responsibilities need to be shared between cooperating parties in a way that promotes development. Whereas it must be considered exclusively the responsibility of Russia to make efficient use of project results, foreigners with a wish to assist Russia have a moral responsibility to provide know-how and well-tried, high-quality methods, as well as to economize Russian resources in the broad sense.

Anyone financing a development project in Russia needs to be aware that, from a moral point of view, the biggest risk of failure is not that the foreign donor might waste money. The moral risk is of wasting the Russian people's scarce resources of time, energy, and devotion by tying them up in a poorly planned project. Furthermore, each development project must be designed with the understanding that a day will come when foreign financing ceases. Unless financing is secured from other sources, the endeavor might result in nothing more than a means of passing time for the foreigners.

It is important to ensure that cooperating foreign partners and their sponsors develop responsible strategies. Grant financing could benefit from effective instruments for appraisal and risk assessment. The possibilities of getting a grant sometimes risk overruling thoughtful planning and prioritizing by the recipient. There is also a risk of counterproductive and resource-consuming duplication of projects if several donors engage in similar activities without responsible coordination.

As a means of ensuring that a project takes priority and is not involuntarily duplicated, Sweden has required noticeable financial and other contributions from the Russian side. The social pilot project described above is one example, where participating districts were chosen on a competitive basis.

Making careful risk assessments of long-term financing possibilities ought to be the responsibility of both sides. Risk assessments also ought to consider whether the success of a project depends only on factors that can be controlled by the project itself or if there are factors in the surrounding environment that might influence its results. Such factors might include the existence of necessary legislation or other effects of state policies. Risks might also be encountered in employing new methods, knowledge, and so forth, or in incorporating new activities that have been realized through a project.

Seek Logical Links Between the Individual and the Structure

Potential risks need to be considered in advance, and strategies for avoiding them must be outlined. Based on Swedish experience, the willingness of responsible leaders, professional or political, is crucial for the success of any project. Acceptance and blessing from any person in a position to help or hinder the activities of a project need to be secured. Unless this can be done, the success of the project is at stake and engagement risks being a waste of resources.

Experience has shown that it is necessary to change structures in order to secure long-term effects and sustainability. Structures can, however, be changed only by the individuals acting within them. It seems necessary to find and rely on agents of change and to consciously assist those agents in linking structures that can support the development of a socially cohesive society. Agents of change might be found among insightful and influential persons who are in a position to act as role models. Examples have been found among journalists, politicians, and leaders in strategic positions in society. It is also important to look for agents of change within strategic structures in society. When considering these things, it is important to consider the following questions:

1. Which structures in society might influence and support social cohesion in the Russian society?

2. What are the roles and opportunities of the individuals acting within them?

The Political Arena

Many Russians express a lack of faith in their public institutions and their political leaders. How power is exercised is an important part of how people perceive political leadership. People's perception of political performance plays an important role in trusting political institutions. Lack of trust in political institutions leads responsible citizens to avoid active participation in political activities, which in turn counteracts the development of a sense of common purpose and shared values that characterize a cohesive society. This issue brings up the following question:

> What would be needed on a structural and on an individual level to break this vicious circle?

As long as a culture of "government through power" prevails, it will be difficult to reach a state of social cohesion, defined as public and private interactions within a framework of common purpose, shared values, and vision for the future. There will be neither a forum for interaction nor the driving forces behind interaction. There is still a huge gap between the leaders and the people at all levels of the Russian society. Without the need to seek authority, political leaders will not take on the role of representatives of the people who elected them. On a structural level, there needs to be a forum for formal and informal interchange. On a personal level, leaders need to develop an attitude to leadership that includes the idea of serving their constituency and their task. Likewise, people need to care and be engaged.

Social Capital Grows in Areas Where Women Act

It might be worthwhile to look for structures in Russian society where social capital thrives; areas of personal interaction such as school, social services, health care, and so on, are likely to reflect norms and attitudes in accordance with the nature and quality of public and private interactions.

In international cooperation on social services, attention has been focused on developing the attitudes of staff toward clients, in particular, in viewing clients as responsible subjects, and this has attracted a lot of interest. It is likely that if those in social services develop the attitude that they are serving their clients, this attitude might permeate relations in society and might contribute to social cohesion. Today, women play a leading role in areas of personal interaction and therefore have the potential to act as agents of change. There is reason to believe that in most cases, decision-makers are men who lack this personal experience. There is also reason to believe that areas traditionally dominated by women play a subordinate role in society.

It could be assumed that social cohesion would benefit from a situation in which male decision-makers have more personal experience with interaction and women have more opportunities to influence development in society. Questions regarding how such changes can be brought about, and how international cooperating partners might contribute, remain to be answered.

With regard to politics, it will be a challenge to support a demand for change of the culture of politics, in which women's opinion of politics is transformed from considering it a "dirty business" to viewing it as an arena for serious debate. It is in this debate that decisions will be made about how to distribute common resources to the benefit of all members of society— women, men, girls, and boys. Women represent a new political culture and new sectors of interest that hold a potential for positive change.

International partners can contribute through providing "status" to those sectors and activities dominated by women and those that show a high potential for social capital. They can also demonstrate good examples of leadership attitudes and of playing by the democratic rules of the game in a pluralistic society. International cooperation may contribute to Russian society through finding and supporting agents of change where they are active today, without losing sight of the strategic arenas in which public and private interaction can take place to develop a cohesive society.

14

The Role of International Financial Institutions During the Transition in Russia

Augusto Lopez-Claros

This chapter aims to provide an early assessment of the role played by international financial institutions during the transition in Russia.[1] The subject is multidimensional, and this paper attempts to identify some of the key issues that emerged during the first ten years of Russia's gradual transformation into a market economy. Because the International Monetary Fund (IMF) provided about three-quarters of total multilateral lending during the 1990s, our primary focus will inevitably be on this organization's programs and operations.[2] We begin by briefly identifying in the next section the primary sources of external financing to the Russian government during the 1990s and highlighting the chief characteristics of each. Having shown that multilateral lending played a central role in the provision of resources to the government, we then turn our attention to the issue of what were the key policy objectives pursued and the instruments used as part of the multilaterals' aid effort. We argue that the Fund's approach, in particular, fell well short of achieving the goals established at the outset of the transition. We then look for some explanatory factors, focusing attention in particular on the gap between theoretical insights into the ingredients of sound approaches to economic development on the one hand, and the practice of the development agencies on the other; the role of geopolitical considerations in multilateral lending; issues of IMF jurisdiction; and the limited administrative capacities of the government during the initial stages of the transition. Given the central role played by the IMF during Russia's transition and the continued importance of the organization in assisting other countries in crisis, the paper's last section provides some initial thoughts on IMF reform.

Main Sources of External Financing to the Russian Federation

Table 14.1 presents the outstanding stock of Russia's public external debt from 1994 to 2001. There were three principal sources of external funding to the government during the 1990s: multilateral credits from international financial institutions, particularly the IMF and the World Bank; export credits from bilateral official sources; and, beginning in 1996 and leading up to the August 1998 financial crisis, portfolio inflows from nonresident investors attracted by the high yields in the domestic treasury bill market.[3] There were additional inflows of foreign direct investment, but these were relatively small and, in any event, not necessarily linked to the public sector. Each of these three sources of finance had its particular characteristics, and it is useful to highlight some of the key differences.

Credits from multilateral institutions were generally linked to macroeconomic policy reforms and, in the case of the World Bank, reforms of a sectoral nature as well (e.g., improving the operations of the coal mines). The IMF disbursed the lion's share of multilateral lending during the 1990s—some $22 billion between 1992 and 1999—and the funds were the least restrictive form of foreign finance available to the government. Once the resources were disbursed (generally in tranches, subject to compliance on the part of the government and the central bank with respect to the conditionality established in the IMF program), the government could use (and did use) these resources in any way it best saw fit; in Russia this usually meant direct support to the federal budget.

Export credits from bilateral official sources are also called "tied credits," to highlight the fact that the loan is tied to the purchase by Russia (or earlier, the Soviet Union) of goods in the creditor country. A typical transaction might involve the purchase of industrial machinery from a German enterprise to be used subsequently by a Russian factory. The Russian government provides the state guarantee, the Russian enterprise assumes a ruble obligation to the federal budget (which may or may not be subsequently paid; the overwhelming majority of such credits disbursed during the last several years of the Soviet Union, for instance, were never repaid by the Soviet enterprises that received the goods, and the state was thus left with the external obligation), and the German export credit agency acts as an intermediary, typically providing insurance cover to the German enterprise.[4] The goods are delivered, and the Russian government assumes the obligation without ever having seen any cash.

There is no "policy" component to such lending operations. The creditor government (Germany in the above example; but there were well over a dozen countries providing such credits, with Germany making up about 50

Table 14.1

External Debt Outstanding (end of period; in billions of US$)

	1994	1995	1996	1997	1998	1999	2000	2001
A. Sovereign debt (B+C)*	127.5	128.0	136.1	134.6	158.1	155.0	139.6	131.8
(in % of GDP)	45.8	36.8	31.6	30.2	48.1	80.2	55.6	42.8
B. Russian-era**	11.3	17.4	27.7	35.6	55.4	51.4	67.3	61.5
Multilateral creditors	5.4	11.4	15.3	18.7	26.0	22.4	18.9	15.5
Including:								
IMF	4.2	9.6	12.5	13.2	19.4	15.3	11.6	8.2
World Bank	0.6	1.5	2.6	5.3	6.4	6.8	7.1	7.1
Official creditors	5.9	6.0	7.9	7.6	9.7	9.8	8.5	7.1
Eurobonds	0.0	0.0	1.0	4.5	16.0	15.6	36.4	35.4
Others	0.0	0.0	3.5	4.8	3.7	3.6	3.5	3.5
C. Soviet-era**	116.2	110.6	108.4	99.0	102.7	103.6	72.3	70.3
Official creditors	69.9	62.6	61.9	56.9	59.4	58.4	58.4	55.5
Including:								
Paris Club	39.6	41.6	42.3	37.6	40.0	38.7	39.0	36.0
COMECON	25.7	16.6	15.4	14.9	14.8	14.9	14.0	14.0
Commercial creditors	36.0	38.3	37.8	33.9	35.3	36.9	5.9	5.9
Including:								
Financial institutions	31.1	33.0	32.5	29.7	31.2	32.8	1.8	1.8
Others	10.3	9.7	8.7	8.2	8.0	8.3	8.0	7.1

*The stocks of debt at 1992 year-end and 1993 year-end were $78.7 and $112.7 billion, respectively. No accurate comparable breakdown of these totals, is however, available.
**Russian debt is post-1/1/1992; Soviet debt is pre-1/1/1992.

percent of the total disbursed) is typically only too happy to lend, as such operations boost exports, establish a local presence for the country's industry in the domestic economy, and can be portrayed as "external assistance." These credits were typically factored into G7 announcements of aid packages to Russia, particularly during the early years of the transition. (Indeed, reschedulings of previously disbursed export credits were also counted as part of these aid packages.)

When, in 1993, during his tenure as finance minister, Boris Fedorov expressed some misgivings about the general utility of tied credits, his remarks were unwelcome in the capitals of the main creditor countries. It is not unfair to say that such credits, with some exceptions, were more about supporting domestic industry and/or agriculture in the creditor country, than about providing tangibly useful help to Russia. This was particularly the case when, after German reunification, one useful way to assist enterprises in the former East Germany, to mitigate the adverse impact of competition from their peers in the more developed West, was to keep alive for a few more years their

Figure 14.1 **Exposure of Export Credit Agencies, 1999**
(in billions of US$)

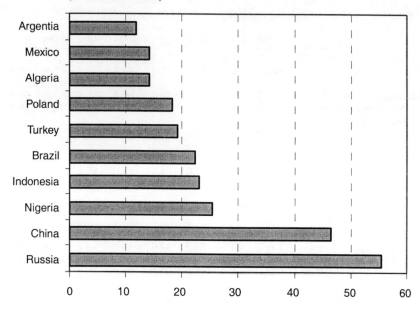

traditional markets in the Soviet Union. As long as the Soviet (and later, Russian) government was willing to assume the obligation and provide the guarantee, this was an excellent business for Germany. Thus, in a very tangible way, Russian taxpayers are still paying for the effects of German economic support. For instance, payments due to official creditors during the period 2002–10 on export credits disbursed to the Soviet Union before 1992 amount to US$31 billion, roughly 11 times the total annual sum spent by the federal government on social transfers, or more than 8 times the yearly amount spent by the local governments on health.[5] Data released by the IMF in 2001 show that by 1999 the largest exposure of export credit agencies to selected major developing countries was to Russia, followed by China, Nigeria, Indonesia, and Brazil (see Figure 14.1).

The development of the treasury bill market in the mid-1990s eventually became an important source of external funding to the Russian government. The amounts, particularly in 1996–98, were large, highly volatile, extremely expensive (dollar returns in excess of 50 percent were not unusual, particularly after 1995 when the IMF and the authorities agreed to peg the ruble, thereby providing investors an effective guarantee of a high-dollar return), and were eventually a precipitating factor in the 1998 financial crisis.[6] As with bilateral official credits, there was no policy reform component to this

Figure 14.2 **Annual Disbursements by the IMF to Russia**
(in billions of US$)

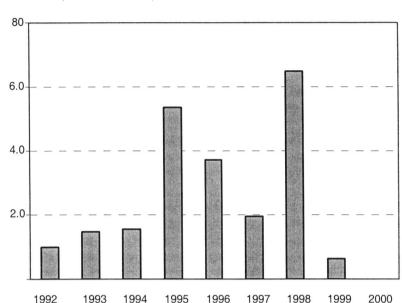

form of lending. With the capital account liberalized, nonresident investors provided the funds, because the returns were among the highest in the world. The government opened the treasury bill market to them because it proved an easier and faster source of funding, supplementary to IMF lending, than collecting taxes from Gazprom, the oil companies, and the public in general. Indeed, as access to foreign borrowing through the sale of treasury bills rose rapidly, the government revenue/GDP ratio fell precipitously; by 1998 the federal government was collecting the equivalent of 10.7 percent of GDP in annual revenues, down from 17 percent of GDP in the early phase of the transition. It was also *barely* able to finance the payment of wages (with some delays) and interest on the public debt.

Of the above three sources, by far the most important was multilateral lending. It was the largest in magnitude. It had the best terms, grace periods, maturity, and interest rates. It was not subject to the extreme volatility of portfolio inflows. Most importantly, it brought with it enormous potential leverage to advance the cause of Russian economic transformation. This was particularly the case for lending by the IMF, due to the fast disbursing nature of its funding and the organization's focus on macroeconomic policy reforms (See Figures 14.2 and 14.3).

Figure 14.3 **Real GDP** (% change)

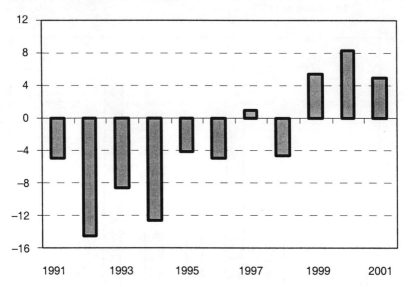

Policy Objectives and Instruments

The IMF seeks the promotion of economic policies that are conducive to sustainable growth. It tries to do this in two ways: helping to strengthen the economic policies of its individual member countries, and safeguarding the soundness of the international trade and financial system, two clearly inter-related objectives. Unlike the World Bank, whose focus is on investment and sectoral policies, the Fund's focus is largely on exchange rate and macro policies and issues of international monetary cooperation. Although the Fund endeavors to assist its members to avoid economic crises altogether, the situation most often encountered is that of a country where inappropriate policies have been pursued for an extended period of time, leading to severe imbalances, in the form of an unsustainable budget deficit, accelerating inflation, and/or distorted prices and exchange rates that discourage productive activity and encourage speculation, the emergence of black markets, capital flight, and so on. These were certainly the starting condition in Russia in late 1991 and early 1992, when the Russian government, with IMF assistance, decided to launch an economic stabilization program.[7]

As in other countries in crisis, the Fund very much saw its role in Russia as that of providing assistance to make the inevitable adjustment away from central planning less traumatic and more conducive to the long-term health of the economy, while providing financing and helping to generate additional resources from other creditors and donors in support of the government's program. The specific measures and overall aims and objectives were essentially the same as those pursued in dozens of other such programs, namely, to control inflation, to improve efficiency in resource allocation, and to help the country attain a more sustainable balance of payments position. These objectives were sought because they were seen as essential conditions for sustainable growth and economic development.

While a discussion of the theoretical foundations of Fund programs is outside the scope of this chapter, it is possible to provide a brief synthesis of the essence of the macroeconomic policy advice provided by the Fund to the Russian authorities beginning in 1992, when the first arrangement was negotiated and the government received its first $1 billion IMF credit. In essence, the Fund's policy advice consisted of four ingredients. First, an economy will be better prepared to adjust to shocks when greater scope is given to market forces. Second, financial policies must be geared to ensure a stable macroeconomic framework. Third, to improve competitiveness, the domestic economy must gradually integrate with the world economy. Lastly, policy reforms must be supported by regulatory and institutional improvements. Each of these four messages in turn brought with it fairly specific policy recommendations which were incorporated into the Fund's programs with the Russian government. A brief elaboration is useful, if only to highlight the key philosophical underpinnings of Fund advice in Russia.

The Role of Market Forces

A system in which prices reflect relative scarcities in the marketplace was presented as one of the most effective instruments of adaptation, providing a decentralized system of signals and incentives for the allocation of resources. The Russian economy would be more dynamic and flexible, better able to cope with external shocks, if decision-making was decentralized and greater scope was given to market forces. Such flexibility was especially important for economies with sharply fluctuating export earnings on account of their dependence on a few primary commodities—oil, gas, and metals in Russia accounting for about 80 percent of total exports. Price liberalization and an easing of administrative controls thus became a key feature of Fund programs in Russia. The definition of price flexibility in the Russian context was quite broad, applying also to those prices having a direct bearing on the macroeconomic environment, such as the exchange rate and interest rates.

A Stable Macroeconomic Environment

A stable financial environment was seen as essential for the successful implementation of other (so-called "structural") reforms, and the establishment of a macroeconomic environment supportive of private sector activity. Russia was to pursue prudent fiscal policies that allowed adequate levels of private sector credit while limiting the growth of total credit to levels consistent with noninflationary growth in the money supply and a viable external position. Cautious fiscal and monetary policies that contributed to low inflation rates and a more stable domestic environment were also to contribute strongly to business confidence and the willingness of domestic and foreign investors to undertake investment projects. Government economic policies that reduced inflation and encouraged macroeconomic stability were thus to play a critical role in fostering economic growth in Russia. Lastly, policies were also to aim at maintaining a competitive exchange rate while establishing a liberal trade and payments regime in which private firms and investors would have free access to foreign exchange and imported goods, with the allocation determined by market forces rather than administrative means.

Integration with the World Economy

A more outward-looking orientation was seen as an essential component of reforms in Russia. In addition to the well-known gains from international trade, relative openness and strong links with the world economy would impose on domestic producers the valuable discipline of international competition and would provide opportunities for new exports. It would also serve as an important channel for absorbing technological advances from abroad. An open orientation would also attract much needed capital and expertise, thus enhancing the prospects for growth through increased efficiency. This approach was regarded as particularly important for Russia, given a long legacy of excessive state interference in the economy involving, for instance, the administrative allocation of foreign exchange and other regulatory requirements, the absence of a competitive banking system, inadequate expenditures for maintenance and investment in a socially productive infrastructure, and the maintenance of inefficient public enterprises.

Institutional Reforms

The gist of the advice here was as follows: The regulatory system, including most importantly the tax system, needed to be freed from excessive intervention, arbitrary decisions, and inconsistent application of rules and policies, all of which were likely to hinder business activity and slow the pace of private sector development. The ultimate aim was to be the establishment of a simple regulatory and tax framework based on transparent rules. Investment decisions, whether by domestic or foreign investors, involved issues of long-range planning; from the investor's perspective a well-identified, simple, and stable set of rules would always be preferable to one perceived to be opaque and subject to unpredictable changes.

The above summary is fairly consistent with the broad thrust of policy advice provided by the Fund to its member countries everywhere. Two points warrant further elaboration. First, the relative weight given to each of the various components described above will vary significantly across countries, depending on the particular circumstances of each individual member, the readiness and/or willingness of the authorities to carry out specific policies, the perceived priorities of the government, the staff of the Fund, and, in some cases and at various times, even those of the Fund's largest shareholders. In Russia, the overwhelming focus of the reforms was on macroeconomic stabilization, that is, to bring inflation down by restraining the budget deficit and hence the need to limit the scope for the authorities to take recourse to monetary financing. While there was discussion of other issues—trade liberalization and the unification of the exchange rate in mid-1992 come to mind as two areas where there was progress early on—these tended very much to take a secondary place to the goal of achieving price stability.[8]

Second, while the content of Fund programs as gleaned from a careful reading of the Letters of Intent of the four programs negotiated between early 1992 and early 1996 would always contain key elements of the four broad policy areas identified above, this did not immediately translate itself into tangible policy reforms in practice. Reflecting the Fund's focus on stabilization, its conditionality in Russia was overwhelmingly focused on traditional macroeconomic targets and parameters, such as the net international reserve position of the Central Bank of Russia, the size of the budget deficit, and the pace of expansion of "net domestic assets" of the central bank—a broad measure of liquidity used by the Fund to monitor credit conditions in the economy. Measures with a structural component requiring long periods of gestation for adequate formulation and design tended either to be largely ignored or, at best, allowed to lapse into future programs.

Thus, while the Fund's approach tended to be fairly broad on paper, in practice the *effective* policy content of its programs was rather more limited, with several glaring omissions. For instance, by failing to incorporate social protection elements in the early phase of the transition, to mitigate the sharp erosion in living standards for large segments of the population, the Fund ended up undermining the effectiveness of its overall approach. First, the government eventually realized that structural reforms were not central to IMF program design (in the specific sense of being incorporated as part of the Fund's conditionality *and* disbursements being actually withheld because of noncompliance) and that the policy focus would likely remain on the stabilization front, that is, reducing the budget deficit, limiting the growth of credit, and so on. Not surprisingly, this led to a weakening of government resolve in this area. Second, lack of adequate progress on structural reforms delayed the economic recovery, prolonged the plight of vulnerable groups, and ended up undermining public support for the reforms.

Explanatory Factors

One possible way to characterize the Fund's policy advice and lending operations in Russia is to say that while the broad thrust of the policies being advocated, however incomplete they may have been, was broadly appropriate, the whole approach fell captive to other considerations, either of a political or an institutional nature. These might include the inherent problems in trying to transform key theoretical insights from the development and economics literature into objective realities in practice, in the context of a country undergoing major systemic changes; the role of strategic political factors and the perceived interests of some of Russia's most important bilateral partners; issues of IMF jurisdiction—specifically, the inability of the Fund to force policy changes in fields outside its "traditional" areas of expertise; and the limited administrative capacities of the government, which may have sharply limited what could objectively be achieved in the short term. We look at each of these issues in turn and assess the extent to which they can be identified as factors that could explain the ultimate inadequacy of the Fund's work in Russia. This discussion has broader implications for the work of the Fund, for instance, its relations with other neighboring countries in the Commonwealth of Independent States (CIS), several of which, having started the 1990s with zero external debt, may soon be joining the group of "highly indebted poor countries" and the developing world in general.

Theory Versus Practice

Partly as a result of falling levels of income per capita in sub-Saharan Africa and rising income disparities everywhere, the last couple of decades have witnessed a remarkable broadening of the debate as to what the ingredients of successful economic development are. This debate has been particularly intense in connection with the lending activities of the World Bank and the Fund, the two central providers of development finance. Perhaps the most tangible shift has been in the extent to which a calculated neglect of "soft-headed" concerns (to use Amartya Sen's characterization), such as the role of safety nets to protect the very poor or the provision of political and civil rights, has given way to an approach that recognizes their importance and actually tries to incorporate them in the design of programs and development strategies.[9] Even in the IMF, for decades committed with single-minded determination to the notion that the best way to achieve macroeconomic stability is to better "manage aggregate demand" (e.g., to reduce the budget deficit, to restrain credit growth), the focus in a growing number of programs has now shifted to creating the conditions for so-called "high-quality growth," a term that explicitly recognizes the importance of policies aimed at reducing poverty, improving opportunity, and protecting the environment.

While this broadening of the debate is most welcome, it is legitimate to ask to what extent it has gone beyond the stage of "heart-warming sentiments" (another Sen term), such as can be found, for instance, in the speeches of the heads of the international financial institutions or other official policy statements. For it is only when poverty, equity, environmental, and other such concerns get *explicitly* incorporated into the design and conditionality of economic programs financed by the development agencies that one can hope to begin to see the benefits on the ground, where it matters most. Regrettably, there continues to be a huge "gap" between theory and practice. The "gentler" approach to development advocated by Sen—the recognition, until recently, that we may have missed out on key elements of the development process and hence ill served the interests of large segments of the world's population—has not yet been reflected in the day-to-day work of these organizations, particularly the IMF and especially during its decade-long involvement with Russia. A couple of examples will clarify the point.

It is now universally accepted that macroeconomic policies can have significant effects on the distribution of incomes and thus on social equity and welfare. A responsible program must therefore take these effects into account, particularly as they impinge on the most vulnerable groups in society. Indeed, proper consideration of the impact of economic policy measures on the poor can produce stronger public support for a particular program and thus improve its sustainability. The provision of nearly $22 billion of IMF loans to Russia during 1992–99 coincided with a pronounced deterioration in living conditions for the Russian population, including a catastrophic reduction in the value of the pensions received by 37 million pensioners, a full 25 percent of the population. While some deterioration in the standard of living was probably inevitable, reflecting the gradual elimination of distortions and rigidities inherited from the Soviet era, it also reflected massive failures in governance. On a number of occasions during this period the government, through the granting of tax exemptions to vested interests or the giveaway of state assets through corrupt privatization schemes, deprived the budget of massive resources that sharply limited its ability to respond to growing social needs.[10] Many of these initiatives took place under the umbrella of fully operational IMF programs. So, in a very tangible way, with serious long-term welfare implications because of the rising external debt burden implied by IMF loans, the "new approach" to development, advocating the importance of good governance and transparency and the central role of the social safety net, was largely empty rhetoric in the case of Russia.

The opportunities that people have to determine who should govern them and on what principles and, more generally, the idea that the legitimacy and credibility of the government matter for the successful implementation of economic policies, is another of those ideas that have become part of the emerging consensus on sound approaches to development. Only governments that have the credibility derived from periodic legitimization of power through elections and that have shown a minimum of competence in economic management have a fighting chance of putting to good use IMF loans and other nonconcessional aid flows. And yet, the IMF has a long history of lending to governments barely (if at all) able to meet the most elementary standards of good governance. The period of fastest IMF lending to Russia was 1995–96, a period that coincided with some of the most glaring abuses in the management of public resources. A single tax exemption in place during this period, granted to the National Sports Foundation, Russia's largest importer of alcohol, tobacco, and luxury cars, deprived the Russian budget of the equivalent of $3–4 billion in annual revenue, a figure only slightly less than the magnitude of annual IMF financial support during this period.

Thus, there would appear to be an urgent need to rapidly bridge the gap between theoretical insights derived from development pioneers such as Sen, and the effective everyday practice of development practitioners like the IMF. The examples above do not reflect failures of economic theory or an inadequate understanding of what makes good development policy (although, surely, this is not to say that we have yet got the full picture right). Rather, they reflect failures of leadership, both by the governments who receive the aid and by the donor institutions who provide it. Ultimately, this gap must be narrowed in a major way if the international financial institutions are to remain relevant to the achievement of the mandate for which they were created: "the promotion and maintenance of high levels of employment and real income and the development of the productive resources of all members as primary objectives of economic policy" (Article I(ii), IMF Articles of Agreement; we come back to this issue in the last section of this chapter).

Lending Driven by Strategic Considerations

There is a growing body of literature on the subject of who the chief beneficiaries of foreign aid are. Alesina and Dollar make several interesting observations about bilateral aid flows.[11] First, patterns of aid seem to be largely
dictated by political and strategic considerations that have little to do with
rewarding good policies or helping more efficient, less corrupt governments.
Second, an inefficient, closed (in an economic sense), mismanaged, non-
democratic former colony that remains loyal to its former colonizer receives
far more aid than a country with similar per capita income and better policies
but no equivalent colonial ties. Third, there is no evidence that foreign aid
encourages the adoption of good macroeconomic policies. Fourth, foreign
direct investment seems to be more closely correlated with the kinds of variables that one would like to see as basic elements of the institutional and
policy framework of developing countries: political stability, democratization, a liberal trade regime, financial stability, a working judicial system,
and, more generally, the rule of law. Lastly, with the possible exception of
bilateral aid provided by the Nordic countries, much of it is actually wasted
or, worse, only serves to legitimize and keep in power people who would
otherwise not deserve to be in power.

From this perspective, to the extent that narrow strategic/political interests figure less prominently in their decision-making process, multilateral
aid may be better. The evidence that this was so in Russia is not compelling.
By the mid-1990s, IMF lending to Russia was less driven by policy content
and the associated conditionality than by geopolitical considerations defined
by the Fund's largest shareholders. Indeed, during much of the 1990s the
Fund was used as the main conduit for G7 support for Russian economic
reforms. "Strategic" lending, however, brings with it a number of risks for
the borrower. First, the strategic interests are those of the shareholder leaning
on the multilateral institution to proceed with the lending, *not* of the borrower. The interests of the borrower and, ultimately, the taxpayers who will
carry the future debt burden, are very much an afterthought, if they enter into
the picture at all. In Russia these interests were multidimensional. They reflected the desire by the Fund's largest shareholders to reward President
Yeltsin's otherwise largely pro-Western foreign policy; the perceived need to
prevent possible political instability in a country undergoing profound political and social change and armed with thousands of nuclear weapons, the
apparent conviction that lending would strengthen the hand of reformist elements within the government who were sympathetic to free market policies
(and who, the argument went, were fighting a rearguard battle against the
forces of vested interests), and the need to support President Yeltsin's reelection

campaign in 1996, against the background of the growing public appeal of the Communist Party, among others.[12]

Second, and perhaps more importantly, the focus of attention for the authorities shifts from how best to advance the economic policy agenda to how best to make sure that the government does the minimum necessary to qualify for the next IMF tranche, given that a proper reading of the strategic considerations underlying the lending has convinced the authorities that the funds will be forthcoming in all probability. This type of consideration in Fund lending operations has ill served the interests of the Russian public; we take up this issue further in the last section of this chapter when the question of IMF reform is examined. Lastly, in times of crisis, such as after the treasury bill default in August of 1998, the countries at whose behest the "geopolitically inspired" lending took place have few options beyond expressing solidarity for the country's authorities, as the public gears up to pay back the loans. In Russia's case, in early 2001, the German government was quite aggressive in rejecting (poorly articulated) Russian requests for debt relief on Soviet-era export credits.

Issues of Jurisdiction

Even if the two factors mentioned above had not been present in the background of multilateral lending to Russia during much of the 1990s, some would argue that the Fund, nevertheless, would have faced issues of jurisdiction in trying to push for reforms in specific areas. There are at least two aspects to this question. First, the Fund has a limited mandate to impose conditionality on policies outside its traditional areas of expertise. Fund executive directors often remind each other during board discussions of programs about "the monetary nature of the Fund." From this perspective, the Fund can push for a lower budget deficit but cannot effectively press governments to introduce social safety nets or prevent the introduction of questionable privatization schemes. Second, the Fund has limited leverage to coerce governments to implement particular policies, even if it felt that these were essential for the success of the program. The Fund is ultimately a cooperative institution lacking in enforcement mechanisms that could ensure a particular outcome, much as a national central bank has, for instance, vis-à-vis the commercial banks under its jurisdiction. As regards "the monetary nature of the Fund" limiting the ability of its staff to venture into areas well beyond inflation control and deficit reduction, the point is largely irrelevant.

Monetary phenomena cannot be examined in isolation from other elements of the macroeconomy. If, in fact, the Fund has a mandate to promote "high-quality growth" (and a careful reading of the Fund's articles makes this an inescapable conclusion), then it cannot walk away from such issues as whether the government is reducing the budget deficit by building up wage and pension arrears, thereby alienating broad segments of the population and undermining its own credibility with the public, or whether the fiscal adjustment is being made more onerous than would otherwise be the case because the government is giving tax breaks to well-connected lobby groups. When the Fund does so, as it most definitely did in Russia during the mid-1990s, the results are heartbreakingly disappointing.

It is an entirely different issue whether the Fund has the *expertise* to address effectively the broad range of concerns identified by Sen as part of an integrated approach to economic development. Here many would argue that where it does not, it would be better to leave these to other donors or to the authorities themselves. So, social protection issues, for instance, in which the Fund has limited expertise, might best be left to the World Bank and its lending operations. The problem with this approach is that the fast-disbursing nature of the Fund's resources give the organization effectively far greater policy leverage vis-à-vis the government than the Bank ever had; indeed the Bank's leverage in Russia was often *derived*. The more important point here is that if strengthening the social safety net was seen as essential to ensure the sustainability and efficiency of Russia's transition to a market economy, then the international financial institutions should have organized their lending operations (including associated conditionalities) during the 1990s so as to ensure this outcome.

That this expertise was not immediately available among the Fund staff is hardly relevant. Such expertise exists and it should have been brought to bear in the design of Fund programs. A tiny fraction, say 0.1 percent of the total amount disbursed by the Fund, is still a very large sum, which could have financed the creation of a high-level task force of the world's best experts.[13] That it was not reflects mainly lack of recognition on the part of Fund staff and management of the central role of social equity issues to successful economic development. Similar comments apply to other elements of Sen's agenda, including the whole range of issues that fall under his category of "transparency guarantees." That loans-for-shares privatization was not stopped in its tracks by the Fund had nothing to do with the inability of its staff to adequately gauge the inefficiency of opaque ownership schemes; it had much more to do with Fund staff and management not thinking that it was a particularly deleterious policy, certainly not one that would have warranted stopping monthly disbursements of debt which continued without interruption as loans-for-shares got underway. Thus, in the end, it represented a massive failure of governance on the part of the Russian government for coming up with a corrupt privatization scheme and of the Fund, which could have stopped it but chose not to.[14]

Administrative Capacities

Some would argue that the ability of international financial institutions to design more elaborate programs was constrained to some extent by the limited
administrative capacities of the Russian government. This reflected a number
of interrelated factors: during the Soviet period the exceptionally talented made
their way into the military industrial complex, not the civil service. By the time
the Soviet Union was dissolved, much of the top echelons of the Union administrative cadre were on their way out, leaving government service altogether
and opting for new careers in some form of private sector activity. This was a
particularly serious problem in 1992–93, the early phase of Russia's transition.
Faced with a serious dearth of suitably qualified personnel, with relevant administrative and managerial experience, the Fund and the Bank did what they
could in terms of policy design and implementation.

My own view is that while this was a serious problem at the outset of the
transition, by the mid-1990s staffing pressures had been considerably relieved in key sectors of public administration. In any event, the Fund's leverage to elicit policy responses from the government was not uniform throughout
the six-year period over which the $22 billion of financial assistance were
disbursed. As is clear from Figure 14.2, total Fund disbursements during the
three-year period through 1994 year-end amounted to $4.2 billion, three-
quarters of it disbursed in two tranches under the Systemic Transformation
Facility, a low-conditionality financing window specially created to assist
countries in the early stages of the transition. The Fund's real leverage began
in early 1995, with the negotiations of the first standby arrangement that
contemplated monthly program monitoring and disbursements and much
higher levels of access to Fund resources. Russian debt to the Fund in the
next two years nearly tripled, and the staffing constraints which had plagued
the early period were much relieved. In those areas where it felt that the
administrative capacities of the government or the central bank needed to be
strengthened through technical assistance, the Fund had no problems making provisions for it. This was particularly the case at the central bank and
the treasury, in a broad range of areas deemed to be essential for appropriate
monitoring of monetary and expenditure control operations. Presumably expertise in other areas could likewise have been boosted through the timely
provision of relevant technical assistance.

Reforming the IMF

The latest events in Argentina raise, once again, serious questions about
the current approach to crisis management in emerging markets, the chief

characteristic of which seems to be large-scale improvisation and ad hoc arrangements with costly social and political repercussions.[15] The IMF has found itself in the middle of each of these debacles, and questions about its effectiveness have been raised every time; indeed some have argued that the organization is no longer needed in an environment of largely floating exchange rates. It is clear, however, that because today's world is one of closely integrated markets, in which linkages are becoming evermore complex, an institution that will have sufficient resources to deal with occasional episodes of financial instability and that will help cushion or prevent the effects of future crises is indispensable. Some ideas follow on the sort of reforms that could make the world's only "financial peacekeeper" a more effective crisis manager.

As presently structured, the IMF falls far short of the role played by central banks in national economies. Like a national central bank, it can create international liquidity through its lending operations and the occasional allocations to its members of Special Drawing Rights (SDRs), its composite currency. Thus, as Richard Cooper has pointed out, the IMF already is, in a limited sense, a small international bank of issue. As seen during much of the past decade, beginning with the Mexican crisis in 1994–5, the Fund can also play the role of "lender-of-last-resort" for an economy experiencing debt-servicing difficulties. But the amount of support it can provide has traditionally been limited by the size of the country's membership quota, and there is obviously an upper limit on *total* available resources; at the end of 2001 this amounted to some $90 billion, a relatively small sum, equivalent to less than 1 percent of cross-border claims of BIS reporting banks.

In addition to the paucity of resources, which do not allow the Fund to respond to more than a handful of crises in a few medium-sized countries, there are other serious structural flaws in its lender-of-last-resort functions. To begin with, its regulatory functions are extremely rudimentary. Its members are sovereign nations that are bound, in theory, by the Fund's Articles of Agreement, but the institution has no real enforcing authority, other than some limited functions through the "conditionality" it applies to those countries using its resources. In particular, the Fund has no authority to enforce changes in policies when countries are engaged in misguided or unsustainable policy paths but are otherwise not borrowing from the Fund—this was the case with the Asian countries in 1997. What little enforcement authority the IMF does have is sometimes eroded when the country in question has a powerful patron, who may try to persuade the Fund and its managers to exercise leniency or "turn a blind eye" if policies appear to be going awry. Contrast this situation with that of a typical national central bank, which has enormous leverage vis-à-vis the commercial banks under its jurisdiction when making resources available to them, particularly in the midst of a crisis. The IMF simply does not have an analogous authority at the international level vis-à-vis the countries that are eligible to use its resources.

There are a number of possible ways to deal with these shortcomings. One proposal is to create an International Financial Stability Fund, to supplement IMF resources. This would be a facility that could be financed by an annual fee on the stock of cross-border investment; a 0.1 percent tax could generate, according to Edwin Truman, a former assistant secretary at the U.S. Treasury, some $25–30 billion per year, which could then be used over time to create a $300 billion facility.[16] This would deal with the relative scarcity of IMF resources and would partially de-link its lender-of-last-resort functions from the periodic allocations of national currencies that currently form the basis of IMF liquidity growth. An alternative proposal would give the Fund the authority to create SDRs as needed, as a national central bank can in theory, to meet calls on it by would-be borrowers.

When this idea was first put forward in the early 1980s, concerns were raised about the possibly inflationary implications of such liquidity injections, but international inflation was a serious problem then in ways that it is clearly not today, and measures could be introduced to safeguard against this. This, of course, would involve giving the Fund considerably more leverage vis-à-vis the policies of those countries willing to have much larger potential access to its resources. Nobody questions the right of central banks to have a major say over the prudential and regulatory environment underlying the activities of the commercial banks under their jurisdiction; it is seen as a legitimate counterpart of its lender-of-last-resort functions. A much richer Fund would likewise have to have much stronger leverage and independence.

The above says nothing about the kinds of policies that the IMF advocates and whether these are generally welfare-enhancing or not. The recent crisis in Argentina, as well as earlier devastating episodes in Russia and Asia, have generated heated debates as to whether the IMF is part of the problem, part of the solution, or a bit of both. Whatever the justice of these respective positions, it is clear that giving the Fund potential access to a much larger volume of resources would have to be accompanied by significant internal reforms, both in terms of the *content* of the policies it advocates, as well as its internal *management*. Both areas have received scant attention in the past decade, with the focus having largely been on the type of facilities through which resources are made available and the bureaucratic underpinnings of each.

It is becoming increasingly clear, however, that at least some of the instances of unsuccessful intervention by the IMF in recent years (that of Russia springs most readily to mind, though Paul Krugman thinks Argentina qualifies as well) may reflect less a lack of resources and more old-fashioned policy mistakes, arising from the Fund's own intellectual biases, its particular views as to what makes for good economic policy, and the vagaries of its internal decision-making processes, which suffer from a number of serious flaws. As noted above, in Russia the IMF disbursed some $22 billion of debt between 1992 and 1999 but clearly it did not elicit much in the way of policy reforms in return. Indeed, six years of IMF involvement collapsed in August of 1998, and, along the way, with the cognizance of the IMF, the government was allowed to give away its best assets under extremely corrupt privatization schemes. Simultaneously, as noted earlier on, the Russian population endured a more pronounced decline in living standards than was warranted by the elimination of some of the distortions of the central plan, greatly undermining public support for market-oriented reforms. During a visit to Moscow last year a senior IMF official characterized the 1995 standby arrangement as "very successful" and "a key achievement" because inflation came down. The consensus in Moscow, however, remains that the 1995 program was an "unmitigated disaster"; for what virtue could there be in bringing inflation down (temporarily—it came back with a vengeance after the collapse of the ruble in 1998) if this is at the cost of the state building up massive wage and pension arrears, thereby signaling to taxpayers that since the state fails to fulfill its own obligations, others may legitimately follow suit?

So, if the Fund is to be given more of the functions of a lender-of-last-resort to the likes of Argentina, Turkey, and Russia, then it needs a new philosophy, bringing into the center of its programs (and its conditionality) the kinds of concerns and policies that, so far, it has only tended to espouse in theory. In their public speeches, the Fund's top managers speak of transparency, social protection, good governance, and "high-quality growth," but they have not yet managed to incorporate these laudable aims into IMF program design. Indeed, it is becoming increasingly evident (as the crisis in Argentina has dramatically demonstrated) that only programs perceived as meeting actual needs and as being just and equitable in their objectives can hope to engage the commitment of the people, upon whom successful implementation ultimately depends. By this yardstick, most IMF programs yield distressingly disappointing results. Not surprisingly, the Fund finds itself increasingly at the center of ineffective programs, blamed for the failure of its policy prescriptions.

Easing the task of evolving new paradigms of intervention, a wealth of illuminating material already exists in the field. A perusal of Sen's *Development as Freedom* provides a compelling list of the ingredients of a successful approach to economic development, soon bearing home upon the reader that fiscal austerity is not the sole remedy available. Indeed, as UK Chancellor of the Exchequer Gordon Brown recently noted, the assumption that "just by liberalizing, deregulating, privatizing and simply getting prices right, growth and employment would inevitably follow" has "proved inadequate to meet the emerging challenges of globalization."[17]

A broadening of the policy content of Fund programs, to meet the challenges of Sen's much wider vision of successful development, to be credible, would need to be accompanied by a structural reorganization, whereby the Fund's shareholders assigned it a greater measure of intellectual independence, making it at the same time more accountable for the consequences of its decisions. It would seem desirable to separate the Fund's surveillance activities from its decisions in respect of lending, so that glaring conflicts of interest might be avoided. Gordon Brown's call for a "more transparent, more independent and, therefore, more authoritative" Fund is certainly a step in the right direction, as is his call for new approaches to sovereign debt restructuring and the implementation of code standards for fiscal, monetary, and other policies to diminish the likelihood of future crises. In these discussions the focus should overwhelmingly shift to crisis prevention rather than crisis resolution.

But even an updated set of policy prescriptions is unlikely to suffice without corresponding reforms in the internal workings of the organization. As a preliminary measure, the international community might finally break with the convention adhered to ever since the IMF's creation, which establishes that its managing director must be an EU citizen. (A similar recommendation applies to the World Bank, whose president has traditionally been a U.S. citizen.) The organization is too important and its mistakes too socially costly for the nationality of the candidate for managing director to be the determining factor in assessing suitability for the job. The unseemly negotiating process that is entered into every few years as efforts are once more set in train to locate the most suitable candidate from a specific country is inherently offensive to the peoples of those countries who have to endure the rigors of IMF austerity, not to mention that it exemplifies that very inefficiency that IMF officials are quick to condemn in dealings with the Fund's member countries. (Doubtless the practice could not be sustained under present-day judicial codes, embodying as it does the particular conceptions of a world recently emerged from the trauma of world war.) Another desirable reform along these lines would be to accord the managing director a nonrenewable fixed term of service, thereby freeing him from the conflict that may otherwise result between the interests of those who hold his appointment in their hands and the countries that it is his mission to serve. In this way, he may never feel himself under pressure to forgo his principles by reconciling these divergent stances.

On the question of the controlling interest in the organization, it may be noted that the salaries of the Fund's managing director and of its entire staff (as well as other administrative expenditures) are financed precisely by the interest paid by taxpayers in Argentina, Turkey, Russia, and other users of Fund resources. Whereas IMF lending operations have no budgetary implications for members such as the U.S. and the EU, indeed they earn a return on their SDR reserve assets. A country such as Russia, by contrast, has paid, since August 1998, over $3 billion in interest charges on previous Fund loans. Such a circumstance alone, one would think, might go some way to counter the existing notion that, because the large shareholders "contribute" more to the organization, they are in some manner entitled to oversee its operations as well, particularly since they have already the largest voting shares at the IMF board.

This raises a second observation, namely, that increasingly there is a tendency for the markets, borrowers, and other economic agents to view the Fund as subservient to its main shareholders, a proxy of G7 foreign policy or, worse, as Paul Krugman recently expressed it, "a branch of the US treasury."[18] Such a perception is deeply damaging to the organization's ability to act effectively. It encourages countries to gauge their relationship with the IMF in terms of short-term political advantage rather than lasting economic gain. In Russia, for instance, in the mid-1990s, the government realized that "the money was coming in any event"; the will for policy reforms died at about the same time. A similar calculation may be under way in Turkey at the moment, as the country amasses a mountain of debt to the IMF at a vertiginous pace, breaking and confounding all previous historical parameters that linked the amount of external funding to the scale of the policy adjustment, and destroying the long-respected Fund principle of equality of treatment across its member countries.[19]

The present organizational structure has implications too for the Fund staff, who cannot under the present regime be held accountable for policy miscalculations. Deprived of full freedom to make intellectually independent assessments, inasmuch as the controlling influence rests with the large shareholders, who, as indicated, may be answerable to various "strategic," meaning political, interests of their own, they are constrained to represent themselves merely as executors—not a role calculated to enhance their standing with their counterparts in the Fund's member countries. And to the extent that they be viewed by the countries concerned as mere functionaries, their ability to act more generally as advocates for change will be impaired.

Emerging from the 1944 Bretton Woods conference at which both the

IMF and the World Bank were created, John Maynard Keynes expressed the view: "As an experiment in international cooperation, the conference has been an outstanding success." The world has changed beyond recognition in the meantime, and, with the emergence of one global economy, the case for an institution that will help further the cause of international cooperation and be identified with the promotion of economic policies supportive of improved efficiency and equity has only become stronger. Conditions seem now propitious for the convocation of a global conference of heads of state to consult on the policy and institutional requirements for a more stable world financial system in the era of globalization. How to promote better ownership of programs, and how to more effectively engage the countries most affected by such crises, in the decision-making process, are clearly two central questions that would need to be addressed. Indeed, the time may be fast approaching for a new Bretton Woods conference aimed at turning our two premier development organizations into more flexible and effective instruments for the promotion of global welfare.

Conclusions

There are at least three ways to look at the role of international financial institutions in Russia during the past decade. Due to the unprecedented policy leverage that the IMF enjoyed during some of the most critical periods of Russia's transition, the much larger volume of resources it provided, their fast-disbursing nature, and the relatively shorter repayment periods (which put a heavier burden on efficient utilization of the loans), this paper has focused on the operations of the Fund. The Fund can be seen to have provided assistance to the Russian government in three broad areas. First and foremost, the Fund was the principal financier of the government; this role was particularly intense during the three-and-a half-year period from early 1995 to July 1998, when a total of $17.5 billion of debt was disbursed. Second, the Fund provided technical assistance to the central bank and other public sector institutions, both in the context of policy formulation during program negotiations and program implementation and through the provision of external advisers with specific terms of reference (e.g., assisting the State Tax Service in tax administration issues and the central bank in monetary operations). Third, membership in the Fund opened to the Russian authorities new avenues of international cooperation, for instance vis-à-vis CIS neighbors, for which Russia was the most important trade partner and creditor.

Of these three forms of assistance, by far the most "valuable" was the technical assistance component, particularly that part of it that was focused on specific needs and delivered at particular institutions. The value of technical assistance provided in the context of program negotiations and subsequent implementation is more difficult to gauge. Some of it clearly forced government officials to look at policy reforms at an earlier stage; the Fund was certainly a useful catalyst in focusing government attention on priority areas and assisting in the design of plans and strategies. That many of these subsequently fell captive to government inertia, the power of vested interests, or administrative limitations in the public sector does not take away the fact that the *process* of formulating policies, identifying priorities, and imbedding these within a consistent program framework was useful in itself. So, the purely nonfinancial aspects of Russia's evolving relationship with the international financial institutions, involving mainly an intellectual dialogue on the policy requirements of economic reform, may be one of the more enduring and valuable aspects of the International Financial Institutions' involvement in Russia during the first decade of the transition. That membership in the Fund and the Bank also opened avenues for the interaction by senior Russian officials with their peers abroad on issues of international economic cooperation is another aspect worth highlighting. It contributed in tangible ways to the acceleration of Russia's integration with the global economy.

Whether it was necessary for the Russian government to acquire $17.5 billion of debt along the way (we exclude here the amounts disbursed during the period 1992–94 which were relatively small and for which the policy reform component was not insignificant)[20] is a separate issue altogether. It is this author's assessment that, on balance, the effects of large-scale Fund financing during the period 1995–98 were largely detrimental. First, the government used IMF loans as a substitute for tax collection; as noted above, the revenue/GDP ratio fell drastically over this period, under the weight of tax exemptions, tax arrears and offsets, and the pernicious effects of expenditure sequestration.[21] Indeed, the period of largest Fund financial support coincided with the most severe erosion in the ability of the state to collect taxes and in the willingness of corporations and households to pay them. Second, this large-scale funding brought with it very little in the way of actual economic reforms. To the extent that Fund lending largely reflected the strategic considerations noted earlier on, it was much easier for the authorities to lobby their G7 patrons for "Fund flexibility" in interpreting the program's agreed conditionality (or for the prime minister to lobby the Fund's managing director), than, for example, to eliminate tax exemptions or collect taxes due from the energy or metals sectors.

Third, there were no safeguards in place to ensure that the resources disbursed would be efficiently utilized. Much of IMF lending during this critical period involved direct support to the federal budget (as opposed to international reserve buildup at the central bank); once the tranches were released it was left to the government to decide how to allocate the funds. Since during much of this period (1995–98) the government was mainly able to finance only the payment of wages and interest payments on the public debt, one can infer that little of it went to finance productive investments aimed at enhancing the economy's growth potential. Lastly, since IMF funds were loans, after 1998 the country was left with a $28 billion future claim on the budget (including interest charges), payable through 2008. That Russia has since been able to fulfill its financial obligations to the Fund on a timely basis is more a reflection of the sharp recovery of oil and other commodity prices that began in early 1999, than the delayed effects of IMF reforms. Both the Russian budget and the Fund's reputation were thus "saved" by higher oil prices, not a particularly cheerful commentary to characterize the Fund's ten-year involvement with Russia.

Notes

1. The author is presently an executive director with Lehman Brothers in London. He was resident representative for the IMF in Moscow during the period 1992–95. The views expressed in this chapter are the author's own and are not necessarily those of the institution with which he is affiliated.

2. World Bank lending was much smaller in scope, largely focused on specific sectoral reforms, and given at much longer maturities.

3. This latter category of debt does not appear in the table, as the underlying obligations were denominated in rubles.

4. For an interesting overview of some of the irregularities associated with the disbursement of export credits, see the article by Sabrina Tavernise, "Russia Trying to Head Off Debt Squeeze," *The New York Times*, 14 April 2001.

5. Annual debt payments on Soviet-era export credits actually rise after 2010 and peak in 2015 at US$4 billion. These figures exclude amounts due to official creditors on export credits disbursed to Russia beginning in 1992; the total debt burden on account of this type of debt is thus much higher.

6. According to the IMF, net nonresident purchases of ruble treasury bills (the so-called GKOs and OFZs) amounted to $6 billion in 1996, $10.9 billion in 1997, and $2.8 billion in 1998.

7. For a description of the starting conditions faced by the Gaidar government in late 1991, see Augusto Lopez-Claros and Mikhail M. Zadornov, "A Decade of Russian Economic Reforms," www.zadornov.com. For a shorter version of the same article, see *The Washington Quarterly 25* (2002): 105–116.

8. For a fuller discussion of these issues, including the limitations of the Fund's "financial programming" approach to program design and the implications for the work of the Fund more generally, see the author's 1996 paper, "The Fund's Role in Russia," available at the Institute for the Economy in Transition's Web site www.iet.ru.

9. For a fuller discussion of these issues see Amartya Sen, *Development as Freedom* (Oxford: Oxford University Press, 1999).

10. For a listing of some of the most important tax exemptions in force in Russia during 1992–96, see Augusto Lopez-Claros and Sergei Alexashenko, "Fiscal Policy

Issues During the Transition in Russia," Occasional Paper 155, International Monetary Fund, March 1998, 18–21.

11. See Alberto Alesina and David Dollar, "Who Gives Foreign Aid to Whom and Why?" NBER Working Paper No. W6612, June 1998.

12. That, by early 1996, the Communist Party should have been perceived by many within Russia as a viable political force is itself an interesting indicator of public disaffection with key elements of the reform process and the particular way in which it was being implemented.

13. Indeed, there were a number of governments who would have been only too willing to defray the bulk of these costs out of their international technical assistance budgets.

14. In what is surely a bitter irony, the scheme's chief protagonists on the Russian side were some of the same "reformers" on behalf of whose efforts much of the "strategic" lending took place.

15. This section draws from other work being done by the author on crisis management in emerging markets and the future of the international financial system.

16. Edwin M. Truman, "Perspectives on External Financial Crises," Institute for International Economics, December 2001.

17. Speech given by Chancellor of the Exchequer Gordon Brown to the Federal Reserve Bank of New York, 16 November 2001.

18. See Paul Krugman, "Argentina's Crisis Is a U.S. Failure," *The International Herald Tribune*, 21 January 2002.

19. To put things in perspective, consider the following statistic. Were Argentina later this year to return to the Fund with a coherent economic program and ask for levels of access to IMF resources broadly similar to those granted to Turkey, it could qualify for a $50 billion loan, equivalent to about 60 percent of total net, uncommitted usable IMF resources. Nobody thinks that Argentina would ever be given a credit of this magnitude, no matter how ambitious and comprehensive its program. However, by the end of 2002 Turkey could well account for 35–40 percent of the total debt of the entire IMF membership. As in Russia, one can be sure that long after the Fund is no longer an active lender, taxpayers will be making the necessary sacrifices to repay more than $30 billion in IMF loans.

20. For instance, the 1992 program, involving a one-time disbursement of $1 billion brought with it the unification of Russia's inefficient and corruption-ridden system of multiple exchange rates.

21. For a discussion of the effects of budget execution and, in particular, expenditure sequestration, on the willingness of corporations and households to pay taxes, see Lopez-Claros and Alexashenko, "Fiscal Policy Issues During the Transition in Russia," 29–34.

15

Programs for Homeless Children

Introduction: Homeless Children in the Former Soviet Union

Kate Schecter

Not since the tumultuous 1920s have the children of Russia and the former Soviet Union suffered so terribly from the political turmoil of their time. Following the Bolshevik Revolution and the Russian Civil War, an estimated seven million children whose parents were either dead or missing roamed the former Russian empire searching for food and shelter. While the situation today is not as dire, estimates from government sources put the number of street children in Russia alone at anywhere between 1 to 4 million. What started out as a trickle of abandoned and runaway children in the early 1990s has turned into a steady flow, especially into major former Soviet cities. The problem is so serious that President Putin recently gave a speech calling for a government response to cope with the national crisis.[1]

A Historic Perspective

Prior to the collapse of Communism, the problem of abandoned and handicapped children was hidden from public view by an extensive institutionalization system. Following the Bolshevik Revolution, World War I, and the Russian Civil War, and in response to postwar chaos, millions of "hooligans" and orphaned children were institutionalized in Soviet children's homes. This huge network and infrastructure of state-sponsored child rearing began with the inception of the Soviet state and helped confirm the Marxist notion that the family would "wither away" with a transition to full socialism.

The reliance on residential institutions—boarding schools, orphanages, and homes for handicapped children—became an entrenched aspect of the Soviet social welfare system. When Gorbachev came to power, glasnost provided an opportunity for many social issues to be discussed more openly, and children's homes became a subject of investigation. In the USSR, it was revealed that the infrastructure of these institutions was collapsing; food and clothing were inadequate, and inmates were ill-treated. In addition, it became evident that hundreds of thousands of children were living in these homes and that a large number of them were not orphans but had been placed there by their parent(s). Today, it is estimated that 95 percent of the children in institutions, shelters, or on the street are "social orphans," abandoned or neglected by living parents who clearly have lost the material or psychological wherewithal to care for them.

Current Conditions and Estimates

In the current environment, it is close to impossible to estimate the actual number of youth living on the streets. The problem is far more evident during the summer months when children flock to major cities to beg from tourists and live outside while the weather permits. In the winter, subways provide shelter, but unlike warmer Brazil and India, the cold climate hides children from the public eye for much of the year. Municipal governments conduct periodic sweeps to round up street children—as well as adults— and send them out of the city on trains or buses. The former Soviet system of internal passports and residency permits—*propiski*—required that every person living in a major urban area had a stamp in their passport allowing them to live there. While this authoritarian holdover has been declared unconstitutional in Russia, in reality it persists, and the majority of street children do not have documentation to prove their identities, let alone residency permits. In numerous cases, social workers and police have found children who are so young or so traumatized that they do not even know their own names or ages. State orphanages, shelters, and detention centers will not accept children without legal documents, children lacking these papers are treated as illegal immigrants and are sent out of the country. A few nongovernmental shelters and organizations try to help these youth but often find themselves sending children back to their country or city of origin, only to have them reappear a few months later.

Russia and Ukraine are the two most populous countries in the region and probably have the highest percentage of street children. One hundred thousand new orphans are registered in Russia each year, the majority of whom are social orphans abandoned by their families. One Moscow neighborhood detention center reported taking in 6,500 children in 2001, with a turnover rate of as many as 200 children every day.

Causes of Homelessness

The central cause of this horrifying phenomenon is the rapid impoverishment that has occurred across the region since the collapse of Communism. Child poverty has increased throughout the region as general economic output has declined. More than 75 million people in these post-socialist regions fell into poverty between 1989 and the mid-1990s as wages dipped for most people to less than 50 percent of their previous earnings.[2] War and armed conflict have caused mass migration throughout the region. Since the late 1980s, 7 million people—more than a third of them under 18 years of age—have been forced to migrate. In the countries of the former Yugoslavia, more than 150,000 women and children were forced from their homes, and many have never been able to return. More than half of the 350,000 refugees who fled Kosovo in 1999 were children. The UN estimates that 30 percent of the world's refugees and displaced people come from this part of the world.[3]

In addition to unemployment and general impoverishment, the growth in single-parent households, the majority of which are headed by women, has exacerbated the situation. In Russia, 14 million children out of a total of 33 million live in one-parent households, 94 percent of them headed by mothers. Almost half of all children in Russia are being brought up by single mothers who are at the highest risk of being unemployed or living close to or in poverty.[4]

Alcoholism, the rise in crime, incarceration of parents and youths, and the health crises facing the region are additional contributing factors. Not only are parents suffering disproportionately from these problems, but adolescent health is on the decline as well. A recent report by the Russian Ministry of Health cited increasing mortality—213.4 per 100,000 for ten- to seventeen-year-olds—in Russia and increasing morbidity, especially through sexually transmitted and other infectious diseases.[5] The lethal combination of homelessness, prostitution, and drug use has led to skyrocketing rates of sexually transmitted infections (STIs) and HIV/AIDS among young people in the region. STIs have reached epidemic proportions in Russia and Ukraine, and the potential for an HIV epidemic looms large in this part of the world. The HIV/AIDS infection rate remains a relatively underreported problem in many parts of the region, and the rate of infection among adolescents and youth, although probably very high among certain at-risk populations, is unknown in most cities.

In addition to the factors cited above, the adult mortality crisis in the Newly

Independent States (NIS) and Central and Eastern Europe is indirectly taking its toll on youth. Parents are at higher risk for premature death throughout the region, and this is contributing to the skyrocketing number of abandoned or orphaned children. While the increase in male mortality is more severe, female mortality has risen in parts of the former Soviet Union; UNICEF estimates that as many as 700,000 children throughout the region have been affected by the premature death of their parents.[6]

The health situation of children in this region is grim in general, and homelessness only exacerbates the threats that they face, because street children are at higher risk of contracting infectious diseases and of premature death. A recent Russian newspaper report in the popular journal, *Nezavisimaya Gazeta*, states that in northern Russia 40 percent of the children suffer from tuberculosis, more than half suffer from lung disorders, 96 percent have some kind of infectious disease, and 92 percent have dental problems.[7] Even if these statistics are exaggerated, there is little doubt that the general health status of children and youth in the NIS is declining.

The rise in crime has also had a devastating effect on the people of the region and is an additional factor that endangers homeless and abandoned children. In 1999 alone, Russia registered 208,000 crimes committed by children, 2,000 suicides by children, and 200 children killed by their parent(s).[8]

Many street children and other young girls desperate for employment turn to prostitution as a means of survival. Moscow and Kiev have become centers for networks trafficking in the sale and pandering of young women, the majority of whom are thought to be between the ages of 15 and 20. It is estimated that two of every three trafficked young women is kidnapped from Moldova and that 64 percent of all prostitutes working in the European Union are from there.[9] Young women are brought to the Czech Republic, Hungary, Albania, and other Central and Eastern European countries where thousands work or are shipped overseas, stripped of their passports, and sold to brothels in such countries as Turkey, Cyprus, Greece, and Israel. Most of the victims are the equivalent of slaves: illegal immigrants, without documentation, forced to work for little or no pay. Because young European women are in demand in the international "white slave trade," these girls—many of them unregistered children living on the streets—are the most vulnerable and the most available source for this market.

Steps Toward Reform

While there is no comprehensive foster care system in any of the former Soviet countries, there are hundreds of nongovernmental organizations (NGOs) and individuals who have responded to the crisis of homelessness by opening shelters and makeshift foster homes for these children. Government-sponsored shelters and programs are emerging, but coordination with NGOs is rare and, in many cases, the official response is to incarcerate these children. Hundreds—perhaps thousands—of youths are detained in prisons where they may never be charged with a crime or given a fair trail, but where they are simply warehoused until the authorities decide what to do with them. In addition to living in terrible, overcrowded prison conditions, the children often contract tuberculosis or other infectious diseases because of their incarceration, diseases that they then transmit to others whom they encounter when they are released.

Until an infrastructure of shelters and foster care is developed and a cadre of social workers and psychologists trained, the old system will continue to take in children. The first step toward reform is to remove the incentives that perpetuate institutionalization. Many orphanages, for example, still receive state funding based on occupancy rates. And while foreign aid to improve the conditions in orphanages is sent by well-meaning donors, it does little to help solve the long-term fate of these children. Like many social problems, this one will take many years to resolve; at present, the solution appears to lie in a mixed model. Although a wholesale dismantling of the current institution system does not make sense, there is sufficient evidence that institutionalization in general is detrimental to both the mental and physical well-being of a person, and that the ideal solution lies in placing children in a nurturing home environment. For those youth who are truly orphaned or for whom returning to their parents or relatives would endanger their well-being, a varied system of options including foster care, adoption, or an institutional setting is still necessary. To this end, many countries in the region are encouraging the development of so-called "homes in the family style," which allow foster parents to adopt or care for up to ten children in a foster home/shelter environment. The foster parents are paid a minimal fee to support each child, who receives individualized care and attention. This system encourages the child to develop relationships and to bond with the foster family, as well as to develop an identity beyond the depersonalized and often dehumanizing environment of an orphanage.

In Russia, the army has stepped in to respond to the problem of abandoned and homeless boys. Three years ago, the central government decreed that the army could "adopt" boys, fourteen or older, from orphanages or single-mother families. This practice of "regimental adoptions" has its origins in World War II when orphaned boys were recruited to fight the Nazis. These newly instituted regimental adoptions are helping to solve the problem of a decreasing number of healthy, available men to fight in Chechnya, but human rights groups have questioned the practice of taking such young recruits. While the boys do not fight until they reach the age of seventeen, they are trained, go through rigid and cruel hazing rituals, and often regret leaving the horrible environment of the orphanage for the even harsher reality of the army. Although some boys have been quoted as saying that at least they are fed in the army and therefore would rather stay than return to an orphanage, regimental adoptions are not a solution to the problem of homelessness.[10]

International Donor Efforts

The international donor community is active in addressing child welfare issues in the former Soviet Union and in Central and Eastern Europe. Large NGOs such as Save the Children and the European Children's Trust are developing a presence in the countries where the need is most acute. The myriad of programs throughout the region face the same challenges that national programs encounter: lack of coordination among donors, bureaucratic resistance from governmental agencies, and limited resources. One essential aspect of this issue that can not be resolved through a top-down reform program is that each child has an individual story and needs focused attention to resolve guardianship and future care. The causes of the problem are systemic, and while improved economies, greater access to health information, and parental education will all help to alleviate the problem for future generations, these are of little help to the current wave of street children.

Notes

The author wishes to thank the publishers of *Common Health* magazine (Summer 2002) for permission to reprint a revised version of this chapter.

1. Francesca Mereu, "Russia: Homeless Children—Helpless Victims of Collapsing Welfare, Family Systems" RFE/RL, June 19, 2002.

2. Omar Noman, "In the Former Eastern Bloc, A Hazardous Transition," *The UNESCO Courier*, March 1999, p. 30.

3. UNICEF, *Children at Risk in Central and Eastern Europe: Perils and Promises* (1997), p. 28.

4. Olga Nesterova, "The Russian Family is Changing," *Trud*, May 17, 2001 (from Russian Interfax Agency, Novosti, *Johnson's Russia List*, #5260, May 18, 2001).

5. Interfax, March 27, 2001 (from *Johnson's Russia List* #5175, March 28, 2001).

6. UNICEF, *Children at Risk*, p. ix.

7. *Nezavisimaya gazeta—Krug zhizni*, June 8, 2001(Radio Free Europe/Radio Liberty [RFL/RE], vol. 5, no. 110, part I, June 11, 2001).

8. RFE/RL, vol. 5, no. 97, part I, May 22, 2001, from an Interfax report from the Russian Children's Fund.

9. As reported by Interfax to Deutsche Presse-Agentur 7/2/2001.

10. Robyn Dixon, "In Russia, Military Helps Orphaned Boys Soldier On," *Los Angeles Times*, February 24, 2001.

"The Road Home" Children's Shelter

Sapar M. Kulianov

A child in a desperate situation can be found in any large city in any country. Children get lost, they become orphaned unexpectedly, they may be abused, they may be kidnapped or leave home on their own—all these situations, along with many others, may occur anywhere people live.

Beginning in the mid-1980s Moscow, along with the rest of Russia, experienced adverse developments related to its economic, political, and spiritual spheres, which brought about the impoverishment of the population, increased alcohol consumption, and spiritual disorientation. These processes, in turn, resulted in the appearance of homeless children who were forced to live on the streets and earn money by odd jobs such as washing cars, stealing, begging, and so on, to survive. State organizations whose official responsibilities include working with children (law enforcement entities, educational and trustee and guardianship bodies, as well as others) were unable to effectively counter these adverse processes, since no laws acknowledged the existence of homeless children and no funds were allocated for homelessness prevention. As a result, the situation got increasingly worse.

In addition, homeless children were increasingly taking drugs and committing crimes, such as drug pushing, prostitution, theft, and so forth. Taking into account that children under fourteen cannot be tried in courts, it is all the more logical that criminals actively recruited them to participate in illegal activities, adding exponentially to the crime rate among minors. Teenagers who took drugs or participated in criminal activities couldn't work, study, serve in the army, or participate in other normal activities. They quickly became invalids and/or ended up in jail. It became obvious that it would cost the government less to work on preventative measures regarding the children and youth in question, than to later pay for their treatment or incarcerate them.

The Appearance of Children's Shelters in Moscow

Social organizations and private individuals were the first to react to signs of distress among children, and they opened several children's crisis shelters in

Moscow. This initiative was supported by the mass media. In the early 1990s, the first directives were issued by the president of Russia and the mayor of Moscow to provide assistance to homeless children by opening free hostels and shelters. Shelters opened by private individuals and social organizations were complemented by shelters opened with state budgetary funds.

The Children's Shelter, "The Road Home"

The Road Home shelter was opened in the autumn of 1992 by the Russian charity "Let's Say No to Alcohol and Drug Addiction." Children were supposed to come to the shelter from families in which parents decided to undergo treatment for alcohol abuse; many of these had not sought treatment due to the lack of child care. As time passed, it became obvious that there were very few such families. The shelter was flooded instead with children detained by the militia or taken from abandoned basements and attics. By the end of 1992 this shelter was the largest and the only one that accepted children from all of Moscow. About 200 children passed through The Road Home during its first two years of operation. In 1994, the administration of Moscow's southwest district allocated some funds to renovate the old building, having recognized the crucial importance of the shelter's work. Upon completion of renovations, in 1995 the shelter opened a joint program of the foundation "Let's Say No to Alcohol and Drug Addiction" and the Health Care Committee of Moscow; thus, the shelter now serves as a branch of the Department for Medical and Social Assistance to Children and Teenagers, partially financed by the state.

The operations of the shelter are financed in a composite manner. Some expenses such as food for the children (which makes up 70 percent of the total), staff wages, medicines, and utilities (such as water, electricity, and trash removal) are covered by the state. Everything else—remaining expenditures for food, clothes, shoes, office supplies, and so on—is obtained through extrabudgetary sources; charitable and commercial organizations, as well as private individuals, assist the shelter in purchasing what is required. Unfortunately, support from nongovernmental organizations is not encouraged by economic incentives from the state (i.e., there are no significant tax exemptions); support is based merely on the moral satisfaction of the entity providing assistance. For this reason, charity is not widespread in Russia.

Goals and Objectives of The Road Home

Taking part in a child's life, the shelter staff seek the reasons behind the crisis situation at hand. As these reasons become clear, tasks in the areas of medical or psychological treatment, or teaching and education are posed for rehabilitation or correction of the condition while the child is living in the shelter, taking into consideration possible further life improvements upon leaving the shelter (e.g., social and legal assistance). The first priority lies in returning the child to his own family; of course, this becomes the main task when there are no abnormalities in family relationships. The abnormalities in question may include mental disorders, cruelty, violence, absence of parental feelings, and so forth. Children who have been abused or treated cruelly can be identified based on their expressing fear of their parents or of one or all family members and a disinclination to see any of them. Frequently a medical examination will reveal signs of beatings. Many of these children have sleeping disorders among other problems. When returning the child to his family is not in the child's best interest, parents may be stripped of their parental rights through the court system. After that, the shelter works together with trustee and guardianship associations to seek placement of the child for custody.

In order to resolve these tasks in the best way, once a child is received at the shelter the problems he or she experiences are divided into four categories, and appropriate professionals—including physicians, psychologists, teachers and educators, and social and legal aid workers begin working with the child. Besides this, there is also a support staff at the shelter, consisting of cooks, laundry staff, and others, whose work is to ensure normal living conditions for children while they are there.

Problems that arise in the course of managing such a diverse staff are resolved in the following ways:

- Detailed instructive job descriptions are composed for different specialists with overlapping tasks (for example, in the case of physicians and educators, their tasks would be protecting the life and health of the children, providing recreational activities for the children, and so on).
- General meetings are held in order to coordinate staff activities.
- Each shift of educators on duty acts as a single team.
- There are shift and department managers, such as chief educator, head nurse, and so on.
- All services are accountable to the general manager of the shelter.
- Bonuses are paid to the staff based on outstanding performance results.

Functions and Activities of the Medical Department

Normally, a child comes to the shelter from an extremely dire situation (such as beggary, living on the street, or living in railroad terminals); frequently those children have skin diseases (e.g., pediculosis, scabies, various forms of herpes, or dermatitis). There is a high probability of the presence of infectious diseases such as hepatitis and measles, as well as diseases of other types. Frequently, no information is available on the child's medical background (i.e., general health condition, shots, and past illnesses). A new child entering the shelter cannot be allowed to come into immediate contact with children who have been living in the "clean" quarters for a while; he or she must be placed in a medical quarantine section to be examined and treated by qualified medical personnel. The medical quarantine section is an isolated area with several bedrooms, a canteen, a playroom, a disinfecting and medical facility, showers, and bathrooms. In this section, members of the medical staff perform necessary tests and provide primary disinfection, which includes treating pediculosis and skin diseases. They also try, from a psychological standpoint, to help the child adapt to life in the shelter.

Upon completion of the examination, if the child is free of infectious disease, he is transferred to the "clean" quarters in the shelter, where he continues to be observed by the medical staff. The medical staff monitors the overall epidemiological situation in the shelter, the nutrition of the children, and the quality of the food and the preparation thereof.

Medical staff members work to discover any use of psychotropic agents by children. Due to their past asocial lifestyle, many of the children smoke and have experience with alcohol. The extent of their dependency is determined, psychotherapy and counseling are provided, and appropriate therapy is applied to prevent relapse.

Functions and Activities of the Department for Psychological Treatment

It is hard to overestimate the importance of psychological services in the shelter. All the children who come there have been through some degree of violence or abuse, from minor cases (living in an asocial family with problems) to extreme cases, in which they have been treated with violence and cruelty. Psychological traumas inflicted by the family are often accompanied by other issues such as problems in school and the experience of living in the street, among others. But even if a child comes from a relatively trouble-free family (for example, if the child's mother is in the hospital), merely ending up in the shelter traumatizes the child, and such situations as those in which a child has no family other than the mother pose a problem. It is worth noting that for a child, every institution is a stress factor, whether it be kindergarten, school, transferring from one school to another, or hospitalization. This stress increases several times if we talk about closed institutions, such as orphanages, boardinghouses, or shelters. Even consistent efforts on the part of the staff of the shelter to mitigate the psychological trauma of being admitted to and living in a shelter cannot completely overcome it.

This trauma can be expressed in any number of ways. Upon being admitted to the shelter, a child faces tight restrictions on his activities (smoking, fighting, and swearing are prohibited, for example) as well as his or her movements (leaving the grounds of the shelter is not allowed). A child is often scared and humiliated by adults making life decisions without regard for his or her wishes, by the medical procedures he or she has to undergo, as well as by many other things. Inevitably, all these factors inflict psychological trauma.

Later, a new child will have to develop relationships with the other children at the shelter, fitting into their system, adjusting or trying to win a place in the group. A child may then become, in turn, a victim or an aggressor. Initially, a child has no one with whom to share emotions, as these children are not used to complaining, and so must resolve problems alone. There is also the possibility of a child being traumatized by the staff of institutions in which employees are improperly trained or are simply indifferent, thinking children are not worthy of respect, being bound to follow in their feckless parents' footsteps.

Resolving problems having to do with the environment (e.g., new roommates, staff, and the necessities of life) enables a child to think about the past and to contemplate events that occurred to him. The child starts asking questions like: "Why did this happen to me?" "Maybe my parents do not love me?" "Maybe I am to blame for the whole situation?" "Maybe it's all those people who are talking about how it's good for me, while meanwhile they are ruining my family and my life?"

Finally, those questions also can be resolved, and the child has a chance to calm down. Then the time comes to leave this haven as well, as the shelter offers only temporary refuge. The child has to keep going into the unknown, losing everything again—new friends, adults who have become familiar, social status, and so on. Again, almost nothing depends on the child. Of course, the child receives explanations that it is done in his or her best interests, that it is the best possible placement, but nobody asks the child's opinion of what he or she thinks is best.

These are but a few of the traumatic situations that are practically inevitable for each child staying in the shelter. There are countless other problems specific to each child. In each of those situations, a child must have an adult available to explain what is happening and what to expect from the future, to understand that child's interests, to help the child learn to use his or her own strengths, to talk to the child in his or her own language, through action, play, and drawing. This is the kind of person the psychologist has to be.

At the same time, it is necessary to convey this understanding to all those who are working with that particular child, and to help other adults follow the path to the child's heart. This constitutes working with other staff, helping educators find a key to understanding, and working with doctors to prepare the child for medical procedures and with teachers to find the most effective ways of providing education.

A child's time in the shelter is only a small part of his or her whole life. Making this time interesting and useful, as well as preparing the child to leave the shelter, are only a part of the psychologist's work. It is also necessary to prepare the parties taking custody of the child, whether they are the child's original family or a new family. The best situation is that in which a child can return to his original family, providing that the parents have changed whatever problems led the child to enter the shelter in the first place (e.g., they stopped drinking, started working, and so on). But when there is uncertainty that the situation will be better and that the problematic psychological patterns have been resolved, the chances are good that the child will land back in the shelter after returning home for a time. A foster or adoptive family is a good option in this and other situations. However, it would be extremely unwise to forget that about two-thirds of adoptive families fail to cope well with bringing up the child they adopt, leading that child to come back into the shelter again with new psychological trauma and rejection, losing more faith in himself or herself and others. A psychologist's participation in working with the child's own parents or the potential adoptive family helps to significantly reduce the risk of a potentially traumatic situation arising. In this area, cooperation between the psychologist and the social worker is, of course, of paramount importance. Therefore, psychological services must consist of the following three elements to be successful: working with the children, interacting with the staff, and working with parents and potential guardians.

All these areas of work are closely connected through the main objective of the shelter on the whole: ensuring the well-being of the child not only within the shelter but throughout his or her entire future life.

In the course of our work at the shelter we have come to some conclusions. They may not be unquestionable, unchangeable, or universal, but they do help us perform our work in such a way that makes us feel confident that that work is of real help to the children. Our position with regard to a child is as follows:

1. Any child, no matter how "difficult" or "troublesome" he or she appears, has social and personal potential;
2. Frequently there are noble motives and feelings behind a child's negative behavior;
3. Often a child just does not know how to express himself or herself in

any other way than by negative expressions, rudeness, and aggression, that usually conceal feelings of dignity and a yearning for fairness and justice that have been warped by a distrust of adults and habitual violation of the child's rights.

4. Practically all of a child's negative behaviors had a practical place in his or her prior life and helped the child to survive, to develop, and to satisfy his or her immediate primary psychological needs. A simple change of situation normally does not result in an automatic behavior change, and habits formed over the years continue to operate. However, frequently by understanding the meaning behind a certain behavior (asking such questions as: What was the child trying to achieve, frequently unconsciously, through this behavior?) enables adults to help a child find other means of attaining the same goal. The behavior may acquire a new meaning in a new situation; aggression for self-assertion, for example, might be modified into a form of protecting the weak, for defending justice, and so forth.

It is possible to list a number of similar values that may turn out to be no less important, all of which are based on one main thesis: A child is a full-fledged person with his or her own rights, including the right to be happy; each child is a unique individual whom we can help develop and realize his or her full potential. We cannot help a child by force, nor can we do the development; a child must make these changes for himself or herself. We do our best to ground all our practical work in these values.

The psychologist's task in the shelter is to restore a child's trust in the world and in society, change his or her attitude to self, discover traumatic events and work through them, and help the child to reevaluate his or her life experience. In the course of this work, a child will discover new horizons for growth. The problems that might have seemed intractable turn out to be much less intimidating once the child feels that he or she is not alone and is being accepted without judgment.

Functions and Activities of the Study and Education Department

Educators start working with a child immediately upon his or her entering the shelter, even during initial treatment in the medical quarantine section. In conversations and games, children calm down, and it becomes possible to gauge their level of social skills, education, and development. Educators then work on correcting the child's condition in preparation for life in the shelter, using conversations and games to encourage the child to become less inhibited. This is the first stage of a child's acclimatization.

After the medical examination, a new student is transferred into the main ("clean") quarters and assigned to a group according to age. All students are divided into three age groups: young students, from four to seven years; intermediate students, from eight to eleven years; and senior students, from twelve to fifteen years. There are about ten children in each group, but this number frequently varies. A separate team of educators works with each group. Young students are separated from the intermediate and senior students. The younger children have their own bedrooms, as well as a playroom, washroom, bathroom, and a separate schedule. Preschool children are educated in accordance with a normal kindergarten program, adjusted for the individual abilities of the children. Every pupil is examined by a speech therapist, who then works with them on an individual basis. The purpose of working with the preschoolers is to develop their intellectual, physical, and psychological abilities. The types of classes include speech development, conversations with children on certain subjects (e.g., seasons, animals, fruits, vegetables, and so on), development of elementary mathematical concepts, and improving their surface and spatial orientation skills. A lot of attention is paid to their creative development: drawing, clay modeling, appliqué, creative play with erector sets, and development of musical abilities. Another purpose of classes with children of preschool age is to teach them how to read and write, in preparation for school in accordance with the program of a kindergarten with speech correction. There are both individual and group sessions.

Intermediary and senior students have shared living quarters. They have one playroom, and they share an assembly hall which is used for physical education classes (there are Swedish wall-bars, mats, a trampoline, and exercise machines), for watching videos (there is a home-theater system), and for listening to music (there is a music center). Each bedroom houses three to five people. Intermediate and senior group students transferred from the medical quarantine section to the clean quarters are examined by a commission, which consists of a teacher and a speech therapist. The test materials are compiled on the basis of the secondary school curriculum. The tasks that are offered to the students are traditional and are explained in easily understandable forms. On the basis of the test results, each student is assigned to an appropriate group for further education.

Under an agreement with the District Department of Education, those children of school age who have previously studied in a secondary school and show an acceptable level of knowledge continue their studies in a secondary school near the shelter.

Otherwise, school-age children with significant lapses in school attendance or those who have never attended school for a variety of reasons, as well as children with various physical or mental disabilities, are schooled in the shelter. There are two classrooms in the shelter for this purpose. Classes are taught by professional teachers who come from the nearby secondary school. Teachers work on the basis of the age and individual abilities of each child, eliminating the gaps in the children's education, and bringing their knowledge up to levels corresponding to their ages. The main task of the teacher in these classes is to get the child interested in studying. To be successful, a teacher needs to know his or her subject well and needs to love children, to be very patient and determined, and to create a warm and friendly atmosphere in class. The teacher strives to find and praise positive changes in a child's knowledge, sometimes even before they happen, and initially tries to overlook any failures, later not focusing on them, but rather assuring the child that it is easily possible to overcome them. Teachers base individual classes on the curriculum of either a secondary school or a school for developmentally impaired children and hold classes in preparation for the high school diploma exams later available for the children to take in a neighboring school. Experts working in the shelter, such as educators, speech therapists, and psychologists, work together with visiting teachers to ensure consistency in their work; they help children in their learning, control their studies, and sum up the progress achieved each week. Educators create monthly plans for academic and other types of training, which take into account the interests of children from all groups.

A number of extracurricular activities are promoted, as well. Much attention is paid to sports, and the children play soccer on the shelter grounds and attend sports classes in a nearby school. They enjoy riding bicycles in the summer and skiing and skating in the winter. There is a children's creative center where they take classes in both ballroom and modern dancing. In order to develop their living skills and strengthen unity and friendships among them, one-day field trips to the country are arranged. Students are frequently taken to the theater, cinema, museums, and exhibitions.

The children's self-management system is a crucial element of the education process. This system is based on three categories of seniority. Any child, regardless of age, may become a First Category Senior if he or she knows and obeys the Charter of the Seniors and is trusted by the educators. The Charter of the Seniors is drafted and discussed at the school assemblies with input from educators and psychologists. Any child who is a First Category Senior may become a Second Category Senior if he or she has not violated the charter during the preceding two months and has passed a number of additional tests. Any child who is a Second Category Senior may become a Third Category Senior if he or she hasn't violated the charter during the preceding four months. In order to attain this category, a child also has to pass some additional tests, for example, designing an activity or project and performing it with other children, giving up smoking, and so on. All tests for attaining a higher category are analyzed very thoroughly by the educators, with mandatory input from the psychologists and medical staff. They are put together taking into account the individual features of each child. Each Friday there is a meeting of all intermediate and senior groups to go over the results of the week, discussing behavior, academic performance, and so on.

Older students may be demoted in category due to misconduct. All events related to the children's self-management are made public on a special display board. Upon receiving seniority, a student is given certain rights and responsibilities, which ultimately help him or her better adjust to life in the shelter.

One of the main responsibilities of students is shelter-house duty. In accordance with the duty schedule, students clean the shelter within their abilities and help educators take care of the younger children, dressing them, helping them wash, putting them to bed, reading them stories, and so on. Older children are allowed to help clean the shelter grounds, sweeping, shoveling snow, or performing other tasks, for a pecuniary reward. The children thus learn the value of work, and they learn to be materially and morally encouraged for work well done.

The main task of the children's self-management system is to create a well-knit group which, together with adults, participates in the educational process. When this process is well organized, it doesn't matter how many students leave the institution or how many new ones arrive; the group of children preserves its good traditions and actively helps the adults.

Functions and Activities of the Social and Legal Services Division

The shelter's social office ensures social rehabilitation of the minors who are in a difficult situation and in acute need of social help. The division of social services works on such issues as recovering lost documents pertaining to the child, submitting letters and petitions to government organizations, making telephone calls to various organizations, appearing in court as witnesses in cases pertaining to restoring the children's residence rights, and so forth.

Social workers gather as much information as possible on the child's life preceding his or her placement in the shelter to create as complete a picture as possible of the reasons for distress. Psychologists and educators help to measure a child's social skill development.

The first and foremost task of the shelter staff is to return a child to his or her own family, not just by sending the child back, but by providing all possible assistance to improve the family situation in the child's best interest.

The main criterion for evaluating the family situation at any given moment and designing the course of further work is to gauge the child's love of his or her parents and the parents' love of the child. If this love exists, our staff will spare no effort to restore the family.

The first meeting with the parents is extremely important. Here, social workers need to befriend parents, gain their trust, and explain that the shelter is not their enemy; also, the social worker offers possible social, psychological, legal, medical, and other help to the parents from the shelter. First impressions tend to be the strongest, and if the social service representatives make a positive impression on the parents, it greatly helps all future work with the family. We try to gather as much information on family life as possible in order to thoroughly analyze the reasons for the crisis. It is important to visit the family home to observe in what conditions the child lived before he or she was placed in the shelter and to what situation he or she is returning.

Once we have sufficient information, the shelter holds an Expert Commission meeting, which includes the most competent and respected staff for comprehensive assessment of the child's condition and effectiveness of rehabilitation programs. Also, the time frame for the length of stay is determined. At this meeting, all information available to members of the shelter staff (the social services staff, educators, psychologists, teachers, medical staff, and support personnel) is summarized and reviewed. Also, priority measures for rehabilitation of the child are defined, the mechanism for working with the child is discussed and approved, and an individual program for rehabilitating the student in question is prepared, wherein is defined specifically what must be done by which expert and at what time.

In the majority of cases (over 70 percent), the family faces problems due to alcohol abuse by one or both parents. During initial meetings with the parents, the objective of the shelter's social services division is to resolve the family crisis so that the child can return home. Drinking parents are offered a free treatment program in an outpatient clinic for substance abuse, the possibility of visiting the child frequently, and help in bringing the child home. Help for the family is coordinated with trustee and guardianship authorities. In cases when the relationship between the child and the parents is normal (e.g., they love each other, the child looks forward to seeing the parents, the parents visit with the child often, the meetings are affectionate, and the child does not think about living independently), the program for helping the family commences. The family is given a chance to restore itself, and if the parents truly love their child, they agree to undergo treatment. The parents are then referred to an outpatient clinic for substance abuse treatment. The clinic treats those patients very carefully; they undergo an initial consultation with a psychologist, and the outcome of that conversation determines the method for treatment. Modern treatment methods are used to help the parents. The most important factor is the parents' willingness to undergo the treatment out of fear of losing the child. At the last stage of treatment, the parents attend Alcoholics Anonymous meetings. In the case of a favorable outcome, the parents receive a document confirming that they have completed a course of treatment, which is an important factor in allowing a child to return home.

Unfortunately, we have to point out that only a small percentage of drinking parents admit that the addiction is pernicious, and an even smaller percentage (only several families each year) complete the course of treatment and are able to have the child return home. The rate of success is so low because usually the guardianship authorities do not start working with a family until late in its destruction, when the parents are in an advanced stage of alcoholism. Frequently the parents, while visiting their child in the shelter, sincerely promise to change their lives. But then they return home, where the old life awaits them: a circle of drinking friends, problems of living in a communal apartment, and so forth, and nothing changes; they keep drinking. Prevention measures undertaken at an earlier stage could help avoid the crisis; unfortunately, official organizations start working with this type of family only when they reach crisis level, at which point they consider removal of parental rights the only solution to the problem. But against all odds, when the shelter comes across a drinking family, we continue to offer the parents a helping hand, and the staff feel great moral satisfaction when it is possible to preserve a family.

If the child is afraid of his or her parents and does not want to return to the family after having been abused, the shelter's social service will start looking for foster parents. The first tier of candidates is family members (an aunt or grandmother, for example) or old friends. If none of these wish to take the child, a search is performed among willing unrelated individuals.

Other steps are also possible, such as placing the child in a new type of foster care establishment, for example, Children's Village SOS, Family Boarding School, foster families, or similar places. However, if it is inevitable that the child be placed in a state-run institution (in order to join siblings, because of the possibility of apartment allocation, when love for his or her parents results in rejecting a foster family, or for other reasons), the shelter's social service will search for an institution with the mildest conditions and a family-like atmosphere (a family-type orphanage, one for musically gifted children, one associated with a circus, or other group). The child will be placed there, and the shelter will continue to follow the child's life.

Reasons for Child Homelessness and Classification of Homeless Children

The practice of the shelter's social services division has determined the following main reasons for child homelessness:

- Parental neglect of their responsibilities due to a dramatic deterioration of their financial situation and/or physical health (e.g., alcohol abuse, schizophrenia, or other condition), or because of cruelty and indifference;
- Lack of legislation (until March 1996) that would enable the guardianship authorities or police to interfere with the life of a child at a time when distress signals are detected, without waiting for a lengthy court procedure;
- Lack of sufficient budgetary resources from the state for homelessness and neglect prevention;
- Illegal purchase of apartments from people by fraudulent individuals, resulting in the children and their parents becoming homeless;
- Abnormal lifestyle of the parents (e.g., refugees, nomads, and so on).

The mass media tend to notice only the "tip of the iceberg" while talking about the problem of street children and describing children who need help: begging in the subways, loitering around railroad terminals, and washing cars at crossroads. These children are not always unsupervised and frequently are not homeless. For example, a teenage beggar is most likely recruited by adults, sometimes providing for the family, but more frequently working for adult criminals who control his or her activities. Frequently, children stay in the streets throughout daylight hours, and even pretend that they are homeless, but in fact return home for the night.

In practice, children in crisis may be from Moscow and registered in their parents' apartments; "non-Muscovite" children who are born in Moscow but are not registered or have lapsed registrations for a number of illegal reasons; children from other locations who were brought to Moscow by their parents and who have been living in Moscow for a long time without registration; or children from out of town who have arrived in Moscow recently from other cities, either alone or with someone, and who spend most of their time in or near the railroad terminals.

These categories of children are subdivided into nine subcategories:

1. Those living under conditions dangerous to their lives or health (in criminal dens, with mentally retarded or alcoholic parents, and so on). This subgroup includes children who are partially or completely

isolated from the outside world and locked up in apartments by their parents (so-called "Mowgli" children);

2. Children whose relations with parents are partially severed but who spend their nights at home. These children loiter aimlessly throughout their waking periods, in parks and other places, earning petty cash by begging or from odd jobs such as washing windshields at crossroads, selling small goods, and so on.

3. "Street children" who have no relationship with their parents, due to the cruelty, indifference, or illness of the latter. These children live in basements, attics, old cars, and other places, fend for themselves, and do not return home for the night.

4. Truly homeless children who have lost their living places, such as when apartments were illegally purchased from their parents;

5. Children who were formerly trouble-free, but are suddenly left without parental custody (due to their parents' death, emergency hospitalization, arrest, or other circumstance), or who are facing a crisis together with their parents (e.g., cruel treatment by relatives);

6. Children brought to Moscow by parents who are not Muscovites and who are lost or abandoned, including Bohemian children and children of other nomadic nationalities (such as Tajiks and others), who earn money independently or as instructed by adults;

7. "Travelers" and "adventurers" from other Russian or CIS cities (sometimes compulsive travelers);

8. Runaways from state orphanages who left due to cruel treatment by other children or staff;

9. Children kidnapped from parents (for ransom, or to be sold to new parents, for example).

Most frequently, children face a multidimensional situation: for example, a child living in a criminal den suddenly loses his or her mother.

Legal Grounds for Placing Children in the Shelter

Prior to 1996, if children's rights were violated, they could be taken from the family only after the court had removed the custodial rights of their parents or guardians. The Marriage and Family Code strictly defined the rights of parents with respect to children but gave no definition of children's rights. The procedure for stripping parents of their rights was extremely cumbersome and complicated and included the need to produce protocols documenting police detainment of the parents, eyewitness testimony by the neighbors, and the mandatory presence of the parents in court. A large number of documents was required, and unless all the conditions were met, the hearing was continued. As a result, few cases went to court, and those that did took years to resolve. Many children were malnourished or abused, and the apartments where they lived were turned into criminal hangouts, but the authorities could do nothing with the neglectful parents and could not remove the children. The prosecution took care not to violate the parents' rights, and there were no facilities in which to place those children anyway. In other words, there were no laws or regulations, not to mention money or staff to counteract child homelessness.

Therefore, more and more children encountered crisis situations. Officials ignored the situation since no directives from the top were forthcoming. Only when the first shelters appeared and started functioning, created by social organizations or private individuals, did the media start taking notice and thus attract public attention to the plight of these children. The first significant change came in the form of the new Family Code Law, adopted in 1995 and enacted in March of 1996. The code included sections aimed at helping children in crisis. The measures included removal of the child in a case in which his or her life or health were in danger, discovery and placement of children left without parental custody, and protection of the rights and interests of children left without parental custody.

The next step toward meeting the needs of children being considered by the state was the adoption of the Federal Law "Basic Measures to Prevent Juvenile Homelessness and Crime," adopted by the State Duma on May 21, 1999. This law outlined the main principles and tasks aimed at preventing juvenile homelessness and crime (e.g., prevention of homelessness, misdemeanors, and asocial actions by juveniles; ensuring protection of rights and lawful interests of minors; and so on). It also designated authorities and organizations that would work on ensuring prevention of juvenile homelessness and crime such as commissions for working with minors, health care management organizations, employment services, and offices of the Ministry of Internal Affairs; and it defined the categories of individuals subject to individual prevention measures (e.g., neglected and homeless, engaging in vagrancy or mendicancy, and so on).

However, despite the overall positive effect of the newly adopted law, Article 22 thereof closed access to the Centers for Temporary Detention of Juvenile Delinquents for those children who had not violated any laws. These institutions fall under the Ministry of Internal Affairs and formerly assisted all children from outside the city by sheltering them for one month, finding out their identity and original place of residence, providing necessary treatment and help, and sending them home. The children in question are aged three to eighteen and appear in Moscow for a variety of reasons:

They may be vagrant, brought by the parents and abandoned, runaways who have left home because of abuse by adults, refugees from nearby countries, and so forth. Legislators who adopted this law felt certain that they should not place these children with the young criminals in the centers. They assumed that by the time the law went into effect, new shelters would have opened in the city for these needy but non-offending children; however, by September of 1999 not a single shelter had opened, and the Centers for Temporary Detention of Juvenile Delinquents complied with the law and stopped accepting them.

This joint action by prosecutors and legislators left thousands of children from out of town homeless. Nobody is available to help them find protection, food, shelter, and then to return them home; currently no one has either the capacity or the expertise equal to that of the Ministry of the Interior in finding, identifying, and sending children home. The city shelters are overcrowded with Moscow children, and even when they accept a child from another location the child has to stay in the shelter for a long time, sometimes years, as the shelters do not have as high a capacity as the Centers for Temporary Detention of Juvenile Delinquents. This means that the number of spaces available for new children is limited. The Moscow City government is working to change this situation by adopting a new resolution (No. 617, dated July 10, 2001) that would create a pilot state-run facility called the City Center for Preventing Vagrancy, Mendicancy, and Crime among Nonresident Juveniles. We can only hope that the children now living in railroad terminals do not have long to wait until the doors of the new center open, giving them an opportunity to start on the way home.

Procedure for Accepting Children in the Shelter

In accordance with Article 13 of the Federal Law "Basic Measures to Prevent Juvenile Homelessness and Crime," the shelter will accept, in accordance with established procedure, minors who:

- are not in the custody of parents or legal guardians;
- are living in families that are in a socially dangerous situation;
- are lost or abandoned;
- left the family voluntarily or ran away from an educational establishment for orphans or children not in parental custody, or who have left other institutions for minors, with the exception of those who have left institutions for juvenile delinquents;
- are left without a place of residence, permanently or temporarily, and/or without means of support;

- are facing another dire situation and need social aid and/or rehabilitation (e.g., emergency hospitalization of a single parent, and so forth).

Reasons for placing a child in the shelter include the personal request of the minor, a petition by the parents or guardian, a referral by the local authorities, police, or social protection services, and the petition of individuals who are witnessing a crisis.

When a child arrives on his or her own and it is unclear which trustee or guardian institutions are responsible for him or her, the shelter's social services division, with the help of the prosecutor's office, will try to discover the former location of the child's residence (for example, cases in which the last place of residence turns up a residence registration in Moscow with consequent sale of an apartment, resulting in homelessness of the child). In such cases where the child's residence address in another city is known, the shelter may get in touch with that city's administration to work out future plans for the child (the shelter may suggest a new place of residence, foster care, or an educational establishment, or request that a place for the child be found in the city or town in which he is registered).

The shelter will not accept individuals under the influence of alcoholic beverages or narcotic substances or individuals with obvious symptoms of acute mental illness. A minor who comes to the shelter voluntarily has the right to leave voluntarily, after requesting to do so.

Prospects for the Development of the Shelter

After eight years of work, we observe that the shelters are gradually approaching an impasse. The prosecutor's office demands that children be kept in the shelter for no longer than 1–6 months. It is not always possible to normalize a child's condition, collect all the documents, wait for the situation in his or her family to normalize, or if needed, to revoke the parents' custody rights, and so on within this time frame.

The main goals of the shelter are to create favorable living conditions for its residents while rehabilitating them as much as possible and ensuring their return home. If this proves impossible, then the shelter attempts to ensure, together with trusteeship and guardianship organizations, an optimal future life for those under its care. These goals cannot always be fully attained within the deadlines established by the prosecutor's office. Shelters are forced to transfer children to state-run orphanages and long-term boarding schools, leaving each of these children's individual rehabilitation programs incomplete.

This pattern not only harms the children; it also undermines the morale of the staff by making them feel that their work is futile. In an orphanage, a child's condition tends to deteriorate quickly, which leads to increased personnel turnover.

Some shelters gradually turn into municipal institutions for transferring children, i.e., they accept only children who are registered in their district, and after keeping them for two or three months, transfer them to orphanages. Others change their goals and objectives by becoming orphanages themselves and discontinuing the practice of accepting children from the street.

As one possible course of action, we offer a way of working with children in crisis that would move them, not along a "crisis-shelter-orphanage" route, but along a "crisis-Social Rehabilitation Center-family or guardian" route. This is particularly desirable, given that Article 123 of the Family Code of the Russian Federation establishes the priority of family upbringing over bringing up a child in an institution.

Social Rehabilitation Center

We propose a program for establishing a Social Rehabilitation Center for minors in crisis as a way of providing a comprehensive solution for preventing child neglect and homelessness in Moscow, fostering conditions for providing medical, psychological, and pedagogical, as well as legal and social, support to children and adolescents facing a difficult situation in their lives, and we encourage further placement of the child with a family. The center will operate in accordance with Figure 15.1.

The proposed comprehensive program outlined here represents a project aimed at creating a system that includes the crucial elements of a Social Rehabilitation Center for minors. As noted below, two of the elements (2 and 7) are already in existence:

1. Social and legal aid division
2. Children's Shelter such as the currently functioning shelter, The Road Home;
3. Family Boarding School Shelter
4. School for Foster Parents;
5. Free Hostel for Mothers and Children;
6. Free Hostel for Young Adults
7. Charitable Foundation such as the functioning foundation, Shelter for Childhood, which was created to support the elements of the center and raise funds for their operations.

Figure 15.1 **Proposed Model of Social Rehabilitation for Families and Children**

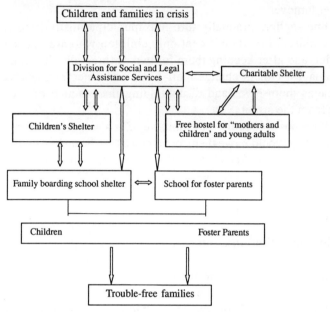

Activities Performed by Each Element of the Center

The *Social and Legal Aid Division* helps children, teenagers, and their families if they are facing a crisis; it works on preventing homelessness and crime among children and minors; and it compiles a data bank on troubled families and provides information to the public on social, legal, and other issues. Together with the trusteeship and guardianship organs, the division refers children in dire situations who were left without parental custody to the children's shelter.

The *Children's Shelter* provides emergency and medium-term (2–6 months) assistance to children who have lost family connections, who are neglected and not cared for by their parents, who have been through any form of abuse, or who are in a situation of physical and psychological crisis that they are unable to overcome alone. Over the course of several months, they receive medical, psychological, educational, social, and legal assistance. The main priority of the social work is to eliminate the crisis in the child's family and help the child return home, or to find a foster family if it is impossible to rehabilitate the child's own family.

Since, as our practice shows, over 70 percent of all children arrive from alcohol-ridden families, substance-abuse specialists should pay special attention to working with the children's parents.

If the shelter resolves a child's problems within 2–6 months, the child will be returned to family, relatives, or another guardian. In more complex cases, when it may take more than 6 months to resolve a child's problems, he or she will be transferred to the Family Boarding School Shelter based on a decision of the Board of Experts' meeting and the concurrence of the trusteeship and guardianship authorities.

In the *Family Boarding School Shelter* (hereafter referred to as the Boarding School), students live in family-type groups of up to eight children in which educators help them adjust to living in a family setting. Children receive education and vocational training and engage in sports. The time frame for acclimatization to a family environment is set at 6–12 months. Experts from the Boarding School and the center educate individuals willing to adopt a child in the School for Foster Parents.

The *School for Foster Parents* uses experts from the Boarding School and the center to educate individuals willing to adopt a child. In Russia there is no positive experience or cultural tradition for transferring children to foster families and rendering professional assistance to those families. Despite a large pool of people willing to adopt children (made up primarily of people with unspent parental potential who have no children or have lost their children, elderly couples whose children have left home, or single men or women), it is practically impossible to obtain even the most basic information necessary for bringing up a child. A number of factors contribute to the need for an overall educational facility for prospective guardians:

- The paperwork approval procedures associated with adoption are extremely complicated;
- The approving party has no personal interest in a positive final outcome;
- There is no qualified assistance available for the adoptive family (there is some financial assistance, but none of it is educational or psychological, for example);
- The insufficient professionalism of many officials working in the child-protection sphere manifests itself in a predilection for sending children to orphanages and state facilities rather than to foster families, as well as in the officials' belief that children from problem families will inevitably repeat the fate of their biological parents;
- No information is available on successful foster families.

We propose creating a School for Foster Parents where those wishing to adopt a child or become foster parents or guardians can study basic parenting information. Educators, psychologists, social workers, and lawyers will work with them, and the training will culminate in practical assignments to the Family Boarding School Shelter as assistant educators. During this period, prospective parents will have a chance to select a child for adoption, and those who adopt will receive comprehensive information on the child and recommendations for parenting, along with the help and support necessary at the time and in the future. Of course, all events will be planned in accordance with the requirements of the laws of the Russian Federation. Through this service, we will have the opportunity to place children who are left without parental care—those students at the Boarding School—into adoptive, guardian, or foster families with a higher chance of a successful life for children in these families until they reach majority age. In addition, attention will be paid to making positive experiences widely known via the mass media.

The free *Hostel for Mothers and Children* provides a place for a family to live while they attempt to overcome the problems that led them into the center in the first place. Our practice shows that the vast majority of children arrive in the shelter from families in which parents have serious problems, such as illness (including alcohol addiction), poverty, violence among family members, and so on. Parents need to be helped out of the crisis so that the children can return to their families, and it is difficult to do so when the parents stay at home and the children are in the shelter. Difficult conditions (such as communal apartment living or drinking friends) hold adults fast in their routines. In addition, a child's situation may be exacerbated by the stress of parting with the family when he or she is removed from it and placed in the shelter.

Creating a free Hostel for Mothers and Children would help resolve both of these problems. Mothers would be placed for temporary residence in individual rooms and would undergo a joint rehabilitation program (the desire for placement must be mutual). This form of help may be particularly successful with regard to single, nondrinking, energetic women who are facing a crisis, such as in a situation where their relatives ousted them, leaving them with no place to live or means of obtaining one. While staying in the hostel, parents may be able to try to find jobs, to work, or to earn some money to rent an apartment.

At the same time, social workers (psychologists and educators) would work with parents to improve their social status (providing assistance in finding a job or professional training or helping them find a new circle of friends, for example) and streamline their future family life. If necessary, they would be involved in an antialcohol program aimed at working out a healthy lifestyle. We expect better results from joint rehabilitation of mother and child, since it eliminates the problems caused by dividing the family.

The hostel also plans to accommodate teenage mothers and pregnant teenagers. They would receive comprehensive training in acquiring parenting skills and would develop prospects for a future favorable outcome for themselves and their children.

Parents and children would stay in the shelter for 3–6 months. Contact would be maintained with the family after that, and consultations and other assistance would be provided if needed.

The free *Hostel for Young Adults* is designated for temporary accommodation (1 to 2 years) for teenagers aged 15–18. It is well known that young people at that age, if they are not cared for by adults, have few prospects: Shelters provide almost no assistance to them, and they are unable to find work as they do not have any professional training. In order to prevent teenagers from becoming associated with criminal organizations (which always readily accept them—a main factor in driving up youth crime rates), adults must actively participate in improving their life situations.

Young men and women staying at the hostel would sign a contract of temporary residence that would include a mandatory clause pertaining to obeying internal rules, studying, working, and so forth. There would be a small staff at the hostel—educators, psychologists, social workers, and others—to work with these teens.

The *Charitable Foundation* supports the funding of the entire center, focusing on raising money for its operations. Presently the government does not have the resources needed to establish and maintain programs of this type. We can only hope that the state will finance expenses for food, clothes, and so on, in a similar manner to that in which it allocates these resources for state-run orphanages.

Given international experience in this area, it may be possible that financial assistance will be forthcoming from social (domestic and international) organizations, commercial companies, and private individuals, given the importance of the center's work. The Charitable Foundation, Shelter for Childhood, was created in 1999 with the purpose of raising funds for the creation, operation, and development of the Social Rehabilitation Center.

The project of the Social Rehabilitation Center does not offer anything particularly utopian or new. For the past nine years the The Road Home has been successfully functioning in Moscow. It is, in effect, a small social aid center for children in crisis. This shelter continually actively works toward returning children to their families; it work with parents, involving substance-abuse treatment specialists where needed; it also constantly searches for families willing to adopt a child or become foster parents.

Over the last few years, several Russian institutions for children have been created based on Western examples. Those that are functioning successfully include, among others, SOS Village for Children and Foster Families.

All of the elements of the center described above can be found in existing institutions to a greater or lesser extent; the project merely suggests that they be gathered into one organization in order to:

- put in place an integral rehabilitation program;
- preserve continuity and consistency of the educational process;
- make a single entity responsible for the results; and
- return or place children with families as soon as possible.

Implementation of the project would require a considerable financial investment, of course, but those funds would soon be paid back through resolution of children's problems.

Alone, this center will not resolve all the issues involving social protection of Russia's needy children, but it will create a precedent for establishing a complete network of related institutions capable of tackling those issues successfully.

Conclusion

The situation of children in Moscow is becoming increasingly dire. More and more children in Moscow are becoming homeless or virtually abandoned. There are also growing numbers of children who are not homeless, but who are washing car windows at stoplights, sniffing glue, and begging in the streets. Trusteeship and guardianship authorities remove more and more children from criminal dens. The courts hear an increasing number of cases attempting to remove children from the custody of parents guilty of child abuse and neglect. The number of children who become homeless due to fraudulent housing schemes is growing. After the autumn of 1999, the number of problem children uncovered by social aid services has risen due to an inflow of thousands of children coming to Moscow from other Russian cities or CIS countries in order to seek out a better life.

Again, as was the case ten years ago, the railroad stations and streets are teeming with homeless children, but the police ignore them because there is no place to take them even if they are picked up. Moscow shelters are crowded with local children, and there are no places for nonresidents; the shelter's social services divisions are unable to contact other cities to identify detained nonlocal children, and there is not sufficient staff or other resources to send them back to their places of residence. All city districts have received directives from the mayor's office instructing them to immediately create shelters capable of accepting nonresident children, but there is neither space nor money to implement them.

In addition to tens of thousands of street children, there are at least as many children locked up in criminal hangout apartments and "Mowgli" children living in heaps of trash, deprived of basic living conditions or communication with other people.

Up until 1998, Moscow was battling the problem of homeless children with fourteen shelters, containing roughly 600 available spaces, while there are currently only seven or eight shelters left, totaling roughly 400 spaces. The rest of the shelters have been converted to orphanages.

Even if a miracle were to occur and ten new shelters with 100 spaces each suddenly appeared in Moscow, this quantitative approach would not resolve the issue; in six months the shelters would be full and again there would be no place available for new children.

In order to change the situation, a qualitative approach is necessary. The "fire department" principle—when firefighters arrive at the peak of a fire or after everything has already burned to the ground, thus dealing with a situation only after it has become a crisis—should be replaced with prevention work with high-risk families everywhere. It is important not to consider an individual child's problem separately from the context of that child's world, as often happens in orphanages and similar institutions. To deal with a child's problems effectively, the elements of that world—family, parents, grandparents, and so forth—must be taken into account. And the best interests of the child should always be the main priority of our work.

16

Russia in Transition
Social Problems in an Atomized Society

Boris Nemtsov

Problem Overview

Poverty

Poverty has become one of the most severe social problems in Russia today. At the beginning of the year 2000, approximately 30 million citizens one-quarter of the Russian population, were living below the poverty level. Figure 16.1 illustrates the scale of this problem. There has been some discussion about how the role of the "shadow market" should be accounted for when estimating poverty rates in Russia; in truth, consideration of the "shadow economy" probably requires an adjustment of less than 1 percent because of the fact that those involved in this system are primarily *not* poor people.

The main source of poverty in Russia is the disparity between salary and pension levels in relation to the minimum subsistence level. The salary minimum makes up only 20 percent of the minimum subsistence level, and the pension minimum is only 59 percent. Unfortunately the disparity has been continually widening (See Figure 16.2.)

The Russian poor are made up of state employees paid from the state budget and pensioners. Demographically, the poorest group in Russia is children. The face of Russian poverty is by and large the face of a child; more than 70 percent of Russian children are living in poor families. The "new poor" in Russia are teachers, doctors, engineers, and scientists—all those members of society who make up the middle class in the West and are the foundation of any highly developed nation (See Figure 16.3.)

State-provided social services cannot combat the level of poverty alone. The

Figure 16.1 **Rate of Poverty**

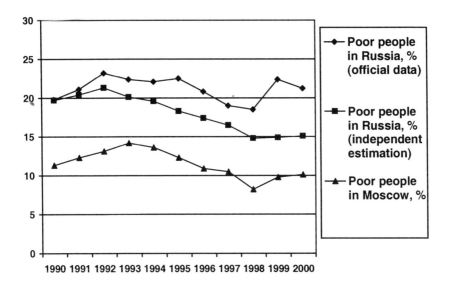

Figure 16.2 **Poor People in Russia**
(Average income is below subsistence minimum)

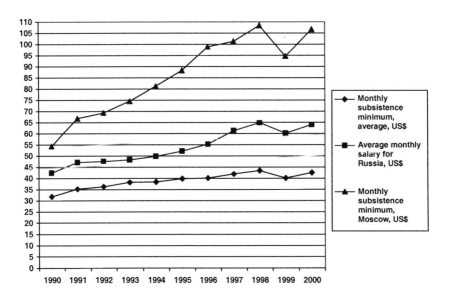

Figure 16.3   **Social Structure of Poverty in Russia in 2000**

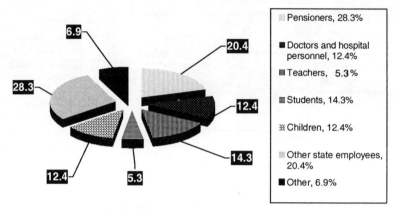

individual-oriented social assistance that is widely used in developed countries is still a distant dream for Russian society. The main tool necessary to fight poverty is the further development of the liberal economy in a democratic society.

Drug Problems in Russia

The spread of drugs across the territory of the former USSR is one of the first and foremost threats to Russia. Over the last five years, the number of drug addicts has increased approximately three and a half times. The number of addicts has now reached more than 3 million according to official data, but unofficial estimates number about 7–9 million persons. The average age of drug addicts ranges from 13–25 years. Over the last ten years, the number of women involved in drugs has increased 6.5 times.

Drugs are spreading among schoolchildren very fast at a rate that has increased 6–8 times over the last four years. According to the latest estimate, every fifth schoolboy in Moscow and St. Petersburg has already had an experience with drugs. About one-third of older children use drugs regularly in Russian schools. On top of this, drug users move from "light" drugs to "heavy" drugs much more quickly in Russia than anywhere else.

In 2000, 1,048 illegal drug production laboratories were closed. The state brought more than 2,000 cases against drug producers, resulting in only 1,850 convictions.

The annual turnover of the drug market in Moscow and St. Petersburg alone is around $120 million. According to official information last year, the amount for all of Russia was more than $2.5 billion. Experts estimate the figure to be, in actuality, $5–$7 billion.

Table 16.1

Demographic Comparison of Select Countries, 1991

No.	Country	Urban population, %	Fertility (coefficient of births per woman)	Increase of population, %
1	France	75	1.7	0.4
2	Germany	87	1.3	0.1
3	Great Britain	89	1.7	0.2
4	Italy	67	1.2	0.0
5	Russia	76	1.3	–0.2
6	Ukraine	67	1.4	–0.4
7	Haiti	33	4.4	1.7
8	India	27	3.1	1.6
9	Kenya	29	4.4	2.0

Source: World Statistics Pocketbook (New York: United Nations Statistics Division, United Nations, 2000).

According to information from the Russian Ministry of Internal Affairs, the number of crimes connected with drugs over the last five years has increased more than sixfold, from 16,000 to 100,000. Out of every ten crimes, six were committed by drug addicts.

The Depopulation Problem

If one compares recent demographic tendencies in Russia with the tendencies in those countries with a similar makeup of urban/rural population, a similar educational level, and a similar pattern of change in the occupational sectors (e.g., the dying off of heavy industry), we observe a similar picture (see Table 16.1). The comparison should be adjusted for the influence of immigration; in Russia this influence is insignificantly positive, while in Ukraine it is insignificantly negative.

Meanwhile, since the very first months of the Gaidar government, the Communists have put forth the fantastic accusation that the government was responsible for the lowered birthrate. The problems of depopulation, an aging population, and an increase in the number of immigrants with their own cultures are faced by all of Europe and by many other developed countries. So far, no solutions that would be at once effective and satisfactory to the majority of the population have been found. Even in the circle of Russia's political allies, there are difficult discussions on this question; there is no unity about even the basic objectives of such a policy. Some economists argue that it would be possible to achieve a rather significant increase in the birthrate by sharply decreasing the level of obligatory pensions, which would lead people to begin to rely on being supported by their children in old age. However, there is no assurance that we really want to achieve this benefit at such a price.

Social Implications

The Crisis of the Family Institution

The family crisis, regardless of what left-wing politicians and journalists now claim, reached a peak in the 1930s–1950s. During these years, the family, which was to disappear according to the plans of the founders of the Bolshevik state, was again added to its armory by the Soviet regime, becoming a cell of the political surveillance system. What in the West seems to be the fruit of Orwell's imagination was life as usual for a typical Soviet family of the mid-twentieth century. From the 1960s to the 1980s, the family reoriented itself into a cell of redistributional coalitions. The presence of a marriage stamp in a Soviet internal passport reduced the costs of access to certain resources distributed by the state. This said, the demographic tendencies characteristic of an industrial urbanized society—the decreasing birthrate and the growing number of divorces—were characteristic of the Soviet Union as well, particularly in Russia and the European republics of the USSR.

The disintegration of the socialist system was followed by a crisis of adaptation to new realities, which was common to each individual. A sharp change in social status, the loss of stability and predictability, and the "shrinking horizon" for day-to-day decisions typical of a transitional revolutionary era, all extremely and painfully affected the family as an institution. At the outset of creating a new family, it became very difficult to make the sorts of long-term plans that new families have to make.

Quite predictably, the number of new marriages decreased. A steep growth in the number of divorces would have not been surprising; however, this was not the case. Although an increase in the number of divorces was observed from 1991 to 1995, even the peak level (4.6 divorces per 1,000 persons in 1994) only insignificantly topped the Soviet record of 1980—4.2 divorces per 1,000 inhabitants. By 1999 the number of divorces had decreased to 3.4, approximately to the level of the first half of the 1970s. More importantly, there has been a reduction in the number of new marriages; in recent years this number has been fluctuating at a level of about 6 per 1,000 in comparison with 9 to 11 per 1,000 in the late Soviet period. The decrease in the number of new marriages is partly accounted for by the increasingly widespread non-nuptial joint residence of young people (a marriage stamp in an internal passport during a stay in a hotel is not required any more, after an initial attempt on the part of the state to demand it all but disappeared).

Children and Adoption

By virtue of the reasons described above, the natural growth in the number of children who have been left without care (considered to be a parameter of immorality during the previous, Socialist epoch) is in part compensated for by a doubling of the number of children who have been adopted. The number of children who were left in institutional care increased from 11,000 to 33,000,[1] illustrating a regrettable gap between the revival of family values and the pace at which the institution of "the basic cell of Soviet society" is decomposing. It should also be noted that official statistics do not take into account specifically the number of children staying in the new family-type children's homes created in recent years.

It is highly probable that the above-mentioned increase in the number of adoptions might be substantially larger if it were not for some oddities in the organization of state and municipal financing of this problem. Under this system, a trustee (that is, the person who assume temporary limited responsibility for a child) receives a handsome allowance, which is certainly necessary, but an adopting family receives no such an allowance. This sharply narrows the adoption options of families of modest means who, based on other essential parameters, would be fit to adopt children.

Support programs for adoption might be substantially expanded, given reasonable legislation on charity and a gradual redistribution in this direction of the resources that today are spent solely on the maintenance of orphanages. These official children's homes are typically "closed institutions" in which the quality of service at best falls far short of minimally acceptable standards, or which simply resemble prisons for minors who have committed no crimes. These conditions naturally stimulate criminality, because any teenager coming out of this system can expect no deterioration in the condition of his life if he were to enter prison, but the chances of improving his lot through successful criminal activity are much greater, leaving what appears to be a rather clear rational choice.

"New Poverty," Political Instability, and Population Adaptability

Behind Russia's "new poverty" lie a number of factors, including the atomization of society, aggressive individualism in the guise of collectivism, the absence of practical knowledge of civil life and self-management (as opposed to having many aspects of life managed by the state), and, in a broader sense, the lack of an ability to adapt. As a result, radical strategies of survival are usually chosen, either in the form of a break with one's former life (e.g., a former scientist becomes a petty trader), or vegetation at a job that has been effectively abolished—although perhaps not in name—resulting in a person clinging to former employment that pays an income barely fit for survival. An intermediate possibility, chosen by many, is the search for work at one of the new private firms, using free-of-charge (i.e., illegal) resources available from the former enterprise to carry out this work.

A number of factors can delay the advent of a new proprietor into a business that might help his situation, including the high costs associated with the transfer of property into new hands and the overestimated investment of hired workers who have become personally dependent on an inefficient administration as a source of security. In the short-term, this strategy may raise the chances of keeping one's job, but it also catastrophically reduces the possibility of finding a place in the market economy in the long term for the scientist, the engineer, or the qualified worker of a former military enterprise.

On the other hand, political instability undermines the incentive to choose a long-term strategy, and the cycle becomes self-perpetuating. Political instability is in turn determined by the choices of the poor themselves, who are frequently inclined to vote for those who promise to "make the old times come again." A characteristic episode of the 1996 election campaign illustrates this. In Russia's southern regions, the ratings of the Communists were very high, and a victory of the Communist Party candidate in the first round looked very impressive. This situation gave rise to the sensation of the inevitability of restoration of the old regime, and in the final weeks before the second round and in the first days after the voting, there was an excessive demand in the area for the type of goods usually bought during "wartime" (e.g., canned food, groats, salt, matches, and sugar). Another phenomenon promoting panic was the economic language after August of 1991 that talked in terms of only very short-term decisions. This sort of panic, in turn, led to choices of less than optimal strategies of behavior, which sharply complicated the adaptation to a market economy.

If we compare Russia to other countries with transitional economies and young democracies, it is striking that, in those places where the population resolutely supported market reforms even before they started, as a rule, these countries gained most from the reforms. Such regularity is manifested even among the Russian regions. Poll data reveal a clear connection between political preferences and the ability to adapt. The non-adapted voters constitute the bulk of the electoral base of the restorationist forces, while the adapted voters constitute the hard core of the supporters of reformist forces (see Table 16.2).

Table 16.2

Voter Adaptation and Voting Behavior Characteristics by Party Vote (December 1999 Elections)

What party ticket did you vote for in December 1999?	Population of Russia	Adaptation level			Sex		Age			Education				Income per family member		
		High	Medium	Low	Male	Female	18–35	36–50	> 50	Up to secondary	Secondary	Secondary special	Higher	Up to R250,000	R250,000–400,000	More than R400,000
Communist party	25	15	23	**32**	25	25	11	21	**37**	**36**	25	19	24	25	**32**	19
Yedinstvo" ("Unity")	23	26	22	21	20	24	**29**	24	17	21	23	24	18	26	21	20
"Otechestvo—Vsya Rossia" ("Fatherland—All Russia")	13	14	12	12	12	13	11	13	13	12	11	13	17	7	12	17
"Right Forces Union"	8	**17**	7	5	9	8	**16**	8	4	4	8	9	**15**	8	6	11
"Yabloko"	6	6	7	5	5	7	5	8	5	3	5	6	10	6	5	7
"Zhirinovsky's list"	6	9	5	5	9	3	**11**	5	3	4	8	7	2	9	4	6
Other parties	11	7	14	12	9	13	10	10	13	13	12	11	9	10	12	13
Voted against all	3	3	3	4	5	2	4	4	2	2	3	4	3	4	3	3
Don't want to answer, don't remember	5	3	6	5	6	4	4	6	5	4	5	7	2	5	5	4

Source: The Public Opinion Foundation, WWW.fom.ru.

The population's inability to use the instruments of democracy to its benefit is compounded by the inability to use mechanisms that provide judicial protection of its rights. Although there are thousands of examples of cases won, ending in employers (sometimes even the Ministry of Defense) being compelled to pay hired workers their due, in most cases workers do not go to courts. This is explained in part by the inefficiency of the judicial system, but can also be seen as the result of an "inefficiency" on the part of citizens themselves in upholding their rights.

An indirect parameter of such inefficiency is the absence of a mass, independent trade-union movement. There is a structure that calls itself the "Federation of Independent Trade Unions," but it is a typical quasi-nongovernmental organization, "made in the USSR," whose existence is based on having property through a satellite of the CPSU (the property of the Communist Party was nationalized in 1991 but not the property of its satellites and affiliates). The old "quasi-social" organizations continue to function as the successors of the children's, youth, and women's Communist organizations, Communist trade unions, and so on. They have no opportunity to rely on public authority and highly motivated activists, but the strength of their heritage enables them to participate in the publication of newspapers, to finance political campaigns, and to carry out lobbying activity. They are joined by small entities of similar origin. The old quasi-social institutions take an active part in the struggle for the preservation of administrative barriers, through which they continue to receive rent. Some of the new redistributive coalitions create their own "social" affiliates (including quasi-human rights champions and quasi-consumer organizations), targeted almost exclusively to the weakening of competitors.

"Revolution of Expectations"

It is also necessary to note that inaccurate stereotypes and strategies of behavior were promoted through some features of a media strategy in the years before the 1991 revolution and in the first years after the beginning of reforms. The fall of Communism was promoted by regular reports from Western supermarkets, which showed the availability of thousands of brands of every possible good. After spending so many years with the empty show windows of socialist state shops, this appeared to be a shocking challenge to a regime that allowed no one to question its operations. But at the same time, such pictures raised hopes that a market economy would be a panacea produced by a kind, loving, democratic state for the benefit of its citizens—a state that gives them everything they wish for. This was in sharp contrast to the portrayal of the malicious intent of Communist leaders who did not wish to share with people and who have hidden treasures in the party's system of "special points for distribution." Economists have named this phenomenon a "revolution of expectations." The appearance of this phenomenon is characteristic not only of Russia, but of other countries as well. Leshek Balcerovich wrote about it thus:

> In conditions of communism . . . before publicity . . . the rigidly controlled mass media did not show negative aspects of the system in its materials. After clearing these means . . . they have focused all of their attention on the things about which it was previously forbidden to speak and write. . . . This was promoted also by the low professional level of journalists who received education under socialism. In result, public opinion day by day appeared under the influence of the mass media, which constantly pursued negative phenomena more and more. Television viewers wrongly accepted the exaggerated visibility of the undesirable phenomena, such as criminality or poverty, as a valid picture of their country's growth. "The effect of visibility," absent in classical democracies, might lead to negative estimates of the undergone and, as a consequence, might affect the results of elections and the future direction of economic transformations.[2]

The post-Soviet economic crisis caused Russian citizens to revise their standpoints on their own lives, having cured them of the syndrome of the "revolution of expectations." A lot of people, including the ex-speaker of the Congress of Peoples' Deputies, discussed seriously what route of capitalist development Russia needed to take (following either the Swedish or American example), as well as how many years after 1992 it would take Russia to achieve a comparable level of prosperity to that of the countries of Western Europe (the majority agreed that this should require no more than five years). The responsibility for Russia's failures was assigned to the Communists. But after the crash of the USSR, naturally, Russians did not begin to live like their European counterparts, and responsibility for the crisis was then shifted to the reformers. Even partial improvement of their economic position was not satisfactory; whatever was achieved by the population, they were told that they deserved more. According to data from VTsIOM (All-Russian Center for Public Opinion Research), in July 1998 a "normal" single adult person needed 1,665 rubles (about 280 dollars) to live, in comparison to the actual average wage, which was estimated by the population to be 688 rubles. In May 1999, at the moment of Primakov's resignation from the government, according to the population, "normal" life began to require 2,442 rubles (about 100 dollars), and the actual average wage was estimated to be 904 rubles. That is, the amount that the population could expect to earn was almost three times less than what was needed to live. Ironically, the end of the "revolution of expectations" may give Russians a basis for hope, as they start to aspire to nothing more than a steady job rather than hoping for such unrealistic things as a "kind government," a "kind president," and so on. In other words, it may be possible to achieve the impression of economic success simply by requiring people to be more realistic.

The Economic Situation

Poverty, Monetary Policy, and Inflation

The economic situation is extremely grave. The consolidated government budget deficit for 1991 reached 30 percent, and hyperinflation loomed large. Besides increasing the state's foreign debt, the government was also taking over the monetary assets of citizens and enterprises that had always been held in Sberbank (the Soviet Union's lone savings institution) and Vnesheconombank (the Soviet foreign-exchange agent). In the cities, people had to stand in line for hours to buy sugar, soap, cigarettes, and vodka. Setting up legitimate businesses through administrative channels was a bureaucratic nightmare; authorization to engage in export-import operations could be obtained only through case-by-case decisions by the cabinet, and licenses to open banks were also contingent on case-by-case decisions by the State Bank of the USSR (the Soviet Union's central bank).

In countries that conduct radical reforms and ensure rapid disinflation, the transitional recession creates important conditions for coming growth. Resources that had been previously tied up in inefficient and nonviable enterprises are quickly redistributed to enterprises and sectors that are capable of competing in harsh market conditions. The general growth in production begins when the growth of output in the new private sector, as well as that in the part of the state sector capable of adapting to the new conditions, proves capable of more than compensating for the continuing cuts in ineffective enterprises inherited from the Socialist period.

The key role of structural changes, along with the emergence of a broad section of enterprises capable of competing in the marketplace, demand that special attention be devoted to the mechanisms that underpin market reforms. An important cause of the economic stagnation and crisis of socialism that led to its collapse was the absence of institutions in the Socialist economy to ensure the generation and introduction of efficient innovations and the automatic redistribution of resources to economic units capable of using them effectively.

Creating an environment that provides such incentives has been a strategic goal of the post-socialist transition. In a developed market economy the most important mechanism for ensuring this is the use of hard budget constraints for enterprises. Enterprises that are incapable of using resources effi-

Table 16.3

Gross Domestic Product Growth (Recession) Rate in Rapid Disinflation Transition Countries (% to previous year)

	1990	1991	1992	1993	1994	1995	1996	1997
Albania	−10.0	−27.7	−7.2	9.6	9.4	8.9	9.1	−7.0
Hungary	−3.5	−11.9	−3.1	−0.6	2.9	1.5	1.3	4.0
Latvia	2.9	−10.4	−34.9	−14.9	0.6	−0.8	3.3	6.0
Poland	−11.6	−7.0	2.6	3.8	5.2	7.0	6.1	6.9
Czech Republic	−1.2	−11.5	−3.3	0.6	3.2	6.4	3.9	1.2
Slovakia	−2.5	−14.6	−6.5	−3.7	4.9	6.9	6.6	5.7
Slovenia	−4.7	−8.9	−5.5	2.8	5.3	4.1	3.1	3.7
Estonia	−8.1	−13.6	−14.2	−9.0	−2.0	4.3	4.0	10.9

Table 16.4

Inflation (to the end of the year) in Rapid Disinflation Transition Countries (% to previous year)

	1990	1991	1992	1993	1994	1995	1996	1997
Albania	—	104.1	236.6	30.9	15.8	6.0	17.4	42.1
Hungary	33.4	32.2	21.6	21.1	21.2	28.3	19.8	18.4
Latvia	—	262.0	959.0	35.0	26.0	23.1	13.1	7.0
Poland	249.0	60.4	44.3	37.6	29.4	21.6	18.5	13.2
Czech Republic	18.4	52.0	12.7	18.2	9.7	7.9	8.6	10.0
Slovakia	18.4	58.3	9.1	25.1	11.7	7.2	5.4	6.4
Slovenia	105.0	247.1	92.9	22.8	19.5	9.0	9.0	8.8
Estonia	—	304.0	954.0	36.0	42.0	29.0	15.0	12.0

ciently and that are not using the most rational production methods become uncompetitive and start to experience liquidity problems and financial losses, and their managers lose their jobs and owners lose their property. The strong link between effectiveness/financial stability and the maintenance of control over corresponding resource flows is the most important mechanism giving the market economy the edge over its socialist competitor. The figures presented in Tables 16.3 through 16.6 illustrate this thesis.

There has not been enough time or stable political support to carry out the majority of these measures in Russia. Shock therapy (as carried out in Poland) did not occur in Russia. The measures Russia has used in its transformation have allowed it to avoid mass famine and to start the market mechanisms working, but they might not result in the long-term steady growth necessary to combat the most severe social problems.

The increase in "new poverty" has been aggravated as a result of the use of "soft budget constraints," in which some businesses, based on "social reasons,"

Table 16.5

Gross Domestic Product Growth (Recession) Rate in Slow Disinflation Transition Countries (% to previous year)

Countries	1990	1991	1992	1993	1994	1995	1996	1997
Azerbaijan	−11.7	−0.7	−22.6	−23.1	−19.7	−11.8	1.3	5.8
Armenia	−7.4	−17.1	−52.6	−14.8	5.4	6.9	5.8	3.1
Belarus	−3.0	−1.2	−9.6	−7.6	−12.6	−10.4	2.8	10.0
Georgia	−12.4	−20.6	−44.8	−25.4	−11.4	2.4	10.5	11.0
Kazakstan	−0.4	−13.0	−2.9	−9.2	−12.6	−8.2	0.5	2.1
Kyrgyzstan	3.0	−5.0	−19.0	−16.0	−20.0	−5.4	7.1	6.2
Lithuania	−5.0	−5.7	−21.3	−16.2	−9.8	3.3	4.7	6.0
Macedonia	−9.9	−12.1	−21.1	−9.1	−1.8	−1.2	0.8	1.5
Moldavia	−2.4	−17.5	−29.1	−1.2	−31.2	−3.0	−8.0	1.3
Russia	—	−5.0	−14.5	−8.7	−12.7	−4.1	−3.5	0.4
Romania	−5.6	−12.9	−8.8	1.5	3.9	7.1	3.9	−6.6
Tajikistan	−1.6	−7.1	−29.0	−11.0	−18.9	−12.5	−4.4	2.2
Turkmenistan	2.0	−4.7	−5.3	−10.0	−18.8	−8.2	−8.0	−25.9
Uzbekistan	1.6	−0.5	−11.1	−2.3	−4.2	−0.9	1.6	2.4
Ukraine	−3.4	−11.6	−13.7	−14.2	−23.0	−12.2	−10.0	−3.2
Croatia	−6.9	−21.1	−11.7	−8.0	5.9	6.8	6.0	6.5

Source: Institute for the Economy in Transition, "Russian Economy: Trends and Perspectives" (Moscow: Institute for the Economy in Transition) Monthly Bulletin, Moscow, December 2001.

Table 16.6

Inflation (to the end of the year) in Slow Disinflation Transition Countries (% to previous year)

Countries	1990	1991	1992	1993	1994	1995	1996	1997
Azerbaijan	—	126.0	1,395.0	1,294.0	1,788.0	84.5	6.5	0.4
Armenia	—	—	—	1,089.6	1,885.0	31.9	5.8	21.8
Belarus	—	—	1,559.0	1,996.0	1,960.0	244.0	39.0	63.0
Georgia	5.0	—	1,177.0	7,488.0	6,474.0	57.0	14.3	7.1
Kazakstan	105.0	137.0	2,984.0	2,169.0	1,160.0	60.4	28.6	11.3
Kyrgyzstan	—	170.0	1,259.0	1,363.0	95.7	31.9	35.0	14.7
Lithuania	—	345.0	1,161.0	189.0	45.0	35.5	13.1	8.5
Macedonia	121.0	230.0	1,925.0	230.0	55.0	9.0	−0.6	2.7
Moldavia	—	151.0	2,198.0	837.0	116.0	23.8	15.1	11.2
Russia	—	161.0	2,506.1	840.0	204.4	128.6	21.8	10.9
Romania	37.7	222.8	199.2	295.5	61.7	27.8	56.9	151.4
Tajikistan	—	204.0	1,364.0	7,344.0	1.1	2,133.0	40.5	163.6
Turkmenistan	—	155.0	644.0	9,750.0	1,328.0	1,262.0	446.0	22.0
Uzbekistan	—	169.0	910.0	885.0	1,281.0	117.0	64.0	50.0
Ukraine	—	161.0	2,730.0	1,015.5	401.0	182.0	40.0	10.0
Croatia	136.0	250.0	938.0	1,149.0	-3.0	3.8	3.4	3.8

Source: Y. Gaidar, see Note 4.

were allowed by the state to function despite failing to meet market requirements and to benefit from covering failures with the assets from another account. As a result, the state budget, and by extension all of the teachers, doctors, military personnel, and others who receive payment through that budget, pay for the operation of these enterprises. Politically less influential partners of the giants of socialist industry also pay for them. In fact, workers of these very enterprises end up paying for their own administration.

Therefore, research that has been carried out by the Department of Finance of the Russian government indicates that workers are considered by directors to be de facto creditors of the lowest rank. Even when factory directors have the ability to pay out money, they pay their workers last, after they have settled accounts with commercial banks, other partners (suppliers), local (regional) governments, and the federal budget.[3] This problem appears to be universal and not confined to the Russian context.

All this shows that everybody wins from inflation and soft budgetary and monetary policies—everybody, that is, except poor people. Thus, Y. Gaidar noted:

> An important difference between Czechoslovakia and Poland or Hungary was the almost complete absence of a private sector in the prereform period. Under the new conditions, the Czechoslovak state enterprises encountered serious financial problems. The strong position of the state budget allowed the authorities to combine tough budget and monetary policies at the macrolevel with tolerance of soft budget constraints in the state enterprise sector. The law on bankruptcy adopted in 1991 was effectively suspended. In 1991–1992 there were no cases of bankruptcy or liquidation of large or medium-sized enterprises. As a result the Czechoslovak enterprises responded to the challenges presented by the radically changing environment in a manner typical of enterprises in market socialism—by expansion of mutual nonpayments. Only in April 1993 was it possible to implement bankruptcy legislation to halt further growth of mutual arrears.[4]

The Central Bank of Russia gave a special low-interest loan (at an annual rate of 25 percent in 1992, when the level of inflation was about 2500 percent) to some enterprises for the purpose of paying off delayed salaries in regions. Subsidized credits were allocated through ten specially selected commercial banks, which had been getting credits for a long time and using them in their own interests. The choice of selected banks was made on a subjective basis, with the personal contacts among those who made the decision and the leadership of commercial banks playing a significant role in the choices made. Working with privileged credits was the main source of additional profits for commercial banks.

Giving illegal tax privileges to commercial structures, quite often functioning under the noblest names, was the original form of budget privatization. The monetary value of this kind of privilege for the period of 1993 through the first half of 1994 exceeded the scale of expected revenue from capital privatization. A sports foundation headed by Tarpishev (a famous tennis coach), by way of example, managed to gain profits in the amount of $4.2 billion as the result of being granted the right to be free of custom duties.

The problem of regional budgets also remains critical. Over 70 percent of regional budgets are subsidized. More than half of regional budgets are bankrupt without any hope for remedying their situations in the foreseeable future.

All this once again shows that inflation and soft budgetary and monetary policies could benefit everybody except poor people. Inflation "deserved" its fame as a most unjust, unfair tax. Poor people suffered the most from the excess printing and distribution of money. The poor, by virtue of the above-mentioned atomization of society, are unable to organize themselves to lobby in their own interests. Because of this, they could not redistribute revenue streams to their benefit, and so they lost all. A similar situation exists even in the most advanced countries, when adjusting for the size of per capita gross national product. In these countries, the well-organized middle class successfully attacks large business, while the poor remain in the same "third place." Therefore the severe monetarist, who suffocates inflation, is the best friend of the poor man.

Debts on State Employees' Wages and Pensions

Among the most difficult problems of post-Soviet Russia is the several months' delay in the payment of wages to "budget employees," i.e., employees of the state. But after the August 1998 crisis (indeed, because of the crisis), debts on wages and pensions have been decreasing rapidly.

However, what well-being has been achieved is under severe pressure now due to: 1) the recent fall of petroleum prices and the decline in tax revenues that will accompany this decrease; 2) the skewing of federal policy with regard to the rate of bureaucratic centralization of authority, the increase of the share of the federal budget in the general charges, and incomes of "Big Government"; and 3) the easing of democratic regulations at a regional level (e.g., governors' right to a third term in office and the initiative to designate governors in regions where the winner has received not less than 50 percent of the vote of all registered voters). All of these factors destroy the stimulus for responsible disposal of financial resources. Therefore the present new wave of nonpayments to state employees (for the first time happening within a context of relative budgetary proficiency—see Table 16.7) will hardly be the last.

Table 16.7

Russian Federal Government Budget Structure, 1998–2001 (billions of rubles)

	Jan.	Feb.	Mar.	Apr.	May	June	July	Aug.	Sept.	Oct.	Nov.	Dec.
1998												
Taxes	16.2	17.4	18.1	19.3	19.7	19.8	19.8	19.4	18.8	18.5	18.6	19.6
Revenues	18.8	20.1	21.2	22.4	23.0	23.2	23.2	22.9	22.3	22.0	22.0	24.5
Expenditures	25.3	23.8	27.0	28.1	28.6	29.5	29.4	28.6	27.4	26.9	27.1	29.5
Deficit/Surplus	-6.5	-3.7	-5.8	-5.7	-5.7	-6.3	-6.2	-5.7	-5.2	-5.0	-5.0	-5.1
1999												
Taxes	16.8	16.6	18.1	19.9	20.1	20.5	20.8	20.8	20.3	20.2	20.9	22.1
Revenues	19.2	18.9	20.6	22.7	23.2	23.9	24.3	24.5	24.1	24.0	24.8	26.3
Expenditures	18.6	20.3	23.6	25.6	26.6	27.3	27.4	27.4	26.7	26.3	26.7	29.2
Deficit/Surplus	0.6	-1.5	-3.1	-3.0	-3.4	-3.4	-3.1	-2.9	-2.7	-2.3	-1.9	-2.9
2000												
Taxes	20.8	21.4	22.6	24.2	25.5	25.4	24.9	24.8	24.1	23.7	24.0	24.6
Revenues	24.4	24.8	26.4	28.2	29.7	29.7	29.3	29.2	28.4	28.0	28.6	30.0
Expenditures	19.6	21.1	23.8	24.8	25.2	25.5	22.3	25.1	24.5	24.2	24.6	27.0
Deficit/Surplus	4.7	3.7	2.6	3.4	4.5	4.3	7.0	4.1	3.9	3.8	4.0	3.0
2001												
Taxes	22.7	23.6	23.9	25.4	26.4	26.0	26.1	25.9	25.0	24.8		
Revenues	25.9	27.1	27.4	29.3	30.5	29.8	29.9	29.7	28.3	28.2		
Expenditures	16.8	22.8	23.7	24.7	25.1	25.3	25.5	25.6	24.9	24.7		
Deficit	9.1	4.2	3.7	4.7	5.4	4.4	4.4	4.1	3.5	3.5		

Social Assistance

Throughout the 1990s, during a period of chronic budgetary crisis and falling GDP, the disproportion between the need for spending on social programs and actual expenditures on medical, educational, and cultural services and social benefits and allowances steadily increased. Dramatic changes in the distribution of income among population groups (that is, in the number of people living below the poverty line) significantly affected the amount of money needed to sustain social assistance. According to official estimates, in 1992 one-third of the population had incomes below the poverty line. From 1994 to 1996, this number went down to about 25 percent, and then increased again in 1999 to about 34 percent, an increase that was caused mainly by the August 1998 economic crisis. The household income differentiation sharply intensified; the Gini index, which according to available estimates was at about 0.2 in 1998, increased to 0.4 by 1994 and fluctuated for the second half of the 1990s from 0.35 to 0.39. Thus, the number of those in need of social assistance, among them the "new poor" (i.e., the lowest paid categories of the working population, including a considerable share of those employed in the state budgetary sphere), increased considerably.

In the 1990s the social policy system in the Russian Federation developed to a considerable degree as a system of responses to newly emerging and aggravated social and economic problems. Many of the present benefits and allowances are the legacy of the Soviet system, under which they performed quite different functions. At the same time, a substantial share of these benefits is paid in compliance with laws, decrees, and regulatory acts approved from 1994 to 1996 (e.g., "On Veterans," "On State Allowances for Citizens with Children," "On Social Protection of Disabled Persons in the Russian Federation," and "On Social Services to Senior and Disabled Citizens"). The normative acts put into place during that period bear the stamp of the time (i.e., the time of election campaigns) and often are of a populist (declarative) nature. These legal and normative acts failed to define clearly their target groups within the population; that is, social assistance and social services as a rule were not related to the economic situation of households. These acts often were too broad, and thus those who need the assistance the most are the least likely to receive it. According to some estimates, there are over 1,000 different programs of social assistance available to the population in Russia that are paid from the public coffers. At the federal level, there exist 156 programs entailing benefits payable to 236 categories of the population. Two social benefits (monthly child allowances and housing subsidies) were enacted during 1998–1999 at the federal level and were provided only to households with per capita incomes below the poverty line.

Because the amounts of social benefits distributed during the 1990s were spread over too broad a population category, the amounts were not substantial enough to help those who needed help the most. For instance, previously the child allowance was at about 13% of the subsistence minimum for children below the age of 16, while in 1999 it was only 6% of the subsistence minimum. A considerable drop in the amount of benefits and allowances to households (by 55% in real terms) was a natural consequence of the crisis of 1998.

The financing of social programs comes out of the social policy sector of the state budget. In 1999, the expenditures of the consolidated budget for these items were R92.2 billion (about 7.3% of the total expenditures of the consolidated budget, i.e., 2% of GDP). A number of state extra-budget social funds (e.g., Pension Fund, Employment Fund, Social Insurance Fund, and Compulsory Health Insurance Fund) also came out of this funding. The total expenditures for the maintenance of the RF social policy system were about 18% of the GDP in the late 1990s.

Social measures to protect the unemployed were begun in the 1990s. The law on employment, which released the state from the responsibility for the total employment of the population, was approved in 1991. The State Employment Fund was created to finance active and passive measures in the labor market. The Federal Employment Service (FES) became the institutional infrastructure of the labor market. The number of unemployed persons registered by the employment service reached its peak (2.5 million) in 1996. At the end of 2000, the number of registered unemployed was only about 1 million. The share of registered unemployed in the total number of the unemployed as defined by the International Labor Organization was about 15% in 2000 (37% in 1996), probably because of the small amount of benefits given to those who are unemployed (about 30% of the subsistence minimum), considerable benefit arrears, the low efficiency of employment agencies in searching for "suitable jobs," limited capacity to implement the program of active measures in regional labor markets, and other circumstances.

The Social Insurance Fund manages the resources of public social insurance. The Fund finances disability benefits, maternity benefits, birth grants, child-care allowance for a period of up to 1.5 years, and some services at health and spa centers. However, the latter group of payments is outside the fund's primary area of responsibility (the bulk of that money is received by higher-income households) but takes up to one-third of the total amount of Social Insurance funds. There is currently a plan to limit the Fund's expenditures to short-term insurance payments. In 1999, to improve the effectiveness of payments, the maximum amount was limited to twelve minimum monthly wages.

The old system offered many schemes that were universal and clearly inefficient, or, in other words, that were not targeted to the needy. Under the old system there were consumer subsidies for housing, energy, and transportation, and privileges and allowances for war veterans, "work heroes," or the like. A great number of these benefits were, in fact, positively correlated with an individual's income.[5] Such inefficiency called for a change as well.

To date, the poverty line has been calculated according to Presidential Decree No. 210 of March 2, 1992, and the "Methodological Recommendations" approved by the Labor Ministry in November 1992. Introduction of a social assistance system was changed to be based on eligibility, but the reforming of the social benefits system still remains on the list of necessary reforms. The most comprehensive accomplishment in this area is the federal law "On State Social Assistance," approved in the summer of 1999. The law was passed to fully redesign the whole system of social assistance on the basis of eligibility. However, in practice this law regulates only the introduction of supplementary social benefits provided in accordance with the verification of eligibility. However, lack of enforcement mechanisms, including financial ones, reduces public social assistance to just another kind of nonfinanced, and therefore unimplemented, system of social benefits and allowances.

Pension Reform

Russia's Pension Fund was established in the 1990s to manage pension resources. The fund's financial standing was not stable, its deficit due largely to the accumulation of budgetary indebtedness coming from pensions financed on a repayment basis and combined with falling revenues from insurance fees. The growth in the number of pensioners (to a considerable degree caused by the significant granting of preferential pensions) was an additional factor contributing to the increase in the pension deficit; adding to this is the disproportionate numbers of those working versus those who need pensions. The lack of comprehensive reforms may result in a dangerous decline in the financial standing of the pension system in the long term.

The social burden on the employed population increased during the 1990s because of both economic (falling number of the employed) and demographic (aging of the population) factors. Looked at in perspective, the impact of the demographic factor will probably only increase. In spite of measures aimed at increasing the amount of pensions, the minimum gross pension remained below 80% of the subsistence minimum for pensioners, a level stipulated by legislation currently in force.

The debates on pension reform illustrate the ongoing struggle for the redistribution of poorly formalized jurisdiction over major financial resources.

The pension reform approved by the Russian government in May 1998 will ensure long-term stability of the pension system by introducing insurance principles within the distribution component. But ideas to have pension funds invested through transparent private means fail to gain unanimous support among either Pension Fund officers or government officials.

In my opinion, the state should be responsible for the transparency of pension funds, for the stability of the national currency, and for the small layer of those in the most desperate need, to whom it is really in a position to offer support. In terms of the latter, encouraging charity by private persons (under simple and transparent schemes) may turn out to be much more effective. The best thing the state could do for its elderly citizens would be to guarantee the stability of conservatively invested pension funds.

The accumulative (insurance-type) pension system will mitigate the acuteness of the disproportion that is formed when most men do not live to pension age, and most elderly people are therefore women. An increase in the birthrate may come about as a by-product of citizens assuming responsibility for their old age by having children to care for them later in life. Children have long since been the classic and most reliable "pension fund" in a good family.

The aforementioned aspects of institutional structure and economic reform will create a qualitatively different investment climate and will lay the foundation for the stable improvement of macroeconomic parameters.

Reforms of Housing and Communal Services

Residential and communal utilities are faced with the problem of restructuring. For the present day, the need for funds in this sector exceeds what is available by 60%. An estimated $1.3 billion is required in the next year just to maintain the status quo, which is far from ideal, with future figures calculated in geometric progression. The communal services system wastes enormous resources now; the state and municipal budget can no longer support housing, which means that the poorest people will likely face the added burden of additional significant expenses. In order to avoid a disaster like this, the state should reform this branch as quickly as possible.

This sphere is currently monopolized by former Soviet municipal enterprises, and the cost of their services is too high for the majority of citizens. But it still receives state grants to compensate for its expenses. Some increase in prices in this sector is inevitable. But it does not have to be large if restrictions on repair activity in the housing and communal services sector are removed, so that competition can keep prices down. Reform of the housing and communal services sector is extremely necessary. Currently, up to one-third of many regional budgets goes toward subsidizing housing and communal services.

There are many opportunities for reform in this sector. For example, a local government might establish a limit on the consumption of water and gas, and any use exceeding this amount would result in a price increase. Some monopolies currently design price structures in recognition of the fact that, at almost any given time, someone in an apartment is, for example, using the gas cooker, turning on the water, or burning electricity. As another example of possible reform, a local government might undertake an initiative to install individual counters for the consumption of water and gas. The reform experience of the housing and communal services sphere in the Baltic countries confirms that paying for what is actually consumed is much easier for a family's budget than paying by a system of normative consumption quotations established by the government or the utility, who tend to highly overestimate the amounts. Moreover, this experience shows that citizens are ready to pay for the purchase of individual counters independently if given the opportunity to replace the normative payment system with payment on the basis of an individual account. But the current situation in many of Russia's regions does not allow for this option.

Conclusion

Mass poverty in Russia, and the social problems connected to it, are, on the one hand consequences of insufficiently consistent application of economic reform. On the other hand, they are caused by the Communist-induced loss of the majority of the population's civil skills (e.g., self-management, mutual aid, including charity, and so forth) and abilities to bear responsibility for themselves and their families. Lastly, the population's loss of the ability to adapt to varying circumstances has contributed to the rise in poverty. The rather low unemployment rate in Russia should be viewed in this context as an indicator of the incompleteness of the process of structural reorganization and adaptation of the economy, rather than as an attribute of well-being.

The general amount of social benefits Russia can afford continues to be spread over too broad a category of the population. The amount of support offered is too low and not substantive enough to help those who need help the most. A number of important problems (e.g., depopulation and the spread of drug addiction) are connected to Russia's national problems in general and to the dilemmas of a transition economy in particular. The prospects for tackling these problems are connected to the stability of a democratic system in Russia, accompanied by an ability to adopt and to accept the values of an open society. The accumulation of social problems cannot stimulate the acceleration of the transition but rather threaten to break it and to send the country into a situation even worse than in the 1990s.

Notes

1. *Rossiiskii statisticheskii yezhegodnik: Statisticheskii sbornik* (Moscow: Goskomstat Rossii, 1999), 100, 186, R 76.

2. Leshek Balcerovich, *Capitalism, Socialism Transformation* (Moscow: *Nauka, URAO*, 1999).

3. See the report of the chief of the Department of Finance of the Russian Federation, M. Afanas'ev, in the collection of reports of the conference "Liberalization and Stabilization: Five Years After," Moscow, IET, 1997.

4. Y. Gaidar, "The Legacy of the Socialist Economy: the Macro- and Micro-economic Consequences of Soft Budget Constraints," IET, Moscow, 1999.

5. On consumer subsidies, see World Bank, "Poland: Subsidies and Income Distribution," World Bank Report 7776–POL, Washington, DC, B1989; on social transfers, see World Bank, "Social Expenditures and Their Distributional Impact in Eastern Europe," Washington, D.C., 1992.

Index